THEOLOGY SIMPLIFIED

THEOLOGY SIMPLIFIED

GOD, HIS SON, and HIS SPIRIT

LONZO PRIBBLE

To order additional copies of this book, contact:
Xlibris Corporation
1-888-795-4274
www.Xlibris.com
Orders@Xlibris.com
62781

CONTENTS

Introduction..i
Pribblonian Creed iv
CHART-Theology: A Study About God vi
Versions and Translations..vii
Explanations and Abbreviations..ix

PART I. GOD AND HIS SON

CHAPTER   PAGE

1. Source of the Mystery 1
2. Opening Testimonies 4
3. Trinitarianism and Unitarianism Identified 8
4. The Great Cloud of Witnesses.. 10
5. God and Divine Nature.. 14
6. Equality With God... 17
7. God With Us... 21
8. Using Prophetic Expressions... 25
9. Mighty God, Everlasting Father 28
10. The Fullness of the Godhead.. 30
11. *Elohim* 31
12. Us and Our... 34
13. Three That Bear Record 37
14. God Manifest in the Flesh 40
15. And the Word Was God 42
16. Origin and Development of "The Trinity".............................. 46
17. Creeds and Orthodoxy.. 51
18. My Lord and My God 58
19. Purchased With His Own Blood... 60
20. God Blessed Forever.. 63
21. The Great God and Savior 65
22. Thy Throne, O God... 67
23. He Is the True God 71
24. The Omnipresence of God 73
25. Preparing the Way of the Lord... 79

CHAPTER   PAGE

26. The Origin and Preexistence of Christ 81
27. Firstborn of All Creation 90
28. Divine Fatherhood and Sonship: Real? or Metaphor?...................104
29. The Name of the Father, Son, and Holy Spirit 107
30. Godhead...117
31. One 122
32. *Achid* and *Yachid* 127
33. Plural Subjects With Singular Verbs...................................130
34. The Alpha and the Omega 133
35. First Person, Second Person, Third Person 139
36. Good Teacher...143
37. Isaiah Saw His Glory...148
38. Salutations, Invocations and Benedictions............................154
39. Communion and Sanctification of the Spirit 157
40. The Angel of Jehovah 160
41. Only Begotten Son 174
42. The Father Is Greater Than I...177
43. The Word Became Flesh...182
44. Lord 187
45. Miscellaneous Arguments Considered 190

PART II: GOD AND HIS SPIRIT

CHAPTER   PAGE

1. The Holy Spirit Personified 198
2. "He" or "It" 205
3. The Holy Spirit as a Witness 208
4. The Holy Spirit Speaks...211
5. The Mind of the Spirit..216
6. Intercession of the Spirit...219
7. Person? or Mere Influence? 225
8. The Holy Spirit and Deity 228
9. The Spirit Knows and Teaches 233
10. Worshiping the Holy Spirit...237
11. The Comforter 241
12. The Spirit Leads and Guides 247
13. The Love of the Spirit..249

APPENDICES

A. God Is Declared to Be the Father (56 Times) 251
B. Jesus Christ Is Declared to Be the Son of God (77 Times) 254
C. Jesus Is Distinguished from God (326 Times) 258
D. Salutations, Invocations, and Benedictions 273
E. Spirit Passages (105 OT; 269 NT) 277

SCRIPTURE INDEX (Appendices not included) 294

BIBLIOGRAPHY 308

INTRODUCTION

To most people, *Theology Simplified* may appear to be the ultimate oxymoron, inasmuch as they have been so long and so completely schooled in the *mystery-of-the-Godhead* concept. To them, the words *theology* and *simplified* may be total contradictions.

Theology is primarily a study about God. And while there are many things about God which are unrevealed mysteries, divine Scripture reveals everything we need to know about God, particularly about the relationship which exists between God, his Son, and his Spirit.

Theology is about doctrine, a word somewhat repulsive to many in this present generation, especially to those who are not willing to spend the necessary time and mental energy required to find what the Bible actually teaches on various given subjects. Many sincere Christians are saying, "I am not interested in doctrine," not realizing that it is doctrine (teaching and instruction) which distinguishes between truth and error. Jesus said, "You will know the truth, and the truth will set you free" (John 8:32). Therefore, doctrine cannot be avoided in one's coming to a knowledge of that truth which sets us free.

A study about God consists of two basic considerations: (1) how the Father, Son, and Holy Spirit relate to each other, and (2) how each of those three distinctions relate to man. This book concerns that first consideration, the subject about which there seems to be the most dogmatism. And while that second consideration is of no less importance, and has by itself filled countless volumes by numerous authors, limitations of time and space here dictate that it not be a primary concern for this book.

Theology was not intended to be nearly so complicated and mysterious as is projected by many theologians. And while most dissertations concerning deity leave the student wondering first, "What did he say?" and second, "What does it mean?" we believe that *Theology Simplified* presents God, his Son, and his Spirit in clear and understandable language, with a concept so biblical and so simple that even the "layman," the novice, and in most cases, even children can understand.

Inspiration for the title, *Theology Simplified*, was suggested in a statement by Elder Barton W. Stone (early 19th Century), a most prominent leader in the Restoration Movement in America, in *"An Address to the Churches,"* where he made the following comment concerning his rejection of the doctrine of the Trinity, and the simplicity of his own point of view, as follows:

> Others, who have labored through mazy volumes of scholastic learning on this doctrine, may be disposed to object to my view of it, because of its simplicity. They have long been taught that

the doctrine was a high, incomprehensible mystery . . . . We are told by some, that it is an evidence of an humble heart to believe it. Can any man believe it, whether he be humble or not? . . . If a doctrine be revealed, however mysterious it may be, I will humbly receive it. My reason shall ever bow to revelation; but it shall never be prostrated to human contradictions and inventions. Pious and good men have received such doctrines. God loves and pities them; and so will I.[1]

—*Works of Elder B. W. Stone*, pp. 57-58.

Without necessarily giving sanction to all of Stone's theology, we hereby give credit to his writings for removing some of those mysteries about God and his Son, which had so long plagued this author's curiosity, and for serving as an encouragement to take Stone's simple and understandable point of view, expand and elaborate upon it, and show how the resulting point of view, more than any other, withstands the scrutiny of divine Scripture.

In accomplishing this task, a project spanning more than 45 years, it was necessary to show how all those arguments, both old and new, being used to support the various forms of Trinitarianism and Unitarianism, conform to neither Scripture nor reason.

Because of the apologetic nature of the material herein presented, the contents may occasionally appear to be quite negative. However, had there been fewer unscriptural arguments used in support of Trinitarianism, as well as other such *isms*, then there would have been much less need for negative arguments to refute those errors.

It is hoped that this book may remove at least some of the dogmatism which traditionally has been associated with this subject down through the centuries, and continues to be so prevalent to this day. We therefore believe that any study or presentation of the doctrine of the Godhead would be incomplete and irresponsible without at least giving due consideration to the concept and supporting arguments contained herein.

It is not our purpose nor intent to indict any particular persons as false teachers, but rather to refute all nonbiblical doctrines on the subject at hand, regardless of who might teach such doctrines.

During the 45 years of off-and-on research, writing only an occasional article on certain phases of the subject at hand, the author, for the first 30 years, gave no thought to ever publishing a book on the subject. Food for thought has come primarily from discussions with ministers, elders and other students of the Bible, as well as from the many Trinitarian publications. Encouragement to put the results of this research into book form has come from numerous sources.

The forthcoming *Statement of Belief*, herein identified (reluctantly) as the *Pribblonian Creed*, is not intended to be a full and complete catalogue of what this author believes, but is rather a brief summation of his belief concerning the subject at hand. The burden of this volume is to show how this *Statement of Belief* corresponds with both Scripture and reason.

Not at all original with this author, it is our prayer that—

In ALL THINGS there should be CHARITY;
In matters of FAITH there should be UNITY;
In matters of OPINION there should be LIBERTY;

AND MAY GOD HELP US TO KNOW THE DIFFERENCE!

PRIBBLONIAN CREED

A STATEMENT OF BELIEF—by Lonzo Pribble

CONCERNING THE GODHEAD (DIVINITY, DEITY)

I BELIEVE in the one only true God, the Father in heaven, known to Israel as Jehovah, the "I am," the existing one, the almighty one; that supreme, spirit being, person or substance who is eternal, without beginning or end, unborn, uncreated, self-existent, omnipotent, omnipresent, omniscient, immutable and infinite; who is independent of, unlimited by, and superior to all other beings; the creator, OF whom are all things, and sovereign of the universe; the Father of our Lord Jesus Christ; the Father of our spirits; and in whom we live and move and have our being.

I BELIEVE that Jesus of Nazareth is the Christ, the Messiah, our Lord, the only begotten divine Son of Jehovah God; born, not created; preceded only by God, and born of God alone without the aid of any other being; possessing by inheritance that same divine nature as God his Father; born before all ages, before any other being, person or thing ever came into existence; the firstborn of all creation, and BY whom all things were created, both in heaven and on earth; who, in the fullness of time, and for our salvation, was sanctified by God and sent forth from heaven into the world, begotten by the Holy Spirit and born of the virgin Mary; was anointed by God with the Holy Spirit and power, went about doing good, and performing all manner of signs, wonders and miracles; was crucified under Pontius Pilate, was entombed, rose again from the dead the third day, ascended back to heaven where he, having been given by God all authority in heaven and on earth, now sits on the spiritual throne of David at God's right hand, being now the only mediator between God and men, continually making intercessions to God on our behalf; called "the Lamb of God" because of his atoning sacrifice, and called "the Word of God" because he declared God's word so completely and so authoritatively; ruling now at God's right hand as King of kings and Lord of lords over God's spiritual kingdom; from whence he shall come again to destroy death, to raise all human dead to life immortal, and to judge all mankind according to their works; and after which he shall deliver up the kingdom to God his Father.

I BELIEVE in the Holy Spirit (Holy Ghost), that one eternal Spirit of God, the Spirit of Jehovah, the Spirit of the Father, the Spirit of the Lord, the Spirit of truth, the Spirit of holiness; a part of that divine essence which makes the one God the God that he is, and by which God is omnipresent; that which hovered over the waters when the earth was waste and void, the power by which God garnished the heavens and inspired the prophets of old; that by which Jesus was begotten in the virgin, with which he was anointed by God, and by which God raised him from the dead; the Comforter (Counselor, Advocate) promised to the apostles; that which ever proceeds from the Father and in or with which the apostles were baptized on Pentecost; that Spirit which convicts and converts sinners today through the influence of God's holy word; that part of the Father by which, in a way somewhat peculiar to the Christian dispensation God's personal presence is felt among us today; that Spirit which dwells in the hearts and lives of children of God, and by which we cry, "Abba, Father."

THEOLOGY: A STUDY ABOUT GOD

In the divine nature we see at least three distinctions; Father, Son , and Holy Spirit.

THREE BASIC CONCEPTS CONCERNING GOD

TRINITARIAN

The ONE GOD is a triune being composed of three coequal and coeternal persons -- God the Father, God the Son, and God the Holy Spirit.

ONE BEING -- THREE PERSONS

ONE GOD = GODHEAD = TRINITY

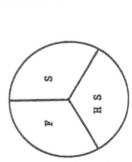

UNITARIAN

The ONE GOD is a singular being (or person) who manifests himself in three personalities -- God the Father, God the Son, and God the Holy Spirit.

ONE BEING (PERSON) -- THREE PERSONALITIES

ONE GOD = GODHEAD

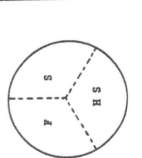

BIBLICAL

The ONE GOD is a singular being (or person), the Father (Jehovah); Jesus Christ is God's only begotten divine Son; and the Holy Spirit is God's Spirit.

ONE BEING (PERSON) -- who has a Son and a Spirit.

GODHEAD = DIVINE NATURE

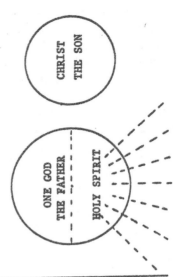

VERSIONS AND TRANSLATIONS

AB—*The Amplified Bible.* 11th printing. Grand Rapids: Zondervan Bible Publishers, 1975.

ASV—*The American Standard Version* (1901). Nashville: Thomas Nelson, Publishers.

Barclay, William—*The Daily Study Bible* (DSB). 17 vol. Philadelphia: The Westminster Press, 1958.

Beck, William F.—*The New Testament.* 8th printing. Saint Louis: Concordia Publishing House, 1967.

Goodspeed, Edgar J.—*The New Testament.* Chicago: The University of Chicago Press, 1923.

ILT—Berry, George Ricker. *The Interlinear Literal Translation of the Greek New Testament.* Chicago: Wilcox & Follet Co., 1950.

JB—*The New Testament of the Jerusalem Bible*, ed. Alexander Jones. Garden City, N.Y., 1969.

KJV—*King James Version* (1611). 49th reprint. Indianapolis: B. B. Kirkbride Bible Co., Inc., 1964.

LXX—*The Septuagint Version of the Old Testament* (Greek). New York: Harper and Brothers.

NASB—*New American Standard Bible.* Chicago: Moody Press, 1963.

NCE—*New Catholic Edition*, New Testament Confraternity Edition. Burlington, Vermont: Catholic Book Publishing Co.; Vermont Church Supply Co., 1953.

NEB—*The New English Bible.* 5th printing. Oxford University Press, 1962.

NIV—*New International Version Study Bible.* Grand Rapids: Zondervan Bible Publishers, 1985.

NKJV—*New King James Version.* Nashville: Thomas Nelson, Publishers, 1992.

NWT—*New World Translation of the Christian Greek Scriptures*, New

World Bible Translation Committee. 2nd ed. Brooklyn: Watchtower Bible and Tract Society, Inc., 1951.

RSV—*Revised Standard Version* (1946-52). New York: Thomas Nelson & Sons, 1953.

RV—*Revised Version.* Boston: W. L. Richardson & Co.

SEB—*The Simple English Bible.* Dallas: International Bible Foundation, 1981.

TEV—*Today's English Version (Good News for Modern Man).* New York: American Bible Society.

TCNT—*The Twentieth Century New Testament.* New York: Fleming H. Revell Company, 1904.

Weymouth, Richard Francis—*The New Testament.* 5th ed. New York: Harper & Brothers.

Williams, Charles B.—*The New Testament.* Chicago: Moody Press, 1960.

EXPLANATIONS AND ABBREVIATIONS

All Scripture quotations, unless otherwise stated, are taken from the *New International Version* (NIV), not because we believe it more accurately adheres to the original Bible text than does the *American Standard Version* (ASV), but because of the increasing popularity of the NIV among today's students of the Bible. However, this should not be of utmost concern, inasmuch as no singular translation is cited as authority without considering a variety of translations, as well as the languages of the original text.

Greek and Hebrew terms are italicized in English characters as shown in Robert Young's *Analytical Concordance to the Bible* (KJV),[2] but without accent and breathing marks.

Items contained in parentheses ( ) include Scripture references and other explanations gathered from the context, and occasionally elsewhere. Brackets [ ] contain textual footnoted alternate readings, and renditions from other versions including Greek and Hebrew texts. Example:

"For God (see v. 17) so loved the world [*kosmon*] that he (God) gave his one and only [Gr. *monogenes*] Son (Christ)" [fn. and ASV: Or *his only begotten Son*] (John 3:16).

Exceptions are those few places where parentheses or brackets are part of the actual version text.

Following the order of the KJV and the NIV, the word "LORD" (in all capitals) stands for Jehovah, as it is so translated in the ASV.

No great significance is being attached to the precise order in which the various chapters appear, as each chapter is purposely designed, for the most part, to stand on its own.

ABBREVIATIONS

ch.—chapter
f. or ff.—verse(s) following
fn.—footnote and/or marginal reading
Gr.—Greek
Heb.—Hebrew
ibid.—in the same place

MS or MSS—manuscript(s)
NT—New Testament
OT—Old Testament
p. or pp.—page(s)
v. or vv.—verse(s)

THEOLOGY SIMPLIFIED

PART I

GOD AND HIS SON

CHAPTER 1

SOURCE OF THE MYSTERY

That the one God is the Father in heaven, that Jesus Christ is God's one and only begotten divine Son, and that the Holy Spirit is God's Spirit, are truths set forth so obviously and so simply in Holy Scripture that even children can understand it. And that simple first-impression concept about God is not to be discarded when one becomes a man, or even a theologian.

The Bible speaks of numerous mysteries; but the relationship between God, his Son, and his Spirit is never said to be one of those mysteries. Paul, the apostle, did say, "The mystery of godliness is great" (1 Tim 3:16). He did not say, "Great is the mystery of the Godhead." How God, who is so good, can be so merciful toward us who are so evil, even sending forth his one and only begotten Son to die for us, that we might become transformed into the image of his own Son, is truly a mystery beyond human comprehension. But the relationship existing between God and his Son, though not so clearly revealed in the Old Testament (OT), is no mystery to even the casual student of the New Testament (NT).

One of the first Scriptures a child learns, popularly and appropriately designated the "Golden Text" of the Bible, makes that distinguishing relationship quite clear: "For God so loved the world that he gave his one and only Son [Or *his only begotten Son*] . . . ." (John 3:16). God was the one who gave; God's Son was the one given. God was the one who sent; God's Son was the one whom God sent. God is not dead as some have supposed, because God never died. It was God's Son who died, yea, but now lives. One would actually need help in order to misunderstand that simple concept.

Most people who make any pretense at all toward Christianity understand the simplicity of that relationship, rightly visualizing God as the Father who reigns supreme on his majestic throne in heaven, with his Son at his right hand, having been given by God glory, honor, dominion, power, and a kingdom. They correctly see God as the giver of that glory, and God's Son as the recipient thereof. They seldom confuse the two; and they understand which of the two is Jehovah God the Almighty. That simple concept is the one most naturally conceived in the minds of most beginning students of the Bible, and contains no great mystery which such unskilled minds cannot comprehend.

But some theologians, more skilled in the art of confusing than simplifying, have taken that beautiful picture of God and his Son, and by isolating certain passages of Scripture from that concept have fancifully created a "triune" God, not only foreign to the Jews of old, but also foreign to the teachings of Christ and his apostles. That new Trinitarian concept—which sprang forth in the latter part of the Third Century A.D. and became more crystallized in the centuries that followed—when simply stated, declares that "The one God is a triune being composed of three coequal and coeternal persons—God the Father, God the Son, and God the Holy Spirit." Truly, such would be an incomprehensible mystery which nobody can understand, defying both Scripture and reason.

Realizing that an ever-present theme running throughout the Bible is the eternal truth that there is only one true God, and realizing further that the Father is called "God" (*ho Theos*), that the Son is also in some sense called "God" (though never called *ho Theos*, the God), and that the Holy Spirit is supposedly called "God," have caused many to conclude that the one God is therefore necessarily a plural being composed of those three distinctions as coequal and coeternal persons. That is the mystery which has plagued theologians since the early post-apostolic centuries of the Christian Era. And while many hold tenaciously to that conclusion as dogma, in their hearts they know that there are numerous unsolved questions which that doctrine poses; thus the often-used expression, "the mystery of the Trinity," supposedly justifies for them all the apparent points of weakness in the doctrine so stated.

But that mystery is removed when it is realized that the word "God" is used in more than one qualifying sense in Scripture, and may indeed refer not only in the absolute sense to the one almighty Jehovah God, the Father, but also in a relative or qualified sense, as well as representatively, to God's Son who possesses the same divine nature as his Father, and who came to earth to represent that Father, without requiring them both to be coequal persons in the one being who is called *ho Theos* (the God) in the absolute sense.

If we can understand how angels—created beings who were sent by God—could speak in the first-person singular mode for God, and be referred to by names belonging to God—without making them divine beings, much less making them identical with Jehovah God the Almighty who sent them—then surely we should be able to understand how Christ, the divine Son of God, could be sent by God to represent God, as in the parable of the Wicked Husbandmen (Matt 21:33-41), being God's own personal representative on earth, and possibly even be referred to by names of the God who sent him, as were some of the angels, without making Christ identical with the God who sent him.

When it is realized that at some point back there in infinite eternity the one God (*ho Theos*) could and did reproduce a divine offspring in the form of a Son, someone to love and to be loved by—born, not made nor created, therefore the divine Son of God, the firstborn of all creation—then that great supposed mystery of the Godhead disappears, and everything else in Scripture about that relationship falls naturally, simply and understandably into place.

And when it is further realized that the Holy Spirit is the ever-proceeding Spirit of that almighty God, the Father—therefore divine in nature, just as everything about God is divine, as distinguished from human, animal or even angelic nature—and that at the Last Supper, God's ever-proceeding Spirit (neuter gender) is personified as an Advocate (masculine gender) for the apostles, then that great unsolved supposed mystery of the Trinity—the idea that there might be three distinct persons in one personal God—is thereby further removed. In this way theology is simplified so that even children and others unskilled in religious dogma may comprehend.

So the burden of proof in *Theology Simplified* is to show how Scripture teaches that the one God is the Father, that Jesus is God's one and only begotten divine Son, and that the Holy Spirit is God's Spirit by which God, who is in heaven, can be (and is) omnipresent, and the means by which the power of the omnipotent God is manifest in the universe, especially toward mankind.

Like millions who are made in his own image, the one and only Jehovah God, the Almighty, is also a Father who has both a Son and a Spirit, and does not need to be a plural being composed of three persons in order to be so.

CHAPTER 2

OPENING TESTIMONIES

Compare a supposed triune God with that which was taught by Jesus and his apostles:

JESUS' TESTIMONY: In one of Jesus' most notable prayers (John 17), as he earnestly prayed to his Father (v. 1), he clearly stated in verse 3, "Now this is eternal life: that they may know you, the only true God, and Jesus Christ, whom you have sent." Jesus clearly did not include himself as being that only true God, nor as being part of that only true God, nor as being one of a plurality of persons in that true God. Instead, Jesus definitely and clearly distinguished himself from that God. If the only true God were a triune being composed of three coequal and coeternal persons, including Jesus himself, surely Jesus would have prayed "that they may know US, the only true God." But he didn't. And why would Jesus specify only the Father, and not also the Holy Spirit, as being the only true God, if indeed the Holy Spirit were also a coequal person with the Father in that only true God?

Furthermore, when the Jews accused Jesus of making himself God (John 10:33), Jesus did not plead guilty to the charge, but instead testified, "I said, 'I am God's Son.'" (v. 36). (The significant implications of this text shall be explored later in much greater detail). Jesus never ever called himself *God*. In fact, on the occasion already mentioned (John 10:36) and only two (or possibly three) others, recorded only by John, did Jesus ever call himself *Son of God*. Elsewhere, without denying his divine Sonship, he called himself *Son of man*, recorded by all the gospel writers no less than eighty times.

GOD'S TESTIMONY: When Jesus was baptized by John in Jordan, and the Spirit of God was seen descending on him, a voice was heard from heaven saying, "This is my Son, whom I love; with him I am well pleased" (Matt 3:16-17; Mark 1:10-11; Luke 3:22).

Again, when Jesus was transfigured before Peter, James, and John there on a mountain, and there appeared before them Moses and Elijah, a voice came from a cloud saying, "This is my Son, whom I love; with him I am well pleased" (Matt 17:5). The disciples knew who was being called God's Son, for "When they looked up, they saw no one except Jesus" (v. 6). Had Jesus been *ho Theos* (the God), then surely the voice would have identified him as such. But instead, God identified Jesus as his Son.

JOHN THE BAPTIST'S TESTIMONY: John gave this testimony concerning Jesus: "I saw the Spirit come down from heaven as a dove and remain on him. I would not have known him, except that the one who sent me to baptize with water told me, 'The man on whom you see the Spirit come down and remain is he who will baptize with the Holy Spirit.' I have seen and I testify that this is the Son of God" (John 1:32-34). The next day when John saw Jesus passing by, he told two of his disciples, "Look, the Lamb of God!" John did not say, "Look, there goes God!" But instead, John testified that "this is the Son of God." There is a difference. John the Baptist, who came to introduce Christ, the Son of God, to the world, never once called Christ *God*, much less, *ho Theos* (the God).

ANDREW'S TESTIMONY: After John the Baptist pointed out "the Lamb of God" to his disciples, one of them, Andrew, went first to tell his brother, Simon Peter, "We have found the Messiah" (John 1:41). Andrew did not tell Peter, "We have found God," for he no doubt knew that "no one has ever seen God" (v. 18).

JOHN'S TESTIMONY: Whatever John the apostle meant by applying the term *God* to the *Word* (John 1:1) which "became flesh" (v. 14), he obviously was not declaring Christ to be *ho Theos*, the God whom he "was with"; for then John proceeded to explain in verse 18, "No one has ever seen God." And then John himself summarized his gospel narrative thus: "But these are written that you may believe that Jesus is the Christ, the Son of God" (John 20:31). Therefore John 1:1 apparently was not written to convince anyone that Christ is God in the absolute sense, as shall be shown conclusively when this text is explained later in greater detail. (See Part I, Chapter 15, *And the Word Was God*).

Some contend that the divine person who "became flesh and made his dwelling among us" (John 1:14) was not the Son of God until he became the Son of man. This conclusion is due to a misunderstanding as to why Jesus was called "the Word" in John 1:1, supposing that the actual and literal word (Gr. *logos*) of God existed coeternally as a separate and distinct spirit, being or person from the God he was the word of, not being at that time a son or offspring, and God therefore not being the Father of anyone, and did not become God's Son until he became the Son of man via the virgin birth. Thus God would not be the Father until Jesus became the Son of man. It shall be shown later by many infallible proofs that Jesus was literally the Son (divine offspring) of God when he was sent to become also the Son of man, but was called "the Word" figuratively because he came to declare that word so authoritatively and so completely. Thus Jesus could say, "That very word which I spoke (not the word that I AM) will condemn him at the last day" (John 12:48).

PETER'S TESTIMONY: When Jesus asked his disciples, "Who do you say I am?" (Matt 16:15), Peter responded, "You are the Christ, the Son of the living God" (v. 16). Jesus then gave sanction to Peter's answer as having been revealed by Jesus' "Father in heaven" (v. 17). Note: Peter did not confess, "You are the living God." If he had, he would have spoken without authority; for God's voice from heaven had said, "This is my Son, whom I love; with him I am well pleased" (Matt 3:17). No Christian or prospective Christian should ever be required to confess that Christ is God (*ho Theos*), but rather the Son of God.

PAUL'S TESTIMONY: Now see how the Trinitarian concept clashes with the teachings of Paul: "For us there is but one God, the Father, from whom all things came and for whom we live; and there is but one Lord, Jesus Christ, through whom all things came and through whom we live" (1 Cor 8:6). Had Paul been either a Trinitarian or Unitarian theologian, he should have said, "There is but one God—the Father, Son and Holy Spirit." But he didn't. Paul said the one God is the Father as distinguished from the one Lord, Jesus Christ. It should not be argued that this distinction of Christ from the one God only applied during Jesus' earthly advent as a human being, for the text extends backward to the Creation, at which time all things were FROM God, but THROUGH Christ. And if the Holy Spirit were a coequal person in the one God, as claimed by Trinitarians, then why would Paul identify only the Father, instead of both the Father and the Holy Spirit, as being the one and only God?

If Christ were distinguished from the one God, only as it pertains to his incarnation, during which time the Father would be the only true God, that would require a conclusion that Christ on earth was not that God, and God would therefore cease to be a triune being. And if the Holy Spirit were a distinct person from the Father, then Christ and Paul both would have been in error when referring to the Father as the only true God, inasmuch as the Holy Spirit never became incarnate, never became a man, and therefore supposedly would still be as much the one true God as was the Father.

Hear Paul again: "There is . . . one Lord, one faith, one baptism; one God and Father of all, who is over all and through all and in all" (Eph 4:4-6). So again, the one God is distinguished from Christ our Lord, even after his ascension and reglorification.

TESTIMONY BY SATAN AND THE DEMONS: Those capable of properly identifying Jesus from his preexistent state prior to his becoming the Son of man include Satan and the demons. They never called him *Son of man*, nor did they call him *God*, but rather, *Son of God*. It is true that Satan is a liar, and the father of lies. But in this case he told the truth. It was to Satan's advantage, he thought, at a time when

Jesus tried to keep his true identity from the Jewish leaders, for Jesus to be thus exposed in order to hasten his death before being able to accomplish his mission on earth. So Satan told the truth, thinking it would spell defeat for Christ. And in the Temptation Satan never said, "If you are God"; but instead he said, "If you are the Son of God . . . ." (Matt 4:3, 6). Satan knew the difference. Most assuredly, if Jesus were God, instead of God's Son, Satan would have known, and would never have even tried to tempt him, knowing that "God cannot be tempted by evil" (Jas 1:13). But Satan knew that God's Son could be tempted; therefore he did his utmost, but failed. Demons always called Jesus "Son of God," or as in Mark 1:24, "the Holy One of God," for they surely must have known him back in the ages of eternity before he ever became the Son of man. Other such references could be multiplied which show that the one God is the Father, and that Jesus Christ is his Son.

We have thus far considered opening testimony by Jesus, God, John the Baptist, Andrew, John, Peter, Paul, and even Satan and the demons; and all their testimony on the identity of Christ is found to be in agreement. Throughout the NT Jesus is consistently distinguished from the one God. We shall be discussing later any references which may on the surface seem to suggest otherwise, and which have been used by Trinitarians in trying to prove that Jesus Christ is the Jehovah *Elohim* of the Hebrews and the *Theos* of the Greeks.

CHAPTER 3

TRINITARIANISM AND UNITARIANISM IDENTIFIED

Reference has already been made to both *Trinitarian* and *Unitarian* theology. The Trinitarian concept, which we may call *Trinitarianism*, has already been defined as declaring that "The one God is a triune being composed of three coequal and coeternal persons—God the Father, God the Son, and God the Holy Spirit." In this definition the one God, the Godhead, and the Trinity are all identical, which we will hereinafter show to be nonbiblical. (See Chart on page vi).

Another approach to Trinitarianism is "The Trinity of the Godhead" theory, which declares that "in the unity or oneness of the Godhead (divine nature) there are three coequal and coeternal persons—God the Father, God the Son, and God the Holy Spirit." But since the word translated *Godhead* is not identical with a being, but rather refers to the divine nature possessed by any such being, this concept would force the inevitable conclusion that there are three separate and distinct spirits, beings, persons or Gods who all possess the same divine nature, and who are all one in agreement, purpose, mission, etc., while at the same time each having his own personal mind, will and intellect with which any one of the three could individually choose not to thus agree. Thus one divine nature, but three coequal and coeternal Gods. That's a form of Polytheism, identified by some as *Tritheism*.

A similar, and yet distinct approach to "the Trinity of the Godhead" is that "in the unity of the Godhead there are three coequal and coeternal persons—God the Father, Christ the Son, and the Holy Spirit." But while this concept is scripturally monotheistic (the one God being, not the Godhead, but the Father, as distinguished from Christ and the Holy Spirit), and while it maintains the divine nature of Christ and the Holy Spirit (as distinguished from human nature, animal nature, and even angelic nature, all of which are created beings), it contradicts itself by making these three distinctions coequal and coeternal spirits, beings, persons or Gods. For if the Father is God, and if Christ and the Holy Spirit were coequally God with the Father in the absolute sense, then there would still be three separate and distinct spirits, beings, persons or Gods. That's still a form of Polytheism or Tritheism.

The term *Unitarian* (or *Unitarianism*) as has been used earlier and shall subsequently be used in this study (having no reference to the religious denomination by that name, nor to any doctrine which might through the years have been identified by that name) is herein being used to identify the doctrine that "The one God is not three separate and distinct spirits, beings or persons, but rather one person who manifests himself, sometimes even simultaneously, as Father, Son, and Holy Spirit. Not three separate persons, but one being or person playing three separate, but not conflicting roles. Again, this doctrine also equates the one God with the Godhead in such a way as to make the one God and the Godhead identical. There is much evidence to justify a conclusion that this form of Unitarianism, and Trinitarianism as first defined, differ only in semantics, all saying essentially the same thing, while expressing it in different ways. But in both cases the one personal God supposedly plays the role of Father, Son and Holy Spirit simultaneously, just as on stage one performer may portray both hero and villain, as long as both characters are not required to appear on stage simultaneously. It is supposed that while man cannot appear in multiple roles simultaneously, God can.

A second and more popular concept called "Unitarianism" has the Father as the one-only divine person, denying the preexistence and divine nature of Christ, arguing that if both Father and Son were divine persons, that would mean two Gods, and to them would be Duotarian (if we may coin that word) instead of Unitarian. The terms Trinitarian, Duotarian and Unitarian refer to the number of divine persons believed to be in each concept. In the chart (page vi) solid lines represent distinct persons, while dotted lines represent distinctions that are not distinct persons.

Trinitarians do not believe in three Gods, but rather three divine persons in the one God. And Duotarians do not believe in two Gods, but rather one God (*ho theos*) the Father (Jehovah) who has an only-begotten divine Son, Jesus Christ. But since none of those three designations are found in Scripture, it is the responsibility of each author to define how he or she is using such designations.

It is not claimed that even children can understand all the relationships described in these doctrines, for they are mysteries indeed. However, these doctrines are not the simple teaching of Holy Scripture, which we have pointed out, namely: "The one God is the Father, Jesus Christ is his only begotten divine Son, and the Holy Spirit is his Spirit." Such is neither Trinitarian, Unitarian nor Tritheistic, but shall be shown to be completely and monotheistically biblical. That's THEOLOGY SIMPLIFIED.

CHAPTER 4

THE GREAT CLOUD OF WITNESSES

Before further dealing negatively with those comparatively few references and arguments which are so often used in an attempt to promote the doctrine of the Trinity, let us first see from the plain teachings of Scripture just how vast and overwhelming are the affirmative proofs that the one God is the Father, to the exclusion of all other beings or persons, and that Jesus Christ is that one God's only begotten divine Son, and that therefore the one God cannot be a triune being composed of a plurality of persons or personages which include his Son.

In the Bible there are no less than 56 references where God is specifically called the Father. (See Appendix A). That tells us precisely who the one God is; and he isn't Christ. God is not the Anointed; he is the Anointer. Seven of those references are in the OT, six of which show that the God who is called the Father is Jehovah. In 2 Sam 7:14 it is Jehovah (the LORD, v. 11) who said, "I will be his father, and he will be my son." Later, the author of Heb 1:5 applied this prophecy to Christ, showing therefore that Christ is not Jehovah as some have supposed, but is rather the Son of Jehovah. And since Jehovah is repeatedly declared in the OT to be the one only true God, then Jehovah God is therefore the Father of Christ, and is not a triune being composed of three persons including Christ.

Of those 56 references where God is specifically called the Father, 44 of them specifically distinguish Christ from God in such a way that even the mind of the simple can understand that Christ is not literally that God, but is rather the Son thereof. For example: "We always thank God, the Father of our Lord Jesus Christ" (Col 1:3).

And not only is God declared to be Christ's Father, but seven out of this group of references (according to both the NIV and ASV) furthermore declare him to be also the GOD of Christ; not just his Father, but also his God. For example, Jesus Christ (Rev 1:5) "has made us to be a kingdom and priests to serve his God and Father" (v. 6).

Out of all those 56 references which show that God is the Father, as distinguished from Christ, only Isaiah 9:6 refers in any way to Christ as being called God: "He will be called . . . Mighty God, Everlasting Father." The ASV has, "His name shall be called . . . ." In whatever sense Jesus is called *Mighty God*, surely in that sense he is also called *Everlasting Father*. If Jesus is not his own Father in the absolute sense, then neither should it be concluded that he is *Mighty God* in the absolute sense. But representatively, Jesus is both. Jesus, the Son of God, came to earth as a representative of the Mighty God, his everlasting Father. (See Part I, Ch. 9, *Mighty God, Everlasting Father*).

In Scripture Jesus is simply and emphatically distinguished from God. In no less than 403 NT references, in addition to those listed in Appendix A, Jesus is clearly distinguished from the God which Trinitarians and Unitarians claim Jesus to be, or to be a part of, or to be one of the persons or personalities in. Every time Jesus is called the Son of God, he is thereby distinguished from the God he is said to be the Son of.

Besides those many references which distinguish Jesus from the Father, a distinction apparently recognized by all, there are also no less than 77 other NT references to Jesus as being the Son of God, thereby distinguishing Jesus from the God he is the Son of. (See Appendix B). Four of those 77 NT references are quotations from the OT where the God, whom Jesus is said to be the Son of, is Jehovah, proving further that Jesus is not Jehovah as some have supposed.

"Son of God" no more makes Jesus God (*ho Theos*) than "Son of David" makes him David. But "Son of God" does give him the nature of God (divinity), just as "Son of David" gives him the nature of David (humanity).

Then in addition to those 77 mentioned references where Jesus is called the Son of God, there are at least 326 other NT references which also clearly distinguish Jesus from God. For example: "No one has ever seen God" (John 1:18); yet thousands had seen Jesus and continued seeing him daily. Again, Jesus "spent the night praying to God" (Luke 6:12). Thus, Jesus, the one doing the praying, is distinguished from God, to whom Jesus prayed. And again, "For there is one God and one mediator between God and men, the man Christ Jesus" (1 Tim 2:5). Thus Jesus, the mediator, is clearly distinguished from the one God between whom and mankind he mediates. For the entire list of 326 such references, see Appendix C.

Many of those, at least 46, are quotations from the OT where the God from whom Jesus is distinguished is Jehovah, proving further that Jesus is not Jehovah, and that Jehovah is not a triune being composed of three persons, including Jesus. For example: "The Lord said to my Lord: 'Sit at my right hand . . .'" (Matt 22:44). This is a quote from Ps 110:1, where it reads, "The LORD (Jehovah) says to my (David's) Lord (Christ)," thus clearly distinguishing Jesus from the Jehovah of the OT. Jehovah was the one doing the speaking; Christ was the one being spoken to. Jehovah said to Christ, etc.

These 403 distinguishing references are by no means limited to Jesus' relationship to God during his earthly advent, his existence as the Son of man on earth, for as many as 118 of them refer to Jesus after his resurrection and ascension back to his Father, and after having been glorified with the glory (or probably even above the glory) which he had with his Father before the world was (John 17:5). Example: "Jesus . . . sat at the right hand of God" (Mark 16:19). Thus Jesus is not God in heaven (*ho Theos*); but instead, he is at God's right hand.

Not only is Jesus thus clearly, simply, and emphatically distinguished from God these 403 times, being repeatedly called the Son of God, and God being repeatedly called Jesus' Father, as well as the very numerous other ways in which these two divine beings are separately and exclusively identified, but also 21 times God is even identified as Jesus' God, four of which show Jesus' God to be Jehovah, and six of which show God to be Jesus' God even after his ascension and reglorification. In Mark 15:34 Jesus cried out, "My God, my God, why have you forsaken me?" showing that God was not only Jesus' Father, but was also Jesus' God. Jesus also said to Satan, "It is also written: 'Do not put the Lord your God to the test'" (Matt 4:7). Jesus is not here calling himself the Lord God of Satan—not telling Satan that it is written in Deuteronomy 6:16 that Satan shouldn't make trial of Jesus—for apparently it was God's will that Jesus be thus tempted ("Jesus was led by the Spirit into the desert to be tempted by the devil," Matt 4:1). But Jesus was saying that he, Jesus, was not to make trial of Jehovah his God, as Satan was tempting him to do by getting him to jump off the highest point of the temple. Therefore Jesus is not Jehovah, but Jehovah is Jesus' God.

Then even after Jesus was restored to his former status with his Father in heaven, he said to the angel of the church in Philadelphia, "Him who overcomes I (Jesus) will make him a pillar in the temple of my God . . . . I (Jesus) will write on him the name of my God and the name of the city of my God . . . which is coming down out of heaven from my God" (Rev 3:12), showing repeatedly that even now, the God of heaven is still Jesus' God. How can one God be the God of another God, and both be coequally God in the same absolute sense, when there is only one God?

In the face of all this mighty cloud of affirmative witnesses, as catalogued in Appendices A, B, and C, about 459 thus far, that the one God is the Father to the exclusion of Christ and any other being or person, and that Christ is the only begotten Son of, and therefore distinguished from the one only true God, Jehovah, how can any truly informed scholar possibly presume that the one God is a triune being composed of three coequal and coeternal persons, including Christ? To fully receive the total impact of that query, one should at this point examine carefully all of Appendices A, B, and C.

A principal rule of logic and reasonable interpretation of Scripture requires that we first take all the many divine witnesses which are clearly and obviously in agreement on any subject under consideration, and let that testimony be presumed to establish the truth thereof. Then any other divine testimony, which may seem on the surface to conflict with the vast majority of evidence, must be interpreted in the light of the overwhelming majority of testimony, unless common logic forbids.

This rule of interpretation, though maybe herein crudely stated, is generally followed by biblical scholars, except that in the case of the Trinity, the opposite apparently has been the case. Disregarding all those 459 affirmative witnesses that the one God is the Father, and that Jesus Christ is the Son of that one God, Trinitarianism has declared, without even one single passage of Scripture that so states, that "the one God is a triune being composed of three coequal and coeternal persons—God the Father, God the Son, and God the Holy Spirit."

But since the truth of the matter is so well established in Scripture in such simple terms that even children or a novice can understand, we must now proceed to show how other evidence being used to the contrary does not in fact support either Trinitarianism or Unitarianism as have been defined, but rather, when properly understood, adds credence to the truth already established—that the one God is the Father, and that Jesus Christ is his only begotten divine Son.

It is not intended that the foregoing massive array of witness thus far considered be understood as exhaustive of all affirmative testimony on the relationship existing between God and Christ, for there is much more yet to come; but what has been mentioned thus far should be sufficient to impress any fair-minded student as to the truth and simplicity thereof.

A failure to understand that distinction between God and his Son has caused many to proclaim "Holy Mary" to be the "Mother of God," or to thank God (and sometimes even more specifically the Father) for dying on the cross, or to wonder if Mary realized that the God to whom she prayed was asleep in his cradle in the next room, or to wonder what Mary thought when she changed God's diapers and let God nurse from her breasts. One might just as well wonder if Mary expected God to hear and answer her prayers when supposedly God was a two-week-old human embryo in the womb of Mary. All such is theological nonsense, and shows how some Trinitarians and Unitarians do not even know the distinction between God and his Son.

CHAPTER 5

GOD AND DIVINE NATURE

While this book points out a very definite distinction between divine nature, angelic nature, human nature, animal nature, etc., it does not presume to explore and define the precise nature of divinity to any great extent beyond those characteristics defining God in the *Statement of Belief (Pribblonian Creed)*. To do so would be reaching beyond that which is written, and would be delving into unknown realms of speculation and fantasy. We believe that such would defeat the very purpose of *Theology Simplified*. We therefore would prefer leaving that subject to others.

Several erroneous hypotheses have kept theologians through the centuries from accepting our simple but biblical explanation. From the time of the Arian controversy late in the Third Century A.D., theologians seem to have concluded that since there is only one God, then everything that is divine must be part of that one God; meaning that if Christ is divine, he must be as much the one God as his Father is. But the word "divine" does not equate with *God*, it equates with the *nature* of God.

For one to be the offspring of God without the aid of any other being, therefore composed of God's very nature or substance as opposed to human nature or substance, does not make that one the God he is the offspring of. Not God in the absolute sense, but rather in a qualified or relative sense.

At the fount of human existence we find only one *Adam*, the Hebrew word for *man*. But since that first man, there have been millions classified as man or human, which mean, "having the nature of Adam." Adam, the being (or person), has no rival as origin of the human race. But all other beings issuing from Adam, including Eve, possess Adam's nature—human nature as distinguished from divine, angelic, animal, or any other nature. Those millions do not nullify the fact that there was only one original Adam, the father of the whole human race. Just as there is only one source of divine nature—God (that's monotheism), there is only one source of human nature—Adam (that's—if we may coin the word—monoanthropism). Cain could be the son of Adam, possessing the very nature of Adam as distinguished from divine or any other nature, without being that Adam he was the son of. Likewise, Christ can be the divine Son of God, possessing the very nature of God as distinguished from human or any other nature, without being that God he is the Son of. It cannot be successfully denied that there is only one being (or person) who is *God* in the absolute sense (*ho Theos*), regardless of how many may be called *God* or *gods* in a qualified sense.

The term *God* is acceptably used in more than one sense by divine authority. Reference has already been made to Jesus' conversation with the Jews as recorded in John 10:24-38. In this conversation Jesus used a very powerful argument to prove that one may rightly be called *god* without being the one God in the absolute sense. Jesus answered them, "Is it not written in your Law, 'I have said you are gods'? If he called them 'gods,' to whom the word of God came—and the Scripture cannot be broken—what about the one whom the Father set apart as his very own and sent into the world? Why then do you accuse me of blasphemy because I said, 'I am God's Son'?" (vv. 34-36). Note: The original text, being written in all capital letters, did not make the distinction between *god* with the little "g" and *God* with the capital "G." That difference is made by translators to make the very distinction of which we speak; that is, *God* in the absolute sense (there is only one such God) as distinguished from *god* in a qualified or relative sense. Jesus said, "I am God's Son" (v. 36). That makes Jesus *God* in the sense that any son who is an actual substance offspring possesses the same nature as his father. As Adam was human, so Cain was human. As Jesus' Father is divine, so Jesus is divine. But such does not mean that Jesus is that one, supreme, self-existent God and Father of whom he is the Son. However, because he is divine, we still prefer to bestow upon him special honor with the capital "G" to distinguish him from others whom God called *gods* in a human representative sense.

In the text under consideration, Jesus argued that God himself used the term *god* in such a broad but qualified and relative sense so as to include even the Israelites "to whom the word of God came" (v. 35). And Jesus used three witnesses to prove the validity of his argument. First, it was written in their Law. Second, God said it. Third, "the Scripture cannot be broken." As we might say, "It's in the Book!"

Jesus here quoted from Psalm 82:6, which no doubt was a reference back to verse 1 of the same Psalm, where "God presides in the great assembly; he gives judgment among the 'gods.'" Specifically, those called "gods" were the judges who had been given the solemn responsibility of judging the Israelites in keeping with that law God had given them through Moses. That exalted position caused them to be called "gods" because only God has the ultimate right to judge. Since those human judges had been given authority by God to represent him in such counseling and verdicts, they were *gods* representatively, but certainly not absolutely. There is still just one God absolute; and that is the Father.

Furthermore, immediately following God's declaration in Psalm 82:6, "I said, 'You are gods,'" he added, "you are all sons of the Most High." In the sense that they were sons of God, they could be called "gods." But this neither means that there are many Gods absolute, nor that the one God is composed of all those persons in Israel whom he called *gods*. There is still just one God absolute, and that one God is the Father of Jesus Christ, his only divine Son, as well as Father of the righteous, his spiritual sons, and even the Father of all mankind who are called "his offspring" (Acts 17:28), being the descendants of "Adam, the son of God" (Luke 3:38). Just as the Israelites were called *gods*, so may Christ be called *God* representatively, as well as because of his divine nature, without the one God being a triune being composed of three persons. There is still just one God; and that one God is the Father.

If God this day were to produce—not create nor make—a thousand offsprings, all persons possessing by inheritance God's divine nature or substance, there would not then be a thousand and two Gods, nor would the one God then become a plural being composed of a thousand and two persons. The one God would still be the Father to the exclusion of every other being. Jesus said, "I am God's Son." He did not say, "I am God."

CHAPTER 6

EQUALITY WITH GOD

It is in the sense of divine nature that Christ is said to be equal with God. The following text bears this out in a very obvious manner: Christ Jesus, "Who, being in very nature [Or *in the form of*] God, did not consider equality with God something to be grasped, but made himself nothing, taking the very nature of a servant, being made in human likeness" (Phil 2:6-7).

Is Christ here being called God? According to the NIV text, Christ was "being in very nature God." This rendition cannot be accepted as a true translation, but is rather a commentary on the meaning of what is actually said. The Greek says, "*en morphe Theou*," which literally translated is, "in (the) form of God." The NIV translators knew this; but instead of translating it that way in the text, they placed it as an alternate rendition in a footnote. That footnote corresponds not only with the Greek text, but also with seventeen out of twenty English translations examined, except that the *New Catholic Edition* (NCE), like the NIV text, has, "he was by nature God." But then the NCE commentary adds: "literally 'by form' in the Greek and Latin."

William F. Beck's mistranslation says, "Although He was God," but then follows with, "He decided not to take advantage of his being equal with God." Which is it? Was Christ God? Or was Christ *equal* with God? According to the other seventeen English translations examined, as well as the Greek text, Christ is not here said to be God. Berry's *Interlinear Literal Translation of the Greek New Testament* (ILT), as well as the ASV, NASB, KJV, NKJV, RV, RSV, and *The Amplified Bible* (AB) all have "in the form of God." The NWT has, "existing in God's form." Goodspeed, Weymouth, the *Simple English Bible* (SEB), the TEV, *The Twentieth Century New Testament* (TCNT), *The Jerusalem Bible* (JB), and Barclay all express the idea that Christ was by nature in the form of God.

And even if the NIV text were correct in saying that Christ is "in very nature God," it is obvious that the reference is to Christ's having the nature of God as opposed to the nature of man, without meaning that Christ is verily that God whose nature he possesses.

Christ is not here said to be the God he was on an equality with. But Christ was (and is) equal with God in that Christ, by actual, literal offspring possesses God's divine nature or substance. Christ, the instant he became God's Son, back in the ceaseless ages of eternity before anything else ever came into existence, he being rightly called "the firstborn over [or *of*] all creation. For by him all things were created" (Col 1:15-16), was equal with God in divine nature as distinguished from human or any other nature. They were not equally fathers, not equally sons, and not equal in sequence. For one person (or being) to be a son, he must of necessity be preceded by both the being doing the begetting and the act of being begotten. The Father is before the Son. They are neither equal in begetting nor in being begotten. They are not equal in supremacy, sovereignty, self-existence nor authority. They are not equal in sending nor in being sent. Neither are they equal in sanctifying nor in being sanctified (John 10:36 ASV). They are not equally the one God; but they are equally divine.

The day a human son is born, both father and son are equal. Beginning at birth a son is as much a living human being as his father is, or as he himself will ever be. He, by offspring, inherits human nature from his human father. He does not possess the nature of the lower animal kingdom, not that of angelic spirit beings, nor any other nature. He may, however, possess different characteristics from those of his father, yet still possess the same human nature. A son may be as dumb as an ox, as stubborn as a mule, as sly as a fox, as busy as a bee, sing like a bird, and play a harp like an angel, all possibly different from his father's characteristics, while he still possesses human nature equal with his father. Both are still human.

When a son is born, he and his father are not equal in age, sequence, size, strength, power, knowledge, wisdom, authority, and a lot of other things; but they are equal in nature, both being human as distinguished from any other nature. Similarly, the founding fathers of the United States of America declared, and we have accepted it as true, "All men are created equal." Likewise, while Christ is as divine as God his Father, that equality has never included divine Fatherhood, nor the authority that goes with being that Father, nor the supremacy of being the almighty God he is the Son of.

The context under consideration here shows that the equality shared by both God and Christ is their divine nature and the result thereof. Christ was not said to be existing as God, but "existing in the form of God" (ASV). Christ was not said to be God, nor equally God, but "on an equality with God" (ASV). Christ obviously was not the God he was on an equality with. But Christ "made himself nothing . . . being made in human likeness." The status, or rank, of the divine Son of God was lowered ("You made him a little lower than the angels" Heb 2:7), when he took on human nature in the form of a human body like his earthly ancestors all the way back to his father Adam. (See Luke 3:23-38). "Therefore, when Christ came into the world, he said . . . 'a body you prepared for me'" (Heb 10:5).

Furthermore, it may even be that the emphasis here is not to be placed so much on equality in nature or substance as on equality in the glorious status which both Father and Son shared in heaven over all other beings as a result of their equality in nature. For whatever that equality was, Jesus gave it up when he "made himself nothing, taking the very nature of a servant" (Phil 2:7). What a change in status! From that glorious, honorable, incorruptible and immortal existence with his Father in heaven, to the indignities and dishonor of a common slave in a corruptible, mortal body of flesh and bones, with all of its aches and woes, even to suffering and death at an early age on a torturous cross by wicked inhumane humans. The loss of that equality in glory with his Father was what Jesus wanted so desperately to be restored; but he knew it would come only by way of the cross. Jesus prayed on the night of his betrayal, "Father, the time has come. Glorify your Son, that the Son may glorify you . . . . And now, Father, glorify me in your presence with the glory I had with you before the world began" (John 17:1,5).

Whatever that equality of Phil 2:7 might have been, Jesus obviously gave it up while on earth in human form. However, it is evident that he was still as much the divine Son of God while on earth as he was before, and still is after his earthly advent. He has never ceased to be the divine Son of God. Jesus never changed from Son of God to Son of man; but that divine Son of God, a spirit being (or person) as distinguished from a natural, physical, human person, came into this world by means of the virgin birth, and dwelt in a fleshly human body, possessing all the characteristics and limitations of humanity. Thus by a supernatural procreation by God in that human virgin, and a normal physical gestation period and delivery in and by that human mother, the Son of God became also the Son of man, thus being both divine and human simultaneously. He is therefore often called (though not in Scripture) the "God-man," because during his earthly advent he was both divine and human.

However, Jesus' being divine on earth does not mean that he always possessed the powers of heaven while on earth. Those powers he gave up when he "made himself nothing." For the first thirty years of his life as the Son of man, even though he was still the divine Son of God through whom God had made all things (John 1:3; Col 1:16), Jesus was limited by his mortal and fleshly physical nature, living as did his fellow man without those powers of the supernatural world. But then when Jesus was baptized by John in Jordan, "At that moment heaven was opened, and he saw the Spirit of God descending like a dove and lighting on him" (Matt 3:16), endowing him with all the powers of heaven. "For the one whom God has sent speaks the words of God, for God gives the Spirit without limit. The Father loves the Son and has placed everything in his hands" (John 3:34-35). And again, "You know what has happened throughout Judea, beginning in Galilee after the baptism that John preached—how God anointed Jesus of Nazareth with the Holy Spirit and power, and how he went around doing good and healing all who were under the power of the devil, because God was with him" (Acts 10:37-38).

It was not until after that anointing that Jesus performed his first miracle when he turned water into wine at a marriage feast at Cana, which John the apostle later called "the first of his miraculous signs" (John 2:11). That power which Jesus had before his earthly advent, and not his divine nature, was taken from him (or was given up by him) when he "made himself nothing," not to be given him again until after his baptism. Jesus, though divine, was not that omnipotent God. The power he received on earth had to be given him by God. Jesus was able to perform all those miracles, not because he was that one omnipotent God, but rather because "God was with him" (Acts 10:38); that is, God gave Jesus power which he did not have for the first thirty years of his existence on earth as both Son of God and Son of man.

So Jesus' being "equal with God" does not mean that Jesus is that God (*ho Theos*) with whom he is equal.

CHAPTER 7

GOD WITH US

The prophetic use of the name "Immanuel" (*God with us*) is grossly misinterpreted by those using the name to prove that Christ is God absolute, instead of being God representatively. But let's examine the text.

When Ahaz was king of Judah (Isa 7), he learned that Rezin the king of Syria and Pekah king of Israel had formed a confederacy to fight against Judah. Because of a lack of confidence that God would rescue them, the heart of Ahaz and his people trembled. God told Isaiah to meet with Ahaz and strengthen his heart.

Isaiah already had a son to whom was given the symbolic name "Shear-Jashub," which means, "a remnant shall return." God told Isaiah to take this son with him to meet Ahaz, probably a prophetic reminder that even from the predicted Babylonian exile (as seen in the first five chapters of Isaiah, especially 5:13) a remnant would return. Thus the kingdom of Judah was not going to be destroyed; therefore Ahaz was not to be afraid of these two kings whom God called "smoldering stubs of firewood." Their plot against Judah would fail; and within 65 years (Isa 7:8) the northern kingdom of Israel would be no more.

Even though God was willing to strengthen the faith of Ahaz through a sign, Ahaz refused to ask for one. But Isaiah gave him one anyway. Isaiah told Ahaz, "The virgin will be with child and will give birth to a son, and will call him Immanuel" (Isa 7:14).

A sign was usually fulfilled in a relatively short period of time, within a few years at the most, or else the sign would serve no useful purpose. If the sign given by Isaiah (v. 14) was not going to come to pass until Christ would be born some 740 years later, it would have come some 722 years after the death of Ahaz, more than seven centuries too late to have done any good at all in strengthening the faith of Ahaz. Isaiah was not here predicting the birth of Christ as a sign to Ahaz.

Who was this virgin (or maiden, ASV fn.) who was going to bear this child called Immanuel? There is no need here to look for some kind of miraculous or supernatural conception or birth. The supernatural aspect of this sign would be on the part of Isaiah's being able to describe what was going to happen before it happened. The fact that the mother-to-be is called a virgin does not mean that the child would be begotten without a human father. It probably does mean, however, that at the time the prediction was made, the maiden under consideration was known to be a virgin.

In both the Greek OT Septuagint and the Greek NT the word for *virgin* is preceded by the definite article, thus *the virgin*. We may not be able to speak with absolute certainty concerning who she was, nor who would be the father of this Immanuel, but obviously both Isaiah and Ahaz knew exactly who was meant by *the virgin*, or else the prediction could not have been a profitable sign to Ahaz.

Some may have supposed that she was a newly acquired maiden in the king's harem, fulfilling the time required by royalty to prove that she was indeed a virgin, and not already with child by someone else, before she would be received by the king into his chambers. (Whose offspring would become heir to the throne was always of utmost concern.) She would thus be *the virgin* in waiting.

However, it is much more likely from the context that she was a young woman betrothed to Isaiah, of which Ahaz must have been well aware, and who subsequently became Isaiah's wife, becoming referred to as "the prophetess" (Isa 8:3). Supposedly, Isaiah's former wife had died after the birth of Shear-Jashub. But later it would be by this *prophetess* that Isaiah would father a male child to fulfill the sign given to Ahaz back in Isa 7:14. She was *the prophetess*, so called because she may very well have been a prophetess and a virgin, as were the four virgin daughters of Philip (Acts 21:9); or she may have been so called because she, formerly a virgin, had become the wife of the prophet Isaiah; hence, *a prophetess*; that is, the wife of a prophet.

Whichever the case might have been, it obviously was by her that Isaiah fathered the predicted son after having written down on a large scroll some sort of document containing the God-given name for that son. And to assure that the birth of that son would be an irrefutable sign for King Ahaz, Jehovah called on two reliable witnesses for the record, Uriah the priest, and Zechariah, probably a prophet, both of whom no doubt had credentials well known to the king.

Several things made this episode a trustworthy sign. First, the maiden was a virgin, never having conceived nor borne a child. Who, other than God, could know for sure that she was capable of conceiving a child? She, like many others, could have been barren. Second, even if she conceived, who could be sure that the conception would proceed normally to a successful birth? Third, even when the child would be born, the chance of its being a son instead of a daughter was only one in two. But when God, through one of his prophets, predicts a sign, all odds are removed. Isaiah's son was born as was predicted; therefore Ahaz could take courage in the remainder of Isaiah's predictions. The son was named by God "Maher-Shalal-Hash-Baz," which means, "quick to the plunder, swift to the spoil" (NIV fn.), or "the spoil speedeth, the prey hasteth" (ASV fn.). This was a symbolic name which told Ahaz that his enemies would soon be plundered. For "before the boy knows how to say 'My father' or 'My mother,' the wealth of Damascus and the plunder of Samaria will be carried off by the king of Assyria" (Isa 8:4). Then Isaiah proceeded to lay out in more detail how the destruction of Damascus and Samaria would be brought about by the Assyrian army, reaching down even into Judah itself (vv. 5-8), concluding with the exclamation, "O Immanuel!" God is with us! God has come to our rescue and has avenged our enemies!

Originally Isaiah had predicted that the child would be called "Immanuel"; but instead, he was named by God "Maher-Shalal-Hash-Baz." This does not mean that Isaiah's prediction was untrue. "Immanuel" was prophetic symbolism, meaning that when the predicted son would be born, his presence would be a sign that God was with the house of David, the kingdom of Judah, and that God had come to their rescue. It by no means meant that Maher-Shalal-Hash-Baz was God in the flesh in the form of Isaiah's son.

Then seven centuries later, when Matthew applied the wording of this prophecy to the birth of Christ (Matt 1:23), he was not saying that Christ was literally God in the flesh, but that the miraculous conception of Christ in the virgin Mary by the power of God's Holy Spirit would be proof that God, after several centuries, had come to the rescue of lost and dying mankind. Just as Isaiah's son was never literally named Immanuel, but Maher-Shalal-Hash-Baz instead, so God's Son was never literally named Immanuel; for "you are to give him the name Jesus" (Matt 1:21), a name which means "Jehovah saves." Thus God came to the rescue of mankind by sending his Son to be our savior. "O Immanuel!" But as far as we know, Jesus was never literally called by that name. Thus the prophetic name *Immanuel* no more means that Jesus is the one God absolute than it did in the case of Maher-Shalal-Hash-Baz. Jesus, like Isaiah's son, was God symbolically and representatively, not literally and absolutely. A thorough study of Isaiah 7:14 in the greater context of the entire seventh and eighth chapters will show conclusively that the birth of Jesus was not the sign being predicted.

There have been many Jewish names which have carried meanings pertaining to God, without those names signifying that the ones so-called were divine, much less God or gods. For example, the military leader who led Israel into Canaan was called "Joshua" (*Jehovah saves* or *Jehovah is salvation*). That name did not mean that Joshua was Jehovah God. In fact, it was probably a reminder of the fact that when he led Israel to victory, it was not he who saved Israel, but rather Jehovah.

The Greek form for *Joshua* is *Jesus*; yet no one seems to claim that because the Son of God is named *Jesus* (*Jehovah is salvation*), therefore Jesus must be Jehovah, for they know that the same reasoning would also mean that Joshua who led Israel would also be Jehovah.

A few other examples could include Josiah (*Jehovah supports*), 2 Kings 22:1; Jotham (*Jehovah is perfect*), Judges 9:5; Jozabad (*Jehovah has bestowed*), 1 Chronicles 12:20; Jozachar (*Jehovah has remembered*), 2 Kings 12:21 (KJV); Jozadak (*Jehovah is righteous*), Ezra 3:2; etc. None of these were God, but they all were called by God's name, just as both Isaiah's son and Christ were said to be called by God's name Immanuel (*God with us*), without their being God.

CHAPTER 8

USING PROPHETIC EXPRESSIONS

Just how could Matthew make such a connection between Isaiah 7:14 and the birth of Jesus, as in Matthew 1:23? One explanation is the fact that OT prophecy many times had not only an immediate application to national Israel, but also embodied a far-reaching and distant application to the coming of the Messiah with his spiritual kingdom. In such cases, not all the details of the prophecy would necessarily fit both occasions, especially not the latter.

But another similar use of such double application of prophecy, a more prominent use than most people realize, is that of NT writers simply borrowing certain familiar expressions from well-known ancient prophecies and applying those expressions, as they became applicable, to events in latter times. Not that the latter events were the object, either directly or indirectly, of the prophet's message; but applying those familiar expressions would oftentimes enhance the meaning and intensity of the contemporary event being described. Thus many times, exceptionally often by Matthew, and in the Revelation to John, when certain OT prophetic expressions, even though taken out of their original setting, seemed to fit the current occasion in at least one point, the NT writers used such expressions as if those prophets had actually had the latter-day applications in mind. Not that the NT writers schemed deception; but rather, such applications were a common part of communication in their time, especially among the Jews to whom Matthew's gospel and the Hebrew epistle were written.

A failure to understand this type of literary composition has caused many modern-day prophetic interpreters to think that the Revelation to John and the prophecies of such men as Ezekiel and Daniel all point to the same latter-day fulfillments, failing to realize that in John's Revelation many OT familiar expressions are merely borrowed and applied symbolically to Christ's spiritual kingdom.

An obvious example of this use of prophetic expressions that could not have been originally uttered with the latter application in mind is Matthew's description of Herod's slaughter of the infants soon after the birth of Jesus. "A voice is heard in Ramah, weeping and great mourning, Rachel weeping for her children" (Matt 2:18). This statement was borrowed from Jeremiah's prediction of the capture of the kingdom of Judah and the destruction of Jerusalem by Nebuchadnezzar (Jer 31:15), which took place about eighteen years after Jeremiah's prediction, in which he endeavored to describe the horrible sadness of the occasion.

The captives were assembled in Ramah, bound in chains, awaiting that long trek to Babylon as slaves (Jer 40:1). As Ramah was about five to seven miles north of Jerusalem, the captives could no doubt look back and see the flames and pillars of smoke rising from the shambles of their beloved city and temple where God had once dwelt so gloriously among them. It would be hard to describe the lamentations and woes of the occasion; but Jeremiah tried by picturing the ultimate in human sorrow, "Rachel weeping for her children."

Rachel's two sons were Joseph and Benjamin. Some 135 years before, the two tribes of Ephraim and Manasseh, Rachel's only grandsons by Joseph, had already been carried away by the Assyrians at the destruction of the kingdom of Israel; and now, what is left of the tribe of Benjamin, her only other son, who had remained with the kingdom of Judah, is about to leave on that long and torturous journey as slaves to Babylon. Thus Rachel, whose sepulcher was nearby, is in this beautiful figure of poetry pictured as coming out of her tomb and lamenting bitterly over the loss of her children who were no longer to be found; for they were either slain or taken into captivity. The prophecy fit perfectly the occasion.

But then when Matthew later applied these words to the slaughter at Bethlehem, the only thing that fit the occasion was the bitter anguish of mothers for their newborn sons who were snatched from their arms and slaughtered at Herod's command. Opposed to Ramah of Jeremiah's prophecy, Bethlehem was six miles to the south of Jerusalem, in the land of Judah, from which tribe Jesus was descended. Judah's mother was Leah, not Rachel. Wrong city, wrong direction from Jerusalem, wrong tribe, wrong mother. Then Jeremiah added, "Your children will return to their own land" (Jer 31:17), predicting the Jews' return from Babylon. No way could this have been said of the slaughtered infants of Bethlehem, for they never came again. In fact, other than the intense sorrow of mothers over the loss of their children, none of the details of Jeremiah's prophecy fit Herod's massacre. As fitly described by Adam Clarke:

> St. Matthew, who is ever fond of accommodation, applies these words . . . to the massacre of the children at Bethlehem. That is, they were suitable to that occasion, and therefore he so applied them; but they are not a prediction of that event. (Adam Clarke's *Commentary* on Jer 31:15).[3]

William Barclay, in his comment on Matthew 2:18, put it this way:

> Here again . . . we see Matthew's characteristic way of using the Old Testament . . . . Very clearly the verse in Jeremiah has no connection with Herod's slaughter of the children . . . . Here again Matthew is doing what he so often did. He is finding a prophecy in his eagerness where no prophecy is. But, again, we

must remind ourselves that what seems strange to us seemed in no way strange to those for whom Matthew was writing in his day.

In similar fashion Matthew also borrowed the name Immanuel from Isaiah's prediction of the birth of Isaiah's son as a sign to Ahaz that God would come to their rescue, and applied the name to Jesus centuries later. For God had again come to man's rescue, this time representatively in his own Son. Thus Jesus, to be called Immanuel, is not thereby proven to be the one only almighty God in the absolute sense any more than was Isaiah's son who was actually the original one predicted to be called Immanuel. But Jesus' very presence on earth via the virgin birth was a sign to man that after about 400 years of no direct communication from God, God is now again coming to man's rescue by sending his own Son. "O Immanuel!"

CHAPTER 9

MIGHTY GOD, EVERLASTING FATHER

Another such Scripture which shows Christ to be God representatively, but one which is often misused in an attempt to prove that Christ is the almighty God absolute is Isaiah 9:6, "For to us a child is born, to us a son is given, and the government will be on his shoulders. And he will be called Wonderful Counselor, Mighty God, Everlasting Father, Prince of Peace." The ASV has, "his name shall be called," another example of poetic symbolism, for we know his name was to be Jesus (Matt 1:21). His mission was to be Savior, which is the meaning of the name Jesus. And his title was Christ, which means "anointed." Jesus was never literally called "Mighty God" nor "Everlasting Father." And it was proper that he not be thus called, for he himself instructed, "And do not call anyone on earth 'father,' for you have one Father, and he is in heaven" (Matt 23:9). Jesus was not at that time in heaven, and was certainly not to be called "Everlasting Father." But he was to be received as God's Son, the on-earth representative of the Mighty God, the Everlasting Father who was and is in heaven. First, let us consider what, according to prophecy, his name was to be called. According to the *Septuagint* (LXX) in Isaiah 9:6, his name is called "the Messenger of great counsel," not "Mighty God." It was in the Alexandrine Text, compiled probably in the Fifth Century A.D., that "Wonderful, Counsellor, Mighty One, Potentate, Prince of Peace, Father of the age to come" was added. Thus, in either case, the LXX in this text calls Jesus neither "Mighty God" nor "Everlasting Father."

However, let's consider the text as quoted from the NIV, where both "Mighty God" and "Everlasting Father" (ASV fn: Heb. "Father of Eternity") are found. If "Mighty God" means that Jesus is literally that one almighty God of whom he is the Son, then likewise "Everlasting Father" must also mean that Jesus is literally that Father of whom he is the Son, therefore being his own Father, and being as much "God the Father" as he is "God the Son." No wonder the doctrine of the Trinity is called a mystery. Who can believe it? No doubt this is the reason for avoiding as much as possible the name "Everlasting Father" when applying the other names in this text to Jesus in an absolute sense.

A certain song, favorite to some, goes like this: "Wonderful, Wonderful, Jesus is to me; Counselor, Prince of Peace, Mighty God is he." But "Everlasting Father" is conspicuous by its absence from the lyrics; absent no doubt because everyone knows that Jesus is not the Father, but is rather the Son. So the absence of "Everlasting Father" is compensated for in the song by using "Wonderful" twice for meter's sake. It should be obvious to all that Jesus is not literally the Mighty God any more than he is literally the Everlasting Father; but that representatively he is both. The one God, the Father, did not leave his home in heaven and come to earth to save mankind; but he sent his only begotten divine Son as his representative to do so. Consider Jesus' parable of the wicked husbandmen (Matt 21:33-41) where this very truth is so vividly illustrated. Thus this text in Isaiah is not declaring that Jesus is two of a plurality of persons in the one God, both the Father and the Son, but that God's Son, Jesus, represents on earth that Mighty God, his Everlasting Father. And even children can understand that simple concept, which is so consistent with the whole theme of the Bible. They know that Jesus is God's Son, and that makes the one God his Father.

Furthermore, the words "Mighty" and "Almighty" are from different words in the original, with *mighty* referring to any number of biblical characters, while *Almighty* refers exclusively to the one and only Jehovah God, and never to Christ. (See Part I, Ch. 34, *"The Alpha and the Omega"*).

According to the ASV marginal note, the Hebrew text means "Father of eternity," instead of "Everlasting Father." The Alexandrine Text has, "Father of the age to come," and the New Catholic Edition has, "Father of the world to come." If these represent the true intent, then Christ is not here being called a Father in the sense that God is the progenitor of Christ his firstborn, and the Father of our spirits (for "We are his offspring," Acts 20:28); but rather Christ, as joint creator with God—for "without him nothing was made that has been made" (John 1:3)—is the origin and cause of the age and world to come. Thus Christ is not the actual Father of anyone, has never given birth to any person, but is the origin and producer of everything that is and is to come.

CHAPTER 10

THE FULLNESS OF THE GODHEAD

About Jesus, Paul declared, "In Christ all the fullness of the Deity lives in bodily form" (Col 2:9), or "In him dwelleth all the fullness of the Godhead bodily" (ASV). From this passage some have supposed that the one true God (*ho Theos*) literally came to earth, clothing himself with that body which came forth from the virgin Mary, concluding that Christ is therefore the one God in the absolute sense, and making Mary in fact the mother of God. But Mary is nowhere in divine Scripture ever called, or said to be, the mother of God. However, she is the mother of the Son of God as pertains to his existence as a human being. But as we have said before, when Jesus took on human nature, he did not change that Father-Son relationship, and did not cease to be the divine Son of God; but he did allow himself to become limited by the normal restrictions of a human existence, until at age thirty God anointed him with the Holy Spirit and power.

So the *fullness* of Colossians 2:9 undoubtedly refers to that divine nature which remained with Jesus even while existing as a human being. While on earth, Jesus continued to be as fully divine as he had ever been or would ever be, a truth which was in direct opposition to Gnostic doctrine to which Paul was directing his arguments. He was not trying to prove that Christ is that one only God, but that Christ, even as a man, still possessed divine nature in its fullness.

But if that *fullness* in Colossians 2:9 necessitates all the powers of the omnipotent God, be reminded that Paul made that present-tense declaration not only after Jesus had received God's Spirit without measure, but also after Jesus' corruptible, dishonorable, weak and natural body had been resurrected as an incorruptible, glorious, powerful and spiritual body (1 Cor 15:42-44), and after that resurrected Christ had ascended back to his original, or even above his original glorious status with the one God his Father in heaven.

Furthermore, Paul referred to the church as "the fullness of him who fills everything in every way" (Eph 1:23). And he bowed his knees to the end that the Christians at Ephesus "may be filled to the measure of all the fullness of God" (Eph 3:19). Paul did not hereby mean that when they had attained that fullness of God, they would then have become that almighty God with whom they were filled, nor even some of the persons in a supposed plural being called God. So for Jesus to have in himself all the fullness of the divine nature does not make him that one God whose divine nature fully indwells him. Again, Jesus was, is and ever shall be God's divine Son.

CHAPTER 11

ELOHIM

Great stress is often placed on the fact that the word *Elohim*, the most common Hebrew word for God, is plural in form, and therefore supposedly proves that God is a plural being composed of more than one person. This argument cannot be used to support the idea that the Godhead is composed of three persons, God being one of those persons; for *Elohim* is the word for God, not Godhead. If *Elohim* proves any plurality at all, it proves the plurality of God, not the Godhead. If it means three of anything, it means three Gods, not three persons. But *Elohim* is the plural for *Eloah*, both of which are translated "God," and both refer to the same being or person. Therefore, *Elohim* no more proves that God is a plural being composed of three persons than *Eloah* proves that God is a singular being composed of one person. Consider the following testimonies:

Peloubet's Bible Dictionary, under "God," says:

> The plural form of Elohim has given rise to much discussion. The fanciful idea that it referred to the *trinity of persons* in the Godhead hardly finds now a supporter among scholars. It is either what grammarians call *the plural of majesty*, or it denotes the *fullness* of divine strength, the *sum of the powers* displayed by God.[4]

The International Standard Bible Encyclopaedia (ISBE), under "GOD," *II-3-(1)* says:

> By far the most frequent form used by OT writers is the plural Elohim, but they use it regularly with singular verbs and adjectives to denote a singular idea. Several explanations have been offered of this usage of a plural term to denote a singular idea—that it expresses the fullness and manifoldness of the Divine nature, or that it is a plural of majesty used in the manner of royal persons, or even that it is an early intimation of the Trinity . . . . These theories are, perhaps, too ingenious to have occurred to the early Hebrew mind, and a more likely explanation is, that they are survivals in language of a polytheistic stage of thought. In the OT they signify only the general notion of Deity.

ISBE, under "GOD, NAMES OF," *II-1*, concerning *Elohim*:

(1) Its *form* is pl., but the construction is uniformly sing., i.e. it governs a sing. vb. or adj., unless used of heathen divinities . . . .

(2) The *derivation* is quite uncertain . . . . The origin must always lie in doubt, since the derivation is prehistoric . . . .

(3) It is the reasonable conclusion that the meaning is "might" or "power"; that it is common to Sem language; that the form is pl. to express majesty or "all-mightiness," . . . [5]

Works of Elder B. W. Stone, in "*An Address To the Churches*," pp. 54-55, says: The doctrine of a plurality of persons in the one God, is argued from the plural termination of the Hebrew word *Elohim*, translated *God*. As great stress is laid on this argument . . . it will be necessary to introduce the rule in Hebrew Grammar . . . . "A plural put for a singular denotes greatness and excellency."

—Robertson's Heb. Gram., p. 240.[1]

The NIV Study Bible, Commentary on Gen 1:1, *God created*:

The Hebrew noun *Elohim* is plural but the verb is singular, a normal usage in the OT when reference is to the one true God. This use of the plural expresses intensification rather than number and has been called the plural of majesty, or of potentiality.

There are numerous examples of others in the OT called *Elohim*, without suggesting a plurality of persons:

(1) Jehovah said to Moses, "See, I have made you like God [*Elohim*] to Pharaoh" (Exod 7:1).

(2) The Israelites called the molten calf Aaron made *Elohim* (Exod 32:4, 8. ASV fn: "This is thy God." See also Neh 9:18).

(3) The Israelites claimed their idol, Baal, to be *Elohim* (Judg 6:31; see also 1 Kgs 18:27).

(4) The Israelites also made Baal-Berith their *Elohim* (Judg 8:33; 9:27).

(5) The *Elohim* of the Amorites and Moabites was the idol Chemosh (Judg 11:24; I Kgs 11:33).

(6) Ashtoreth was the goddess (*Elohim*) of the Sidonians (1 Kgs 11:5, 33).

(7) Molech (Milcom, ASV) was the *Elohim* of the children of Ammon (1 Kgs 11:33).

(8) The Philistines said that their *Elohim*, Dagon, delivered Samson their enemy into their hand; so they praised their *Elohim*, Dagon (Judg 16:23-24. See also 1 Sam 5:7)

(9) Baal-zebub is called the *Elohim* of Ekron (2 Kgs 1:2, 3, 6, 16).

(10) Sennacherib, king of Assyria, worshiped in the house of Nisroch his *Elohim* (2 Kgs 19:37: 2 Chr 32:21; Isa 37:38).

(11) Nebuchadnezzar's god in Babylon is called *Elohim* (Dan 1:2).

(12) Jonah's frightened shipmates cried every man unto his *Elohim* (Jonah 1:5).

Surely Moses was not thought by Pharaoh to be a plural being composed of a plurality of persons. And surely all these idols (though each is in the singular) are individually referred to with the plural *Elohim* because of their supposed dignity, majesty and excellence in the minds of their worshipers, and not because they each were believed to be composed of a plurality of persons.

Further examples of this rule in Hebrew grammar (the plural of majesty) are seen in the plural title *Adonim* (master, lord). The following quote is from Barton W. Stone, Ibid., pp. 55-56:

> "And the servant put his hand under the thigh of Abraham, his *master*," his *Adonim* in the plural—Gen 24:9, 10, 51. So Potiphar is called Joseph's *Adonim, master*—Gen 39:2, 3, 7, 8, 16, 19, 20 . . . . So Joseph, the ruler of Egypt, was called *Adonim, a lord*—Gen 42:30, 33 and 44:8. In all these places the plural is used for the singular, according to the well known rule; because the word expresses dominion, dignity and greatness. It would be unnecessary to multiply quotations. These surely are sufficient to prove to any unprejudiced mind, that the plural word, put for a singular, does not imply a plurality of persons.[1]

Furthermore, with the exception of references to the many gods of pagan polytheism, the Hebrew plural *Elohim* is correctly translated in the *Septuagint* (LXX) by the Greek singular *Theos*, because those seventy Greek and Hebrew scholars knew that the plural *Elohim* did not suggest a plurality of persons in the one God. According to Thayer's *Greek Lexicon*, p. 287b, the LXX uses *Theos* to translate both *El* (singular) and *Elohim* (plural).[7]

If the LXX mistranslated *Elohim*, Jesus and his apostles failed to make any mention of it; but instead, the NT writers, when quoting from the OT, likewise translated the Hebrew *Elohim* with the Greek singular *Theos*, even though they had access to the plural Greek form for God (*Theoi*). And we know of no English version, either ancient or modern, which does not translate the plural *Elohim* with the singular "God."

Therefore, the inevitable and reasonable conclusion is that no one should ever use the plural *Elohim* to prove, or even suggest, that the one God is a plural being composed of a plurality of persons or personalities. Jehovah God is ONE, not two nor three.

CHAPTER 12

US AND OUR

In addition to the plural *Elohim*, "us" and "our" (in such passages as Gen 1:26; 3:22; 11:7; Isa 6:8) are considered by some to be of great weight in establishing the notion of a plurality of persons in the one God. We shall here show why such a conclusion is unwarranted.

What these plural pronouns do infer in the passages mentioned is that there must have been at least two parties (persons or beings) involved: (1) the party doing the speaking, and (2) the party or parties being spoken to. It was God (*Elohim, Theos*) who said, "Let us make man in our image, in our likeness" (Gen 1:26). In Genesis 3:22 it is the LORD God (Jehovah Elohim). In Genesis 11:7 it is the LORD (Jehovah). In Isaiah 6:8 it is the Lord, called "the LORD (Jehovah) Almighty" in v.5.

But if there had been no party of the second part, the party being spoken to, surely God would have declared, if anything, "I will make man in MINE own image." So setting aside the improbable "corporate" or "editorial" WE, what are the possible (or even probable) conclusions as to the party or parties being spoken to? Since the Scriptures mentioned do not tell us specifically to whom God thus spoke, any answer given should be based on sound reasoning. First, what persons or beings could possibly have been present to have been thus spoken to?

POSSIBILITY #1: God could have been speaking to "all the host of heaven standing around him on his right and on his left" (1 Kgs 22:19). On this referenced occasion a conversation ensued between Jehovah and this "host of heaven," concerning who would fulfill a particular chore. We are not told how long this heavenly host had been in existence, but we may conclude that these were intelligent spirit beings, including angels, created by Christ (Col 1:16; John 1:3; 1 Cor 8:6), before God ended his work of creation, and rested on the seventh day (Gen 2:3). And because such spirit beings, including angels, were nowhere mentioned as having been created on any one of the days of the creative week, they, like the heavens and the earth (Gen 1:1), must have already been created at some point or points—who knows when?—prior to the days of the creative week.

The devil (Satan) and his angels apparently at one time had been part of this "heavenly host" (2 Pet 2:4; Jude 6; Rev 12:9), but were cast out of heaven, accounting for Satan's presence in the earth soon after Adam and Eve were created. Those angels which did not thus sin apparently remained as part of the heavenly host present when God spoke of US and OUR. "Our image" could not have referred to the nature of the man to be made; for man possesses human nature, while

God possesses divine nature. Therefore angels are not to be excluded from "OUR image" just because angels are not divine; for neither is man divine. So in what way is man made in God's image?

Both divine and human natures possess the power of reproduction. If this were the only way man is made in God's image, then the angels must be excluded from US and OUR in Genesis 1:26, because Jesus said that after the resurrection there will be no such thing as marriage (the means for reproduction), but instead, we will be like the angels in heaven (Matt 22:30), implying the lack of ability to reproduce.

But that which God, the angels, and man do all have in common includes intellect, mind, will, power of choice, being, individuality, personality, etc. In this sense God could have included "the host of heaven" in US and OUR image.

The NIV Study Bible, commenting on Genesis 1:26, concerning US and OUR, has this to say: "God speaks as the Creator-King, announcing his crowning work to the members of his heavenly court."

Question: If *Elohim* were a triune being composed of three persons, and as man is made in the image of *Elohim*, is man likewise a triune being composed of three persons? Would anyone dare propose the idea that the body, soul, and spirit of man are three separate and distinct persons who make up the one being which each man is? We think not.

POSSIBILITY #2: We know that when God said, "Let us make man in our image," Jesus Christ, God's Son, later to be called "the Word," was present (John 1:1-3, 14; 17:5; 1 John 1:1-2). We know also that as a result of this statement by God, the Father, OF or FROM whom all things came, man was therefore made by the Lord, Jesus Christ, BY or THROUGH whom all things came, including man (1 Cor 8:6; John 1:3; Col 1:16).

So the obvious conclusion is that Christ must have been that second party (person or being) to whom God spoke, and whom God included to constitute the plural US and OUR. This second explanation seems to be the more probable of the two.

POSSIBILITY #3: God could have been speaking to any one or more beings included in that host of heaven referred to in our POSSIBILITY #1.

POSSIBILITY #4: God could have been speaking to a combination of any or all of the first three possibilities.

Any one of these four suggested possibilities is far more probable than the idea that the plural pronouns suggest a plurality of persons in a God who was both doing the speaking and being spoken to. And if Moses, recording this information, divinely inspired by God's Spirit, was trying to tell the Israelites that the Spirit of God was one of three persons in the *Elohim* who was both doing the speaking and being spoken to, then Moses failed miserably. For to the Israelites, who knew the Hebrew language best, such a suggestion would have been most incredible. And nowhere do NT writers ever suggest such an explanation for Genesis 1:26.

Any father who is a custom home builder might say to his son who supervises their construction crew, "Let us build a house according to these plans and specifications." The son takes the plans and proceeds accordingly. And when the project is completed, either father or son could proclaim, "We did it!" Who on earth would conclude that either of them, including the father who had said, "Let US," was claiming to be a plural being composed of more than one person, because he used the plural pronoun?

Simply stated, Genesis 1:26 must have been addressed by God to his Son, who then carried out the order as he was told. Surely, even children can understand that simple concept. Why would anyone want to turn such a simple statement into something so complicated and mysterious?

CHAPTER 13

THREE THAT BEAR RECORD

It is interesting to note how theological bias has crept into the various language texts, copies, versions and publications of the Bible down through the centuries, most of which alterations were apparently thought to be needed to help support the traditional doctrine of the Trinity, a doctrine which needed all the support it could get because of the lack of genuine support from the Scriptures themselves as they were originally written.

Prior to the Twentieth Century, and even today among those who are uninformed, the statements found in 1 John 5:7-8 as they appear in the King James Version (KJV), seem to have been used as exhibit No. 1 in favor of the case of Trinitarian doctrine: "For there are three that bear record [in heaven, the Father, the Word, and the Holy Ghost: and these three are one. And there are three that bear witness in earth], the spirit, and the water, and the blood: and these three agree in one." The brackets inserted here are not found in the KJV, but have been placed here to offset that portion which is now known to deserve no place in the biblical text. According to *The NIV Study Bible* at this point, "the addition is not found in any Greek manuscript or NT translation prior to the 16th century." The RV, ASV and RSV omit it without even considering it to be worthy of a footnoted explanation.

William Barclay gives the following explanation in his *Daily Study Bible Series:*

It is quite certain that it does not belong to the original text . . . . First, it does not occur in any Greek manuscript earlier than the 14th Century. The great manuscripts belong to the 3rd and 4th Centuries, and it occurs in none of them. None of the great early fathers of the Church knew it. Jerome's original version of the Vulgate does not include it. The first person to quote it is a Spanish heretic called Priscillian who died in A.D. 385. Thereafter it crept, bit by bit, into the Latin texts of the New Testament, although, as we have seen, it did not gain an entry to the Greek manuscripts . . . . Since it seemed to offer good scriptural evidence for the doctrine of the Trinity, bit by bit it came to be accepted by theologians as part of the text, especially in the early days of scholarship before the great manuscripts had been discovered.

Albert Barnes, in his *Notes on the New Testament*, at this passage, observes that—

It is never quoted by the Greek fathers in their controversies on the doctrine of the Trinity—a passage which would be so much in point, and which could not have failed to be quoted if it were genuine; . . . It was at first written perhaps, in the margin of some Latin manuscript, as expressing the belief of the writer . . . . Some transcriber copied it into the body of the text, perhaps with a sincere belief that it was a genuine passage, omitted by accident; and then it became too important a passage in the argument for the Trinity, ever to be displaced but by the most clear critical evidence. It was rendered into Greek, and inserted in one Greek manuscript of the 16th century, while it was wanting in all the earlier manuscripts . . . . this passage is not a genuine portion of the inspired writings, and should not be appealed to in proof of the doctrine of the Trinity.[6]

But then let us, for the sake of argument, consider the passage to be genuine. What part of the doctrine of the Trinity does it actually prove? Verse 5 had just asked and answered the vital question, "Who is it that overcomes the world? Only he who believes that Jesus is the Son of God." Not, "he who believes that Jesus is God."

Nothing in the questionable text says anything about the one God as a triune being composed of three persons. The word "person" is not even found in the text. Nor does the text say that the three record bearers in heaven are one God. They three are said to be one; but the oneness under consideration is the agreement of the record being borne by each of the three. If all bear the same record, then the three are in agreement; they are one in the record they bear. They do not record conflicting testimony. So it is with the three that testify in the earth who agree in one, in that portion of the text, the genuineness of which is not challenged. The three agree in one; that is, they do not bear conflicting testimony.

Some have argued that only a person can bear witness; therefore the Spirit which is said to bear witness must be a person. But that same genuine part of the passage says that the water and the blood also testify, or bear witness. Does that mean that the water and the blood are also each persons? Certainly not. And neither does the Spirit's bearing record in heaven with the Father and the Word prove that the Spirit is a person. Nor does the fact that the Bible bears record of God's will toward man prove that the Bible is a person. In both the genuine and spurious portions of this passage, the Word, the Spirit, the water and the blood are each personified as either record bearers or witness bearers. But personifying a thing does not literally make that thing a personal entity. Under a later topic we shall further see in what sense the Spirit of God may be called a person, but certainly not in the sense implied and taught by the doctrine of the Trinity. Therefore, this passage, whether genuine of spurious, does nothing to prove that the one God is a triune being composed of three persons. If it can be proved at all, it will have to be done with evidence found elsewhere.

CHAPTER 14

GOD MANIFEST IN THE FLESH

Another very unfortunate rendering, based on spurious evidence which crept into the KJV, is found in 1 Timothy 3:16. But even more unfortunate and more unexplainable is the fact that even today in our age of textual enlightenment, a few who would consider themselves scholars on the subject still cling to that unwarranted rendition as found in the KJV, only because they believe that it supports Trinitarianism and/or Unitarianism by calling Christ "God," as follows: "God was manifest in the flesh, justified in the Spirit, seen of angels, preached unto the Gentiles, believed on in the world, received up into glory." From this comes the often-used expression that Christ is "God manifest in the flesh."

Out of eighteen English translations examined, none of which predate the KJV, only the KJV has at this place, "God was manifest in the flesh." None of the seventeen later versions even have the word "God" in the statement under consideration. The following list gives the renderings of those versions, along with their accompanying footnotes:

> RV (*Revised Version*) and ASV: "He who" (fn: The word *God*, in place of *He Who*, rests on no sufficient ancient evidence. Some authorities read Which).
> NCE (*New Catholic Edition*): "which" (fn: The Greek reading is "who," i.e., the Christ, instead of "which," i.e., the gospel.)
> NEB (*New English Bible*), Barclay, and Weymouth: "He who" (no fn).
> NASB (*New American Standard Bible*): "He who" (fn: Some later mss. read *God*.)
> RSV: "He" (fn: Greek *Who*; other ancient authorities read *God;* others, *Which*.)
> NIV: "He" (fn: Some manuscripts *God*).
> AB: "He" (fn: Some authorities read "God.")
> Williams: "He" (fn: Likely from an early Christian hymn in praise of the person and work of Christ.)
> TEV, NWT (*New World Translation*), Beck, Goodspeed, and TCNT: "He" (no fn).
> SEB (*Simple English Bible*): "Christ" (No fn.)

So the vast weight of evidence among English translators is that the apostle is saying, "He who (that is, Christ) was manifest in the flesh." Then let's hear testimony from Greek texts which were compiled, using all the fragmentary evidence available. Out of eight such Greek texts examined, seven of which are represented with all their variations in Berry's *Interlinear Literal Translation of the Greek New Testament* (ILT), only Elzevir has *Theos* (God) in place of *os* (the masculine form for "who," i.e., "He who"). Elzevir (1624) was much too early to have access to the better and more ancient MSS discovered in the Nineteenth Century. The various texts by Griesbach, Lachmann, Tischendorf, Tregelles, Alford, Wordsworth, and Nestle all have *os* ("He," or "He who") at this place; and there is no sufficient evidence to the contrary which could warrant its use as an argument in favor of the Trinity.

William Barclay at this point in his *Daily Study Bible* says that—

> Here we have a fragment of one of the hymns of the early church . . . . Right at the beginning this hymn stresses the real manhood and the real humanity of Jesus. It says: "Look at Jesus, and you will see life as God would have lived it, if God had been a man."

Such a statement is in direct opposition to the idea that God ever became a man, while recognizing that Christ, God's Son, did truly become man. And even if there were equal evidence in the Greek manuscripts for either "God" or "He who," both Scripture and reason would rule in favor of the latter, inasmuch as it was Christ (the Son of God) and not God himself (of whom Christ is the Son) who was manifest in the flesh; for "No one has ever seen God" (John 1:18).

Furthermore, even if the word *God* were justified at this point, obviously it would have reference to the divine nature existing in Christ, which is often the case when *Theos* is not accompanied by the definite article (as we shall establish more fully in our study of John 1:1; see Part I, Ch. 15), and would not refer in the absolute sense to God, the being, whom both Paul and Christ identified as "the Father" as distinguished from Christ, the Son of that God.

So the irrefutable conclusion, therefore, is that 1 Timothy 3:16 should never be called upon as an argument in favor of the doctrine of the Trinity by calling Christ *God*. It isn't; and it doesn't.

CHAPTER 15

AND THE WORD WAS GOD

Probably the most obvious Scripture in the NT which tells us that Christ is God, in a passage, the genuineness of which is in no way challenged, is John 1:1-2, "In the beginning was the Word, and the Word was with God, and the Word was God. He was with God in the beginning."

As has been pointed out previously, John's purpose for writing this biography of Christ was to prove "that Jesus is the Christ, the Son of God" (John 20:31), and not to prove that Christ is actually and literally that one God he is said to have been with, not the God he is the Son of, nor one of a plurality of persons in that one God. John's burden, writing toward the close of that First Century A.D., was to combat the Gnostic heresies which denied the divinity of Christ.

Much time had lapsed since Jesus had walked on earth; and most of the witnesses of his miracles, his resurrection, and his ascension had passed on. John, apparently the only surviving apostle at that time, by inspiration saw the need for reaffirming that Jesus of Nazareth really is "the Christ, the Son of God," therefore divine in nature by inheritance. This he declares again in verse 14 where "We have seen his glory, the glory of the One and Only, who came from the Father" [fn and ASV: Or *the Only Begotten from the Father*], thus divine by inheritance.

John did say in verse 1 that "the Word was God"; and we know that it was Christ whom John called "the Word," for in verse 14, "the Word became flesh and made his dwelling among us." But we also know that John did not mean that Christ was that one and only God whom he was said to be with, whether referring to "the God" or to the divine nature of that God, for "No one has ever seen God" (v. 18). Many had seen Jesus, for "We have seen his glory" (v. 14); but no man had seen God. This proves that the word "God" which Jesus was said to BE in verse 1 could not have been used in the absolute sense in which the word "God" is used in verse 18 to refer to that one invisible God Almighty of whom Christ is then called the only begotten Son, as well as in verse 1 to refer to the God whom Jesus is said to have been with.

Consider also that John the baptizer, who was sent to bear witness of Christ, when he saw Jesus coming, said, "Look, the Lamb of God" (v. 29). John did not say, "Look, here comes God." But he did say, "I have seen and I testify that this is the Son of God" (v. 34). Then Nathanael confessed to Jesus, "Rabbi, you are the Son of God" (v. 49); not, "You are God."

When Jesus came into the temple, the house of God, he called it "my Father's house" (2:16); not "my house" nor "our house," for Jesus knew that it was God's house. Remember also that it is in John's Gospel that the Golden Text is recorded (3:16), showing that God was the giver and that Christ was the one given, and showing that God was the sender and that Christ was the one sent (v. 17), but never confusing the two.

Thus is set the tone for John's entire message in his gospel narrative, proving that Christ is indeed the divine Son of God, but never attempting to prove that Christ is verily that invisible God whom no man had ever seen. Therefore, why would the very first verse of John's gospel convey an idea different from that by saying, "and the Word was God"? The answer: What John actually said does not in fact convey any such conflicting idea, but does fit precisely into his very purpose for writing; that is, to reaffirm the fact that "Jesus is the Christ, the Son of God."

Joseph Henry Thayer's *Greek-English Lexicon of the New Testament*, under *Theos*, states:

> Whether Christ is called *God* must be determined from Jn. i. 1; xx. 28; 1 Jn. v. 20; Ro. ix. 5; Tit. ii. 13; Heb. i. 8 sq., etc.; the matter is still in dispute among theologians. (p. 287b).[7]
>
> *Theos* is used of *whatever can in any respect be likened to God, or resembles him in any way:* Hebraistically i. q. *God's representative or vicegerent,* of magistrates and judges . . . . (p. 288a).[7]

This we have already seen to be true in Part I, Ch. 5 concerning Jesus' discussion with the Jews in John 10:24-38, where Jesus said that God, speaking to those Jewish judges, said, "You are gods" (v. 34). Then Jesus added, "If he called them 'gods,' to whom the word of God came—and the Scripture cannot be broken—what about the one whom the Father set apart as his very own and sent into the world? Why then do you accuse me of blasphemy because I said, 'I am God's Son'?" (vv. 35-36).

When John said that Christ "was God," he could have meant only that Christ was divine, the Son of God, for that was his stated purpose. What was actually said is hidden in the process of translation, because most translators have failed to deal precisely with the definite articles used in the Greek text. What John actually said in this text was, "In beginning was THE Word, and THE Word was with THE God, and THE Word was God. He was in beginning with THE God" (see Greek text). The "God" whom Christ was with in beginning was "the God," with the definite article; but the "God" whom Christ was said to BE was "God" without the definite article. In NT Greek that can make a very significant difference. According to A. T. Robertson—

Most translations treat the Greek article in a careless fashion.[8]

—A New Short Grammar of the Greek Testament, 10th Edition, p. 283.

Commenting on this very Scripture, William Barclay, in *The Daily Study Bible*, said:

> When Greek uses a noun it almost always uses the definite article with it. The Greek for God is *theos,* and the definite article is *ho.* When Greek speaks about God it does not simply say *theos;* it says *ho theos.* Now when Greek does not use the definite article with a noun that noun becomes much more like an adjective; it describes the character, the quality of the person. John did not say that the Word was *ho theos*; that would have been to say that the Word was *identical* with God."

Spiros Zodhiates, in his book, *Was Christ God?* pages 104 and 105, quotes from *A Grammar of the Greek Language*, by William Edward Jelf, John Henry, and James Parker, 1859, p. 124, as follows:

> The effect of the omission of the article is frequently that the absence of any particular definition or limitation of the notion brings forward its general character . . . . Some words are found both with and without the article, and seemingly with but little difference; but without the article they signify the general notion conceived of abstractly, and not in actual existence; with the article the objective existence is brought forward, as *Theos* (God), the Divinity; *Ho Theos* (the God), the God we worship."[9]

The author (Zodhiates) then explains John's statement:

> He wants to emphasize that His nature, His substance, is the same as that of God the Father. It is not His separate personality that is stressed here in the third clause, but his nature; not *who* he is, but *what* He is.[9]

Other like testimonies could be added; and for this reason numerous translations, including those by E. J. Goodspeed, James Moffatt, and *The Complete Bible—an American Translation* (1943 Reprint) say, "the Word was with God, and the Word was divine," or "the Logos was divine." The *Simple English Bible* (SEB) says, "The Message was deity."

Such is to say that Jesus was not only back there in the beginning with God (which most probably could also be said of angels), but he also even possessed the same divine nature or substance as the God whom he was with (which could NOT have been said of angels). In this way, "God" without the definite article here means *divine*, just as "man" without the definite article often means *human*. This fact of grammar is clearly and understandably illustrated in the following improvised but true parallel statement:

> In Gen 4:1 was THE son (Cain),
> and THE son (Cain) was with THE man (Adam),
> and THE son (Cain) was man (human).
> He (Cain) was in Gen 4:1 with THE man (Adam).

Notice how the absence of the article before "man" in the third line changes the meaning from the person (Adam) to the person's nature (human). Now compare this with our text (see Greek):

> In beginning was THE Word (Christ),
> and THE Word was with *ho Theos* (THE God),
> and THE Word was *Theos* (divine).
> He was in beginning with *ho Theos* (THE God).

Just as Cain was man (human) without being THE man he is said to have been with, so is Christ said to be God (divine) without being THE God he is said to have been with. That's theology simplified, logical, understandable, and scriptural. Further attention will be given to the reason for Christ's being called "the Word," when we discuss more particularly Christ's preexistent relationship with God, in Part I, Ch. 26, *The Origin and Preexistence of Christ*.

CHAPTER 16

ORIGIN AND DEVELOPMENT OF "THE TRINITY"

With the overthrow and downfall of the multiple ancient false deities and their temples came the most universal conquering concept of monotheism—the belief that there is only one true God. The seed for this concept was first strewn throughout the ancient empires by the dispersion of the Jews, even though Israel had not always held consistently to their idea of monotheism until after the purging effect of their Babylonian captivity and exile. That seed was later cultivated and harvested by the spread of Christianity throughout the pagan Roman Empire.

Christianity, unlike Judaism, was not just *among* the Gentiles, but actually received Gentile converts from paganism to the extent that the pagan deities met their doom, leaving behind the remains of only a few of their temples as relic reminders of an ancient polytheism. Today monotheism is almost universally accepted by all deists.

However, this observation is not to suggest that true Judeo-Christian monotheism successfully survived the rapid spread among the Greco-Roman world without some tainting of the accurate biblical concept of that one only true God. Historically, the Christian church and its theology have always been somewhat influenced by each culture whose adherents became converts to Christianity. As the pagan world gravitated toward the Christian community, that gravity also sometimes moved the church toward the world. Early Christian theology did not entirely escape the effects of that bipolar attraction.

It can hardly be denied that the development of ancient Catholicism, and that of the middle ages, was actually the result of centuries of merger between Christianity and paganism, as well as Judaism, even though Christianity no doubt played the greater role. As dominance in church membership shifted gradually from Jews toward Gentiles, Christian thought and theology drifted in the direction of paganism. There seems to have been a noticeable correlation between the three-century development of Greco-Roman theology in the church and the diminishing of Jews among its membership. Christian Jews seem to have been able to comprehend and accept the biblical concept of Jesus' being the Son of their monotheistic God (Jehovah), but could hardly accept him as being that God he is the Son of, or as being one of three coequal and coeternal spirits, beings or persons in a triune God.

During the First Century A.D., that period of church history which was graced by the presence of Holy Spirit inspired apostles, the burden of true Christendom was primarily to convince the world that Jesus is the Christ, the divine Son of God. However, before the end of that First Century, many were denying the true deity of Christ. By inspiration, the apostle John saw the need for reaffirming the deity of Christ; so he stated that his Gospel was written "that you may believe that Jesus is the Christ, the Son of God" (John 20:31).

But then, under the influence of Greek and Roman theologians, the next two or three centuries would see the pendulum swing to the other extreme, arguing that Jesus is not only the divine Son of God, but that he is also as much that one supreme God in the absolute sense as his Father is the one God, forcing the conclusion that Jesus himself is that one God whom he is the Son of, since there is only one God. To such theologians, no longer was Jesus Christ simply the only begotten and divine Son of the one true God his Father, possessing the same divine nature with that one true God, but Jesus became theologically one of three coequal and coeternal *persons* in a triune God—God the Father, God the Son, and God the Holy Spirit, a formula never so stated in divine Scripture.

Even though this changed concept was not found in the earliest known uninspired Christian declaration of faith, the *Apostles' Creed*, nor later in that 325 A.D. first-ecumenical-council creed at Nicaea, it was, however, embodied heavily in the Athanasian Creed of that era. And even though Athanasius and Arius, champions of two opposing and extreme factions at Nicaea, were both overruled in favor of a more biblical declaration, yet the contents of the Athanasian Creed gradually became more and more the "orthodox" theology of the Roman church in the centuries following.

Not everyone accepted the Athanasian *Trinity*, but those who rejected it were faced with suppression, excommunication, and extinction at the hands of a politically empowered clergy.

Athanasian Trinitarianism, in varying forms, also retained its prominence during the Protestant Reformation, with some Christians being burned at the stake by Protestant leaders for not accepting the doctrine of the Trinity. And even today, in what many call a "Restoration Movement," many who have taken in hand to uphold and defend the divine nature of Christ seem to have inked their quills in the stains of Roman "orthodoxy" and Protestant creedalism.

One primary purpose for this writing, *Theology Simplified*, is to give assurance that one does not have to believe the doctrine of the Trinity in order to believe and uphold the true deity and divine Sonship of Jesus Christ. So let us examine the Scriptures to see just what the Bible has to say about the Trinity.

Most Christians today are completely shocked to find that neither the word *Trinity* nor any of its relatives, such as *triunity, triad, triune being*, etc., are found anywhere in the Bible. The very word *Trinity*, as applied to God, reeks of ancient Catholicism and Athanasian creedalism, and is repulsive to the Restoration principle of "Speak where the Bible speaks, and be silent where it is silent." That may sound like awfully strong language; but let us see what Trinitarians themselves have said. It is admitted by Trinitarians that—

> The term "Trinity" is not a Bib. term, and we are not using Bib. language when we define what is expressed by it as the doctrine that there is one only and true God, but in the unity of the Godhead there are three coeternal and coequal Persons, the same in substance but distinct in subsistence . . . . the doctrine of the Trinity is given to us in Scripture, not in formulated definition, but in fragmentary allusions.[5]
> —*The International Standard Bible Encyclopaedia* (ISBE), Vol. V, p. 3012b.

Thus the doctrine of the Trinity is admittedly an arrived-at conclusion based upon "fragmentary allusions." Again—

> It is a plain matter of fact that none who have depended on the revelation embodied in the OT alone have ever attained to the doctrine of the Trinity . . . . The mystery of the Trinity is not revealed in the OT.[5]
> ISBE, Vol. V, p. 3014.

And again—

> We cannot speak of the doctrine of the Trinity, therefore, if we study exactness of speech, as revealed in the NT, any more than we can speak of it as revealed in the OT.[5]
> —ISBE, Vol. V, p. 3015a.

The earliest recorded use of the word "trinity" (Gr: *triados*) is found in the writings of Theophilus (A.D. 115-181), Bishop of Antioch in Syria, to Autolycus, Book II, Ch. 15, concerning the fourth day of creation:

> The three days which were before the luminaries, are types of the Trinity, of God, and His Word, and His Wisdom. (A footnote on this statement says: "The earliest use of the word 'Trinity.'"
> —*The Ante-Nicene Fathers*, Vol. II, p. 101a.

So the first recorded use of "the Trinity" was not even composed of Father, Son, and Holy Spirit, but was God, His Word, and His Wisdom. The doctrine of the Trinity, as well as the name *Trinity*, is obviously the product of some of the many pagan influences that infiltrated the church during the widespread conversion of Greeks, Romans and other pagans, resulting in an apostate religion with nonbiblical concepts as to who the one God really is, as well as innumerable other doctrines and practices which have clearly distinguished the Roman church and her hierarchy through the centuries. There are very few, if any, NT doctrines which the Roman church has not thus polluted.

Hear H. Leo Boles, a noted leader of Trinitarian concepts for several decades among those of the Restoration movement:

> "The Trinity" is another term that man has given to the Godhead . . . . In nearly all heathen religions there are triads of supposed divinities; man has given this name to the Godhead in keeping with terms used in other religions.[11]
>
> —*The Holy Spirit*, H. Leo Boles, p. 21.

Furthermore—

> Triads of divinities, no doubt, occur in nearly all polytheistic religions, formed under very various influences. Sometimes, as in the Egypt triad of Osiris, Isis and Horus, it is the analogy of the human family with its father, mother and son which lies at their basis . . . . Sometimes, as in the Hindu triad of Brahma, Vishnu and Shiva, they . . . symbolize the three stages of Being, Becoming and Dissolution. Sometimes they are the result apparently of nothing more than an odd human tendency to think in threes . . . . It is no more than was to be anticipated, that one or more of these triads should now and again be pointed to as the replica (or even the original) of the Christian doctrine of the Trinity. Gladstone found the Trinity in the Homeric mythology . . . . H. Zimmern finds a possible forerunner of the Trinity in a Father, Son, and Intercessor, which he discovered in its (Babylonian) mythology.[5]
>
> —ISBE, Vol. V, p. 3012b.

So it isn't difficult to see how these pagan triad concepts, fused with the biblical monotheistic doctrine, resulted in an unintentional compromise of *one God (one being)* composed of *three persons*; thus *the Trinity*.

Hear Elder Barton W. Stone in the early stages of the Restoration Movement:

> The word *Trinity* is not found in the Bible. This is acknowledged by the celebrated Calvin, who calls the Trinity "a popish God, or idol, a mere human invention, a barbarous, insipid and profane word"; and he utterly condemns that prayer in the litany—O holy, glorious, and blessed Trinity, etc., as "unknown to the prophets and apostles, and grounded upon no testimony of God's holy word." Admon. 1st. ad Polonus—Cardale's true Doct.[1]
>
> —*Works of Elder B. W. Stone*, p. 51.

To which Stone then added, "The language, like the man, I confess is too severe."

How could these possibly be the words of that "celebrated" John Calvin who in 1553 pressed to have Michael Servetus beheaded, but settled for having him slowly burned alive for denying the doctrine of the Trinity? Apparently one need not deny the doctrine of the Trinity in order to realize that the name *Trinity* is of nonbiblical origin. Even in numerous contemporary writings in which the doctrine of the Trinity is freely expounded, the absence of the name *Trinity* is most conspicuous, as if deliberate efforts were made by those writers to never refer to the Godhead with such a nonbiblical name as the *Trinity*. And some publishers of nondenominational hymnals have avoided the use of the word *Trinity* by changing the wording in the first and fourth verses of "Holy, Holy, Holy" from the old creedal "God in three persons, blessed Trinity," to the more scriptural and accurate concept of "God over all, and blessed eternally."

Actually, we might find many triads in the Scriptures and multiply Trinities with the same propriety by calling them "the Trinity," such as

> spirit, soul and body (1 Thes 5:23);
> faith, hope and love (1 Cor 13:13);
> Spirit, water and blood (1 John 5:8);
> Paul, God and Christ (1 Tim 1:1);
> grace, mercy and peace (1 Tim 1:2);
> grace, love and fellowship (2 Cor 13:14); etc.

In fact, many such triads might with the same propriety even be called "the *Holy* Trinity," as long as each portion of the triad is actually holy.

The burden of this composition is to proclaim that reference to God as *the Trinity* is not only nonbiblical language, but is also language which either expresses or suggests nonbiblical concepts.

CHAPTER 17

CREEDS AND ORTHODOXY

Orthodoxy, like beauty, is in the eye of the beholder. "Orthodox" means "conforming to established doctrine." But the problem of uncertainty rests in the question, "Who established the doctrine being conformed to?" The doctrine of the Trinity has been the "orthodox" doctrine of the Christian church for centuries. But what is the authority which determines what is orthodoxy and what is heterodoxy? Is it the church which is to make the decision? If so, then which church? And if it is the church in history, then at what point in history?

Instead of the church at any point in history being the ultimate authority in religious doctrine, only divine Scripture, which is what gives the church its only divine right to exist, may be cited in determining true orthodoxy. And as it has already been pointed out that since the doctrine of the Trinity is nowhere stated in Scripture in a formulated definition, but is an "arrived-at conclusion" based upon "fragmentary allusions," then the question is, "Who arrived at the conclusion?"

Someone has suggested that orthodoxy is always MY doxy and heterodoxy is YOUR doxy. So let not "orthodoxy" be heralded as a reason for holding onto any doctrine. True orthodoxy can only refer to the God-ordained doctrines clearly revealed in the Scriptures on any given subject, regardless of what the church in history has or has not believed about them.

The word "creed" (Gr: *credo*, to believe) refers to some form of statement of that which is believed, usually a brief and concise statement with precise wording of well-guarded language expressing the basic and fundamental tenets of one's belief. Creeds in history have primarily dealt with the relationship existing between God, Christ, and the Holy Spirit.

Because the Bible has been so variously interpreted on this subject, with each interpretation found lacking in conclusive evidence to substantiate all of its arguments, it seems to be man's nature to want to wrap up one's own conclusions in a brief statement and insist that all others accept it. And the lesser the concrete evidence to support a conclusion, the more dogmatism is required to bridge the gap. It's like the preacher who wrote at a certain point in the margin of his sermon outline, "Weak point; talk real loud!" And strong language is often used to make up for a weak argument; such as, "It is a grievous blunder growing out of dense ignorance to believe da-di-da-di-da!"

In all propriety one may write his own creed as an explanation or apology of what he believes. But creeds have traditionally been written to tell others what they are required to believe. Little emphasis is ever placed on whether or not a creed is actually understood.

> The mystical and devotional values believed to be guarded by the
> formula (of the Trinity), rather than its intelligibility, have made the
> trinitarian doctrine the cornerstone of orthodoxy in Roman Catholic,
> Eastern Orthodox, and most Protestant theology.[12]
>   —*The American People's Encyclopedia*, Vol. 19, p. 30.

Too often, understanding such a creed seems not to be of great significance;
just accept it and you're IN. But question or reject it, and you're unorthodox,
an infidel, heretic, barbarian, fit only to be ostracized, excommunicated, or
burned at the stake. Thus has been the result of many creeds, even in the
absence of such an intent. Hopefully, that will never be the result of the
Pribblonian Creed.

Sometime, about the middle of the Second Century (as early as 140 A.D.),
after the death of the last apostle, a statement of belief was anonymously
developed, later to be commonly referred to as *The Apostles' Creed*. Because of
the prevalence of numerous heresies within the church, such a statement seemed
necessary; and it probably served a very useful purpose. But no creed which
contains any more or any less than the entire Bible can be said to be infallible.
However, creeds are not really intended to be a statement of all that which one
believes or is required to believe, but are to clarify some of the basic elements
of those beliefs.

Such creeds seem to have never solved all problems by bringing unity of
faith, as evidenced by the numerous creeds which have had to be written to
explain, clarify or reaffirm previous creeds. It reminds us somewhat of that
glorious document, the original Constitution of the United States, which has
had to be amended time after time, and about which decision upon decision
has been handed down by Supreme Courts to clarify their own decisions which
they previously made about the meaning and implications of the numerous
amendments to that original Constitution. Few libraries could contain all the
volumes of decisions thus written, along with all the various interpretations
given by myriads of judges, attorneys, lawmakers and politicians. No sooner is
such a decision handed down than the question arises, "What does it mean?"
Most creeds have sparked the same question. So then another creed is often
written to explain the previous one.

The *Apostles' Creed*, by far the oldest known creed in the Christian church,
probably formulated to preserve the church from Second-Century Gnosticism, has
taken on many forms. It probably was not intended to be the official creed of the
church, and its author or authors probably expected many to reject it. Therefore to
give credence to the statement, it came to be called *The Apostles' Creed*, implying that

either the apostles wrote it, or at least it contained the belief of the apostles. Since it was not the official creed for the church, those who used it no doubt made any changes necessary to properly express their own beliefs, resulting in a variety of texts.

The earliest known text, written in Greek, and by far the most generally accepted form, known as the Old Roman Form, is translated thus:

> I believe in God the Father Almighty. And in Jesus Christ His only (begotten) Son our Lord, who was born of the Holy Ghost and the Virgin Mary; crucified under Pontius Pilate, and buried; the third day He rose from the dead; He ascended into heaven, and sitteth at the right hand of the Father, from thence He shall come to judge the quick and the dead. And in the Holy Ghost; the holy Church; the forgiveness of sins; and the resurrection of the body; (the life everlasting).[5]
>
> —ISBE, Vol. I, p. 204b.

Various translations of the creed differ only slightly and insignificantly. And even the enlarged form of much later origin makes very little modification in the description of God, Christ, and the Holy Spirit.

The *Apostles' Creed* is believed to have been originally used as a confession by converts receiving baptism. The original confession (if indeed there was such) used in the Apostolic Age may have contained no more than, "I believe that Jesus is the Son of God." Creeds, just as the writings of the Ante-Nicene Fathers, were purest when closest to the fount. But as they got farther away in time from the Apostolic Age of the First Century, they invariably became more and more contaminated with unscriptural language, doctrine and concepts.

Surely no true Bible scholar would deny the Scriptural accuracy of the earliest texts of the Apostles' Creed, whether the short form or the longer form, as pertaining to God, his Son, and his Spirit. The doctrine of the Trinity—that the one God is a triune being composed of three persons—is not even remotely suggested by either form. Instead, the Creed takes Paul's stance of 1 Corinthians 8:6, declaring that there is one God, the Father, and one Lord, Jesus Christ. If the apostles, and even those of the Second Century, believed that the one God is a triune being composed of three persons, surely they, like Athanasius a century later, would have so stated. Instead, they made it quite clear that the one God is the Father. They did not refer to Jesus as being that one almighty God, but rather the Son of that God. And had they believed that the Holy Spirit was a separate person from the Father, as Jesus was and is a separate person from the Father, their creed would have been saying that the Holy Spirit is the personal Father of Jesus. Notice: "born of the Holy Ghost and the Virgin Mary." This statement parallels that of Matthew 1:18, "she was found to be with child through the Holy Spirit

[ASV: child of the Holy Spirit]." Obviously the NT writers and the Second-Century creed makers never thought of the Holy Spirit as the personal Father of Jesus, but rather as the *power* of the almighty God of whom Jesus was Son. "The Holy Spirit will come upon you, and the power of the Most High will overshadow you. So the holy one to be born will be called the Son of God" (Luke 1:35). Here we see a linguistic parallelism: that which "came upon" Mary was that which "overshadowed" her; therefore the Holy Spirit (God's Spirit) is "the power of the Most High," the power (not the person) by which God the Father in heaven was able to impregnate the virgin on earth. Therefore, the one begotten could be called "the Son of God," not the Son of the Holy Spirit. The fatherhood of God and the sonship of Christ were obviously not by proxy involving pregnancy by a third person. If God were the "First Person," Christ the "Second Person," and the Holy Spirit the "Third Person," then according to Matthew, Luke, and the *Apostles' Creed*—if language means anything at all—Christ would be the Son of the so-called "Third Person," the Holy Spirit.

What can possibly be more orthodox than the Apostles' Creed as herein stated? This Creed accurately, though not exhaustively, depicts the teaching of both Christ and the apostles; and nothing taught in this writing, *Theology Simplified*, contradicts it.

Then moving onward in history, around the beginning of the Fourth Century, a great controversy was rising in the church concerning the relationship between God and Christ, questioning the true deity of Christ. This breach in the church became so intense and widespread that the "recently-converted" Roman Emperor Constantine insisted on calling the first ecumenical (worldwide) council to solve the problem and reunite all Christians in the Empire. This council met at Nicaea in 325 A.D., and produced the first "official creed" for the church, commonly known as the *Nicene Creed*, as follows:

> We believe in one God, the Father almighty, maker of all things visible and invisible: and in the Lord Jesus Christ, the Son of God, begotten from the Father, only-begotten, that is, from the substance of the Father, God from God, light from light, true God from true God, begotten not made, of one substance [Gr. *homoousion*] with the Father, through whom all things came into existence, things in heaven and things on earth, who because of us men and because of our salvation came down and became incarnate, becoming man, suffered and rose again on the third day, ascended to the heavens, and will come to judge the living and the dead; and in the Holy Spirit.[13]
>
> —*Encyclopaedia Britannica*, Vol. VI, p. 719a.

This original *Nicene Creed* (325 A.D.) was later expanded by the

Council of Constantinople (381 A.D.), becoming the most generally accepted formula of faith by East and West alike, including the leading Protestant churches. Additions to the original *Nicene Creed* include such descriptions of Christ as, "begotten from the Father before all ages," and "begotten, not made, of one substance with the Father, through whom all things came into existence."

As already mentioned, two opposing champions of two extreme views at Nicaea were Arius and Athanasius. These two theological generals were up in front in the heat of the battle, each pushing the other more and more into incomprehensible and extreme positions. Athanasius, not content with the age-old *Apostles' Creed*, proposed the doctrine of the Trinity as set forth in the creed which bears his name, but which was of much too late origin to have been written entirely by him. The Revised translation of the *Athanasian Creed* is as follows:

> Whosoever would be saved: before all things it is needful that he hold fast the Catholic Faith. Which Faith except a man have kept whole and undefiled: without doubt he will perish eternally. Now the Catholic Faith is this: that we worship the one God as a Trinity, and the Trinity as a Unity. Neither confusing the Persons: nor dividing the Substance. For there is a Person of the Father, another of the Son; another of the Holy Ghost; But the Godhead of the Father, the Son, and of the Holy Ghost is one: their glory equal, their majesty co-eternal. Such as the Father is, such is the Son: and such is the Holy Ghost; The Father uncreated, the Son uncreated, the Holy Ghost uncreated; The Father infinite, the Son infinite: the Holy Ghost infinite; The Father eternal, the Son eternal: the Holy Ghost eternal; And yet they are not three eternals: but one eternal; As also they are not three uncreated, nor three infinities: but one infinite and one uncreated. So likewise the Father is almighty, the Son almighty; and the Holy Ghost almighty; And yet they are not three almighties: but one almighty. So the Father is God, the Son God, and the Holy Ghost God; And yet they are not three Gods, but one God. So the Father is Lord, the Son Lord: The Holy Ghost Lord; And yet they are not three Lords: but one Lord. For like as we are compelled by the Christian verity: to confess each of the persons by himself to be both God and Lord; So we are forbidden by the Catholic religion: to speak of thee Gods or three Lords. The Father is of none: not made, nor created, nor begotten. The Son is of the Father alone: not made, nor created, but begotten. The Holy Ghost is of the Father and the Son: not made, nor created, nor begotten, but proceeding. There is therefore one Father, not three Fathers; one Son, not

three Sons: one Holy Ghost, not three Holy Ghosts. And in this Trinity none is before or after: none is greater or less; But all three persons are co-eternal one with another: and co-equal. So that in all ways, as is aforesaid: both the Trinity is to be worshipped as an Unity, and the Unity as a Trinity. Let him therefore that would be saved think thus of the Trinity. Furthermore it is necessary to eternal salvation: that he also believe faithfully the Incarnation of our Lord Jesus Christ. The right Faith therefore is that we believe and confess: that our Lord Jesus Christ, the Son of God, is at once both God, and Man; He is God of the Substance of the Father, begotten before the worlds: and he is Man, of the Substance of his Mother, born in the world; Perfect God; perfect man, of reasoning soul and human flesh consisting; equal to the Father as touching his Godhead: less than the Father as touching his Manhood. Who, although he be God and Man: yet he is not two, but is one Christ. One, however, not by change of Godhead into flesh: but by taking of manhood into God; One altogether: not by confusion of substance, but by unity of person. For as reasoning soul and flesh is one man: so God and Man is one Christ; Who suffered for our salvation: descended to the world below, rose again from the dead; Ascended into heaven, sat down at the right hand of the Father: to come from thence to judge the quick and the dead. At whose coming all men shall rise again with their bodies; and shall give account for their own deeds. And they that have done good will go into life eternal: they that have done evil into eternal fire. This is the Catholic Faith: which except a man have faithfully and steadfastly believe, he cannot be saved.[14]

—*Schaff Encyclopaedia of Religious Knowledge*, Vol. XI, p. 202.

While this creed does contain much truth, it is saturated with incomprehensible and sometimes even contradictory assertions and ambiguities entirely unknown to Christ and the apostles. Athanasius calls it "the Catholic Faith." And even though his concept later came to be somewhat the basis for the theology of the Roman Catholic Church, it was by no means the catholic (universal) faith, as seen in the fact that it was neither adopted nor incorporated into the *Nicene Creed* of 325 A.D.

Both the NT, the *Apostles' Creed*, and later the *Nicene Creed* clearly described God as being the Father, with Jesus Christ as his only begotten Son; while Athanasius describes God as a triune being composed of three persons. Athanasius does have Jesus as "begotten before the worlds" (as we show under another heading to be biblically true), but also has him to be "co-eternal"; for "in this trinity none is before or after." For Christ to have been "begotten before the worlds," he had to be preceded by the being who begot him, as well as by the act of his being begotten. Before the worlds, Jesus was either preceded by his Father, or else he was never begotten at all until begotten in the virgin.

Divine Scripture, unlike Athanasius, has never directed us to worship a Trinity. We are to worship God's Son, and are to worship God through his Son; but we are never told to worship the Holy Spirit. There is no record in Scripture of anyone ever worshiping the Holy Spirit, singing praise to the Holy Spirit, praying to the Holy Spirit, giving thanks to the Holy Spirit, offering sacrifice to the Holy Spirit, nor even speaking to the Holy Spirit; nor is there any record of anyone ever being told to do so. Songs like "Spirit, we love you; we worship and adore you," have no biblical precedence or authority. (Much more will be said along this line in Part II, Ch. 10, *Worshiping the Holy Spirit*).

Contrasted against the *Athanasian Creed*, an historical source of the doctrine of the Trinity, we challenge you to compare the *Pribblonian Creed* (on page iv of this book), and determine which is more consistent, more understandable, more logical, and more scriptural.

Athanasian Trinitarianism presents Christ as the one almighty God himself, just as the Father is the one almighty God, yet separate and distinct coequal and coeternal, infinite and almighty personal beings. That's polytheism. At the other extreme, Arianism even denies the divinity of Christ by presenting him as the first thing God created, and through him all other things were subsequently created or made. But between these two unbiblical extremes lies the biblical truth: The Bible presents Christ as the one God's firstborn and only begotten divine Son, neither created nor made, but uniquely born as the offspring of God's divine substance or person, therefore divine by generation, yet distinct from and subordinate to the one and only almighty God, his Father. That's monotheism, pure and simple.

CHAPTER 18

MY LORD AND MY GOD

In addition to John 1:1, another textually accepted Scripture in which Jesus is thought to be called "God," is John 20:28, where Thomas, having been convinced that Jesus had truly come forth bodily from the tomb, exclaimed, "My Lord and my God!" What Thomas did not say is, "You are my Lord and my God." Whether or not that is what Thomas actually meant is the question before us. If Thomas were saying, "You are that one almighty God" in the absolute sense, whom John said no man had ever seen, then Thomas would have been as doctrinally incorrect as he had been just a few moments before, when he exhibited his disbelief that Jesus had been raised from the dead. And if Jesus had understood that such was Thomas' intent, Jesus probably would have corrected him on the spot as he did the young man who addressed him as "Good Teacher" (see Part I, Ch. 36), or as he did the Jews who accused him of making himself God (John 10:33-36).

The resurrected Jesus was definitely a living demonstration of the power of God, just as his miracles had been, including raising Lazarus from the dead, no doubt witnessed by Thomas himself; but there was certainly nothing about Jesus' resurrection which necessarily required Thomas to conclude that Jesus therefore had to be that almighty God in the absolute sense, who alone could raise him from the dead, especially since Jesus had never called himself "God," nor claimed to be God, plus the fact that God could have even used human prophets to perform those same demonstrations of power without their even being divine, much less being referred to as the almighty God.

But Jesus not only knew Thomas' heart, he also knew that the term "God" is used in various qualified senses. We have already seen previously that Jesus is called "God" representatively. So if Thomas called Jesus "God," he could have meant that he not only accepted Jesus as his Lord, ruler or master, but that he also accepted him as the on-earth personal representative of the almighty God in heaven. The term "God" or "Jehovah" sometimes even referred to angels, when it was understood that those angels were messengers from God. (See Gen 16:7-13; 32:24-30; Judg 13:21-22).

Unlike John's statement in John 1:1, "the Word was God," a statement apostolically produced after decades of divine inspiration by the Holy Spirit, Thomas' statement came before his Holy Spirit baptism on Pentecost, and thus before his utterances would be produced by divine guidance. Therefore, even if Thomas had actually said, "You are my God," the accuracy of the statement would not necessarily have been established.

Thomas disbelieved the resurrection of Christ; and only by seeing and touching the crucifixion imprints would he be convinced otherwise. But when he had thus witnessed, he exclaimed, "My Lord and my God!" Sixteen English translations examined conclude the statement with an exclamation mark (!), suggesting that it was not simply a declarative statement, but was rather an exclamation of astonishment. If so, Thomas may have been so joyously overwhelmed by the excitement of the occasion that he burst forth in exuberant praise and adoration to both Jesus his Lord for being raised, and to his God in heaven for raising him. As Thomas directed his first statement to Jesus by saying, "My Lord," it is not at all unreasonable to allow his next statement to be directed to their heavenly Father when he exclaimed, "My God!"

On seeing Lazarus being raised from the dead, Thomas, along with the rest of the apostles, as well as all others present, might have appropriately exclaimed in unison, "My Lord and my God!" without any of them believing that the one being raised was either Lord or God. Many times astonished people, on witnessing some marvelous event, have been known to exclaim, "My Lord and my God!" and in so doing glorify both Lord and God for causing or allowing such marvelous things to happen.

In this same twentieth chapter of John, verse 17, the resurrected Jesus had told Mary Magdalene to "Go instead to my brothers (disciples, v. 18) and tell them, 'I am returning to my Father and your Father, to my God and your God.'" Jesus had thus made it clear that instead of his being God himself, his Father in heaven, to whom he was about to ascend, was Jesus' own personal God, as well as being his disciples' God. And then only three verses after Thomas' exclamation, John states his purpose for writing all these things, including what Thomas had said; that is, "that you may believe that Jesus is the Christ, the Son of God" (v. 31). So whichever the case might have been, surely this statement by Thomas in no way proves that Jesus is the one only God Almighty, but rather the divine Son thereof.

CHAPTER 19

PURCHASED WITH HIS OWN BLOOD

It has long been taught by some that Jesus is called "God" in Acts 20:28, based primarily on the KJV, which translates as follows: "to feed the church of God, which he hath purchased with his own blood." All know that it was Jesus who shed his blood on the cross. And it is furthermore known that the church belongs to Christ who said, "On this rock I will build my church" (Matt 16:18); and, "All the churches of Christ send greetings" (Rom 16:16). Therefore it is argued that since the church belongs to Christ, and since it was Christ who shed his blood on the cross, therefore the God referred to in Acts 20:28 must be Christ. Thus Christ is supposedly called "God."

However, the problem with this text, as quoted from the KJV, involves unsolved questions concerning both the Greek text and the translation thereof. And the controversy focuses on two areas:

(1) the word "God," and (2) the phrase "his own blood." A number of Greek texts, including Griesbach, Lachmann, Tischendorf and Tragelles, have "Lord" instead of "God"; and those same named texts, plus Alford and Wordsworth, have "blood of his own" in place of "his own blood." Those who have "the Lord" purchasing the church "with his own blood" obviously mean that Christ is that Lord; while those who have "the Lord" purchasing the church "with the blood of his own" apparently mean that God is that Lord, purchasing the church "with the blood of his own" (Son understood). Still others have "God" purchasing the church with "the blood of his own" (Son understood). None of these last three renderings calls Christ "God."

Albert Barnes, commenting here on "The church of God," said—

> This is one of three passages in the New Testament in regard to which there has been a long controversy among critics, which is not yet determined . . . . The reading which now occurs in our text (KJV) is found in no ancient MSS. except the Vatican Codex, and occurs nowhere among the writings of the fathers except in Athanasius, in regard to whom also there is a various reading . . . . The most ancient MSS., and the best, read *the church of the Lord* . . . . The authority for the name *God* is so doubtful that it should not be used as a proof text on the divinity of Christ . . . ."[6]
>
> —*Notes on the New Testament*
> by Albert Barnes, Vol. Acts, pp. 296-297.

Adam Clarke, commenting at this point on "Feed the church of God," said—

This verse has been the subject of much controversy, particularly in reference to the term *Theou, of God*, in this place; and concerning it there is great dissension among MSS. and versions . . . . It appears that but for *few* MSS., and none of them very ancient, have the word *Theou, of God*.[3]

—*Clarke's Commentary*, Matthew to Acts, p. 854.

The following are a few examples of English versions and footnotes differing from, or at least recognizing the uncertainty of the KJV:

ASV: "church of the Lord, which he purchased with his own blood."
NIV: Footnote: "Many manuscripts *of the Lord*."
Commentary: "*his own blood*. Lit. 'the blood of his own one' . . referring to his own Son."
RSV (*Revised Standard Version*; See also NEB): "of the Lord . . . with his own blood."
Footnote: "Many ancient authorities read *of God*," and "*with the blood of his Own*."
Barclay: "of God . . . the blood of His own One."
Williams: Footnote: "Some good MSS. read, *the church of the Lord*."
AB (*The Amplified Bible*): "of the Lord . . . with his own blood."
TEV (*Today's English Version*): "of God . . . through the death of his own Son."
NWT (*New World Translation*): "of God . . . with the blood of his own [Son]."
SEB (*The Simple English Bible*): "Lord's people whom he bought with his own blood."
Footnote:"Some manuscripts have 'God' for 'Lord.'"
"Some manuscripts have: 'the blood of His own.'"

An examination of the ancient Christian writings revealed two obvious references at Acts 20:28, found in the *Ante-Nicene Fathers*, Vol. VII, in *Constitutions of the Holy Apostles*, Book II:

Let the bishop pray for the people, and say: "Save thy people, O Lord, and bless Thine inheritance, which thou hast obtained with the precious blood of Thy Christ."[10]

—p. 422a.

. . . to the Church of the Lord, "which He purchased with the blood of Christ, the beloved, the first-born of every creature.[10]

—p. 424a.

These ancient statements show that the writer understood that the Lord (God) purchased the church with the blood of Christ, his own Son; and no other statements were found to be contrary to this conclusion.

But even if there were equal evidence for each of the possible translations herein considered, both Scripture and reason would rule in favor of either "church of God which he purchased with the blood of his own," or "church of the Lord (Christ) which he purchased with his own blood," inasmuch as the church belongs to Christ, as well as to God; and inasmuch as it was Christ, and not God, who shed his blood. There is no evidence that God ever had any blood to shed, except that of Christ or other physical beings. So in the sense that all things belong to God, it may even be said that "God purchased the church with his own blood," without such a declaration meaning that Christ is the almighty God. Therefore, regardless of the way this passage may be translated, it lends no support whatsoever to the doctrine of the Trinity by calling Christ "God." It doesn't.

CHAPTER 20

GOD BLESSED FOREVER

Another Scripture subject to various translations and interpretations, often used in an effort to prove that Christ is indeed the almighty God, is Romans 9:5, which says, "Theirs are the patriarchs, and from them is traced the human ancestry of Christ, who is God over all, forever praised!" There seems to be no challenge brought against the validity of the Greek text at this point, unless it be in the manner in which the punctuation is used. However, there is considerable variation in the way the Greek text is translated and interpreted.

By the time Paul made this statement, already in this epistle to Rome he had made a clear distinction between God and Christ no less than eighteen times, and between God and his Son seven times, and then followed in the remainder of the epistle distinguishing between God and Christ at least another six times. So it would have been quite confusing to the Romans for Paul in this one place to identify Jesus as the God whom he elsewhere so clearly distinguished him from. Examples: "Grace and peace to you from God our Father and from the Lord Jesus Christ" (1:7); "I thank my God through Jesus Christ for all of you . . . ." (1:8); " . . . God will judge men's secrets through Jesus Christ" (2:16); "God presented him (Christ Jesus) as a sacrifice of atonement, through faith in his blood" (3:25); "heirs of God and co-heirs with Christ" (8:17); "Christ Jesus, who died—more than that, who was raised to life—is at the right hand of God and is also interceding for us" (8:34); etc. (For a more complete list, see Appendices B and C). So in the context of such a distinction between God and Christ, it would be unthinkable and quite confusing for Paul to insert a statement that would call Christ "God." It was this Paul who made it so clear to the Corinthians that " . . . for us there is but one God, the Father . . . and there is but one Lord, Jesus Christ . . . ." (1 Cor 8:6).

If indeed Christ were, in Romans 9:5, being called "God," surely it would be in the sense in which he is called "God" in John 1:1, where "God," without the definite article, carries the idea of God's divine nature instead of God the being or person: "and the Word was divine." (see Part I, Ch. 15). In this sense the text here would mean, "Christ, as concerning the flesh, who is over all, a divine being, blessed forever."

However, there are other ways in which this passage of Scripture is translated without Christ being called "God" at all. In fact, the ASV has a footnote as follows: "Or, *flesh; he who is over all, God, be blessed forever.*" When such a variation in translation appears in a footnote, it does not necessarily mean that the better of the possibilities appears in the text, because many times translators make such choices between equally valid translations, influenced greatly by their own theology, or by public opinion and popular acceptance. The NIV gives two alternate readings in its footnotes: "Or *Christ, who is over all. God be forever praised! Or Christ. God who is over all be forever praised*." The NIV *Study Bible* then characterizes this passage as "One of the clearest statements of the deity of Jesus Christ found in the entire NT, assuming the accuracy of the translation (see NIV text note)." This comment admits that it is an assumption, and not a fact, that what is placed in the translated text is more likely to be accurate than what is placed in the footnote as alternate readings. Some other translations are as follows:

> RSV: " . . . according to the flesh, is the Christ. God who is over all be blessed forever."
>
> NEB: " . . . from them, in natural descent, sprang the Messiah. May God, supreme above all, be blessed for ever!"
>
> TEV: "Christ, as a human being, belongs to their race. May God, who rules over all, be praised for ever!"
>
> *The Simple English Bible*: "Christ, in the human sense, came from them. However, God is over everyone. Praise him forever."
>
> Goodspeed: " . . . from them physically Christ came—God who is over all be blessed forever!"
>
> William Barclay: " . . . from them, on His human side, came the anointed one of God. Blessed for ever be the God who is over all!"

These translations and footnoted alternate readings show definitely that the evidence presented in Rom 9:5 is far too insufficient to be used in favor of either Trinitarianism or Unitarianism, for it is not at all certain that Christ is here called God. But we do know certainly that Christ is God's divine Son.

CHAPTER 21

THE GREAT GOD AND SAVIOR

"We wait for the blessed hope—the glorious appearing of our great God and Savior, Jesus Christ" (Titus 2:13). Similar to Rom 9:5, the accuracy of the Greek text for this Scripture seems not to be significantly challenged, except possibly the punctuation thereof. But translations and interpretations do differ, making it uncertain as to whether or not our Savior, Jesus Christ, is here called "the great God." Nothing in the passage as here quoted from the NIV (the same being footnoted in the ASV) would necessarily require such a conclusion.

In this same epistle God is indeed called "our Savior" (1:3; 2:10; 3:4), as well as in numerous places throughout the NT, just as he was Israel's Savior in the OT. And we know that regardless who or what might have a significant part in saving anyone, it is God ultimately who is Savior; for it was God who initiated and stipulated the means for redemption, sending his own Son to die as the redemptive price. Therefore Jesus, whose name means "Savior," is also rightly thus called (1:4; 3:6); for God is the source of salvation, while Jesus is the means thereof. For " . . . when the kindness and love of God our Savior appeared, he saved us . . . . through Jesus Christ our Savior . . ." (3:4-6). So God saves through his Son Jesus Christ. This means that each of them is therefore Savior without both being the "great God" almighty and absolute.

In spite of the fact that in three other places in this short epistle Paul makes a very clear distinction between God and Christ, some translate our text in a way which might (but not necessarily) show Christ to be called our "great God and Savior": "We wait for the blessed hope—the glorious appearing of our great God and Savior, Jesus Christ" (NIV). Even this rendering allows Jesus Christ to be identified with "Savior" only, without being both God and Savior. However, *The* NIV *Study Bible* remarks, "It is possible to translate this phrase 'the great God and our Savior, Jesus Christ' (KJV)," which more precisely identifies Jesus as being not God, but Savior, in keeping with the overwhelming and concurring testimony of the entire Bible. The ASV text, as well as the RSV footnote, also agrees with this rendition.

According to the Greek construction, as rendered by the ASV, RSV, NASB, TEV, NEB, JB, etc., that which is spoken of here seems to be the "appearing of the GLORY of the great God," and not necessarily the appearing of the great God himself in person. Jesus had prayed, "And now, Father, glorify me in your presence with the glory I had with you before the world began" (John 17:5); and we may reasonably assume that God answered that prayer. It is this glory of God, and not necessarily God himself, that will accompany Christ when he comes;

"For the Son of Man is going to come in his Father's glory with his angels . . . ." (Matt 16:27); and "They will see the Son of Man coming on the clouds of the sky, with power and great glory" (Matt 24:30). This would be true whether referring to the final coming of Christ, or to some other coming in judgment, such as the destruction of Jerusalem and the Jewish nation in 70 A.D.

In 2 Peter 1:1 there is a statement similar to Titus 2:13: "To those who through the righteousness of our God and Savior Jesus Christ . . . ." (see also ASV fn). However, the ASV text has, " . . . our God and *the* Savior Jesus Christ."

> Elzevir's Greek text, literal translation: "of our God and our Savior."
> KJV: "of God and our Saviour Jesus Christ."
> RSV footnote: "Or *of our God and the Savior Jesus Christ.*"
> Weymouth: "of our God and of our Saviour Jesus Christ."
> *The Simple English Bible*: "of our God and of our Savior, Jesus Christ."

So the real question is whether Peter is speaking of one being or person, calling him both God and Savior, and identifying both as Jesus Christ, or if he is referring to two separate beings or persons, (1) God, who needed no identification, and (2) Savior, whom he identified as Jesus Christ. The latter interpretation, of course, is the one which much better fits the overall evidence in Scripture which clearly distinguishes Jesus from the almighty God, Jesus being the Son thereof.

Without contradiction, the "like precious faith" (ASV) which Peter speaks of in this passage, is received in or through the righteousness of both God and Christ. And lest there be a question as to whether or not Christ is here called "God," let that question be answered in the very next statement (v. 2), "Grace and peace be yours in abundance through the knowledge of God and of Jesus our Lord." Here the singular "knowledge" is unquestionably common to the two distinct beings, both God and Jesus. With few exceptions, if any, the English versions, as well as the Greek texts, bear this out.

There are entirely too many possible translations and interpretations to allow either Titus 2:13 or 2 Peter 1:1 to be used in any way as a proof text for the doctrine of the Trinity. The overall evidence in Scripture is that Jesus is distinguished from the almighty God, being the divine Son thereof; and both of these passages should be interpreted in that light, an interpretation which certainly does no violence to the original Greek text.

CHAPTER 22

THY THRONE, O GOD

Even though Hebrews 1:8 (God speaking to Christ) in many versions is translated, "Your throne, O God, will last for ever and ever," a thorough study of the entire epistle shows that this letter is one of the most obvious enemies of the doctrine of the Trinity. If it were true that the one only God Almighty, known to the Hebrews as Jehovah, were a triune being composed of three coequal persons, including Christ, no one would have needed to be taught that doctrine more than the Hebrews; for they were all indoctrinated from early childhood to know, understand, and recite that great monotheistic text of their Scripture, "Hear, O Israel: The LORD our God, the LORD is one" (Deut 6:4). [Fn: Or *The LORD our God is one LORD*; or *The LORD is our God, the LORD is one*; or *the LORD is our God, the LORD alone*]. Those words (referring to Jehovah) were worn about their bodies and were written on the doorposts and gates to their houses. They learned those words with greater enthusiasm than children in Christian families today learn, "For God so loved the world . . . ."

But in the letter to the Hebrews the author not only presents the Father and Son as separate persons (1:5), but about 39 times presents God and Christ as two separate beings in such a way as to exclude any idea that one is in fact the other, or that both are separate but equal persons in one being known as God. Those 39 references are among the 326 similar references listed in Appendix C. Not only is God, in this epistle, repeatedly distinguished from Christ, but twice God is even shown to be the God of Christ: " . . . therefore God, your God, has set you above your companions . . . ." (1:9); and, "I (Christ) have come to do your will, O God" (10:7, taken from Ps 40:7-8). So if Jesus is in any way called God or Jehovah in this epistle, surely it must be in some qualified sense so as not to contradict all those many references which clearly show them to be separate and distinct beings or persons, one even being the God of the other, never coequal in authority, neither before, during, nor after Christ's earthly advent.

The prevailing theme of this epistle to the Hebrews is the superiority of Christianity over Judaism, written to help stem the tide of Jewish Christians losing faith and reverting to Judaism. The author proves that superiority first by showing Christ to be superior in every way to all of God's messengers who had ever gone before, whether prophets or angels. Never was his purpose to prove that Christ is actually that God whom they had always worshiped, supposedly having literally come down from heaven in human bodily form; but instead, their God, Jehovah God of Israel, had sent his only begotten and truly divine Son to be their spiritual Messiah, Prophet, and High Priest of a superior order. For them to accept God, they must continue to accept his Son as God's own personal representative from heaven, called "the apostle and high priest whom we confess" (Heb 3:1).

As the Apostle, he was God's envoy or personal ambassador sent from God himself to mankind; and as High Priest he bows before God's majestic throne in heaven with the incense of our prayers, petitions, praise, and thanksgiving, having already presented his own blood as our atoning sacrifice. As Messiah he is seated at God's right hand. Nothing in this epistle should ever be interpreted in such a way as to alter that beautiful picture of God and his Son by confusing their identity. Jesus is not that one God, and not even one of a plurality of persons in that one God. Therefore, the question is: What is meant by, "Your throne, O God, will last for ever and ever"? (1:8).

If this translation be correct, then surely Christ must be called "God" in one or more of the qualified senses which have been previously described:

> (1) He could have been called "God" in the sense of his being divine, as distinguished from mere man. This would not make him equal with God except in divine nature, being the substance offspring of God. Such is the meaning of divine Fatherhood and divine Sonship.

> (2) He could have been called "God" as were other representatives of God, such as those judges appointed over Israel, or angels who brought God's message. Jesus was God's personal representative to mankind, especially the proclaimer of God's holy word, the New Covenant.

On the other hand, the statement as quoted may not even be the best translation at all. The uncertainty has to do with whether *ho Theos*, as found here in the Greek text, means "the God" or "O God." *Ho* is usually the Greek definite article "the," as in, "God (*ho Theos*) so loved the world" (John 3:16), *ho Theos* meaning "the God." However, the same Greek construction is used here, whether in the nominative case (the God), or in the vocative, the case of direct address (O God). In both the ASV, and the NIV as quoted, the expression is translated as though it were in the vocative case; but in the ASV footnote, the alternate translation is nominative: [Or, *Thy throne is God for & c.*]. Similarly it is translated in the text by Goodspeed: "God is your throne forever and ever." So it is also by Barclay, TCNT, NWT, RSV footnote, and NEB footnote. On Psalm 45:6, from whence the Hebrew author here quotes, the ASV footnote has: [Or, *Thy throne is* the throne of *God & c.*].

These alternate renditions occur because there is nothing in the Greek text that determines that *ho Theos* must here be considered as vocative instead of nominative. That is a matter of interpretation, not translation; and therefore of those possible renderings which could be employed, the one which best fits the teaching elsewhere in the epistle should be used. But as has been pointed out, to call Jesus "God," especially in any absolute sense, would contradict the remainder of the epistle which repeatedly distinguishes Jesus from the God who has so highly exalted him above all others, including even the angels.

When it is realized that the 45th Psalm is "a song of praise to the king on his wedding day" (*The* NIV *Study Bible*), aptly describing some king belonging to David's dynasty in ancient times, "Your throne, O God" is an inappropriate choice, while the ASV footnoted alternate, "Thy throne is the throne of God," fits the occasion perfectly. David was God's anointed king over a continuing kingdom, therefore the father of a long dynasty which eventually included Christ.

Considering the poetic language of the Psalms, there is no difficulty in understanding "God is your throne forever" to mean "Your throne is the throne of God forever." And the very next statement concurs: " . . . and righteousness will be the scepter of your kingdom" [ASV fn: The two oldest Greek Manuscripts read *his*], that is, God's kingdom. So just as Christ's throne is the throne of God in heaven, so is Christ's scepter the scepter of God's kingdom. Christ's source of authority and ruling power, as with all of David's dynasty, was and is God. That simple concept, the Hebrews could easily understand and accept.

It is somewhat a mystery to us today how the Hebrew author could take Psalm 45:6, which supposedly referred to Solomon, as well as Psalm 102:25, which referred to Jehovah, and apply both to Christ. But it seems that in the Hebrew letter a secondary application is being made from the Psalms. Hebrews 1:10 has, "In the beginning, O Lord, you laid the foundations of the earth," taken from Psalm 102:25, where the word "Lord" as here used refers to God. Or if verse 25 is a continuation of the prayer which began in verse 1, then "Lord" refers to Jehovah, which of course is the same being as God. In Hebrews a secondary application is again made, applying this passage to Christ. But as has been explained before, the OT statements need not fit the secondary applications in all respects. So in quoting from the Psalms, the Hebrew author made the transition from "God" to "Lord" when applying it to Christ.

William Barclay's *The Daily Study Bible* commenting on Heb 1, says—

> To us some of the proof texts he chooses seem very strange. For instance, 2 Sam 7:14 is in the original a simple and direct reference to Solomon and has nothing to do with the Son or the Messiah. Ps 102:26, 27 is a reference to God and not to the Son. But whenever the early Christians found a text with the word *son* or the word *Lord* they considered themselves quite entitled to take it right out of its context and apply it to Jesus. Whatever that method may seem like to us, it was entirely convincing to them.

We have seen earlier that this was also the practice of Matthew who likewise wrote primarily to Jews.

So the conclusion is that the entire book of Hebrews should rather be used to disprove the doctrine of the Trinity, instead of using only 1:8-10 contrarily to prove that Christ is actually that one God in the absolute sense. The *name* Jesus received, which is more excellent than even the angels, came by inheritance from the God who said, "You are my Son" (vv. 4-5); thus one divine being, God, speaking to another divine being, God's Son; equally divine, but not equally the one almighty God in the absolute sense.

CHAPTER 23

HE IS THE TRUE GOD

"And we are in him who is true—even in his Son Jesus Christ. He is the true God and eternal life" (1 John 5:20). Because Jesus Christ in this passage is the immediate antecedent to the pronoun *he*, many have interpreted the statement to be calling Christ "the true God"; therefore it is often used as a proof text in support of Trinitarian teaching. And indeed, both the Greek and English grammatical construction allows such an interpretation. However, for it to qualify as a genuine proof text for the Trinity, it must first be proved beyond reasonable doubt that there can be no other logical or possible interpretation. But such a negative proposition cannot be thus confirmed.

First, a pronoun does not necessarily refer to its immediate antecedent; it can, and many times must, refer back to some more remote person, place or thing, depending on the context under consideration. It has already been shown by a *Great Cloud of Witnesses* that in the broadest context, the entire Bible, God is the Father, Christ is his Son, and they should never be confused by supposing one of them to be a part of the other, or by having them both to be coequal parts of still another supposed Triune Being.

In the smaller context of John's first epistle, containing only five chapters, there are at least fifteen references which show Christ, one being, to be the Son of God, another being, never fusing nor confusing the two. In fact, 4:15 explains: "If anyone acknowledges that Jesus is the Son of God, God lives in him and he in God." Yet some today would require a confession that Christ is actually that God whom John says Christ is the Son of. Again, in 5:5, "Who is it that overcomes the world? Only he who believes that Jesus is the Son of God," not he who believes that Jesus is God (*ho Theos*).

Then coming down to the immediate context, we are "born of God" (5:18); and we are "children of God" (5:19). God is indeed the person under consideration at this point. But in verse 20, "We know also that the Son of God (not God himself) has come and has given us understanding, so that we may know him who is true." "Him who is true" refers back to the God of whom John had been speaking in vv. 18-19, the God who sent his own Son into the world to speak God's word (not Christ's word), to teach man more completely about that God. That's why Jesus is "called The Word" (Rev 19:13, ASV, referring back to John 1:1, 14), because he came to more completely declare God's word.

"And we are in him who is true (that is, we are in God)—even in his Son Jesus Christ" (1 John 5:20). For one to be in God, one does so by being in God's Son. "Him who is true" is both the appropriate and immediate antecedent for the possessive pronoun "his" in the succeeding phrase. Therefore God, the Father of Jesus, is the being who is here called "him who is true." Then John says, "He is the true God and eternal life"; that is, "He who is true," the Father of Jesus. So it is God, the Father of Jesus, and not Jesus himself, who is here called "the true God," a concept which best fits the contexts mentioned, both immediate and extended.

Thus interpreted, the meaning must be: "We know that the Son of God is come, and has given us an understanding, that we know God who is true, and we are in God who is true, even in the true God's Son, Jesus Christ. This God, the Father of Jesus Christ, is the true God, and eternal life." By this interpretation the divine Sonship of Christ is maintained without calling Christ "God." We know the true God because Christ has declared him to us.

CHAPTER 24

THE OMNIPRESENCE OF GOD

Many laborious and ambiguous statements have been propounded through the centuries in efforts to explain the presence of God. Scripture teaches that for some 33 years Jesus, the Son of God, whom Trinitarians claim to actually be that one almighty God in the flesh, was present here on earth in a corporeal body which was variously located and visibly seen in such localities as Jerusalem, Bethany, Samaria, Capernaum, walking on water, riding in boats, standing on mountains, hanging on a cross, and even lying in a tomb. Jesus was definitely located. To get from one place to another, he changed locations. And when he moved, he was no longer present where he had been before he changed locations.

At that time God was in another location, in heaven. Jesus, while on earth, told his disciples to pray, "Our Father in heaven" (Matt 6:9). This confirms that God, who is the Father, was not on earth as Jesus was, but was in heaven. In other words, God and Jesus were in different places, if indeed heaven is in reality a place, and not just a state of being. If heaven were merely a state of being, and not a located place, then Jesus would not have needed to leave the earth to get to heaven. But Jesus told Mary Magdalene, "Go instead to my brothers and tell them, 'I am returning to my Father and your Father, to my God and your God'" (John 20:17). The ASV and others, as well as the Greek, have, "I ascend." In order for Jesus to get from earth to heaven where God his Father was located, he had to ascend, which necessitated a progressive upward movement from the earth. To ascend is to go up.

Some might suggest that since the earth is round, if heaven is in an upward direction from one given point on earth, then heaven would have to be in a downward direction from a point on the opposite side of the globe. No one really knows just what direction heaven is from the earth; but it is certain that wherever on earth one might be, he will have to go up to get to heaven. Anyone who understands our space program knows that to reach the moon a rocket must go up, even if the moon is on the opposite side of the earth. So since heaven is not on earth, then heaven must be a located place up there as distinguished from down here. And since Jesus said that his God and Father is in heaven, then God must be a located being in a located place, with Jesus now located at his right hand.

Jesus asked his disciples, "What if you see the Son of Man ascend to where he was before!" (John 6:62). Later, "After he said this, he was taken up before their very eyes, and a cloud hid him from their sight" (Acts 1:9). "After the Lord Jesus had spoken to them, he was taken up into heaven and he sat at the right hand of God" (Mark 16:19). "While he was blessing them, he left them and was taken up into heaven" (Luke 24:51). All these Scriptures deal with heaven as a location beyond this earth with both God and his Son located there. On and on we could go, multiplying Scriptures which teach that heaven is a place, the place where God is, and the place from whence Christ came, to whence he returned, and from whence he shall come again.

In spite of all these very clear and understandable statements about the location of God, as well as the location of Christ before, during, and after his earthly advent, some have endeavored to prove the omnipresence of Christ, claiming that even while Christ was on earth, he was at that same time also still in heaven. Jesus, on earth, said, "No one has ever gone into heaven except the one who came from heaven—the Son of Man" (John 3:13). (Fn. and ASV add, "who is in heaven," based on some manuscripts). But the ASV footnote states: "Many ancient authorities omit 'who is in heaven.'"

The RSV and NIV both omit the phrase from the text, and state in footnotes that some authorities or manuscripts do have it. The NASB, Williams, *The Twentieth Century New Testament*, Goodspeed, Beck, TEV, and the SEB all omit the phrase entirely without offering any footnoted explanations. *The Amplified Bible* has it in italics, to denote questionable authority. The *New Catholic Edition* footnote states, "These words are wanting in the best Greek codices." The NEB and Weymouth both have, "whose home is in heaven," which would not necessitate Jesus' actual presence in heaven while on earth away from his heavenly home. But then the NEB footnote says, "Some witnesses omit 'whose home is in heaven.'"

But even if it could be established that the phrase rightly belongs in the text, there is nothing in the original text which compels it to be the words of Jesus on earth, being more likely an added explanation by John who recorded the Lord's statement long after Jesus had returned to heaven. And even if it could be proved that Jesus actually made the statement, meaning that he was on earth and in heaven at the same time, it would not necessarily follow that he would be in both places simultaneously in the same sense. One might be in one place literally while in another place figuratively; in one place bodily while in another place in spirit. "Even though I am not physically present, I am with you in spirit" (1 Cor 5:3). Even we ourselves, like Paul, might be in multiple places simultaneously in spirit, without our being omnipresent. Some commentaries understand Jesus to have been saying that he, after having received God's Spirit without measure, was is constant communication with God in heaven.

"Omnipresent" simply means being in all places at all times. The word is not found in Scripture, therefore God is never said in Scripture to be omnipresent. However, the idea is taught in numerous passages without contradicting the fact already established that God is located in heaven in a sense in which he cannot be said to be everywhere. Location does not necessitate confinement. God can be in heaven hypostatically, that is, in person, as an individual, a distinct entity, without being confined thereto.

Consider some of the passages usually cited to prove the omnipresence of God: "For this is what the high and lofty One says . . . 'I live in a high and holy place, but also with him who is contrite and lowly in spirit'" (Isa 57:15). God not only dwells in heaven, but also in the heart of the righteous. But it does not necessarily follow that God dwells in both places in the same sense. Certainly God does not dwell in the heart of the wicked as he dwells in the heart of the righteous. Therefore, taken hypostatically, this passage does not prove the omnipresence of God, as he obviously does not so dwell in the heart of the wicked, as inferred by singling out those who are "contrite and lowly in spirit" to thus indwell.

There is a sense, however, in which God does dwell in all mankind, both righteous and wicked, God being the Father of our spirits, as we are the offspring of God, and our bodies being the temple of God. Jesus said, "Destroy this temple, and I will raise it again in three days" (John 2:19). "But the temple he had spoken of was his body" (v. 21). A temple is a sanctuary, biblically, a dwelling place for God. "Do you not know that your body is a temple of the Holy Spirit, who [ASV: which] is in you, whom [ASV: which] you have from God?" (1 Cor 6:19). While this epistle is addressed to Christians, in whom God's Spirit dwells as a result of their being born again, there is nothing in the text which keeps the statement from referring to God's Spirit in every person, whether righteous or wicked, that spirit which animates the body of every person; that spirit which, at death, separates from the body and "returns to God who gave it" (Eccl 12:7), there to await the resurrection of all mankind. Paul does not infer in 1 Cor 6:19 that only the bodies of the righteous are temples of God. Furthermore, "You are not your own; you were bought at a price. Therefore honor God with your body" (vv. 19-20). That purchase price was paid for the wicked as well as for the righteous; and when the wicked use their bodies for sin, they desecrate the temple of God's spirit which animates their bodies. But there must be more to the omnipresence of God than is inferred in Isaiah 57:15, where God lives "with him who is contrite and lowly in spirit."

Consider also Paul's statement to the Athenians, how that God is "not far from each one of us. For in him we live and move and have our being" (Acts 17:27-28). This statement shows a multiple presence of God, being near each person, without proving the omnipresence of God in those places where no humans are found, such as the remote expanses of our planet, as well as the vast outer spaces in and beyond our universe. Omnipresence means more than being near all mankind.

Some passages often used to prove the omnipresence of God speak merely of his omniscience. However, other Scriptures seem quite conclusive. "'Do not I fill heaven and earth?' declares the LORD" (Jer 23:24). And the psalmist not only points out the omnipresence of God, but also shows in what sense or in what way God is omnipresent. Addressing Jehovah, he asked, "Where can I go from your Spirit? Where can I flee from your presence? If I go up to the heavens, you are there; if I make my bed in the depths [fn. Hebrew *Sheol*], you are there. If I rise on the wings of the dawn, if I settle on the far side of the sea, even there your hand will guide me, your right hand will hold me fast" (Ps 139:7-10). That's omnipresence.

However, it has already been established that God is in heaven, located in a way or sense in which he is nowhere else (unless heaven is everywhere). But God need not leave heaven in order to be present some place else in a very real sense. The psalmist uses "your Spirit" and "your presence" interchangeably in such a way as to let us know that even though God is in heaven, he is omnipresent by his Spirit. One cannot escape the presence of God, because God's Spirit is everywhere. Whatever God does, he does it by his omnipresent Spirit, which is as much a part of the person of God as each man's spirit is a part of the person of each man. If the person, God, is omnipresent in some way other than by his Spirit, the Bible failed to say so. And if God's Spirit were a separate person from God himself, it would be most difficult to establish the omnipresence of Jehovah God.

A clear example of God in heaven accomplishing something elsewhere through his Spirit is the conception of Jesus in the virgin. God, the Father, did not have to leave heaven in order to impregnate Mary on earth. He accomplished this by his omnipresent Spirit. "This is how the birth of Jesus Christ came about: His mother Mary was pledged to be married to Joseph, but before they came together, she was found to be with child through the Holy Spirit" (Matt 1:18). [ASV: "child of the Holy Spirit"]. And, "what is conceived in her is from [ASV: of] the Holy Spirit" (v. 20). Luke's record seems to even picture the conception as though it were intercourse between the Holy Spirit and Mary, "The Holy Spirit will come upon you, and the power of the Most High will overshadow you. So the holy one to be born will be called the Son of God" (Luke 1:35). What a dilemma for Trinitarians! If the Holy Spirit, the Spirit of God, were a separate person from God, the Father, as Trinitarians claim, then the Holy Spirit, the so-called "Third Person of the Trinity" would definitely be the personal Father of Jesus, or else language means nothing at all. "She was found with child of the Holy Spirit." How could that possibly make Jesus the Son of the "First Person of the Trinity" instead of Son of the "Third Person" which "came upon" and "overshadowed" her? But if God, the Father in heaven, came upon, overshadowed and impregnated Mary by his omnipresent Spirit, then clearly God, the Father, not his Spirit, is the personal Father of Jesus. Otherwise, the "First Person" would be the Father of the "Second Person" only by proxy, by the "Third Person." No wonder the doctrine of the Trinity is admitted to be a mystery. More along this line will be considered later when we study the relationship between God and his Spirit in Part II.

Some might answer, "But God is a Spirit" (John 4:24, ASV). The ASV footnote and the NIV have "God is spirit." In the Greek text there is no article modifying "spirit" at this place. And as we have seen before in our study of John 1:1, "the Word was God," how that the noun without the article takes on somewhat the character of an adjective, describing the nature of the subject. Thus "God is spirit" would suggest that God IS a spirit being as distinguished from a natural, physical being, but HAS a Spirit as distinguished from a body. The resurrected Jesus had tangible flesh and bones (Luke 24:39), which apparently is different from "flesh and blood" which "cannot inherit the kingdom of God" (1 Cor 15:50). "Flesh and blood" in this text is used to signify a corruptible body as distinguished from an incorruptible body. But "flesh and bones" signifies the reality of the resurrected body of Jesus, as distinguished from a mere disembodied spirit. For "a spirit hath not flesh and bones, as ye behold me having" (Luke 24:39, ASV. The NIV, without justification, has "ghost" instead of "spirit." The Greek is *pneuma*, spirit). "Flesh and bones" did not suggest corruptibility; for even though the resurrected Jesus was capable of eating food (Luke 24:43), he was no longer dependent on food which was necessary to sustain a "flesh and blood" existence. His flesh-and-bones resurrected bodily existence is described as imperishable, glorious, powerful and spiritual (1 Cor 15:42-44).

Because Jesus was raised a spiritual body, that body, like angels, is invisible. But the resurrected Jesus, like angels, was also able to materialize, to become visible and consume physical food, as did the angels when they appeared to Abraham. The resurrected Jesus, as "spiritual flesh and bones," made numerous appearances to his disciples, to more than five hundred at one time. Because spiritual bodies are invisible, Jesus had to materialize (become visible) in order for his disciples to be witnesses of his resurrection. That's the body he left this earth with. And if he didn't get to heaven with it, it must be out there in orbit somewhere. Because it is a spiritual body, not a natural body, it defies gravity. Thus Jesus can now again be described as a spirit being. God, his Father, is likewise such a spirit being, whether he has a real body or not; but God, like Christ, also has a spirit, the Holy Spirit, the means by which God is omnipresent.

The Jews pictured the ever-presence of God as the sun with its rays. The *Mishnah* is the written record (collated about 200 A.D.) of Jewish oral tradition from about 200 B.C. to about 200 A.D. Much of it represents the thinking of the Pharisees in the First Century A.D. The *Talmud* (collated about 500 A.D.) is a commentary on the *Mishnah*. *Everyman's Talmud*, A. Cohen, concerning the Transcendence and Immanence of God, states:

> The Rabbis invented certain terms to express the Divine Presence without giving support to a belief in His corporeality. The most frequent of these terms is *Shechinah*, which literally means "dwelling." It denotes the manifestation of God upon the stage of the world, although He abides in the faraway heaven. In the same way that the sun in the sky illumines with its rays every corner of the earth, so the *Shechinah*, the effulgence of God, may make its presence felt everywhere . . . . Another Rabbinic concept to indicate the nearness of God and His direct influence on man is that of *Ruach Hakodesh* (the Holy Spirit). Sometimes it seems to be identical with the *Shechinah* as expressing the divine eminence in the world . . . ."[15]

We understand that the sun, in one sense, is located at a mean distance of 93,000,000 miles from the earth. Yet in another sense, it can be said that the sun comes into a house through its skylights and windows. Just as the sun's rays are an essential part of the sun itself and the means by which the sun reaches far beyond its location as the center of our galaxy, similarly God's Spirit is an essential part of God himself, and the means by which God in heaven can be said to be omnipresent. Hence, the presence of God's Spirit is equated with the presence of God himself.

That's theology simplified, clear and understandable. But to proceed further with a long parade of theological quotations, filled with ambiguities and dark sayings, would no doubt serve only to bewilder and confuse beyond comprehension rather than to simplify. This simple concept of the omnipresence of God by his Spirit is in accord with all the Scriptures on the subject.

CHAPTER 25

PREPARING THE WAY OF THE LORD

John the Baptist preceded Jesus on earth by about six months. And according to Scripture the beginning of John's public ministry preceded that of Jesus. But Scripture does not tell us just how much time lapsed between the time John began to preach and when Jesus came to him for baptism. However, the indications are that it was not a very long period of time. Even if Jesus had not made a special trip from Galilee down to the Jordan River in the Wilderness of Judea to be baptized by John, it is inconceivable that Jesus would have passed along that route on one or more of his three required annual pilgrimages to Jerusalem without heeding John's message and being baptized as John commanded, in preparation for the coming kingdom which was then said to be "near" (Matt 3:2). Jesus' awareness of John's mission, without his responding immediately, would have suggested rejection by Jesus of that notable prophetic message. By such a rejection Jesus would have placed himself somewhat alongside the Pharisees and lawyers who "rejected for themselves the council of God, being not baptized of him" (Luke 7:30, ASV). But it is most likely that when Jesus in Galilee heard that John had begun his ministry in Judea near the Jordan River, he went without hesitation, making a special trip "to fulfill all righteousness" (Matt 3:15), enabling him to then begin his own personal ministry.

Opposed to the idea that Jesus might have been going that direction to Jerusalem anyway, Mark records that after Jesus was baptized, "At once the Spirit sent him out into the desert" (Mark 1:12), where he fasted for forty days and was tempted by Satan. It seems that not until after the end of those forty days did Jesus make his way into Jerusalem, probably to consummate his fasting period at the temple. These ideas, though somewhat speculative, are here given to infer the urgency of the ministries of both John and Jesus as they each worked separately, but not conflictingly, in preparing the hearts of Israel to receive the coming kingdom.

John's stated mission was to "Prepare the way for the Lord" (Matt 3:3; Mark 1:3; Luke 3:4), as quoted from Isa 40:3, where the Lord is Jehovah God. Because of this, some have concluded that Jesus therefore must be Jehovah God. In this figure of speech by Isaiah, John is pictured to us today somewhat as a bulldozer operator, or pictured to those in olden times more as a supervisor of hosts of slave laborers, constructing a freeway through Israel up to Zion, the city of the Great King, where a triumphant entry could be made with great fanfare for the establishing of that kingdom, or the reestablishing of David's kingdom in a new and more glorious sense. But there is nothing in the prophecy nor in its fulfillment which indicates that it would be Jehovah

God who would personally walk or ride on that highway. Instead, God was preparing it for his Son. Isaiah had said, "And the glory of the LORD will be revealed, and all mankind together will see it" (Isa 40:5). However, Isaiah was not saying that all mankind would see Jehovah on that road, but that they would see the *glory* of Jehovah. They shall see IT, not HIM. That glory was revealed through Jehovah's Son.

So when John carried out his mission, he was preparing the way for Jehovah to accomplish his own will through sending his Son to be the Messiah. Therefore, when John prepared the way for Christ, he was preparing the way for Jehovah to fulfill his purpose through Christ. In no way was this a prediction that Jehovah would personally come down from heaven to travel that road.

After that threefold temptation in the Wilderness, Jesus returned to Galilee. And "From that time on Jesus began to preach, 'Repent, for the kingdom of heaven is near'" (Matt 4:17). Just as John had been preparing the way for Jehovah and the coming Kingdom, Jesus likewise continued to do the same. Instead of being Jehovah, Jesus, like John, prepared the way for Jehovah. The message by both was, "Repent, for the kingdom of heaven is near." By this, both John and Jesus were preparing the way for Jehovah to accomplish his mission by establishing his Son Jesus over an everlasting and spiritual kingdom, whose throne would be in heaven at Jehovah's right hand.

Therefore, Isaiah was not calling Jesus "Jehovah." Jesus is Jehovah representatively, but not literally nor personally. Jesus is Jehovah's Son. And John prepared the way of Jehovah by preparing the hearts of Israel to receive Jesus as King, anointed by Jehovah God himself.

CHAPTER 26

THE ORIGIN AND PREEXISTENCE OF CHRIST

Christ, as a human being, had his beginning on earth when he was born in Bethlehem. But that was not the beginning of Christ as a person; for Jesus himself said, "before Abraham was born, I am!" (John 8:58). Before Jesus became a human being, he was already a distinct individual spirit being or entity, a person separate from all other beings or persons. Jesus did not need to be born of Mary to become a person; he already was one. But one additional thing he needed in order to accomplish his mission on earth was a physical human body. That's what he got from God through Mary. "Therefore, when Christ came into the world, he said: 'Sacrifice and offering you did not desire, but a body you prepared for me'" (Heb 10:5).

Toward the end of his life here on earth, Jesus prayed, "And now, Father, glorify me in your presence with the glory I had with you before the world began" (John 17:5), which speaks of the preexistence of Christ. That preexistence obviously consisted of a Father-Son relationship, and not a God-God relationship. When time came that man would become reconciled to God, there was no question as to which divine person man was to be reconciled to. If, as some have supposed, the so-called "Second Person" were as much the one ever-existing almighty God as is the "First Person," then man would have needed to be reconciled to the "Second Person" as much as to the "First Person"; and the "Second Person" could have as appropriately sent the "First Person" to reconcile man to the "Second Person." But he didn't. Man had sinned against God, who is the Father of Christ; therefore God sent his Son, Christ, to reconcile man to God, not to Christ.

"For God was pleased to have all his fullness dwell in him (Christ), and through him to reconcile to himself (God) all things, whether things on earth or things in heaven, by making peace through his blood, shed on the cross" (Col 1:19-20). God, in this passage in the ASV, is designated as *the Father*; but being in italics, it creates a possible doubt concerning the exact identity of certain pronouns; but Ephesians 2:15-16 removes any doubt concerning who reconciled mankind to whom: "His (Christ's) purpose was to create in himself one new man out of the two (Jews and Gentiles), thus making peace, and in this one body to reconcile both of them to God through the cross . . . ."

Again, "All this is from God, who reconciled us to himself through Christ and gave us the ministry of reconciliation: that God was reconciling the world to himself in Christ . . . . We implore you on Christ's behalf: Be reconciled to God" (2 Cor 5:18-20). And again, "For if, when we were God's enemies, we were reconciled to him through the death of his Son" (Rom 5:10). God didn't die; his Son did. And

Christ didn't die to reconcile man to himself, but to God, his Father.

This whole plan for the redemption of man through Christ was made "before the creation of the world . . . . In love he predestined us to be adopted as his sons through Jesus Christ" (Eph 1:4-5). And while this text does not specifically say that Christ was in on that foreordination planning session, it is inconceivable that God would foreordain such a plan without the specific consent of his Son who would be the one to do the suffering and dying. Thus is established the preexistence of Christ.

Even the OT prophets declared the preexistence of Christ: "But you, Bethlehem Ephrathah, though you are small among the clans [Or *rulers*] of Judah, out of you will come for me one who will be ruler over Israel, whose origins [Hebrew *goings out*] are from of old, from ancient times [Or *from days of eternity*]" (Micah 5:2). This shows that Christ existed before he was born in Bethlehem, but does not specify precisely how long before. Two phrases in this passage are worthy of special consideration: "origins" and "from ancient times," declaring both *what* and *when*.

First, let's consider *what*: "Goings forth," as quoted from the ASV, occurs in the plural form, which suggests numerous goings forth. This tells us that Jesus has "gone forth" more than once, more than when he went forth from heaven to earth to be born of woman. "Goings forth" suggests action, more than mere contemplation to do something. And it probably can be said that every time Jesus has ever purposely acted, he "went forth" from contemplation to do so. When God, speaking to his Son, said, "Let us make man in our image" (Gen 1:26), we can assume that, since all things were created by Christ (Col 1:16), he went forth to do so; he didn't just stay where he was and think about it. Before time began, Jesus was already actively "going forth" in the presence of his Father.

However, there are other renditions which suggest other meanings: The NIV has "whose origins are from of old," possibly referring to the many things Jesus originated or created, including even angels, back in eternity before time began. And *The* NIV *Study Bible* explains, "His beginnings were much earlier than his human birth."

Still another idea is suggested by the RSV and NWT: "Whose origin" (singular), which may be best interpreted in the context of Micah's prediction, that even though Jesus would be born in Bethlehem, his origin was much earlier, back in the ages of eternity, when he became the divine offspring (Son) of God before anything or anyone else ever came into existence.

"From of old, from ancient times" does not suggest that Christ had no origin. The ASV footnote has, "Or, *from ancient days*." The *New Catholic Edition* has, "from the beginning, from the days of eternity." The RSV and *The Amplified Bible* have, "from of old, from ancient days." Clarke's Commentary has, "*olam*, 'From the days of all time'; from time as it came out of eternity." The Hebrew word *olam*, translated "ever" in the KJV about 267 times, is used much more to mean "time indefinite" than to mean "infinity" or "eternity." It does not necessarily mean without beginning or end.

There are numerous examples which prove conclusively that *olam* does not always signify infinity. In Genesis 13:15 God promised Abraham, "All the land that you see I will give to you and your offspring forever [*olam*]." Yet Peter tells us that "the day of the Lord will come like a thief. The heavens will disappear with a roar . . . and the earth and everything in it will be laid bare [Some manuscripts *be burned up*]," and that "everything will be destroyed in this way" (2 Pet 3:10-11). That will be the end of all that land which God promised to Abraham as a possession forever (*olam*). Thus God made to Abraham an *age-lasting* promise, but not a promise that would have no end.

The Passover was to be unto Israel for a memorial, to be kept throughout their generations forever (*olam*) (Exod 12:24). Keeping a lamp burning continually in the tabernacle was to be "a lasting ordinance among the Israelites for the generations to come" (Exod 27:20-21). The ASV has, "a statute for ever [*olam*]." The "linen undergarments" to be worn by the priests was "to be a lasting ordinance," (Exod 28:42-43); ASV: "a statute for ever [*olam*]." The ASV "heave-offering" of "the ram of consecration" was "to be for Aaron and his sons as their portion for ever [*olam*]" (Exod 29:27-28). Aaron and his sons were to wash their hands and feet in the brass laver between the tent of meeting and the altar before going into the tent, which was to be a statute forever (*olam*) (Exod 30:18-21).

On and on we could multiply ordinances, such as meal offerings (Lev 6:14-18), abstinence from wine by priests inside the tabernacle (Lev 10:9), the annual day of atonement (Lev 16:29-30), offerings of the firstfruits (Lev 23:10-14), etc., all of which were said to have been statutes forever (*olam*), but all of which were laws and ordinances which Jesus abolished "in his flesh the law with its commandments and regulations" (Eph 2:15); laws which Jesus took out of the way, nailing them to the cross (Col 2:14). "Therefore do not let anyone judge you by what you eat or drink, or with regard to a religious festival, a New Moon celebration or a Sabbath day" (Col 2:16). All these things were to be kept forever (*olam*), from generation to generation, but not without end; indefinitely, but not infinitely.

For Christ to be *olam* does not mean that he had no beginning as a separate person from the Father. That divine substance which became a distinct personal entity had no beginning; but the person which that substance became had to have a beginning. And the beginning or origin of that separate person was the beginning of Fatherhood and Sonship. Christ was not created in the technical sense; he was born. If

Christ were created, he might be God's son as Adam was God's son (Luke 3:38), but he wouldn't be divine without being the actual substance offspring of God. And if Jesus is the actual substance offspring of God, nothing about him needed to be created nor to be the product of creation, until he took on that human body through Mary, making him also the Son of David, the Son of Abraham, the Son of Adam, as well as the Son of God.

In opposition to an espoused idea that it was Jehovah God himself who clothed himself in human flesh via the virgin birth, Micah makes a very clear distinction between that ruler who came forth from Bethlehem (Micah 5:2) and Jehovah God himself. Concerning that ruler "whose origins are from of old," Micah went on to say, "He will stand and shepherd his flock in the strength of the LORD, in the majesty of the name of the LORD his God" (v. 4). Christ is therefore not Jehovah God; but instead, Jehovah is actually Christ's God, just as he is Christ's Father. Jehovah did not become his own Son, nor did Christ become his own Father.

"In the beginning was the Word" (John 1:1), "He was with God in the beginning" (v. 2), and "Through him all things were made" (v. 3), all attest to the preexistence of Christ, having him present with God prior to the creation of anything. But these statements do not suggest that Christ never had a beginning of existence back there in eternity as a distinct person, the Son of God. In fact, they do not speak of origin at all, but rather of existence. However, Colossians 1:15 does speak of the origin of Christ, calling him "the image of the invisible God, the firstborn over all creation." And we know that this "firstborn" refers not to his birth by Mary, for millions were born before that, but rather to his relation to his Father before the creation, "For by him all things were created" (v. 16). "Firstborn" speaks of origin. And the fact that Christ was born before any other being was ever born proves his preexistence. A further study of "firstborn" will be made in Part I, Ch. 27.

When Jesus said, "before Abraham was born, I am!" (John 8:58), he was saying that his birth in Bethlehem was not the beginning of his personal existence. Before Abraham came into being, Christ already existed. By saying "I am" instead of "I was," Jesus removed any speculation that he might have existed at some point before Abraham, and then existed again as a result of his birth by Mary. "I am" meant that Jesus' existence is a continual existence, spanning all the way from before Abraham to his then present life as a human being. And that's all the expression here can be used to prove. "I am" does not prove, as some have supposed, that Jesus is Jehovah God, without beginning, just because Jehovah God had identified himself to Moses as "I AM WHO I AM" [Or *I WILL BE WHAT I WILL BE*] (Exod 3:14). Such would mean that any other person who might ever say "I am" or "I exist" would be guilty of blasphemy by making himself God.

When God told Moses, "I AM WHO I AM," (see LXX, "*ego eimi* [I am] *ho On* [THE I AM], that first "I am" is a simple statement consisting of a subject and the present tense of the verb "to be." But Moses was looking for a name to identify the God who sent him. The answer to Moses' question is found in the second "I am," identifying God as "THE I AM," to be used somewhat as a name. Thus God identified himself as "THE I AM." The LXX translates, "I am THE BEING," that is, the existing one.

In John 8:58, Jesus simply said, "I am," meaning that he existed before Abraham; but he never told anyone at any time that he is THE I AM. And to use that statement to prove that Jesus is the God who spoke to Moses from the bush, or any other God, is an illogical misuse of both grammar and Scripture. As we have already seen (John 10:30-36), Jesus denied that he made himself God as the Jews had accused him, but instead said, "I am God's Son" (v. 36). With the statement "I am," Jesus claimed to be many things: the bread of life, the light of the world, the door, the vine, the way, the truth and the life, and even the Son of God; but he never once said that he was God. So "before Abraham was born, I am" was intended to prove the preexistence of Christ, but was never intended to prove that Christ is that eternal God who had no beginning, nor that he has always existed with God as a distinct person without beginning, as if he had never been born of God until he was born of Mary.

Some have placed great significance to the idea that this verb of existence (Gr: *eimi*), translated "am" in John 8:58, is in the indicative present tense, and therefore supposedly means that Christ both was, is and shall always be that ever-existing being, Jehovah God, or else the personal literal *Logos* of God, while believing at the same time that Christ never became God's Son until that *Logos* was born of Mary. But this conclusion contradicts another affirmative statement by Jesus, found in John 10:36, where he said, "I am the Son of God." Here again, that same verb of existence (*eimi*) is in the indicative present tense. Therefore, if John 8:58 means that Christ was, is and shall always be that ever-existing being, then John 10:36 means that Christ was, is and shall always be the Son of God, which contradicts the very idea that he never became the Son of God until he became the Son of man via the virgin birth. Such contradiction in reasoning is no doubt why the doctrine of the Trinity is so often called a mystery.

Consider this passage in the Proverbs which through the centuries has been variously translated and interpreted, and in which it is the voice of "wisdom" speaking poetically:

The LORD brought me forth as the first of his works, before his deeds of old; I was appointed from eternity, from the beginning, before the world began. When there were no oceans, I was given birth, when there were no springs abounding with water; before the mountains were settled in place, before the hills, I was given birth, before he made the earth or its fields or any of the dust of the world. I was there when he set the heavens in place, when he marked out the horizon on the face of the deep, when he established the clouds above and fixed securely the fountains of the deep, when he gave the sea its boundary so the waters would not overstep his command, and when he marked out the foundations of the earth. Then I was the craftsman at his side. I was filled with delight day after day, rejoicing always in his presence, rejoicing in his whole world and delighting in mankind" (Prov 8:22-31).

What a beautiful and accurate description of the origin and preexistence of Christ, the Son of God. However, in the surrounding context, the first-person speaker here, as has already been mentioned, is wisdom, and not Christ. But when all is considered, it is evident that wisdom, even though in the feminine gender grammatically in the Greek Septuagint (LXX), is here being personified as an offspring of God before the creation of the universe. The only such personal divine offspring ever mentioned elsewhere in Scripture is Christ, the only begotten Son of God, "the firstborn of all creation" (Col 1:15). Because of this, no doubt, Bible students through the centuries, beginning as far back as the early Ante-Nicene Fathers, have interpreted this passage as being a projected reference, in one way or another, to Christ, the ultimate in perfect wisdom, the infinite wisdom of God extended to mankind.

Justin Martyr (A.D. 110-165) in his "Dialogue With Trypho, A Jew," speaking of the one to whom God said, "Let us make," explains:

This Offspring, which was truly brought forth from the Father, was with the Father before all the creatures, and the Father communed with Him; even as the Scripture by Solomon has made clear, that He whom Solomon calls Wisdom, was begotten as a Beginning before all His creatures and as Offspring by God . . . . [10]

—*The Ante-Nicene Fathers*, Vol. I, p. 228b.

Then after quoting this passage from Proverbs 8, concluding with, "He begets me before all the hills," Justin added:

You perceive, my hearers, if you bestow attention, that the Scripture has declared that this Offspring was begotten by the Father before all things created; and that that which is begotten is numerically distinct from that which begets, any one will admit.[10]

—Ibid., p. 264b.

Tertullian (A.D. 145-220), in his discourse "Against Praxeas," states:

> The Son likewise acknowledges the Father, speaking in His own person, under the name of Wisdom: "The Lord formed Me as the beginning of His ways, with a view to His own works; before all the hills did He beget Me."[10]
>
> —Ibid., Vol. III, p. 602a.

Origen (A.D. 185-230-254), under the title of "Origen De Principiis," states:

> The nature of that deity which is in Christ in respect of His being the only-begotten Son of God is one thing, and that human nature which He assumed in these last times for the purpose of the dispensation (of grace) is another . . . . He is termed Wisdom, according to the expression of Solomon: "The Lord created me—the beginning of His ways . . . . He founded me before the ages . . . before all the hills, He brought me forth." He is also styled First-born, as the apostle has declared: "who is the first-born of every creature." The first-born, however, is not by nature a different person from the Wisdom, but one and the same. Finally, the Apostle Paul says that "Christ (is) the power of God and the wisdom of God."[10]
>
> —Ibid., Vol. IV, pp. 245b-246a.

Had it been the Word (*logos*) instead of Wisdom (*sophia*) who was doing the first-person speaking in this text in Proverbs, almost anyone would have readily accepted it as a reference to the origin and preexistence of Christ, based on the fact that in John's writings Christ is called "the Word." However, just as Christ is the personification of the Word of God, and not the actual word itself, similarly Christ is also referred to as the Wisdom of God: "we preach Christ crucified . . . to those whom God has called, both Jews and Greeks, Christ the power of God and the wisdom of God" (1 Cor 1:23-24). Christ is the wisdom of God, just as he is the word of God. God's word and God's wisdom are inseparably associated in Scripture.

The Greek *logos* (word) does not mean basically the word as being spoken; but *logos* extends backward to include the very idea conceived, whether or not that idea is ever expressed in articulate language. And there is no such thing as an idea in the mind of God without that idea being the wisdom of God. They are inseparable. "To one there is given through the Spirit the message of wisdom [*logos* of *sophias*; ASV: word of wisdom]" (1 Cor 12:8). Christ, who is called "the Word" (John 1:1), "has become for us wisdom from God" (1 Cor 1:30). Consider Christ (called the Word), "in whom are hidden all the treasures of wisdom and knowledge" (Col 2:3). "Let the word [*logos*] of Christ dwell in you richly as you teach and admonish one another with all wisdom [*sophia*]" (Col 3:16). Thus Christ is the wisdom of God as he is the word of God. Both the word and wisdom of God are personified in Christ. Christ is called the Word of God because he came to declare that word so completely and so authoritatively. Christ is called the wisdom of God because the word he declared was so filled with God's wisdom that none of even the greatest of philosophers could ever compare.

Consider some of the variables in the text of Proverbs 8:22-31. "The LORD brought me forth as the first of his works" (v. 22). "When there were no oceans, I was given birth" (v. 24); "before the hills, I was given birth" (v. 25). Considering both the NIV and ASV with their footnoted alternate readings, we see such expressions as "Jehovah formed me," "I was set up," "I was fashioned," "I was brought forth," "I was given birth." If God is all wise, and we know he is, his infinite wisdom is never increased nor diminished. It is impossible to imagine such a God ever existing without that infinite wisdom. Yet this text speaks of wisdom as being formed, set up, fashioned, brought forth and given birth, as if wisdom had not always existed. It seems much more reasonable that in this text wisdom is being personified in Christ whom Jehovah formed from his own divine nature, set up, fashioned, brought forth and gave birth to. That's why Christ is called the Son of God; Christ, not wisdom, is God's offspring. Wisdom was never actually born; but Christ was. Wisdom has always existed infinitely.

Consider also WHEN that something in Proverbs was formed, brought forth and given birth to: It was in (or as) the beginning of God's ways, the first of his works, from everlasting, from the beginning, before the earth was, when there were no oceans, or fountains abounding with water, before the mountains were settled, before all those things which were subsequently created or made by Christ (John 1:3; Col 1:16), after Christ, the firstborn of all creation, was first formed, brought forth and given birth to.

Here also we see a Bible explanation of the meaning of "from everlasting." It is here explained as "from the beginning, before the earth was." "From everlasting" has reference here to the age of eternity as distinguished from measured time which followed creation. It does not refer to something which had no beginning. Here it is indefinite, not infinite.

However, even in the face of all this mass of evidence, because of the poetic nature of this passage in Proverbs, and the linguistic liberties which often accompany such poetry, the accurate meaning of this passage may be too uncertain for it to be used unquestionably as a proof text for the origin and preexistence of Christ, but may be used more as a most probable explanation as to why Paul calls Christ "the firstborn over all creation. For by him all things were created" (Col 1:15-16). All that is said in this passage concerning wisdom may indeed be said even far more literally and understandably of the Son of God. Christ existed before the creation, for "all things were made by him." And he originated from God, being "the firstborn of every creature."

Surely no one would deny that God could have been capable of producing a divine offspring from his own divine substance, in the form of a divine Son, to be his only divine companion from the ages of eternity. And to deny such a possibility would be to deny the omnipotence of God.

CHAPTER 27

FIRSTBORN OF ALL CREATION

An integral part of the origin and preexistence of Christ, and a Scripture already mentioned several times, is Paul's identification of God's Son as "the image of the invisible God, the firstborn over all creation" (Col 1:15). When Paul calls Christ "the image of the invisible God," he is saying in effect that Christ is not that invisible God, but is rather the image thereof. And since there is only one true God, the invisible one, then Christ obviously cannot be that one true God. However, because of the extraordinary likeness between God and his divine Son, though a likeness certainly not including Christ's human nature and physical features, Paul could rightly call Christ "the image of the invisible God." Obviously Christ is not the invisible God he is the image of; for herein are portrayed two separate beings or persons: (1) the Father, the invisible God, and (2) his Son, the image of that invisible God. They are not two Gods, one visible and the other invisible, for there is only one God; and Christ is the image of that one God.

The word "image" (Gr: *eikon*) means a true likeness or resemblance. It does not signify an exact identity. Consider Paul again as he speaks about "image": "For those God foreknew he also predestined to be conformed to the likeness [ASV: image, *eikon*] of his Son, that he might be the firstborn among many brothers" (Rom 8:29). It is God's will that we become conformed to the *image* of his Son; that is, to allow the traits of righteousness found in Jesus to also characterize our lives. When we do this, we become conformed to the *image* of Christ, but we do not become Christ himself. Nor does being in his image imply any likeness to his divine nature; for we are human and shall never be divine. Neither does "image of the invisible God" identify Christ as being that God.

However, we do know that in addition to Christ's having God's characteristics, living as an example on earth as God would have lived if God had become a man, he also even has God's divine nature. Paul's very next statement in Colossians 1:15 goes on to identify that likeness to include divine nature by calling Christ "the firstborn over all creation." Certainly Christ is not that God of whom he is the firstborn. But just as certainly, if Christ is truly God's firstborn, which he has to be if he is God's only begotten Son, then Christ also bears the image of God's divine nature by inheritance.

Furthermore, if "firstborn" here, as some have espoused, means "preeminence" without signifying a birth, this passage could not be used to prove the deity of Christ. God could have given preeminence to any one of his created angels, without making that angel divine. This passage does not specifically say that Christ is divine, nor does his being the image of God prove his divinity, any more than man's being conformed to Christ's image gives man the divinity of Christ. Man was originally made in the image of God, but has never been, nor will ever be divine. But it is evident that Paul is here saying that Christ is the image of the invisible God as a result of his being God's firstborn, thus inheriting his Father's divine nature of whom he is the offspring. It is also evident that Paul is saying that Christ came into a personal existence as God's Son back in the ages of eternity, before anyone or anything else ever came into existence, "For by him all things were created" (v. 16).

The meaning of the word "firstborn" is basically found in the compound word itself—"first" and "born." It has reference to any being which is the first being to come forth from another given being in a way as to constitute a birth. Firstborn simply means born first. The term is used in reference to both humans and beasts alike, as well as to divine offspring. The word within itself contains no primary idea of preeminence, but has to do with being first in time or sequence. But then a secondary usage adds the attained significance of preeminence, due only to the fact that God elected that the firstborn, instead of the second born or some other born, would be given preeminence, and that all such preeminent ones, both man and beast, would belong to God in a very special way. "The LORD said to Moses, 'Consecrate to me every firstborn male. The first offspring of every womb among the Israelites belongs to me, whether man or animal'" (Exod 13:1-2). Not that the firstborn was necessarily any better than all others; but the fact that God legislated that it be that way, the firstborn would have preeminence over all others proceeding from the same womb.

"The first offspring of every womb belongs to me, including all the firstborn males of your livestock, whether from herd or flock. Redeem the firstborn donkey with a lamb, but if you do not redeem it, break its neck. Redeem all your firstborn sons" (Exod 34:19-20). Not necessarily because donkeys and humans were either inferior or superior to cattle and sheep, were their firstborn to be excluded from being sacrificed, and instead were to be redeemed, but rather because God did not allow donkeys and humans to be either sacrificed or eaten. Neither qualified as being ceremonially "clean."

During the Patriarchal Dispensation, from Adam to Moses, there seems to have been a very marked significance attached by those ancient fathers to their firstborn sons. Whether that was by divine requirement or merely by divine sanction, the Bible is not quite clear. It seems that the Patriarch (father ruler) would pass on to his firstborn son that office of patriarchy as a most significant part of the blessed inheritance, especially after God's promise to Abraham. And it seems that following that custom, whether required or merely developed through numerous centuries, God made the practice a part of his law to

Israel, "for all the firstborn are mine. When I struck down all the firstborn in Egypt, I set apart for myself every firstborn in Israel, whether man or animal. They are to be mine. I am the LORD" (Num 3:13). So preeminence is only an attained significance attached to being a firstborn. And only four places in Scripture is it evident that firstborn bears that attained significance of preeminence in the absence of the inherent meaning of being born first.

The word "firstborn" (Heb: *bekor*; Gr: *prototokos*) occurs in the original Bible text at least 132 times, including where three similar Hebrew words (*bekirah, bekorah* and *peter*) are translated *prototokos* nine times in the Greek Septuagint version. Of this total, 123 occur in the OT and 9 in the NT, about 31 of which refer to animal births other than humans. And never does *firstborn*, as pertains to animals, have any reference to preeminence, other than the fact that God said, "They are mine." It always has only the basic significance of being born first. An owner could not reason that since his second born animal proved to be more valuable or of superior quality than his firstborn one, he should offer the second born. The offering of the firstborn did not call for the best nor the preeminent; it called for the one born first. That's the meaning of the word *firstborn*.

Only three times in the OT and once in the NT is it apparent that the word *firstborn* is ever used to refer to exalted status in the absence of being born first:

(1) God told Moses to say to Pharaoh, "Israel is my firstborn son" (Exod 4:22). Jacob, the man, whose name was changed to Israel, was not Isaac's first son to be born. Jacob's twin brother Esau preceded Jacob from the womb (Gen 25:24-26), and was therefore Isaac's firstborn before Jacob. Under patriarchy the birthright seems to have included a sacred right to the divinely appointed office of patriarch as both priest and prophet, as well as tribal ruler. But Esau sold that sacred right to his brother Jacob, making Israel God's *firstborn*, not in the basic sense of being born first, but figuratively, in the sense of possessing the birthright which by inheritance belonged to the son who was born first. Then in God's law to the Israelites, the birthright, with its special rights and privileges, included a double portion of any divided inheritance (Deut 21:17); and in the case of kings, it usually (but not always) included the right to the throne.

However, *firstborn* in the message to Pharaoh refers rather to the people of Israel in Egypt instead of to Israel the patriarch, because Jacob had already died years before, and Moses was to speak on God's behalf to Pharaoh, saying, "Let my son go, so he may worship me." Here, *firstborn* and *son*, even though both are in the singular form, refer to the people of Israel as a whole, who were in no sense literally born first, but were God's favored and chosen people over Egypt, as well as over all other nations and tribes. *The* NIV *Study Bible* at this place, and with justifiable cause, describes *firstborn* as "a figure of speech indicating Israel's special relationship with God." Thus *firstborn* in this passage makes use of the secondary and attained meaning of exalted status without the primary significance of being born first. It was a figure of speech.

(2) In that same sense God said, "I am Israel's father, and Ephraim is my firstborn son" (Jer 31:9). God, of course, is the Father of all mankind; but surely Jeremiah is here revealing the fact that the nation of Israel sustained a special relationship with God which their contemporaries did not enjoy. Then to further emphasize that valued relationship, God added, "and Ephraim is my firstborn son."

Joseph's two sons were Manasseh and Ephraim, in that order, Manasseh being born first (Gen 41:51). So Ephraim could not be firstborn in the sense of being born first. However, when the patriarch Jacob blessed these two grandsons (Gen 48), he purposely crossed his arms, against Joseph's protest, so as to give the birthright to Ephraim instead of Manasseh, acknowledging the future preeminence of the tribe of Ephraim over that of Manasseh. Thus Ephraim is called *firstborn* figuratively without his being born first. God, of course, who foreknows all things, could cause or allow a birthright to go to one who was not born first, and could so signify through his patriarchal representative; but later, his law to Israel declared that a birthright was never to be given to one who was not born first (Deut 21:16-17), specifically not during the lifetime of him who was born first (see ASV fn. on v. 16). And even though the birthright was given by Jacob to Ephraim, Manasseh was still called "Joseph's firstborn" (Josh 17:1), because Manasseh was born first.

This was likewise true of Reuben, Jacob's firstborn. Even though Reuben's birthright was taken from him because of an evil which he had done, and was given to the sons of Joseph, Reuben was still called "the firstborn of Israel" (1 Chr 5:1), where it is also declared that "he could not be listed in the genealogical record in accordance with his birthright." In this way one might possess a birthright without his being born first.

Furthermore, it is quite likely, as believed by numerous scholars, that the name Ephraim is here used representatively as a symbol for Israel, inasmuch as the tribe of Ephraim was so prominent in the leadership of God's people. From Ephraim had come such leaders as Joshua, and Samuel (a Levite), as well as Jeroboam, the first king and dynasty founder for the northern Kingdom of Israel, composed of ten of the twelve tribes. Still others may consider "I am Israel's father, and Ephraim is my firstborn son" to be a form of poetic dualism, with both expressions containing a single message, but using different terminology, with Israel and Ephraim used interchangeably, and with father and firstborn describing a singular exalted relationship which exists between a father and son, especially a firstborn son. In either case, neither Israel nor Ephraim were firstborn in the sense of being born first.

(3) God once spoke concerning David, "I will also appoint him my firstborn, the most exalted of the kings of the earth" (Ps 89:27). David, having seven older brothers, was the youngest son of Jesse, and certainly not a firstborn in the common sense of being born first. This is acknowledged by the statement, "I will also appoint him my firstborn," showing that he had not been, but would become God's firstborn. God, like anyone else, can have only one firstborn in the literal sense (and that's Christ); but in a qualified or figurative sense, he may have as many firstborn as he chooses to give exalted status. Such exalted status he gave to David, described as "the most exalted of the kings of the earth." David did not inherit that status by being born first, whether of God or of man; it was given him by God.

(4) Then in the NT, God's spiritual Israel, the church, like national Israel of old, is referred to as firstborn. "To the church of the firstborn, whose names are written in heaven" (Heb 12:23). Some may think that since Christ is God's firstborn, this passage in essence is calling the general assembly the church of Christ; and truly this general assembly is the church of Christ, the church of him who was born first, who is both the firstborn and only begotten of God. However, "firstborn" here is plural in the Greek, referring not to Christ, but to those firstborn ones "whose names are written in heaven." The author, writing to Hebrew Christians who were familiar with national Israel's being called God's firstborn, also effectively depicts the church (spiritual Israel) as being composed of God's firstborn ones in a more spiritual and more personal sense, meaning that all those who have been born again (John 3:3), born of water and the Spirit (v. 5), are by that new birth deemed *firstborn*, who constitute the church, God's spiritual family. Therefore God's children today are not his firstborn in the common sense of being born first, but in the spiritual sense of having been given exalted status with God, above those fellows who have not thus been born again into God's spiritual family.

Christians are also figuratively firstborn in that they have been "baptized into Christ" (Rom 6:3; Gal 3:27); and therefore being in him who is firstborn, they thereby figuratively become God's firstborn.

These four Bible references discussed show that *firstborn* may at times be used in the attained sense of preeminence in the absence of being born first; but these four are the only such references in the entire Bible where *firstborn* is devoid of being born first. Other than these, none of the 128 other references to *firstborn* can be shown to mean preeminence in the absence of being born first. In one other reference, one of poetic imagery, Job refers to "the firstborn of death" (Job 18:13), but without necessarily eliminating the idea of sequence. Therefore, when Christ is called "the firstborn over all creation" (Col 1:15), it must be concluded that he was the first being to be born, unless there is positive proof, as we have shown in the matter of these four references discussed, that he could not have been born first. Without proof beyond any question that Christ could not have been born of God before any other being or thing ever came into existence, it violates all rules of reasonable interpretation to conclude that *firstborn* in Colossians 1:15 means preeminence without being born first. In Scripture there is no such negative proof to be found; but rather, all evidence points to the fact that he was truly born of God before any other being was ever born or created, "for by him all things were created" (v. 16). Nowhere does Scripture teach that Jesus, as a person, had no beginning.

Some have supposed that *firstborn* here must mean only preeminence without signifying a birth, thinking that "firstborn of creation" (ASV) or "firstborn of every creature" (KJV), in the sense of actually being born, would make Christ a creature, a created being, like all those with whom he is here compared. In fact, through the centuries, based primarily on this passage, some have classified Christ as the first being God created, and subsequently the agent through whom God created everything else. This doctrine in reality denies the true divinity and Sonship of Christ. Christ is either (1) the one God (which we have shown and shall continue to show him not to be), or (2) he is the divine Son (offspring) of that God, born before all ages, or else (3) he is a created being and therefore not divine at all. Between these two first and last extremes lies the truth: Christ is God's firstborn and only begotten divine Son, "the firstborn over [or *of*] all creation. For by him were all things created."

"Firstborn of all creation" does not make Christ a creature. The subject under consideration here is not who are creatures and who are not, but rather, who was born first, and would thereby have preeminence. Of all beings that have ever been born, Christ is the only such being who is not a creature (created being). In considering who was born first, Christ could be compared only with creatures. Therefore, of all the beings ever to be born, all of which were creatures except Christ, Christ was born before them all. That does not make Christ a creature like those whom he was born before, and with whom he is here compared.

Yet some have thought it necessary to have *firstborn* here to mean *preeminence* instead of *born first* in order to keep Christ from being classified as a creature. But the genitive "of" remains the same in either case. If "of all creation" or "of every creature" makes the one born first a creature, it also makes the one who is preeminent a creature. Consider these two statements:

(1) Of every creature, Christ is born first.

(2) Of every creature, Christ is preeminent.

Whichever *firstborn* means in this passage, whether "born first" or "preeminent," the genitive phrase, "of every creature," remains the same and applies equally to both. If one makes Christ a creature, so does the other.

This passage cannot be saying that Christ is included as a created being, "For by him all things were created." If Christ were a created being or thing, and all such beings or things were created in or by him, then he himself would have been created in or by himself. What a preposterous dilemma!

The following are some of the various English translations found in this passage:

ASV, NASB, RSV, NWT, Weymouth: "the first-born of all creation"
KJV and *New Catholic Edition*: "the firstborn of every creature"
TEV: "the first-born Son, superior to all created things"
TCNT: "first-born and head of all creation"
Goodspeed: "born before any creature"
Barclay: "Begotten before all creation"
NEB fn: "born before . . ."
Beck: "born before and above everything created"
Berry's ILT (representing 7 Greek texts): "firstborn of all creation."

Several of these translations emphasize the preeminence of Christ, while others emphasize the sequence of being born first; but none of them excludes the fact that a birth took place prior to creation. As was said earlier, *firstborn* took on the attained idea of preeminence, and therefore includes preeminence whether or not it is so stated. Therefore Goodspeed's "born before any creature" and Barclay's "begotten before all creation" include not only Christ's origin and preexistence, but also his preeminence, as a result of his being born first.

Removing the idea of being born first, and substituting mere preeminence, creates an obvious tautology in the context under consideration. The apostle lists several things which prove the preeminence or supremacy of Christ (Col 1):

(1) Christ is the Son God loves (v. 13)
(2) The kingdom belongs to Christ (v. 13)
(3) In Christ we have redemption, the forgiveness of sins (v. 14)
(4) Christ is the image of the invisible God (v. 15)
(5) Christ is the firstborn over all creation (v. 15)
(6) By and for Christ all things were created (v. 16)
(7) Christ is before all things (v. 17)
(8) In Christ all things hold together (v. 17)
(9) Christ is the head of the body, the church (v. 18)

(10) Christ is the beginning (v. 18)

(11) Christ is the firstborn from among the dead (v. 18)

All these are "so that in everything he might have the supremacy" (v. 18). If *firstborn* in verse 15 means supremacy (preeminence) instead of *born first*, the two verses would be saying that Christ has supremacy (v. 15) so that in all things he might have supremacy (v. 18). But instead, verse 15 says that Christ was firstborn so that in the matter of being born first, as well as in all the other things stated, verse 18 can conclude that in ALL things Christ has supremacy, or preeminence.

Furthermore, if *firstborn* in verse 15 means preeminence, it would seem that the same *firstborn* in verse 18 would also mean preeminence, therefore excluding the idea that Christ was the first person to be raised from the dead to die no more. Such would mean that of all those who have been thus raised from the dead, Christ is preeminent, but not necessarily the first. *The* NIV *Study Bible* on this passage concerning *firstborn* states:

Christ was the first to rise from the dead with a resurrection body. Elsewhere Paul calls him the "firstfruits of those who have fallen asleep" (1 Cor 15:20). Others who were raised from the dead . . . were raised only to die again.

Therefore, if Christ were not the first to be raised from the dead in that ultimate sense, then he should not have been called the "firstfruits of those who have fallen asleep."

While *firstborn* can (as in those four cases cited) mean preeminence, not so with *firstfruits*. Christ can be the firstfruits of those who have fallen asleep only by being the first to be thus raised.

As to whether or not Christ was already the Son of God before being born of Mary, consider this statement found in Hebrews 1:4 concerning Christ: "So he became as much superior to the angels as the name he has inherited is superior to theirs." A name is inherited by a son from his father at the time of his birth; therefore Christ inherited a more excellent name than the angels when he became God's Son. If he did not become God's Son until he was born of Mary, then he could not have inherited that more excellent name prior to his becoming the Son of man. Until God could say to Christ, as in verse 5, quoting from Psalm 2:7, "You are my Son; today I have become your Father" [fn: Or *have begotten you*], which the writer infers to have never been said of any of the angels, Christ could not have had that more excellent name. But obviously, since the creation of angels, Christ's name has always been more excellent than theirs, because "the name he has inherited is superior to theirs," when he became "the firstborn of every creature" (KJV), such creatures including even the angels. Surely Christ already had that more excellent *name* (signifying a relationship) at the time he created those angels, and continued to have it through the centuries, ages before he was born of Mary. Therefore Christ was already the Son of God and inherited that name (or relationship) before he was born of Mary.

Verifying the interpretation herein given concerning *firstborn* (Col 1:15), consider the following statements:

The People's New Testament With Notes, by B. W. Johnson:

> The thought is that he existed before creation began; born of God instead of being created . . . born before any creature was called into existence.[16]

Notes on the New Testament, by Albert Barnes (From editor's notes in brackets at this text):

> [The most commonly received, and, as we think, best supported opinion, is that which renders (the Greek words) "begotten before all creation." This most natural and obvious sense would have been more readily admitted had it not been supposed hostile to certain views on the sonship of Christ.][6]

Thayer's *Greek-English Lexicon*, under *prototokos* (firstborn):
> a. the first-born whether of man or of beast, Heb 11:28. b. Christ . . . who came into being through God prior to the entire universe of created things, Col 1:15 . . . . In the same sense, apparently, he is called simply *ho prototokos*, Heb 1:6 . . . . the first of the dead who was raised to life, Col 1:18 . . . Rev 1:5 . . . who was the Son of God long before those who by his agency and merits are exalted to the nature and dignity of sons of God, with the added suggestion of the supreme rank by which he excels these other sons . . . Rom 8:29 . . . . [7]
> —pp. 555b-556a.

Consider Marvin R. Vincent, concerning Col 1:15, "the first-born of every creature":

> "*First-born*" points to *eternal preexistence*. Even the Rev. is a little ambiguous, for we must carefully avoid any suggestion that Christ was the first of *created things*, which is contradicted by the following words: *in him were all things created*. The true sense is, *born before the creation*. Compare *before all things*, vs 17.[17]
> —*Word Studies in the New Testament*, Vol. III, p. 468.

Of all the various doctrines within Christendom, none can be considered more orthodox than the idea that Christ was born of God back in eternity before the creation of anything or anyone. The ancient church fathers had much to say on this subject, as recorded in the *Ante-Nicene Fathers:*

"Epistle of Ignatius to the Ephesians" (30-107 A.D.):

> For the Son of God, who was begotten before time began, and established all things according to the will of the Father, He was conceived in the womb of Mary, according to the appointment of God, of the seed of David, and by the Holy Ghost.[10]
>
> —Vol. I, p. 57b.

"Tertullian Against Marcion" (207 A.D.):

> If Christ is not "the first-begotten before every creature," as that "Word of God by whom all things were made, and without whom nothing was made" . . . How, again, is He before all things, if He is not "the first-born of every creature" . . . . [10]
>
> —Ibid., Vol. III, p. 470b.

Tertullian "Against Praxeas," (208 A.D.):

> He became His first-begotten Son, because begotten before all things; and His only-begotten also, because alone begotten of God, in a way peculiar to Himself. . . . *The Father* took pleasure evermore in Him, who equally rejoiced with a reciprocal gladness in the Father's presence: "Thou art my Son, today have I begotten Thee"; even before the morning star did I beget Thee. The Son likewise acknowledges the Father, speaking in His own person, under the name of Wisdom: "The Lord formed me as the beginning of His ways, with a view to His own works; before all the hills did He beget Me."[10]
>
> —Ibid., Vol. III, pp. 601b-602a.

Origen (230-254 A.D.):

> The nature of that deity which is in Christ in respect of His being the only-begotten Son of God is one thing, and that human nature which He assumed in these last times for the purpose of the dispensation (of grace) is another.[10]
>
> —Ibid., Vol. IV, pp. 245b-246a.

Novation (257 A.D.):

Before whom (Christ) there is none but the Father.[10]

—Ibid., Vol. V, p. 620a

Novation again:

> If by the apostle Christ is called "the first-born of every creature," how could He be the first-born of every creature, unless because according to His divinity the Word proceeded from the Father before every creature? And unless the heretics receive it thus, they will be constrained to show that Christ the man was the first-born of every creature; which they will not be able to do. Either, therefore, He is before every creature, that He may be the first-born of every creature, and He is not man only, because man is after every creature; or He is man only, and He is after every creature.[10]

—Ibid., p. 632.

Novation continued:

> For who does not acknowledge that the person of the Son is second after the Father, when he reads that it was said by the Father, consequently to the Son, "Let us make man in our image and our likeness."[10]

—Ibid., p. 636b.

Novation continued, pp. 643-644:

> Thus God the Father, the Founder and Creator of all things, who only knows no beginning, invisible, infinite, immortal, eternal, is one God; to whose greatness, or majesty, or power, I would not say nothing can be preferred, but nothing can be compared; of whom, when He willed it, the Son, the Word, was born . . . . it is essential that He who knows no beginning must go before Him who has a beginning . . . . having an origin because He is born, and of like nature with the Father in some measure by His nativity . . . . He is born of that Father who alone has no beginning. He, then, when the Father willed it, proceeded from the Father, and He who was in the Father came forth from the Father . . . . that is to say, that divine substance whose name is the Word, whereby all things were made, and without whom nothing was made. For all things are after Him, because they are by Him. And reasonably, He is before all things, but after the Father, since all things were made by Him, and He proceeded from Him of whose will all things were made . . . . For if He had not been born—compared with Him who was unborn, an equality being manifested in both—He would make two unborn beings, and thus would make two Gods . . . . whatever He is, He is not of Himself, because He is

not unborn; but He is of the Father, because He is begotten, whether as being the Word, whether as being the Power, or as being the Wisdom, or as being the Light, or as being the Son; and whatever of these He is, in that He is not from any other source, as we have already said before, than from the Father, owing His origin to His Father, He could not make a disagreement in the divinity by the number of two Gods, since He gathered His beginning by being born of Him who is one God.[10]

Cyprian (251 AD) in his "Treatise XII," in the Second of "Three Books of Testimonies Against the Jews":

> Although from the beginning He had been the Son of God, yet He had to be begotten again according to the flesh.[10]
>
> —Ibid., p. 519a.

Dionysius of Rome (259-269 AD), "Against the Sabellians":

> Was then "the first-born of every creature" something made?—"He who was begotten from the womb before the morning star?"—He who in the person of Wisdom says, "Before all the hills He begot me?" Finally, any one may read in many parts of the divine utterances that the Son is said to have been begotten, but never that He was made. From which considerations, they who dare to say that His divine and inexplicable generation was a creation, are openly convicted of thinking that which is false concerning the generation of the Lord.[10]
>
> —Ibid., Vol. II, p. 365b.

"Constitutions of the Holy Apostles," Book VIII, under the heading of "The Constitution of James the Brother of John, the Son of Zebedee," pp. 486b-487a:

> God . . . who only art unbegotten, and without beginning . . . who didst bring all things out of nothing into being by Thy only begotten Son, but didst beget Him before all ages . . . . [10]

Even the ancient creeds are clear on the matter of the origin of Christ. The *Athanasian Creed*, although mostly unscripturally founded in its speculative and fanciful presentation of the doctrine of the Trinity, does accurately describe Christ as being "of the Substance of the Father, begotten before the worlds." Also, "The Father is of none: not made, nor created, nor begotten. The Son is of the Father alone: not made, nor created, but begotten."

The *Nicene Creed*, resulting from that first Ecumenical Council (325 A.D.), and later expanded by the Council of Constantinople (381 A.D.), accurately describes Christ as "the only begotten Son of God, born of the Father before all ages." At that Nicene Council, Eusebius of Caesarea presented the creed already in use where he worshiped, which described Christ in part as "the only begotten Son, the first-born of all creation, begotten of the Father before all ages, through whom also all things were made." This creed became somewhat the basis for the *Nicene Creed*. Therefore, as we have said, no Christian doctrine can claim to be more orthodox than this simple, understandable and scriptural concept of the origin and preexistence of Christ, "the firstborn of all creation."

However, true orthodoxy is determined not by what such early church fathers have said, but rather by what divine Scriptures say. But at least we may learn from those ancient theologians, who best knew the Greek language, what the word "firstborn," as in Col 1:15, meant to them.

Some may object to Christ's being the offspring of God without a mother, erroneously thinking that all births must be produced by both a father and a mother, a male and a female. This is true, of course, concerning physical human births, such as Christ's human birth through Mary. But not all forms of life are produced by a male and female reproduction process. Just because human reproduction requires both male and female, it does not follow that all forms of reproduction, including divine reproduction, would require the same male-female combination. For example, the amoeba, one of the simplest forms of life, a one-cell animal, reproduces by fission (splitting), by spontaneous division of the body into two parts, each of which grows into a complete organism without one of the two being considered as the parent and the other the offspring. So if not even all forms of physical life require both a male and female in order to reproduce, surely one should not conclude that divine reproduction would require the same. Furthermore, Thayer lists the Greek *theos* as being both masculine and feminine genders.[7]

With God, there is no reason to suppose that any other being, female or otherwise, would be required for divine reproduction; but in the case of divine reproduction, which requires an offspring of divine substance, resulting in plural entities, beings or persons, there is no mystery as to which is the parent (God, the Father) and which is the offspring (Christ, the Son). Not until the Son of God would become the Son of man was there any need for a female in the generation process of Christ. Mary did not enable Christ to become the Son of God; he already was the Son of God. But Mary enabled Christ, the Son of God, to also become the Son of man.

In a discussion between Jesus and the Pharisees, Jesus asked,

"'What do you think about the Christ? Whose son is he?' 'The son of David,' they replied. He said to them, 'How is it then that David, speaking by the Spirit, calls him "Lord"? . . . If then David calls him "Lord," how can he be his son?' No one could say a word in reply . . . ." (Matt 22:42-46). We all know that Jesus, as the Son of man, was a descendant from David: "Jesus Christ, the son of David, the son of Abraham" (Matt 1:1). But David, under the inspiration of God's Spirit, called Jesus "my Lord" (Ps 110:1). Jesus' argument here implies that a father never calls his son his Lord; consequently, Christ could not have been David's son in the sense in which Jesus was here speaking. Christ was David's son only according to the flesh; and based solely on that sonship, David would have never called Jesus "my Lord." However, based on the Sonship of the preexistent Christ, the Son of God, instead of the son of David, David appropriately called him "my Lord." This proves conclusively that Christ was the Son of God before he ever became the Son of David, the Son of man.

No doubt even more would have been said in Scripture about Christ's preexistence as the Son of God, were it not for the fact that what is said is so clear and simple that it should never have been misunderstood in the first place. "For God so loved the world that he gave his one and only Son [Or *his only begotten Son*]" (John 3:16); "God did by sending his own Son in the likeness of sinful man" (Rom 8:3); "But when the time had fully come, God sent his Son, born of a woman" (Gal 4:4); "But in these last days he has spoken to us by his Son . . . through whom he made the universe" (Heb 1:2). And in the parable of the husbandmen, "He had one left to send, a son, whom he loved" (Mark 12:6), or "I will send my son, whom I love" (Luke 20:13). All these, as well as many others attest to the fact that God had a Son before Christ was born of the virgin. It is unthinkable that these statements would be saying that God produced a Son which he did not already have, just for the purposes stated in these passages. The most natural understanding is that God already had a beloved, only begotten and divine Son,—whom he loved, and by whom he was loved—and that when the occasion arose and the fullness of time came, God was willing to send that only Son forth from heaven to earth to accomplish God's purpose among men.

"Regarding his Son, who as to his human nature was a descendant of David, and who through the Spirit of holiness was declared with power to be the Son of God by his resurrection from the dead: Jesus Christ our Lord" (Rom 1:3-4). According to the flesh, Jesus was the seed of David. But as to Christ's preexistent Sonship as a personal entity, he is the Son of God, and is declared to be so with power by the resurrection. Not that Jesus became God's Son when he was raised from the dead, but rather, his resurrection provided living proof that he is who he claimed to be, the divine Son of God, the first ever to be born.

CHAPTER 28

DIVINE FATHERHOOD AND SONSHIP: REAL?
OR METAPHOR?

Because Scripture places Christ with God before the creation of anything (John 1:1-3; 1 Cor 8:6; Col 1:16-17; Heb 1:2), and because the Fatherhood of God and the divine Sonship of Christ are so well established, even before the creation, some students of theology, in their desperation to maintain their doctrine of the infinite coexistence of both Father and Son, have concluded that the Father-Son relationship existing prior to creation was not indeed the origin of true fatherhood and sonship, but that their relationship is merely pictured metaphorically as Father and Son.

But if both the Father and Son existed as two separate and distinct coequal and coeternal infinite spirit entities, neither preceding nor being preceded by the other, then there would be two infinite beings without beginning, and thus two Gods, even though they may be one in agreement, purpose and intent. Are they not both intellectual and intelligent entities whose continuing agreement in purpose and intent—at any point of their existence—is by their own individual choice, and not by inherent coercion? If by choice, and if one or the other were to choose not to thus agree, therefore no longer be one in agreement, would there then be two coequal Gods because they did not agree? If not, then which of the two supposed coequal entities would be the one true God Almighty?

Be aware that the Bible does not merely teach that there is only one Godhead (divine nature), regardless of the number of persons who possess that divine nature; but rather the Bible also affirms clearly that there is only one true God (*ho Theos*) in the absolute sense, and that that God is the Father to the exclusion of all other beings or persons (John 17:3; 1 Cor 8:6; etc.), even distinguishing the one God from his Son Jesus Christ.

Furthermore, if the Fatherhood of God and the Sonship of Christ are metaphors, and no actual Father-Son relationship existed until Jesus was born of Mary, then God would not be the Father of that divine person who already existed, but would be the Father of only the physical body that was born of Mary ("A body you prepared for me" Heb 10:5). In which case the Sonship of Christ could not be used to prove the divinity of Christ. Yet that was the stated purpose for which John's Gospel was recorded: "That you may believe that Jesus is the Christ, the Son of God" (John 20:31). John opened his Gospel with the affirmation that Christ was with *ho Theos* (the God), and was *Theos* (divine). See Part I, Ch. 15, *And the Word Was God*. Therefore, to prove that the preexisting Christ (not his physical body) is literally the Son of God in origin, is to prove the divinity of Christ.

Also, if that preexisting relationship between Father and Son is interpreted as a metaphor, then when Christ was born of Mary and was "called the Son of God" (Luke 1:35), who is to say that that relationship was not, and is not, also a metaphor, as no physical copulation had taken place?

Jesus' physical body, being miraculously begotten in the virgin by the power of God's Spirit, does not conclusively prove the divinity of Christ, just as John's being miraculously conceived in Elizabeth, and Isaac's being miraculously conceived in Sarah by that same power of God, do not prove that either John or Isaac was divine. But to deny that the preexistent Christ, or even that body which was miraculously begotten in Mary, was literally born of God, is to essentially deny the divinity of Christ; namely, the Sonship of Christ. And to conclude that the Sonship of Christ, at any point in his existence, is only a metaphor, is to essentially deny the divinity of Christ, which denial was evidently a mark of the Gnosticism John's Gospel was written to refute.

Some have set forth the idea that because Jesus' royal nomenclatures, such as Christ, Messiah, Lord, King, etc., appear in Scripture far more often than *Son of God*, therefore we should not visualize Christ through a "Son-of-God" filter, but rather see first and foremost his royalty as verily Jehovah God himself. They are not able to visualize God and Christ in an actual Father-Son existence, which, to them, would necessitate God's having actual male genitalia in order to be able to produce such an offspring in the form of a Son. But that's making God in man's image. We are not speaking of human offspring, but of divine offspring.

Inasmuch as Scripture not only places Christ back there with God before the beginning of all things created, Scripture also presents Christ as God's "firstborn over [of, ASV; see Gr.] all creation. For by him all things were created" (Col 1:15-16. See Part I, Ch. 27, *Firstborn Of All Creation*).

That real Father-Son relationship is the only logical explanation accounting for the subordination of one divine being to another divine being—Christ submitting to God—the Son submitting to his Father—not only as the Son of man here on earth, but also both before and after his earthly advent. We see him now as subordinate to God, not seated on God's throne in heaven, but at God's right hand, still a Son subordinate to God his Father who anointed him King of kings and Lord of lords. Not on God's throne, but on David's spiritual throne at God's right hand.

Likewise, before coming to earth, Christ is seen in a subordinate role with God his Father, even before the worlds were made. It was God, not Christ, who said, "Let us make man in our image, in our likeness" (Gen 1:26). There were not two Gods who brought all this about. It was the one Jehovah God Almighty, with the assistance and instrumentality of his divine Son. Not that God could not have done it all by himself; but God chose that his Son be his trusted but subordinate partner in the project. The Son's subordination in creation is further seen in Paul's declaration, "There is but one God, the Father, from whom all things came and for whom we live; and there is but one Lord, Jesus Christ, through whom all things came and through whom we live" (1 Cor 8:6). God was the origin and architect, while Christ was the agent and medium. Therefore both God and Christ—Father and Son—are said to have created all things, without making Christ and God identical, and without making two Gods. While they were both equally divine, not angelic, human, nor animal, the Son was, and always remains subordinate to his Father in power and authority. The only power or authority Jesus ever claimed to have was given him by his Father (Matt 28:18). If before creation, there existed a God-God relationship instead of a Father-Son relationship, then there would have been one God subordinating to another God, thus two Gods—a greater God, and a lesser God.

It is most reasonable that God already had an actual offspring back there in eternity, whom he brought into existence from his own being and substance, one whom he could love and be loved by. One who for ceaseless ages had been by his side as his only divine companion. One whose tortuous death on the cross tore at the heartstrings of his divine Father as with Abraham when he was told to take the life of his beloved son. Was it not truly God's Son on the cross that caused God to look the other way and blanket the earth with darkness? To say that their relationship was and is merely a metaphor greatly diminishes the most beautiful picture and demonstration of love that could ever be conceived in the mind of God, much less in the mind of man.

And the idea that God sacrificed one who was not literally his own Son, but merely called him a Son metaphorically because God had miraculously produced a human body for him through Mary, would essentially negate the tremendous effect of the Golden Text of the Bible (John 3:16), and leave a gapping chasm in the impact which that truth has had in the hearts and lives of all Christians since John penned those profound words nearly two millennia ago. To Christians, the idea that Jesus is not, and never has been the actual Son of God is nothing short of heresy, and can be the first step in concluding that the whole Bible, and even God himself are simply metaphors, a conclusion to which some theologians have already arrived.

CHAPTER 29

THE NAME OF THE FATHER, SON, AND HOLY SPIRIT

Just before leaving the earth to return to heaven from whence he had come some 33 years before, Jesus gave to his apostles an unlimited commission, commonly known as "the Great Commission." That commission is recorded in Matthew 28:19-20 (see also Mark 16:15-18; Luke 24:46-49). According to Matthew's record, Jesus said, "Therefore go and make disciples of all nations, baptizing them in [Or *into*] the name of the Father and of the Son and of the Holy Spirit, and teaching them to obey everything I have commanded you."

This statement contains that which, through the centuries, has come to be known as "the baptismal formula," presumably a formal statement to be made at the time a person is being or about to be thus baptized. However, no Scripture ever calls the statement a "baptismal formula," nor does Scripture ever command or even suggest that the statement be verbalized by anybody on such an occasion. The command told the apostles what to do, but not what to say, if anything, at the time they would be doing it. So in Scripture, if there is such a *baptismal formula*, it does not formulate what they were to say, but rather what they were to do.

In this statement by Jesus, "the name of the Father and of the Son and of the Holy Spirit," some see what they believe to be evidence of what they call "the Holy Trinity." And indeed, this could be a useful illustration of the existence of the Trinity if it could be proved that such a Trinity actually exists. It cannot be denied that three distinctions are here involved. It may even be said that grammatically this passage does present a tri-unity, inasmuch as the singular "name," which is the object of the preposition "into," is compound, specifically triune, in that it is grammatically applied equally to each of the three distinctions mentioned—the Father, the Son, and the Holy Spirit.

However, to conclude from this phrase that the one God is a triune being composed of three separate and distinct coequal and coeternal persons is unwarranted, to say the least. They are not here called "the Trinity"; the Bible nowhere calls them "the Trinity"; and the three are nowhere said to be three persons who constitute the one God. In this commission they are called neither persons nor God.

It has already been shown conclusively by a *Great Cloud of Witnesses* (Part I, Chapter 4) that the one God is the Father to the exclusion of all other beings or persons, that Christ is his divine Son, and that the Holy Spirit is his Spirit. Furthermore, the word "person" is never found anywhere in the Bible in connection with the Holy Spirit, and specifically not in the statement herein being considered.

Some have erroneously concluded that because both the Father and the Son are each distinct individual persons or entities, therefore the Holy Spirit must likewise be a separate person or entity apart from the God it is the Spirit of, just as Christ is a separate person from the God he is the Son of. We shall herein show why such a conclusion is unwarranted.

Several things need to be considered in connection with this statement in the so-called *baptismal formula*. First, the translators are uncertain as to how the Greek preposition *eis* at this point should be translated, whether it should be "in" or "into" the name. It does make a definite difference in the meaning of the statement; but in neither case does it prove the doctrine of the Trinity. It is rendered "in the name" by the NIV, KJV, RSV, NWT, NASB, NEB, TEV, JB, NCE, Goodspeed, and Barclay. And the SEB has "by the authority," which is an interpolation, and possibly a correct interpretation, but not an actual translation.

The usual Greek word for "in" is *en*, properly signifying the location where the action of the verb takes place. It suggests that the action starts, proceeds, and culminates within the same scope or area. However, in the phrase under consideration the preposition is *eis*, the common Greek word for "into," which properly signifies a change in location, relationship, or status, resulting from the action of the verb, such as from without to within, or from one point to or toward another point (into, unto, to, toward, etc.). When *en* is used in an adverbial prepositional phrase concerning baptism, such as when John baptized people "*en* the Jordan River" (Matt 3:6), *en* refers to the contents of Jordan (water) as being the element within which those baptisms took place. John did not baptize them *eis* (into) Jordan, but *en* (in) Jordan. They no doubt moved themselves from the river's bank INTO the water; but it was IN the water where the baptisms took place.

But if the apostles were told to baptize people "in the name," surely they did not understand that the name, instead of water, would be the element within which the baptisms would take place; for later we find that water was the baptismal element used. In Acts 8:36-39, a vivid description of Christian baptism is recorded:

> As they traveled along the road, they came to some water and the eunuch said, "Look, here is water. Why shouldn't I be baptized?" And he gave orders to stop the chariot. Then both Philip and the eunuch went down into the water and Philip baptized him. When they came up out of the water, the Spirit of the Lord suddenly took Philip away, and the eunuch did not see him again, but he went on his way rejoicing.

Both went down from the chariot INTO the water where the eunuch was then baptized by Philip IN the water INTO which they had descended. So "the name" was not understood to be the element for baptism.

However, a possible interpretation which does allow the phrase to be translated "in the name," is one which means "by the authority." Both "*en* (in) the name" (John 10:25) and "*epi* (upon) the name" (Luke 24:47) are used frequently to mean "by the authority." In such case our text would be telling the apostles to baptize people by the authority of the Father and of the Son and of the Holy Spirit. So let us first consider the passage from that point of view.

The Jews supposedly wanted to accept God without accepting Jesus as God's Son and anointed ruler over them. But Jesus constantly reminded them that they could not have one without the other. Everything Jesus spoke was by the authority of God, his Father: "When a man believes in me, he does not believe in me only, but in the one who sent me" (John 12:44). "For I did not speak of my own accord, but the Father who sent me commanded me what to say and how to say it" (v. 49). "The words I say to you are not just my own. Rather, it is the Father, living in me, who is doing his work" (John 14:10). "These words you hear are not my own; they belong to the Father who sent me" (v. 24). "No one comes to the Father except through me" (John 14:6).

For the benefit of those who might not understand that unity of purpose and authority, Jesus made it clear that whatever authority he had was given him from God. Therefore, Christ's commission to the apostles, giving them authority to baptize believers in all nations, was likewise the authority of God his Father. They therefore never baptized some by the authority of God and others by the authority of Christ. The authority of Christ was the authority of God, without making Christ that God from whom Christ received his authority. Had Christ been God in the absolute sense, or a coequal person in that one God, he would not have needed to receive his authority from anyone; he would have already had it. But after his resurrection, and just before giving his Great Commission, he said, "All authority in heaven and on earth has been given to me" (Matt 28:18).

The one God is supreme. He has always had all authority. But Christ, who is not that God, but is rather the Son thereof, has only the authority given him by God. Thus, "in the name of" (or, by the authority of) the Father and the Son would in no way prove that Christ is that God from whom he received his authority. God can give authority to whomever he chooses, even to the apostles, without making the apostles God, or plural persons in the one God. There is neither proof nor implication in this text that the one God is composed of more than one person, the Father.

Furthermore, this commission of which we speak was to be carried out "in the name of" (or, by the authority of) the Holy Spirit, as well as the authority of God and Christ. God was already hypostatically in a place removed from the earth, being in heaven in a sense in which he was not on earth; and Christ was about to join God in heaven, to be enthroned there at God's right hand. But Jesus had already promised to send upon the apostles God's Holy Spirit to supernaturally guide them in carrying out that seemingly impossible commission, and to empower them with the necessary miraculous gifts needed to establish their message as being authoritative and divine. Jesus wanted it to be clearly understood by all that whatever message the apostles would thus proclaim by the power of that Spirit would be exactly the message which both Christ and God wanted them to proclaim, just as the prophets of old had always spoken "from God as they were carried along by the Holy Spirit" (2 Pet 1:21). Those miraculous powers visibly demonstrated by the apostles would confirm that their authority was from God, given to the apostles by Christ.

Inasmuch as the Holy Spirit is invisible, and would not be seen visibly as a person, only the demonstrated powers could prove the presence of God's Spirit in the apostles. That confirmation of authority by the Holy Spirit would be the same, whether it was done by the power of God's omnipresent Spirit, God's means of being everywhere in one sense while in heaven in still another sense, or whether it was done by the Holy Spirit as a person separate from the God it is the Spirit of. When that fact is realized, the great significance which has been historically attached by Trinitarians through the years to the necessity for the Holy Spirit's being recognized as a person distinct from the Father, will have faded into obscurity; and only the gnawing memory of bygone wars, executions and excommunications will be around to haunt Christians for the needless and senseless bloodshed and misery inflicted upon God's children who refused to accept man-made creeds and dogmas which never should have been written and adopted in the first place. How could the Holy Spirit as a person separate from the Father be any more omnipresent, more knowledgeable, more convincing or more powerful than the Holy Spirit as God's Spirit, the means by which God the Father is omnipresent and omniscient, and by which God's omnipotence and authority would be demonstrated in the apostles as they would accomplish that great commission? That authority, demonstrated in the apostles by the power of God's Holy Spirit was the same authority as the authority of Christ and the authority of God. Therefore, baptizing people in the name of (by the authority of) the Holy Spirit no more makes the Holy Spirit a separate person than baptizing by the authority of the Scriptures makes the Scriptures a person. Nor does baptizing by the authority of the Holy Spirit make the Holy Spirit any more a distinct person in the one God than baptizing by the authority of the apostles makes the apostles each persons in that same one God.

And if the Holy Spirit is a person separate from the Father, does the Father, like any other person who is made in his image, have a Spirit which is not such a separate person? Furthermore, if the Holy Spirit is a personal entity distinct from the Father, does the Holy Spirit, like all other persons, have a Spirit which is not a separate person from the Spirit which the Holy Spirit is? Such questions will be pursued and explored most extensively in Part II, *God and His Spirit*.

While some of the English versions, as we have seen, translate *eis* in the Great Commission with the preposition "in," others give the more literal translation "into," signifying not "by the authority," but rather signifying a change in relationship or status, from without to within "the name of the Father and of the Son and of the Holy Spirit." Such translations include the RV, ASV, TCNT, Beck, etc. Williams has "into" (fn: Expresses transfer of relationship). Weymouth has "into" (fn: Or 'unto'). Berry's ILT has "to the name." Therefore let us consider the text from that point of view.

The singular "name" here refers not to some proper name by which the three distinctions are individually or collectively known, as God was known to Israel in the OT by the name *Jehovah*. There is no such proper name by which those three distinctions are now to be known or designated. Instead, "the name" here, as in many places, especially in prophetic language, has reference to a relationship sustained, instead of a proper name by which one or more are to be called. "Father" is a title, not a proper name.

When the world was dominated by polytheistic paganism, God evidently saw the need for some name that would, for the people of Israel, distinguish him from the many gods of a polytheistic society. Thus *Jehovah*, the "I am" or "the existing one," was an appropriate name to distinguish him from those many gods who did not actually exist. But then in the NT era, when idolatry would no longer dominate, God did not designate some proper name by which he would be known, nor is God anywhere in the NT called by the Hebrew name *Jehovah*. When it is recognized that there is only one God, he needs no name but "God." As when there was only one man, that man's name was "Man," the English translation for the Hebrew word *Adam*.

Since God is the Father, "God" is probably here pictured as the family name into which people were to be baptized as they became spiritual children of God. Thus, baptism "into the name of the Father" would signify a change in relationship from outside God's family to inside God's family. Baptism would be that visible act which would demonstrate one's being born again (John 3:3), born of water and the Spirit (v. 5) into the family of God; or as Jesus said in that Great Commission, "into the name of the Father." Such would be a movement from outside God's spiritual family to within that family, thus, "into the name of the Father and of the Son and of the Holy Spirit."

Since Jesus is declared to be the Son of God, he, by inheritance, possesses that family name. As we might say today, not Jesus Carpenter, but Jesus God. And because Jesus is the only begotten and divine Son of God in a very unique way which cannot be said of any other person, he is even more so than others Jesus God or Jesus Jehovah. In this sense it would be entirely proper to call Jesus by the name of his Father, whether that name be "God," by which the Father is known today, or "Jehovah," by which God made himself known to the Israelites of old. And while it is doubtful that Scripture ever thus calls Jesus "God" or "Jehovah" in this precise sense, the implication in the Great Commission is that such could be proper. But the lack of Scriptural precedence keeps us from doing so. Whatever is the name of the Father, so is the name of his Son by inheritance. However, the more likely figurative application signifying a relationship is probably here intended.

Having the same name as the Father does not make Jesus the God he is the Son of, or even one of a plurality of persons in that one God. As Paul declared, "for us there is but one God, the Father" (1 Cor 8:6). And if Christians have been baptized into God's name, therefore into God's family, and also wear that family name, it does not mean that God is therefore a plural being composed of all those persons who thus wear his name. Nor does Jesus' being God's Son and wearing God's name mean that Jesus is that God whose name he inherited and wears. But the name Jesus inherited is superior to even the angels (Heb 1:4).

Furthermore, "Holy Spirit" is not a proper name as may be suggested by it's being capitalized by translators. Such capitalizations are interpretations, not translations. No such distinctions were found in the original Greek NT text, which was written in all capital letters.

The neuter word "Spirit" tells us what it is. It is a Spirit. And the neuter adjective "Holy" tells us which Spirit it is. It is the Holy Spirit, which is the Spirit of God. And to further distinguish God's Spirit from any other spirit, most translators choose to capitalize both Holy and Spirit, thus attributing special reverence to that Spirit over all other spirits. Such is proper, as long as it is understood that such capitalizations do not prove nor even suggest that "Holy Spirit" is the name of some individual person apart from the personal God it is the Spirit of, any more than man's spirit is a separate person from the man it is the spirit of.

God's Spirit, the Holy Spirit, is an extension of God himself, the means by which God is omnipresent (Ps 139:7-8). Whatever the Holy Spirit says or does, it is God himself saying or doing it by means of his omnipresent Spirit. Whenever the Holy Spirit spoke, it was God, the Father, doing the speaking through his omnipresent Spirit, just as God spoke through those prophets of old, as distinguished from those few occasions when God's voice was heard directly from heaven, saying, "This is my Son, whom I love" (Matt 3:17 and 17:5). Just as man's spirit is an extension of man himself, that part of man which at death is separated from the body it inhabits and returns to God who gave it (Eccl 12:7), there to await the resurrection when that spirit will be reunited with its resurrected and glorified body, restoring life to that person forever, so is the Holy Spirit an eternal extension of that immortal God who never dies, whose Spirit never separates from him, but rather "the Spirit of truth, which proceedeth from the Father" (John 15:26 ASV). Notice at this place the change in tenses of the Greek verbs: "I will send (future tense) the Spirit of truth, which proceedeth (present tense) from the Father."

As Jesus was dying on the cross, he said, "Father, into your hands I commit my spirit" (Luke 23:46). Then he died. When a man's spirit separates from his body, that man dies. It is also understandable that God, in whose image man is made, has a Spirit. But unlike man's spirit, God's Spirit, being omnipresent, ever proceeds from God himself. But if that Spirit were ever to be completely separated from the person who God is, understandably, God would die. However, there is no indication that God's Spirit ever separates from God to form a distinct entity or person, but instead, ever "proceeds from the Father."

Consider the following quotation from the ISBE, Vol. III, p. 1413b, regarding John 15:26:

> The present tense here suggests timeless action and has been taken to indicate an essential relation of the Spirit to God the Father . . . . the language is unusual, and the change of tense in the course of the sentence is suggestive. Perhaps it is one of the many instances where we must admit we do not know the precise import of the language of Scripture.[5]

However, as the Holy Spirit is indeed the Spirit of God, the Spirit of the Father, instead of a supposed separate and distinct person from that God and Father, then there is nothing at all strange about the change of tense in this passage. Jesus was simply saying that in the near future, after he returns to heaven, he would send upon the apostles that Spirit, the Spirit of God, the Holy Spirit, which ever proceeds, or keeps on proceeding from the Father. The language of Scripture at this point could not have been more precisely stated than is here seen in the change in verb tense. Only those who deny the doctrine of the procession of the Spirit find difficulty in understanding the passage.

This latter interpretation, based on the more literal translation of the pronoun *eis* ("into the name," instead of "by the authority") seems to better fit the context under consideration. That Great Commission came immediately after Jesus had revealed the source of the authority for the commission he was about to give: "All authority in heaven and on earth has been given to me" (Matt 28:18). "Therefore go and make disciples . . . ." (v. 19). Jesus here stated his authority to give such a commission. He had all authority in heaven and on earth, not because he himself was God, but because God, his Father, gave it to him. Since Jesus had been given all authority in heaven and on earth, why would he then tell the apostles to baptize by the authority of the Father, Son and Holy Spirit, when he himself had all the authority necessary? It would be much more likely that Jesus would be saying that since he now had been given all authority, it is by that authority, the authority of Christ, they were to go and baptize people into the family of God, into the name of the Father, his Son and his Spirit. The authority would be Christ's authority, but the baptism would be into the family of God. Later references to Christian baptism in (*en*) or upon (*epi*), that is, by the authority of the Lord Jesus Christ, such as in Acts 2:38 and 10:48, are without any specific reference to the authority of God and the Holy Spirit. No such additional authority was necessary, as Jesus had been given ALL authority in heaven and on earth.

Then consider other passages, as listed in the NIV footnote, where baptism is into (*eis*) someone or something, resulting in a change of relationship or status: "they had simply been baptized into the name of the Lord Jesus" (Acts 8:16); "On hearing this, they were baptized into the name of the Lord Jesus" (Acts 19:5); "all of us who were baptized into Christ Jesus were baptized into his death" (Rom 6:3); "Were you baptized into the name of Paul?" (1 Cor 1:13); "They were all baptized into Moses in (*en*) the cloud and in (*en*) the sea" (1 Cor 10:2); "for all of you who were baptized into Christ have clothed yourselves with Christ" (Gal 3:27). In these passages, baptism into the name of Jesus appears to signify the same as baptism into Christ himself.

Tertullian (145-220 A.D.), quoting the statement under consideration, said, "into the Father, and into the Son, and into the Holy Ghost"[10] (*Ante-Nicene Fathers*, Vol. III, p. 252a), without any mention of "the name," showing that he understood the passage to mean, not "by the authority," but rather a transfer of the person being baptized from outside to inside the Father, Son and Holy Spirit.

In reference to "the name . . . of the Holy Spirit," let it not be said that only persons have names, because many things that are not persons have names. Cities, counties, states and nations have names. Rivers, lakes, oceans and mountains have names. Businesses, companies, corporations and estates have names. Schools, churches, clubs and fraternities have names. Songs, books, magazines and encyclopedias have names. Not everything that has a name is a person.

Both my spirit and my body have a name; and that name is the same for both. They are two distinctions—one a body and the other a spirit. But they constitute only one person; and their singular name applies to both. One might ask concerning a deceased acquaintance, "Where is John?" The answer might be, "John is gone on to heaven to be with God," having reference, of course, to John's spirit, not his body. While another answer might be, "John is buried at the Hill-Top Cemetery," having reference to John's body, not his spirit. Both the body and the spirit of a person are essential parts of that person; and both may properly be referred to with the personal pronoun "he" or "she," as well as by the name of that person. Whether living or dead, the name of that person applies to both, without either of them being separate persons from each other, or from the person from which they are the body and spirit.

Likewise, the Holy Spirit, an essential part of God's divine essence, but continually proceeding from the Father—therefore a proceeding extension of God himself, the means whereby God is omnipresent, performing signs, wonders and miracles in the apostles, and having the name of God, and possibly even being referred to with the personal pronoun "he"—need not be a separate person from the God it is the Spirit of and from whence it proceeds.

Furthermore, not all grammatical equals in a compound subject need to be persons. Some may be things along with persons in a compound subject: "The man, his wife, his son, his dog and his car were in the driveway." That compound subject contains five distinctions; but only three are persons. Likewise, not even all the things having the same name in a compound subject need to be persons. I myself, my wife, my son, my estate, my construction company and my corporation all have the same name—"Pribble." However, only three of these six distinctions are persons; the other three are nonpersonal distinctions through which I as a person function. And to do something in their name, whether individually or collectively, would be doing such in that singular name

—"Pribble."

Persons have names; but not all things that have names are persons. "Stop! In the name of the law!" People have laws; but laws are not persons. A man on trial may be either acquitted or found guilty "in the name of justice." But justice is not a person. Certain things are to be done or not done "in the name of common sense." But common sense is not a person. The church is the bride of Christ and wears his name; but the church is not a person. A ship may be addressed with the feminine gender and have the name of some famous person; but ships are not persons.

The Holy Spirit is here mentioned as a third distinction, in addition to the Father and Son, to let it be known that the demonstrated presence of the Holy Spirit which they could see working miraculously in the apostles, made the message of the apostles as authoritative as if God or Christ were actually present in person delivering the message.

So after all is considered, whether "into the name" or "by the authority of the name," there is nothing to be found in that Great Commission, including the baptismal formula, which offers any substantial support at all for the doctrine of the Trinity, which states that "the one God is a triune being composed of three coequal and coeternal persons—God the Father, God the Son, and God the Holy Spirit." Such an interpretation is based purely on assumption, not on any Scripture that says so.

One other consideration, one which shows that the Holy Spirit is personified in both the Great Commission and the promise of the Holy Spirit at the Last Supper, as propounded by Joseph Henry Thayer in his *Greek-English Lexicon,*[7] under *pneuma,* will be covered at length in Part II, Chapter 1, *The Holy Spirit Personified.*

CHAPTER 30

GODHEAD

Some Trinitarians and Unitarians hold to the idea that the Godhead in Scripture is identical with the one God, instead of merely identifying the nature of that one God. Such therefore believe that the Godhead is a person, a personal being or entity, that one only true God known to ancient Israel as Jehovah.

If the Godhead were such a personal being, and supposedly composed of three distinct persons—the Father, Son and Holy Spirit—then it would appear that there would be four divine persons instead of only three. Otherwise, such a concept would be Unitarian, with the one God, a singular personal Godhead, merely manifesting himself as three personalities. But neither concept has any Scriptural basis, as shall be shown.

The three Greek words from which the word "Godhead" is translated, occur only five times in the NT, as follows: *theotes* (Col 2:9), *theoites* (Rom 1:20), and *theios* (Acts 17:29; 2 Pet 1:3-4). All these are translated "Godhead" in the KJV except those found in 2 Peter 1:3-4, where *theios* is consistently rendered "divine." While these three are different Greek words, they do all seem to carry the same general significance. Thayer's *Greek-English Lexicon* describes them thus:

> *theotes:* the state of being God, *Godhead.*
> *theiotes: divinity, divine nature.*
> *theios: divine . . . divinity, deity . . . .* used by the Greeks to denote divine nature, power, providence, in the general, without reference to any individual deity.[7]
>
> —pp. 285a and 288b.

In both passages from 2 Peter 1, *theias* is an adjective, the genitive, singular, feminine form of *theios*, and is uniformly translated "divine" in the English versions, describing God's power (v. 3) and God's nature (v. 4).

The English translators use the three words synonymously, variously translating them as follows:

Greek Word: Inflection:	*THEOTES* *theotetos*	*THEIOTES* *theiotes*	*THEIOS* *theion*
Number:	Singular	Singular	Singular
Gender:	Feminine	Feminine	Neuter
VERSION	Col 2:9	Rom 1:20	Acts 17:29
KJV	Godhead	Godhead	Godhead
RV	Godhead	divinity	Godhead
ASV	Godhead	divinity	Godhead
NCE	Godhead	divinity	Divinity
RSV	deity	deity	Deity
SEB	divinity	divinity	God
NASB	deity	divine nature	Divine Nature
NIV	Deity	divine nature	divine being
TEV	divine nature	divine nature	God's nature
Goodspeed	God's nature	divine character	divine nature
Weymouth	God's nature	divine nature	His nature
NWT	divine quality	Godship	Divine Being
NEB	Godhead	deity	deity
AB	Deity (the Godhead)	divinity	Deity (the Godhead)
Williams	Deity	divine nature	His nature
TCNT	Godhead	divinity	Deity
JB	divinity	deity	deity
Barclay	divine nature	divinity	Divine
Berry (ILT)	Godhead	divinity	divine

From the foregoing list it can be seen that each of these three Greek words is variously and indiscriminately translated "Godhead," "divinity," "deity," and "divine nature." Other renditions, not common to all, include "divine being," "divine quality," "divine character," "God," "God's nature," "His nature," and "Godship." Thus the overwhelming evidence is that none of these three Greek words is identical with the being who is known as the one God (*ho Theos*), but rather signifies the essence or nature of that God, as distinguished from the nature of angels, man, animals, etc. "Nature" is defined as "the inherent character or basic constitution of a person or thing: ESSENCE."

Notice also that the word "Godhead" is found primarily in the earliest translations but is replaced in most later versions with "divinity," "deity," "divine nature," etc. "Godhead" is an archaic and antiquated English word which possibly suggests an unscriptural concept in the minds of the modern reader, as does the old word "Ghost," which was later replaced by "Spirit." "Godhead" originally meant the same as "Godhood," *having the nature of God*, just as "manhood" means *having the nature of man*. As man is made in God's own image (Gen 1:26-27), both God and man are persons, while "Godhood" and "manhood" merely identify the distinguishing nature of those persons. But when changed from "Godhood" to "Godhead," the word seems to somehow conjure up in the minds of some people a sort of mysterious plural being with three heads (as has been depicted by numerous artists). The later renditions much more accurately focus on the nature or essence of God, rather than on God the being.

Notice that in each of these five references, the three words under consideration are always singular in number, not at all suggesting any kind of plurality, especially not suggesting a plural personal being which is composed of three other distinct persons.

Some theologians have even gone so far as to have two separate words for "God." When referring to the Father, Son, and Holy Spirit individually, it is God with a short vowel, as in "rod" or "sod"; but when referring to the three combined in the Godhead, it is God with a circumflex vowel, pronounced "Gawd," as in "broad," or "fraud," sometimes even pronouncing the word in two syllables (Gaw-dah) with equal emphasis on the last syllable. Such a distinction, of course, is theological nonsense, and is without any Biblical precedence or authority.

Furthermore, in these five identified references, the only places in the NT where these three Greek words are found, none occurs in the masculine gender. Four are in the feminine gender, and the other in the neuter gender, obviously not identical with the masculine being, *ho Theos* (the God), but rather refer to the nature of that being, as well as the nature of any divine offspring of that being, especially the Son of God.

Let us now examine each of these passages individually, quoting from the RSV, which translates all three Greek words "deity":

Colossians 2:9, "For in him (Christ) the whole fullness of deity dwells bodily" (*tes theotetos*, divine nature; feminine gender). From this passage we may conclude that Christ is truly divine. Soon after Jesus returned to heaven, God's Holy Spirit (the divine Spirit) came upon the apostles (Acts 2:4), to dwell in them (John 14:17). But that divine Spirit in the apostles did not make the apostles divine. Nor does our having the Holy Spirit in us (1 Cor 6:19) mean that we are divine. We do not have, nor did the apostles have "the whole fullness of deity" dwelling within. But Christ had, and continues to have it all. Christ was truly divine before, during and after his earthly advent. That divine being came to earth and dwelt in a human body ("a body you prepared for me" Heb 10:5). He died, was entombed, arose from the dead and ascended back to God in that resurrected body, enabling Paul to later say that "in Christ all the fullness of the Deity lives in bodily form" (present tense). While on earth Jesus was given the divine Spirit without measure (John 3:34-35). But even after he received that Spirit at baptism, everything about him, except his human body, was fully divine, being the unique Son of God, Son of Jehovah, but not Son of the Godhead, nor Son of "the Trinity."

Romans 1:20, "Ever since the creation of the world his (God's) invisible nature, namely his eternal power and deity, has been clearly perceived in the things that have been made" (*theiotes*, divine nature; feminine gender). Paul here uses God's eternal power and deity (Godhead) as synonymous, not with God's being or person, but with "his invisible nature."

Acts 17:29, "Being then God's offspring, we ought not to think that the Deity is like gold, or silver, or stone" (*to Theion*, divine nature; neuter gender). Barnes' Commentary here, concerning "the Godhead" as found in the KJV, says that it means "The divinity, the divine nature, or essence. The word used here is an adjective employed as a noun."[6] Paul's argument here is not that man is divine. In fact, the implication is that even though man is not divine, we are still made in the image of God, and are God's offspring, in that God's Spirit dwells in (1 Cor 6:19) and animates our bodies. Therefore, if not even man's nature can be compared with the nature of gold, silver or stone, which the Athenians would readily admit, then surely divine nature could not be thus compared.

2 Peter 1:3, "His divine (*theias*) power has granted to us all things that pertain to life and godliness."

2 Peter 1:4, " . . . you may . . . become partakers of the divine (*theias*) nature." Our becoming "partakers" of the divine nature obviously does not make us divine in the sense that Jesus was and is divine. The Greek

word here (*koinonos*) means "*a partaker, sharer*, in any thing"[7] (Thayer's *Greek-English Lexicon*). The NIV says that "you may participate in the divine nature." In essence we can never become like God, but in character we may. The more we think like God, speak like God, and act like God, the more we love and care like God, and the more truthful and just we become like God, the more we "participate in the divine nature." Peter here states that such have "escaped from the corruption that is in the world by lust" (v. 4).

The Godhead is not identical with the one God (*ho Theos*). It is never presented in Scripture as a personal being or entity. It is never referred to with a personal pronoun. The Godhead is never said to have spoken nor to have been spoken to. Never prayed to nor sang to. Never worshiped nor adored. The Godhead is never even personified. Therefore the Godhead is not a personal plural being or entity composed of such persons as may be said to be divine; but Godhead is the divine nature of God, and of everything of which that God is composed, including his omnipresent Spirit, as well as the divine nature of his only begotten Son.

The divine nature of the Son was inherited from the God he is the Son of. Both God and his Son are divine persons. Both speak and are spoken to. Both receive prayers, praise and thanksgiving. Both appear in the masculine gender and are referred to with masculine pronouns. The Godhead is never called the Father nor the Son, and is never referred to with a masculine pronoun. Christ is the Son of God, not the Son of the Godhead.

The Godhead is no more a person than manhood is a person; but God, a person, has divine nature (Godhead, or Godhood), just as man, a person, has human nature (manhood, or mankind). The Godhead is therefore neither a person nor a being, and therefore cannot be a triune personal being composed of three persons, as Trinitarians claim, nor a singular personal being manifesting himself in three personalities, as some Unitarians claim. But God (*ho Theos*) is a singular divine being, the Father (1 Cor 8:6), who has a divine Spirit, as well as a divine Son.

CHAPTER 31

ONE

Concerning how many Gods there are, consider the following Scriptures:

Deut 4:35,   "the LORD is God; besides him there is no other."

6:4,   "The LORD our God, the LORD is one [Or *The LORD our God is one LORD*; Or *The LORD is our God, the LORD is one*; Or *The LORD is our God, the LORD alone*]." (See also Mark 12:29).

2 Sam 7:22,   "How great you are, O Sovereign LORD! There is no one like you, and there is no God but you" (See also 1 Chr 17:20).

Ps 83:18,   "Let them know that you, whose name is the LORD—that you alone are the Most High over all the earth."

86:10,   (Speaking to Jehovah, vv. 6 and 11) "you alone are God [*ho Theos*, LXX]."

Isa 44:6,   "This is what the LORD says . . . apart from me there is no God."

45:18,   "I am the LORD, and there is no other."

John 17:3,   (Christ praying to his Father, v. 1) "that they may know you, the only true God, and Jesus Christ, whom you have sent."

1 Cor 8:4,   "there is no God but one."

8:6,   "for us there is but one God, the Father . . . and there is but one Lord, Jesus Christ"

Eph 4:6,   (There is) "one God and Father of all"

1 Tim 2:5,   "For there is one God and one mediator between God and men, the man Christ Jesus"

For both Jews and Christians, these Scriptures firmly establish forever the concept of monotheism, the doctrine or belief that there is but one God. These Scriptures further tell us exactly who that one God is, identifying him to the Israelites in the OT as the LORD (Jehovah), and to us in the NT as "the Father," while at the same time distinguishing that God from all other persons, even specifically distinguishing him from his own Son, Jesus Christ. The word "God" is obviously here used in that absolute, almighty, and exclusive sense in which none other could ever compare.

However, on one occasion Jesus testified to a group of questioning Jews, "I and the Father are one" (John 10:30). But those Jews, as well as some Bible students today, misinterpreted the statement to mean that Jesus was claiming to be that one God, as if that were the only way the two could be one. The Jews took up stones to kill him (v. 31), accusing him of blasphemy, because, they said, "You, a mere man, claim to be God" (v. 33).

But Jesus had said nothing that made himself God. He did not say, "I and the Father are one God." In fact, Jesus never said at that time that he is, ever was, or ever would be God (that is, in the absolute sense). But he didn't deny his divine nature. The Jews wanted him to say that he is God, so they might accuse him of blasphemy. But of all the "I am's" in this tenth chapter of John, "the gate" (v. 7), "the good shepherd" (v. 11), "God's Son" (v. 36), Jesus never said that he is God, as was so erroneously concluded by those accusing Jews, and by Trinitarians and possibly others today. Jesus never claimed to be the one God, nor one of three persons in the one God. But he did make it quite clear that he is the Son of that one God.

How could Jesus be both the Father ("I and the Father are one") and the Son? If Jesus had been saying, "I and the Father are one God," and since that one God is declared to be the Father, he would have been claiming to be both the Father and the Son; that is, he would be his own Father, and therefore Son of himself. Such an interpretation contradicts the whole idea of fatherhood and sonship, and is both unreasonable and unscriptural. The Father was not the one who died. It was his Son.

Then what could Jesus have meant when he said, "I and the Father are one"? Some have concluded that since the word "one" (Greek: *hen*) at this place is neuter gender, it cannot mean one person or one personality, and therefore must mean one substance. Of course, the antithesis to this conclusion is that where the masculine gender (*heis*) is used, it means one person or one personality, instead of one substance or being. Therefore, when such passages as Deut 6:4, Mark 12:29, 1 Cor 8:4 and 6, Eph 4:6, and 1 Tim 2:5 use *heis* (masculine gender) to refer to one Jehovah, one Lord, one God, and one mediator, they must mean that Jehovah is one person, the Lord is one person, and God is one person, just as our mediator is one person. This, of course, is in contrast to Trinitarian dictrine which says that the one God (Jehovah) is one being (substance) composed of three persons.

The original word for "substance" (Gr: *hupostasis*), as it pertains to God, is found only once in the NT. Thayer defines *hupostasis* in Heb 1:3 as "the substantial quality, nature, of any person or thing."[7] God's Son is here said to be "the radiance of God's glory and the exact representation of his being" [substance, ASV]. This passage, instead of saying that Christ and God are one substance, declares rather that Christ is the very image (*charakter*: an impress, exact representation) of God's substance.

An impression made by a stamp (die or seal) is not the same substance as the stamp which makes the impression; that is, the mark made by such a stamp is not the stamp that makes the mark. The

ASV has, "the very image." Therefore, Christ is not that substance which he is said to exactly represent, or to be the image of. However, while a stamp and its imprint are not one substance, they, like God and his Son, are definitely one in the message they proclaim. That message may be seen by looking at either the stamp, or the imprint made by the stamp. God does not say one thing, and Christ another. The reason John calls Christ "the Word" of God (John 1:1; 1 John 1:1; Rev 19:13) is that Christ came to declare, not his own word, but the word of his Father. "For I did not speak of my own accord, but the Father who sent me commanded me what to say and how to say it" (John 12:49. See also John 14:24 and 17:8).

Furthermore, the *hupostasis* in Hebrews 1:3, translated "substance" (ASV), "person" (KJV), and "being" (NIV), is feminine gender, not neuter. So if the neuter gender "one," which Christ and God are said to be, cannot mean one person or personality because of conflicting genders, then neither could the neuter "one" refer to the feminine "substance" or "being" as in Hebrews 1:3. Surely there must be some other way in which the Father and Son are one.

For the sake of semantics it should be noted that if indeed Christ is truly the offspring of God, not created nor made, but born of God before anything else ever came into existence, then that substance of which Christ consists is truly one with the Father, in that it was actually God's eternal substance before becoming separated from God in a way as to constitute a distinct personal offspring or entity, properly identified as the Son of God. But since that unique precreation birth, resulting in Jesus' becoming "the firstborn over all creation" (Col 1:15), the Father and the Son are not the one substance, being or person mentioned in Hebrews 1:3. Instead, the Son is here depicted as sustaining a relation to God's substance as an imprint sustains a relation to the stamp that made the imprint.

As *hupostasis* is translated "being" (Heb 1:3), the definition of "being" should be explored. The Greek word for "being" is usually *eimi*, never used as a noun, but always as a verb, "to be." It is never used as a person or thing. However, in English the word "being," as a noun, means something that actually exists; conscious existence: *life*, *essence*, a living thing; especially a *person*. "Essence" is defined as the property necessary to the nature of anything; the most significant property of a thing. Something that exists: *entity*. And then "entity" is defined as a *being, existence*; especially independent, separate, or self-contained existence. Therefore *hupostasis* is the appropriate Greek word for "substance," "being," or "person," as found in Hebrews 1:3, depending on the translation used. So the distinction made by Trinitarians between a "being" and a "person" is unjustified. A person is a substance being or entity. If the Father and Son were one being, they would be one person, inasmuch as both of them are persons. Yet

Trinitarians claim that God is one being, but three persons; that is, three persons in one being. No wonder the Trinity is called a mystery.

Two other Greek words which plagued the Nicene fathers, and over which that 325 A.D. Council fought so bitterly, were *homoousios*, "of the same substance," and *homoiousios*, "of like substance; essentially like but not the same substance." Some have suggested that the war over these words was primarily a matter of semantics, both sides saying essentially the same thing, but neither able to communicate their individual concepts in words understandable to their opposition. Looking at the two words, and seeing that they are distinguished only by one little "i" (the smallest letter in the Greek alphabet), someone has suggested that the real controversy probably came when the little "i" was made into a big "I" in the minds of conceited and self-willed bishops in ecclesiastical power struggles. Be that as it may, *homoousios*, "of the same substance," was the one which made its way into the Nicene Creed, even though that word is nowhere found in the Greek NT.

If the Creed is saying that the Father and the Son are one substance, it is obviously unscriptural. But if the Creed is saying that the Son's substance is OF (meaning "from," that is, "having originated from") the substance of the Father, then it accords precisely with the true biblical concept of Fatherhood and Sonship, and with the origin and divine nature of Christ.

The other word, *homoiousios*, was rejected because the majority party (the Emperor-supported group) understood the word to be saying in effect that if the substance of the Son is essentially like, but not the same substance with the Father, then Christ's origin would have been a creation, not a birth; and he would not in fact be divine. This word is found several times in the NT, such as in James 3:9, which says that men "have been made in God's likeness (*homoiosin*)." Man, unlike Christ, is not divine, being not from the divine substance of the Father, as was Christ.

In further confirmation of the fact that the Son is neither one person with the Father, one being with the Father, nor one substance with the Father, the following references should be sufficient: As recorded in John 17, Jesus prayed to God on behalf of his disciples, "that they may be one as we are one (*hen*, neuter gender)" (v. 11). Then again, on behalf of those who would believe on Jesus through the apostles' word, he prayed "that all of them may be one, Father, just as you are in me and I am in you . . . . that they may be one as we are one" (vv. 21-22). Then the ASV has, "that they may be perfected into one" (v. 23). In each case the word "one" is *hen*, neuter gender. Surely no one would suppose that Jesus prayed for his apostles and other disciples to all become or remain one substance or being. Such would have required a most remarkable miracle indeed. Obviously, the oneness for which Jesus prayed was, at least in part, unity of their testimony to the world about Jesus, that "the world may believe that you have sent me" (v. 21), and that "the world know that you sent me" (v. 23). Divided testimony proves nothing; but Jesus knew that the success of his cause would depend most of all on the united testimony of his disciples. Therefore he prayed that they all be one, just as he and his Father are one. If God had testified one thing, and Jesus testified another, then Jesus would never have been accepted as the Son of God.

Another reference, which proves that the word "one" does not mean one substance, being or person, is found in 1 Corinthians 3, where Paul, rebuking the Corinthians for being divided over teachers, namely Paul, who planted, and Apollos, who watered (v. 6), said in verse 8, "The man who plants (Paul) and the one who waters (Apollos) have one purpose" (ASV : "are one," *hen*, neuter gender). Surely no one would accuse Paul of claiming that he and Apollos were one substance or being. Instead, Paul was emphasizing their unity in purpose and message. The NIV actually translated verse 8 to be saying that Paul and Apollos "have one purpose." They were not one substance nor one being; but they did have one purpose. That purpose, as Paul had stated in verse 5, was to cause the Corinthians to become believers.

To the Philippians Paul said, "by being like-minded, having the same love, being one in spirit and purpose" (Phil 2:2). Here again, the word "one" (*hen*, neuter gender) refers to such things as unity in mind, love, accord, spirit and purpose, but certainly not suggesting that they be one substance or being. There are numerous ways in which persons may be one without their being one substance.

So when Jesus said, "I and the Father are one," there is absolutely no reason to conclude that Jesus was saying that he and his Father are one person, one being, one substance, or one God. But instead, he was confirming their unity of mind, purpose and goal, working harmoniously in that ancient and divine plan for the redemption of mankind.

When Philip said to Jesus, "Lord, show us the Father" (John 14:8), Jesus answered, "Anyone who has seen me has seen the Father" (v. 9). Philip was asking for the impossible, for no one could see God and live (Exod 33:20). But Jesus, without claiming to be the Father he is the Son of, was simply explaining what God would be like if God were to become a man and could be seen. He would be just like Jesus. Philip couldn't see the Father, because the Father is that one almighty God (*ho Theos*), invisible to the human eye. But Jesus was saying, "I can't show you the Father, but I can show you what the Father is like. Just look at me."

CHAPTER 32

ACHID and YACHID

Some claim that there is a significance in the precise Hebrew word for "one" as used in Deuteronomy 6:4, distinguishing the word used here, *achid*, from another Hebrew word, *yachid*. They suppose that *achid*, as listed in Robert Young's *Analytical Concordance* as *echad* (*achad, achath*),[2] can only mean "a united one," and that the other word, not used here, is *yachid*, meaning "an only one, or an absolute one." Their argument infers that the word *yachid* would have been used if the one Jehovah God in Deuteronomy 6:4 referred to the Father alone. But since the word *echad* was used, they claim it refers to a "united one," a triune being composed of three persons, or to the divine essence with its three distinct but inseparable personalities.

Several examples of other Scriptures are often given to prove that *echad* means "united one" exclusively, such as: (See ASV)

Gen 1:5 "there was evening and there was morning, *one* day."
Gen 2:24, A man and his wife "shall be *one* flesh."
Gen 11:6, "they are *one* people, and they have all *one* language."
Exod 26:6, "the tabernacle shall be *one whole*," composed of numerous coupled curtains. "Couple the tent together, that it may be *one*" (v. 11).

No doubt other examples could be cited to show that *echad* may, and sometimes does mean "one," even when that "one" is composed of numerous parts, whether separable or inseparable. Ironically, the examples usually given involve separable components, things which can exist separate and independent from each other, such as evening and morning, a man and his wife, people, languages, curtains, etc., while using them to prove the inseparable nature of a supposed plurality of persons in the one Jehovah God.

But even more significant is the fact that these few examples are used in a way as to obscure or ignore the presence of hundreds of other references where *echad* is an only one, or an absolute one, without any suggestion or possibility of being a plurality in unity. Here are a few of many examples where *echad* cannot mean "united one" as distinguished from an "only one" or an "absolute one":

Gen 2:21, God "took *one* of the man's ribs and closed up the place with flesh." Surely this is to be interpreted to mean only one rib, as distinguished from a whole section of bone structure composed of a plurality of ribs. Presumably, Eve could have determined whether or not she had any rivals by merely counting

Adam's ribs. This was not a "united" rib; it was one individual rib.

Gen 4:19, "Lamech married two women, *one* named Adah and the other Zillah." Surely this is not saying that Adah was a "united one" in a sense in which Zillah was not. Such might have suggested that Zillah just "didn't have it all together."

Gen 21:15, Hagar "put the boy under *one* of the bushes," not under a whole united clump of bushes.

Gen 22:2, God told Abraham, "Take your son, your only [*yachid*] son . . . . Sacrifice him there as a burnt offering on *one* of the mountains I will tell you about." The interpretation under consideration does correctly have Isaac as a one and only son, an absolute one (when considering Ishmael as a servant as distinguished from an heir), but incorrectly has Abraham offering Isaac on some "united" mountain, instead of the one designated individual singular mountain specified by God. The mountain range (if there was one) might have been composed of a union of several mountains; but the sacrifice was to be made, not on "one" united mountain range, but on "one" specific mountain as distinguished from all other mountains. Therefore *echad* cannot always mean "a united one."

Gen 40:5, "they dreamed a dream, both of them . . . in *one* night" (ASV). Obviously this has reference to one and the same specific night, not a "united" night.

Gen 42:11, 13, "We are all the sons of *one* man . . . . the sons of *one* man, who lives in the land of Canaan." "One" here does not refer to a union of the twelve sons, but to their singular personal father who had begotten them. That one man was Jacob, not a united plural being (See also v. 16).

Deut 17:6, "On the testimony of two or three witnesses a man shall be put to death, but no one shall be put to death on the testimony of only *one* witness." In this passage it is obvious that the "one witness" cannot refer in any sense to a united testimony by plural witnesses, but rather to an individual uncorroborated testimony by one person. When two or more persons give their individual statements, and those testimonies are all in agreement with each other, such witnesses are said to be "one." That one united testimony by a plurality of witnesses was sufficient to invoke the death penalty. This is the kind of united testimony spoken of in 1 John 5:7-8, "For there are three that testify: the Spirit, the water and the blood; and the three are in agreement" [the three agree in one, ASV]. This is obviously a "united one." But the "one witness" in Deuteronomy 17:6 refers instead to a single testimony which is not corroborated by, nor united with at least one other testimony, and therefore was not to result in a conviction. So "one" (*echad*) in this text refers not to united testimony, but rather to testimony which is not united. (See also Deut 19:15).

All these, along with many other similar examples, far too numerous to mention, are positive proof that *echad* does not always mean "a united one." And there is no reason at all to conclude that the "one" Jehovah God in Deuteronomy 6:4 is a united plural being composed of three persons.

According to the listings in Young's *Analytical Concordance*, *echad* occurs approximately 850 times in the Hebrew OT, approximately 600 of which are translated simply "one." *Echad* is most often used to distinguish one person, place or thing from another, or from many, or to distinguish one from two or some other number, very few of which have anything to do with a unity of plurality. In only a comparatively few instances does unity become an added significance to the number "one" as signified by *echad*. The word itself obviously does not so signify; but rather the context in which it is used must be the determining factor.

Yachid, on the other hand, occurs only 12 times, none of which is translated "one" in the KJV, being rather translated by such terms as "only," "only child," or "only son." It is by no means the Hebrew word for "one" in those hundreds of places where "one" does not include the idea of "unity" of some plural being or substance.

Echad, in Deuteronomy 6:4, referring to the one Jehovah God, is translated *heis* (the masculine gender for "one") in the Greek Septuagint Version (LXX). Jesus quoted that famous passage, probably in the contemporary Aramaic dialect of the Hebrew language of his day. But Mark later recorded the incident and quotation as found in 12:29 of his Gospel, doing so word for word in the Greek language as it has already been translated in the LXX. If the LXX, prevalent in Jesus' day, mistranslated Deuteronomy 6:4 on such a vital issue by using the Greek *heis* for the Hebrew *echad*, neither Jesus or Mark made any mention of the error. The word *heis*, masculine gender (or *hen*, neuter gender) is the usual word for "one," whether singly or by union, and therefore offers no proof, nor even a suggestion, that the "one" Lord God of Mark 12:29 is a plural being composed of three persons.

So any definition given for *echad* or *heis* must conform to the way divine inspiration used those words in Scripture. It matters not if in the Twelfth Century A.D., Moses Maimonides changed the word *achid* to *yachid*; that does not prove that *echad* in Deuteronomy 6:4, fifteen centuries before Christ, meant "a united one" rather than simply telling how many Gods there were in a world filled with idols.

CHAPTER 33

PLURAL SUBJECTS WITH SINGULAR VERBS

Special attention is here directed toward two NT passages wherein plural subjects have singular predicates, as follows:

1 Thess 3:11, "Now may our God and Father himself and our Lord Jesus clear the way for us to come to you."

2 Thess 2;16-17, "May our Lord Jesus Christ himself, and God our Father, who loved us and by his grace gave us eternal encouragement and good hope, encourage your hearts and strengthen you in every good deed and word."

Each of these passages contains a plural (or compound) subject; (1) God, the Father, and (2) our Lord Jesus Christ. And according to the Greek text, in each case the predicate contains singular verbs: *clear, loved, gave, encourage,* and *strengthen.* This use of singular verbs with compound subjects has caused some to conclude that the compound subject in each case must in some way be singular, specifically two persons in one God, in order to agree with the singular verbs. But grammatically, it could as easily prove that there are two persons in the one Lord, as it could prove that there are two persons in one God.

However, even the statements themselves dispel either idea, inasmuch as God, in each case, is specifically identified as the "Father" in such a way as to exclude any other person from being that God. Even the Lord Jesus Christ is clearly not included as being God, but instead is named in addition to God, thereby forming the compound subject: "our God and Father" and "our Lord Jesus Christ."

It is generally known among Greek students that ordinarily a subject agrees with its verb in both person, number and gender. But what some evidently do not know is that the general rule is by no means always the case, as is specifically pointed out in various Greek grammars, such as:

> A neuter plural subject may have its verb in the singular . . . . This strange idiom, however, is by no means invariable in New Testament Greek; the neuter plural subject often has its verb in the plural like any other plural verb.[18]
>
> —Machen's *New Testament Greek for Beginners,* pp. 70-71.

Also—

> As a rule the predicate agrees with the subject in number, person and gender . . . . Neuter plural substantives occur with

singular or plural verbs indifferently . . . The verb may agree with the first subject expressed and be understood with the rest.[8]

—Robertson's *A New Short Grammar of the Greek Testament*, pp. 201-202. See also p. 57).

One need not be overly knowledgeable in the NT Greek language in order to be aware of these exceptions to the general rules. These named sources are used as textbooks for NT Greek 101, and should be known by those who rely on the Greek text to prove their points.

The following are some of the examples given for such plural subjects with singular verbs in the Greek text (For easy reference, SUBJECTS are here given in ALL CAPITALS; *verbs are italicized*):

Luke 4:41 "DEMONS (plural) *came out* (singular) of many people."
Luke 8:30 "Many DEMONS (plural) *had gone* (singular) into him."

Compound subjects may contain a variety of genders, and are treated as neuter plural subjects. Some examples given for such compound subjects with singular verbs in the Greek text are:

Acts 11:14, "He will bring you a message through which YOU and ALL YOUR HOUSE (plural) *will be saved* (singular)."

This compound subject is composed of (1) YOU and (2) ALL YOUR HOUSE, making it a plural subject with a singular verb.

Luke 2:33, "The child's FATHER and MOTHER *marveled* at what was said about him."

This compound subject is composed of (1) father and (2) mother, plural subject with a singular verb. As already quoted from the Greek grammar, "The verb may agree with the first subject expressed and be understood with the rest."[8] Therefore this passage is to be understood as saying, "His father marveled, and his mother marveled."

In addition to these examples given in the Greek grammars, consider just a few others:

Luke 8:19, "Now Jesus' MOTHER and BROTHERS *came* to see him." "Came" is singular according to Greek texts by Tischendorf, Tregelles and Nestle.
Col 4:14, "LUKE, the doctor, and DEMAS *send* (singular) greetings."
1 Cor 16:19, "AQUILA and PRISCILLA *greet* you." "Greet" is

singular according to Greek texts by Tischendorf, Alford and Nestle.

1 Tim 1:20, "Among them *are* (singular) HYMENAEUS and ALEXANDER (plural)." (See also 2 Tim 1:15; 2:17).

In these references the various persons in their compound subjects are Cornelius and his household, Jesus' father and mother, his mother and brethren, Luke and Demas, Acquila and Priscilla, Hymenaeus and Alexander, Phygelus and Hermogenes, and Hymenaeus and Philetus. In no way could the persons appearing in each of these compound subjects be considered as constituting any sort of singular substance, essence or being. Neither does the use of singular verbs with compound subjects in 1 Thessalonians 3:11 and 2 Thessalonians 2:16-17 offer any suggestion at all that God and Christ constitute a singular substance, essence, being or God, as claimed by Trinitarians. Using singular verbs with neuter plural subjects was an acceptable practice in the Greek language of the NT.

No less than sixteen times in his two letters to the Thessalonians, Paul made a clear distinction between Christ and God; not merely distinguishing between Christ and his Father as two separate persons in one substance or being called God, but between Christ and God himself. (See Appendices A, B and C; or else read those two short epistles). Nowhere did Paul teach the Thessalonians that Christ is the one God, nor one of a plurality of persons in the one God, but rather that Christ is the Son of that one God.

CHAPTER 34

THE ALPHA AND THE OMEGA

In the prologue of the Revelation we find this declaration: "'I am the Alpha and the Omega,' says the Lord God, 'who is, and who was, and who is to come, the Almighty'" (Rev 1:8). But before focusing on the Alpha and the Omega, it will be helpful to first identify "who is, and who was, and who is to come, the Almighty," not only to know who he is, but also to understand who he is not.

Comparing this passage with God's statement in 2 Corinthians 6:18, "I will be a Father to you, and you will be my sons and daughters, says the Lord Almighty," we see that the word "Almighty" refers to one who is not only called "Lord," but who is also identified as "Father." It is essential here to keep in mind that it was to these same Corinthians that Paul had previously declared, "For us there is but one God, the Father . . . and there is but one Lord, Jesus Christ" (1 Cor 8:6). How both God and Christ can be called "Lord," and there still be only one Lord, is explained in Part I, Chapter 44, under the caption "LORD."

"Almighty" occurs 48 times in the OT, referring always to God and to none other. Jehovah appeared to Abram and said, "I am God Almighty" (Gen 17:1), confirming the fact that God, who is the Almighty, is Jehovah, the "I AM" (Exod 3:14), the existing one, or the Eternal Living One. (The Septuagint here translates, "the BEING.").

"Almighty" also occurs 10 times in the NT, once as we have seen in 2 Corinthians 6:18, referring to God, the Father; again in Revelation 19:6 where it refers to "the Lord God," and is translated "omnipotent" in the KJV; and the other 8 times, all in the Revelation, always refer to God, never to Christ. (See Rev 1:8; 4:8; 11:17; 15:3; 16:7, 14; 19:15; 21:22).

It is understandable that Christ is never called the "Almighty," as there cannot be two Almighties who are each more mighty than the other.

The Father, who is the Lord God Almighty in Revelation 1:8, is further here defined as the God "who is, and who was, and who is to come," evidently identifying with Jehovah, the "I AM," the existing one, the one and only infinite and self-existing Almighty God. Back in verse 4, this same description is applied to one who is clearly distinguished from Jesus Christ; therefore it is God, not Christ, "who is, and who was, and who is to come," in both verses 4 and 8.

In Rev 11:16-17, the twenty-four elders, who were seated on their thrones before God, fell on their faces and worshiped God, saying: "We give thanks to you, Lord God Almighty, the One who is and who was." Here, "who is to come" is not included, but is no doubt intended to be understood. See also Rev 16:5-7, where that same abbreviated definition is used, again referring to God, not Christ. In Rev 15:3, those singing "the song of Moses . . . and the song of the Lamb," were no more singing to Christ than to Moses; they were instead singing to the "Lord God Almighty."

In Rev 16:7, John heard the altar respond: "Yes, Lord God Almighty." If Christ is to be seen at all in this picture, he is surely to be seen at the altar, offering up his and our praise to God, inasmuch as Christ is our High Priest (Heb 3:1; 4:14) and our only mediator between God and man (1 Tim 2:5). Christ is not the Lord God Almighty receiving the praise from the altar, but is rather to be visualized as the High Priest at the altar offering praise to the Lord God Almighty on our behalf.

Rev 16:14 speaks of "the battle on the great day of God Almighty." That day of God will come when Jesus comes unexpectedly as a thief in the night to execute God's judgments. But there is no evidence to indicate that it is Jesus who is here being called "God Almighty."

In Rev 19:11-15, he who is seen riding a white horse, and whose "name is the Word of God" (not "God Almighty"), is seen judging and making war, as "He treads the winepress of the fury of the wrath of God Almighty." Jesus is therefore not here called God the Almighty, but is rather the one on the white horse, ruling with an iron scepter as King of kings and Lord of lords, having been anointed Lord and King by God, the Almighty.

In Rev 21:22, John "did not see a temple in the city, because the Lord God Almighty and the Lamb are its temple." Here, the Lord God Almighty is clearly distinguished from the Lamb, who is our sacrifice, Jesus Christ.

So in all the 58 Scripture references to "the Almighty," not one time does "the Almighty" ever refer to Christ, but always to Jehovah God, the Father of Christ. For this reason, every time "the Alpha and the Omega" refers to God the Almighty, we can know that it is not talking about Christ.

We have already learned from Rev 1:4, 8; 4:8; and 11:17, that "who is, and who was, and who is to come" (apparently meaning "the existing one") always refers to the Lord God Almighty, but never to Christ. There surely must be a sense in which this description fits God completely, but not Christ, which explains why it was never said about Christ. If the expression means "the existing one," in the sense of having always existed as a distinct personal entity, self-existent, neither born, created nor made, without beginning or cessation of existence, then the description fits perfectly the Lord God Almighty.

But if indeed Christ was and is "the firstborn over all creation" (Col 1:15), born of God alone without the aid of any other being, before all ages, "For by him all things were created" (v. 16), being God's offspring, therefore divine, then Christ would truly have a beginning as a separate and distinct personal entity from him who had no beginning; therefore the description could not properly refer to Christ, who had a beginning, in the way it refers to the almighty God who had no beginning. For if at some point back in the ages of infinite eternity, Christ the person (not the divine substance of which he was firstborn) had a beginning, then it could not be said that "he was," because there would be a point before which he was not a distinct personal entity, therefore not "the existing one" in the sense that the almighty God is. Otherwise there would be two infinite eternals, and therefore two Gods, instead of only one God with his divine Son. That explains why God, but not Christ, is said to be the one "who is, and who was, and who is to come, the Almighty." This explanation is completely compatible with both Scripture and reason.

Returning now to Rev 1:8, we find that in addition to God's being referred to as both "the Almighty" and the one "who is, and who was, and who is to come," descriptions applied to God exclusively and never to Christ, we find God also being described as "the Alpha and the Omega," a description which, like the title "Lord," is in other references also applied equally to Christ.

As Alpha and Omega are the first and last letters of the Greek alphabet, not Hebrew, it is understandable that the expression never appears in the OT to define either God or Christ. In fact, it was not until the latter part of the First Century A.D., and only in the last book of the NT, written in the Greek language within the environment of an Hellenistic society, that Alpha and Omega are used to define a divine being or person. The expression is found only three, or possibly four times, all in the Revelation. See Rev 1:8, (11); 21:6; 22:13.

But then there are two other encompassing expressions which are used synonymously with "the Alpha and the Omega," namely, "the first and the last" and "the beginning and the end." All three of these dual expressions mean the same thing, with "Alpha and Omega" being the "first and last" letters of the Greek alphabet, and therefore being the "beginning and end" of that said alphabet. These latter two compound expressions are given simply to explain what is meant by "the Alpha and the Omega." Therefore to whomever any one of these compounds is applied, so likewise may the other two be understood as being applicable as well.

These three parallel expressions are not to be confused with him "who is, and who was, and who is to come," a description of the Lord God Almighty and none other, inasmuch as he is the one and only infinite self-existing and without-beginning personal entity, the Great "I AM." They do not suggest that either God or Christ was the first or last being created, for neither of them was created. Neither do Alpha and Omega suggest that either God or Christ had a beginning and therefore will also have an end. Nor do they suggest that either of them was before the other, and therefore will still exist after the other ceases to exist. Alpha and Omega have nothing to do with the relationship existing between God and Christ, nor whether either of them preceded the other, but rather with their relationship to all things created. "Who is, was and is to come" signifies God's *existence* without beginning or end; while Alpha and Omega, with their corresponding parallels, signify only the *presence* of both God and Christ as cause, origin and creator of all things created (1 Cor 8:6), in heaven and on earth, and who will still be present to be the cause of the consummation of all things, as partially described in 1 Cor 15:24: "Then the end will come, when he hands over the kingdom to God the Father after he has destroyed all dominion, authority and power." Furthermore, when "The heavens will disappear with a roar; the elements will be destroyed by fire, and the earth and everything in it will be laid bare" (2 Pet 3:10). That will be the *Omega*, the *last*, the *end* of all things which are destined to have an end, including this present age. And both God and Christ will be there causing it all to happen. This most logical and reasonable explanation allows both God and Christ to be both Alpha and Omega, without in any way making Christ identical with God.

Now consider each reference to "the Alpha and the Omega," with their corresponding parallels—"first and last" and "beginning and end":

Rev 1:8, "I am the Alpha and the Omega, says the Lord God . . . the Almighty." This passage does not refer to Jesus, but instead refers to God, who is both the God and the Father of Jesus (see v. 6).

The "Alpha and Omega, the first and last," as found in Rev 1:11 in the KJV, is omitted without explanation in both the NIV and the ASV, due to the lack of ancient textual authority. The "loud voice" speaking to John (Rev 1:10-11) was the voice of Jesus who described himself as "the First and the Last," "the Living One" (vv. 17-18), therefore by definition making Jesus also the Alpha and the Omega, the beginning and the end. "The Living One" in this passage is not to be interpreted as "the existing one," an appropriate description of God alone, but is rather given in contradistinction to one who was dead; for he continues in verse 18 to explain, "I was [Gr: became] dead, and behold I am alive for ever and ever!"

The "first and last" in Rev 2:8 also refers to Christ, who was dead and lived again, and may be explained the same as in 1:17-18.

In Rev 3:14, Christ calls himself "the ruler of God's creation" [ASV: the beginning of the creation of God]. This cannot mean that God was in any way created, nor can it mean that Christ was the first thing God created, for all *things* were made by Christ (1 Cor 8:6; John 1:2). "The beginning of the creation" evidently means either that Christ was present at the beginning of the creation, or that he was the one through whom God created all things. In either case, he was surely there to be the Alpha, the beginning, the first. He was present before anything was ever created. Another possible explanation could be that the Greek word for "beginning" (*arche*), as used here, can also mean "ruler," and is so translated in the NIV: "ruler of God's creation." This latter interpretation can also even accommodate a corresponding end to such a relationship, as described in 1 Cor 15:24-25, "Then the end will come, when he hands over the kingdom to God the Father after he has destroyed all dominion, authority and power. For he must reign until he has put all his enemies under his feet . . . . then the Son himself will be made subject to him who put everything under him, so that God may be all in all."

But it is God, not Christ, who declares in Rev 21:6, "I am the Alpha and the Omega, the Beginning and the End," therefore also by definition, "the first and the last." We know it is God speaking, for he continues in verse 7, "I will be his God and he (who overcomes) will be my son."

It is uncertain in Rev 22:10 if the angel is still speaking, changing the mode in verse 12 to be speaking for God with the first-person pronoun, or if it is Christ who begins speaking in verse 10. We do know that it is Christ speaking in verse 16; but it is uncertain whether it is God, or Christ, saying in verse 13, "I am the Alpha and the Omega, the First and the Last, the Beginning and the End."

However, as has been shown, all three expressions are equally applicable to both God and Christ, for reasons already stated; and therefore when Christ says that he is the Alpha and Omega, the First and Last, the Beginning and End, he is in no way claiming to be the Lord God Almighty, "who is, and who was, and who is to come," a description most appropriate for Jehovah God, "the existing one," the Great "I am," without beginning or end. Jesus did say, "before Abraham was born, I am!" (John 8:58), which probably meant no more than the fact that his existence is a continual one, from before Abraham until the then present time, without specifying how long before Abraham he existed. It cannot be forced to say that Jesus had no beginning of existence as a separate person from God his Father. (See Part I, Chapter 26, *The Origin and Preexistence of Christ*). But Jesus was never described as "the existing one" nor the "I am." Nor was he ever said to be he "who is, who was, and who is to come." That description is applied exclusively to the Lord God Almighty who is clearly distinguished from Christ.

Some have taught that since Alpha and Omega, first and last, and beginning and end, are each used in Revelation as describing both God and Christ, therefore God and Christ must be one and the same being, since there cannot be two firsts and two lasts, nor two beginnings and two ends. Based on this assumption, some have concluded that Christ is therefore the Jehovah God who in the OT said, "I am the first and I am the last" (Isa 44:6; 48:12). But if these descriptions refer to their both being present in the beginning and at the end, as has already been presented, then there can be two beginnings and two ends, two firsts and two lasts, both God and Christ. This interpretation accords with the entire book of Revelation, in which Christ is nowhere called "God," nowhere called "the Almighty," and nowhere referred to as "he who is, and who was, and who is to come."

But instead, the Revelation clearly distinguishes between God and Christ no less than 36 times (see Appendices A, B and C), six of which specifically refer to God as Jesus' God, not just his Father:

> Rev 1:6, Christ "has made us to be a kingdom and priests to serve his God and Father."
> 3:2, "I (Christ) have not found your deeds complete in the sight of my God."
> 3:12, "I (Christ) will make (him) a pillar in the temple of my God."
> "I (Christ) will write on him the name of my God."
> "and the name of the city of my (Christ's) God."
> "the new Jerusalem, which is coming down out of heaven from my (Christ's) God."

So the conclusion is apparent: both God and Christ are called "the Alpha and the Omega, the first and the last, the beginning and the end." But that in no way means that Christ is God (*ho Theos*), because Christ was never called "the Almighty," nor "he who is, and who was, and who is to come."

In the Revelation, in addition to the Alpha and Omega, first and last, the beginning and end, Jesus is called a lot of things. He is called "Christ" (1:1), "faithful witness" (1:5; 3:14), "firstborn from the dead" (1:5), "ruler of the kings of the earth" (1:5), "Son of God" (2:18), "the Amen" (3:14), "the ruler of God's creation" (3:14), "Lion of the tribe of Judah" (5:5), "the Root of David" (5:5; 22:16), "the Lamb" (26 times), "Master" (6:10 ASV), "Lord" (11:8), "Lord of lords" (17:14; 19:16), "King of kings" (17:14; 19:16), "Faithful and True" (19:11), "the Word of God" (19:13), "the bright Morning Star" (22:16); but never one time in the Revelation is Jesus ever called "God," much less, "the God" (*ho Theos*).

CHAPTER 35

FIRST PERSON, SECOND PERSON, THIRD PERSON

In Christ's Great Commission (Matt 28:19), Paul's benediction to the Corinthians (2 Cor 13:14), and Peter's salutation to God's elect (1 Pet 1:2), we see set forth three distinctions. In Christ's Commission they are listed as Father, Son and Holy Spirit; in Paul's benediction they are the Lord Jesus Christ, God and the Holy Spirit; and in Peter's salutation they are God the Father, the Spirit and Jesus Christ. There are also a few other passages where these three distinctions are in some way mentioned in a singular setting or context, such as when Jesus was baptized (Matt 3:16-17), and when he was anointed (Acts 10:38), etc. The first three of these references are as follows:

> Matt 28:19, "Therefore go and make disciples of all nations, baptizing them in [Or *into*] the name of the Father and of the Son and of the Holy Spirit."
>
> 2 Cor 13:14, "May the grace of the Lord Jesus Christ, and the love of God, and the fellowship of the Holy Spirit be with you all."
>
> 1 Pet 1:2, "according to the foreknowledge of God the Father, through the sanctifying work of the Spirit [in sanctification of the Spirit, ASV], for obedience to Jesus Christ."

These passages are often cited, supposedly as proof of the doctrine of the Trinity. But several observations should first be made before concluding that they prove something which none of them specifically states nor suggests.

None of them calls these distinctions "the Trinity." None says that the one God is a triune being composed of three persons. None refers to the three as God the Father, God the Son and God the Holy Spirit. None refers to either Christ or the Holy Spirit as being God, nor as being part of the one God, nor as being one of three persons in the one God. In fact, in Peter's salutation, God is clearly identified as "the Father," not "God the Spirit," and not "God Jesus Christ" nor "God the Son." If all three are equally God in the absolute sense, coequal persons in the one God, it seems most inappropriate that Peter would identify God with the Father only. So this very Scripture, which is used by Trinitarians supposedly to confirm the Trinity, is instead one to be used to refute it.

To further establish this point, Peter goes on to say, "Praise be to the God and Father of our Lord Jesus Christ!" (v. 3), not only distinguishing God from Christ, and not only identifying God as the Father of Christ, but also making him the God of Christ, according to both the NIV, the ASV and others. In the Greek text here, as in numerous other places, "God" is preceded by the definite article "the"; whereas "Father" is without a separate modifying article, therefore making both "God" and "Father" the compound recipients of the same article; thus, "the God and Father of our Lord Jesus Christ"; not "the God" as one designation, and "the Father or our Lord Jesus Christ" as another. This conclusion is in complete harmony with the rest of Peter's writings, which include at least ten additional references that make a clear distinction between God and Christ. (See Appendix C).

Then turning to Paul's benediction, we see again that God is clearly distinguished from Christ, just as in Peter's salutation, and just as the Father is distinguished from the Son and the Holy Spirit in the Great Commission. If that commission can be used to prove that both the Son and the Holy Spirit are personal entities separate and distinct from the Father, then Peter's salutation and Paul's benediction, by the same logic, prove that the Son and the Holy Spirit are personal entities separate and distinct from God; which further proves that God is not a triune being composed of three coequal persons.

In all three of these references, the three named distinctions are made, not to prove that they constitute equal persons in a plural being called God, but rather to show that these three distinctions all have a vital and unified significance as pertains to the Christian system and community.

A second observation that leaps out at us in those first three references is the difference in the order in which the three distinctions appear. A very popular (but nonbiblical) description of these three distinctions makes reference to the First Person, Second Person, and Third Person of the Trinity, referring to the Father as the First Person, Christ the Second Person, and the Holy Spirit the Third Person. And many Trinitarians use that terminology apparently without ever considering what makes one first, another second, and the other third, evidently thinking it is so stated in Scripture, therefore needs no explanation. But since these designations are nowhere found in Scripture, but are rather the inventions of theologians, they by all means do deserve an explanation.

While *first, second* and *third* definitely suggest some kind of progressive order, there are several ways in which these three distinctions might supposedly be classified as first, second or third. One has to do with the order of existence, which would mean that the Father existed first, then came the Son, and after that came the Holy Spirit. But the Trinitarian concept has all three as "coeternal," meaning to them that none of the three ever had a beginning, and that none preceded the other; therefore they cannot accept the order-of-existence concept. Nor should they.

A second explanation might be the order of rank or authority, meaning that the Father has more authority than the Son, and that they each also have more authority than the Holy Spirit. But that idea contradicts their own concept of the three being coequal. If they are coequal, how can one be of a higher rank than the other? Or how could one exercise authority over another?

A third explanation might be the order in which they make their appearance in the Bible: "In the beginning God" (Gen 1:1), the first person. But the Spirit of God (v. 2), instead of Christ, would have to be the second person mentioned, if indeed the Holy Spirit were a personal entity separate from God, instead of its being rather the mode of omnipresence of God himself. The third person, Christ, would not appear until his possible mention as the seed of woman (Gen 3:15), and after Adam, Eve and Satan had also made their appearance, making Christ the sixth person mentioned, instead of the second. So surely there must be some other reason for referring to God, Christ, and the Holy Spirit as the first, second, and third persons respectively in the Trinity.

Some theologians have fancifully put forth the grammatical order of personal pronouns: the first person "I," God, the one speaking; the second person "you," Christ, the one spoken to; and the third person "he," the Holy Spirit, the one spoken about. However, we know that both God and Christ have repeatedly used the first person pronoun to refer to themselves, making Christ as much the "first person" as God himself. And incidentally, out of the approximate 374 Scripture references to the Spirit, not once does the Spirit ever refer to itself with a first-person pronoun, which should tell us something about the non-personal nature of the Holy Spirit as contrasted with the personal nature of both God and Christ. Nevertheless, the grammatical progression explanation proves to be lacking in common logic and Scriptural basis.

Still, a fifth possible explanation of the numerical order might be their dispensational order in Scripture. Someone might erroneously suggest that the OT period of 4,000 years was the dispensation of God; the 33-year life of Christ on earth, or even his limited 3-year personal ministry was the dispensation of Christ; and that since the coming of the Holy Spirit on Pentecost (Acts 2), we are now under the dispensation of the Holy Spirit. Some of the concepts of the modern-day Charismatic Movement appear to relegate Christ into a position of comparative insignificance by placing so much emphasis on the Holy Spirit, referred to by them as "the Third Person of the Trinity." They therefore often speak to, pray to, sing to, worship and praise the Holy Spirit, even though such was never done in either the OT or the NT, nor was anyone ever told to do so. But let it not be forgotten that it is Christ, not the Holy Spirit, who has been anointed by God to be King of kings and Lord of lords (Rev 17:14; 19:16) until the end of time.

The Holy Spirit is not the person ruling the Christian dispensation in which we now live. In fact, the Holy Spirit, instead of being a third person in the Trinity, was the very thing which God used with which to anoint Jesus as King of kings. "God anointed Jesus of Nazareth with the Holy Spirit and power" (Acts 10:38). Therefore the Trinitarian numerical progression of persons would have the First Person anointing the Second Person with the Third Person. And that borders on absurdity. One person might be anointed BY another person, but never WITH another person. When God anointed Jesus with the Holy Spirit and power, the omnipresent Spirit of God was the means by which God empowered his Son on earth to be King of kings and Lord of lords, that power which remains with him to this day on his throne at the right hand of God in heaven.

Furthermore, that anointing apparently took place immediately following Jesus' baptism by John, when "heaven was opened, and he saw the Spirit of God descending like a dove and lighting on him. And a voice from heaven said, 'This is my Son, whom I love; with him I am well pleased.'" (Matt 3:16-17). If two divine and coequal persons were bodily present together on earth, both Christ and the Holy Spirit, regardless of the difference in the physical forms or likeness they assumed, when the voice from heaven was heard saying, "This is my Son," how would it be known which of the two divine coequal persons was being called "Son"? And how would it be known which was the First Person, the Second Person, and the Third Person?

Then finally, a sixth explanation for the numerical progression of the three distinctions mentioned, and probably the one most used by Trinitarians, is the order in which the three are listed in the Great Commission. But why should that order be used to the exclusion of the order given in Peter's salutation: God the Father (the First Person), the Spirit (the Second Person), and Jesus Christ (the Third Person)? Or why not use the order given in Paul's benediction: The Lord Jesus Christ (the First Person), God (the Second Person), and the Holy Spirit (the Third Person)?

So you can see that the whole idea of the one God as a triune being composed of three coequal and coeternal persons, God the Father being the First Person, Christ the Son being the Second Person, and the Holy Spirit being the Third Person, is without Scripture foundation, and should be eliminated from the Christian's theological vocabulary.

CHAPTER 36

GOOD TEACHER

Jesus, while on earth, was many things to many people. He was their Lord, their Messiah, their Christ, their healer, their hope, their physician. And one thing that really stands out about Jesus, and the reason he later came to be called "the Word of God" (Rev 19:13), Jesus was their master, their teacher, their Rabbi. He taught them at every opportunity, both one-on-one and before great multitudes of people.

On one occasion, "As Jesus started on his way, a man ran up to him and fell on his knees before him. 'Good teacher,' he asked, 'what must I do to inherit eternal life?' 'Why do you call me good?' Jesus answered, 'No one is good—except God alone'" (Mark 10:17-18. See also Matt 19:16-17 in various Greek texts, and Luke 18:18-19).

Jesus' response to this title of great respect is most remarkable indeed; for we all know that Jesus was good, that he was "a teacher come from God" (John 3:2 ASV), and was definitely a good teacher. But it seems apparent that this rich young ruler was not just giving his appraisal as to Jesus' rabbinical skills in the art of teaching, but rather was referring to the unquestionable and inherent moral excellence of Jesus as a good person. And who, after coming to know Jesus from the Gospels, could ever doubt that moral excellence and goodness? To whom, more than Jesus, could it ever be said, "Well done, good and faithful servant"? (Matt 25:21).

So why did Jesus respond as he did to the title (if it was intended as a title), "Good Teacher"? Surely there must have been some sense in which Jesus should not be called "Good" or "Good Teacher" without that prohibition being a denial that he is truly good in some other sense.

Numerous attempts have been made to explain the implications of Jesus' response. William Barclay, at this point in his *Daily Study Bible* series, paraphrases Jesus' response in these words: "No flattery! Don't call me good! Keep that word for God!" Then in his comments on Luke 18:18-19, Barclay goes on to say that "This ruler addressed Jesus in a way which, for a Jew, was without parallel. In all the religious Jewish literature there is no record of any Rabbi being addresses as, 'Good Teacher.'" So with that thought in mind, there can be no doubt that when comparing Jesus with any other Rabbi, Jesus was by all means the "Good Teacher."

It is possible that Jesus' modesty prompted his unusual response; but when all is considered, that proves to be highly unlikely. A denial of due praise could be equivalent to the insincere giving of undue praise, and borders on guile, a form of deceit. Yet Jesus "committed no sin, and no deceit was found in his mouth" (1 Pet 2:22).

The foremost question to be answered is this: Was Jesus offering a mild rebuke to this young ruler, inasmuch as God alone is to be called "Good" in that ultimate and absolute sense in which none other, including even Jesus, is to be compared? Or was he being complementary to this young ruler for having properly identified Jesus as being that God who alone is to be called "Good"? The two concepts are as opposed as night and day. The first is a denial, while the latter is an affirmation, that Christ is that one only God who alone is to be called "Good." It shall be shown that the former is the true intent, and that the latter is indeed an unnatural and forced interpretation by Trinitarians to support their idea that Christ is as much that one true God as is the Father, and may therefore equally be called "Good."

First, it should be observed that if Jesus complemented this young ruler for having recognized him as being God, and therefore rightly called him "Good Teacher," then why is it that the very next time he addressed Jesus (Mark 10:20), he called him simply "Teacher," not "Good Teacher"? The answer is obvious: Jesus was denying that he is that God who alone is good in that ultimate sense. This young ruler got the message that he had improperly addressed Jesus, and made sure that he didn't repeat his error. This was more than a mere violation of diplomatic protocol; it was a pure matter of mistaken identity. Whether or not he actually thought Jesus was that God who alone is good, we are not told; but we may be assured that when he went away, he no longer thought so.

Had Jesus wanted us to understand that he is God (*ho Theos*), he could have said so; but he didn't. In fact, Jesus never once told anyone that he is God, neither before, during nor after his earthly advent, but rather is the Son of God (John 10:36).

When Jesus said that only God is "good," could he have meant that only the Trinity is good? That only the Godhead is good? That only God the Father, God the Son, and God the Holy Spirit are good? Or did he mean that only God, who is the Father, is good, and therefore did not include himself as being either God or good? In this same chapter (Mark 10:33, 45) Jesus went on to call himself "Son of man," not "God." If he taught his disciples that he was both the Son of man, and the Son of God, then why would he teach this rich young ruler that he is actually that God? But for Jesus to mean, "I am not good (that is, in the absolute and ultimate sense) for only God is good," would in no way disclaim his own divinity, any more than denying that he spoke from his own will, but rather by the will of his Father, would be a denial of his divinity.

It must have been very obvious to those early post-apostolic theologians that Jesus was referring only to his Father in heaven as being "good," and not to Jesus as being God. See how they identified that God who alone is "good" (Gr. *agathos*):

Justin Martyr (110-165 A.D.), *Dialogue With Trypho, Ante-Nicene Fathers*, Vol. I, p. 249:

> Why callest thou me good? One is good, my Father who is in heaven.[10]

Irenaeus (120-202 A.D.), *Against Heresies*, Ibid., p. 345:

> To the person who said to him, "Good Master," He confessed that God is truly good, saying, "Why callest thou Me good: there is One who is good, the Father in the heavens."[10]

Hippolytus (170-236 A.D.), *The Refutation of All Heresies*, Ibid., Vol. V, p. 50:

> He says that this (one) alone is good, and that what is spoken by the Saviour is declared concerning this (one): "Why do you say that I am good? One is good, my Father which is in the heavens."[10]

Origen (185-254 A.D.), *De Principiis*, Ibid., Vol. IV, p. 280:

> There is none good but one, God the Father.[10]

Origen Against Celsus, Book V, Ibid., p. 548:

> Our Lord and Saviour, hearing Himself on one occasion addressed as "Good Master," referring him who used it to His own Father, said, "Why callest thou Me good? There is none good but one, that is, God the Father."[10]

The Clementine Homilies, Ibid., Vol. VIII, pp. 248-249:

> As the Scriptures say, He said, "Call not me good, for One (only) is good." And again, "Be ye good and merciful, as your Father in the heavens."[10]

Again—Ibid., p. 325 (See also p. 324 for the same statement):

> Our teacher Himself first said to the Pharisee who asked Him, "What shall I do to inherit eternal life?" "Do not call me good; for one is good, even the Father who is in the heavens."[10]

It seems quite certain from these ancient writings that those early church fathers in no way believed that Jesus was saying that he himself is that God who alone is good. In fact, one might rightly surmise that those early writers could have even had access to some earlier Greek texts which actually identified God who is good as being the Father in heaven, considering the uniformity with which they all identified the good God as the Father, not Christ. Otherwise, if they were merely paraphrasing, instead of actually quoting the words of Jesus, the conclusion that necessarily follows is that they uniformly believed that "the God" (*ho Theos*) refers only to the Father, and not to Christ, and were therefore justified in substituting "Father" for "God."

Origen furthermore explains how the goodness in Christ may be distinguished from God's goodness, as follows

—Ibid., Vol. IV, p. 251:

> The Saviour Himself rightly says in the Gospel, "There is none good save one only, God the Father," that by such an expression it may be understood that the Son is not of a different goodness, but of that only which exists in the Father, of whom He is rightly termed the image, because he proceeds from no other source but from that primal goodness, lest there might appear to be in the Son a different goodness from that which is in the Father. Nor is there any dissimilarity of goodness in the Son. And therefore it is not to be imagined that there is a kind of blasphemy, as it were, in the words, "There is none good save one only, God the Father," as if thereby it may be supposed to be denied that either Christ or the Holy Spirit was good. But . . . the primal goodness is to be understood as residing in God the Father, from whom both the Son is born and the Holy Spirit proceeds, retaining within them, without any doubt, the nature of that goodness which is in the source whence they are derived.[10]

According to Origen's explanation, the goodness in the Son is not a different goodness from that which is in the Father, but is instead a goodness derived from the Father. And inasmuch as the Son is born of the Father, and the Holy Spirit proceeds from the Father, it follows that both the Son and the Holy Spirit possess that same goodness, while only God the Father is the actual source of all goodness. Therefore they do not differ in type or kind of goodness, nor in the degree of goodness, but only in the fact that God the Father is the primal source of all goodness. "Every good and perfect gift is from above, coming down from the Father of the heavenly lights" (Jas 1:17).

When comparing Jesus with man, Jesus, of course, is good. And no man has ever reached that degree of goodness. But when comparing Jesus with God, Jesus said that only one is good; and that one is God, not Jesus.

That latter comparison is what Jesus is dealing with, because the young man had come running "and fell on his knees before him" (Mark 10:17), indicating an act of deep reverence, adoration or worship. But he was not rebuked for kneeling down to Jesus. Even while on earth, Jesus accepted worship, but only as the Son of God, and not as being himself that God. Jesus is to be worshiped as God's divine Son; and God is to be worshiped through his Son. Only in this way does God ultimately receive all the glory. But to worship Jesus as being that one only good and almighty God would take away glory from that God who Jesus said is the only one to be called "good" in that absolute sense.

One other observation should be made on this subject about the "Good Teacher." Especially inasmuch as Jesus is one of the underlying subjects of the Psalms, we may be assured that Jesus was most familiar with their contents. From the Psalms, more than any other source, we know that God (Jehovah) is repeatedly called "good":

"Good and upright is the LORD" (Ps 25:8).
"Taste and see that the LORD is good" (34:8).
"You are forgiving and good, O Lord" (86:5).
"For the LORD is good and his love endures forever" (100:5).
"Give thanks to the LORD, for he is good" (106:1; 107:1; 118:1, 29; 136:1).
"You (Jehovah) are good, and what you do is good" (119:68).
"Praise the LORD, for the LORD is good" (135:3).

How many times must Jesus have sung, or heard those Psalms over and over again in the synagogue every Sabbath, until they became a melody in his heart throughout each day? And in order to overcome, especially when evil, persecution and suffering came his way, his soul was no doubt filled with that constant reminder, "Jehovah is good," "Praise Jehovah, for Jehovah is good! Jehovah is good!" Or maybe. "You, Jehovah, are good and ready to forgive." And even if God's name, "Jehovah," were replaced with the title "Lord," as was their custom, and as in the LXX, the message would still be the same: The Lord is good! Even if things are going terribly, God is still good!

If this is an accurate description of the heart of Jesus, one can understand his deep disappointment to hear himself addressed as "Good Teacher," and that by one who by all means should have known from the Psalms who alone is good. To Jesus, this might have bordered on blasphemy. Only God his Father, as in the Psalms, was to be called "good."

This is further undeniable proof that Jesus is not Jehovah, as some have supposed, for only Jehovah God, not Jesus, is "good" in that absolute sense, after which Jesus successfully patterned the goodness in his own life. No, Jesus did not claim to be that God who alone is good.

CHAPTER 37

ISAIAH SAW HIS GLORY

In the year that King Uzziah died (Isa 6:1), Isaiah "saw the Lord seated on a throne, high and exalted," after which the prophet then proceeded in the next few verses to describe in detail that glorious and awesome heavenly scene, identifying the King who sat upon the throne as "the LORD Almighty" [Jehovah of hosts, ASV, vv. 3, 5]. This was no doubt a vision which Isaiah saw, and not in reality the substance person of Jehovah God himself, for "No one has ever seen God" (John 1:18).

However, it is not clear that Isaiah at that moment realized that it was only a vision, for he immediately concluded, "Woe to me! . . . my eyes have seen the King, the LORD Almighty" (v. 5). It had always been commonly believed, probably reinforced by Exodus 33:20, that anyone who saw God could expect to die immediately.

Such was never believed concerning the promised Messiah, the Christ, whether called the Word of God, the Wisdom of God, the Lamb of God, or even the Son of God. So had it been Christ whom Isaiah saw in the vision, there would have been no occasion for alarm.

In the vision revealed to Isaiah, some supposedly see a plural God, inasmuch as the Lord said, "Whom shall I send? And who will go for us?" (v. 8). But such a conclusion presumes that no other beings were present on that occasion who, with God himself, could constitute the plurality referred to by God as "us." We do know that other intelligent spirit beings were present, for at least two seraphim were there worshiping God (v. 3), and participating in the activities of the occasion (vv. 6-7). *The* NIV *Study Bible* at this point says, "The heavenly King speaks in the divine council," without speculating of whom that council consisted. For further explanation of God's use of the plural possessive pronoun, see Part I, Chapter 12 of this treatise, entitled *"Us and Our."*

Furthermore, according to the Greek Septuagint Version (LXX), "for us" is not even found in the passage, but is rather translated, "Whom shall I send, and who will go to this people?" But neither rendition even suggests that the God who is asking the compound question is in any sense a plural being, nor that it was Christ whom Isaiah saw or heard doing the speaking.

What little bit Isaiah might have understood about the Messiah or the Son of God, it is evident that he knew that there is a clear distinction between Jehovah God and Christ, and therefore did not confuse the two. For example, in Isaiah 53, most outstanding among the messianic prophecies, Isaiah retains a clear distinction:

"He (Christ) grew up before him (another being, Jehovah, v. 1) like a tender shoot, and like a root out of dry ground" (v. 2).

"We considered him (Christ) stricken by God (Jehovah), smitten by him, and afflicted" (v. 4). "And the LORD has laid on him (Christ) the iniquity of us all" (v. 6).

"Yet it was the LORD's will to crush him (Christ) and cause him to suffer" (v. 10).

"He (Jehovah) will see his offspring (Christ) and prolong his days, and the will of the LORD will prosper in his (Christ's) hand" (v. 10).

In verse 11, Christ is referred to as "My (Jehovah's) righteous servant."

"Therefore I (Jehovah) will give him (Christ) a portion among the great" (v. 12).

So it is most apparent that when Isaiah saw the vision in chapter 6, and later penned the description of Christ in chapter 53, he knew that it was Jehovah God of hosts, and not Christ, whom he had seen in the vision of chapter 6.

In Isaiah's vision under consideration, Isaiah volunteered to carry God's message of doom to the people of Israel. God's instruction was not actually telling Isaiah to make the people deaf, blind and ignorant, as it may at first appear here and in John 12:40, but was rather predicting how the people would reject the message being delivered. It was a sad commentary on the godlessness of that generation.

Then in John's biography of Christ, John points out a second application for Isaiah's vision, how the Pharisees and rulers rejected Jesus centuries after Isaiah's vision and message. (See John 12:39-43). John here paraphrases Isaiah as having said, "He has blinded their eyes and deadened their hearts, so they can neither see with their eyes, nor understand with their hearts, nor turn—and I would heal them" (v. 40). To which John then adds, "Isaiah said this because he saw Jesus' glory and spoke about him" (v. 41), an obvious reference to Christ.

From this statement, some have erroneously concluded that John was saying that in Isaiah's vision he saw Jesus' glory; and since it specifically states that the Lord whom Isaiah saw was Jehovah the Almighty, then Jesus is therefore that almighty Jehovah whom Isaiah saw enthroned in the heavenly vision. And while it might be possible that God's Son was present on the occasion, to be included in the "us" for whom Isaiah would go, there is no evidence whatsoever that Isaiah either saw or recognized him. Nor is there any evidence that God's Son ever reigned on a throne until after his death, resurrection and ascension back to heaven, where he is now seated at God's right hand, where he shall continue to reign until he delivers the redeemed kingdom back to God (1 Cor 15:24-28). For this and other reasons, we know that Jesus, the Son of God, was not the King whom Isaiah saw on the heavenly throne in the vision.

Then what did John mean when he said that Isaiah "saw his glory"? Obviously, Jesus was not the object character in Isaiah's vision; but Isaiah was. And his commission was to the people of his day. But Isaiah, as with all true prophets, being endowed with the Spirit of God, was able to see (yet maybe not fully understand) what others could not see. With visions from God, prophets could not only look backward in time and tell what had happened, but they could also look into the future and tell what was going to happen. That's why prophets were also called "seers." Isaiah saw Jesus' glory. But what does that mean? In what way did Isaiah see Jesus' glory?

The answer is simple: it means that when Isaiah saw that vision, and received a commission to go to the people and declare that God-given message which he knew would be rejected by the prominent people and rulers of his day, he also, whether knowingly or unknowingly, was predicting a second application in the far distant future, when Jesus, the promised Messiah, would be God's messenger whom the rulers would reject and crucify. For Isaiah to be able to look into the future more than 700 years to the advent of Christ, and to see Christ being rejected, crucified and glorified, was to see Christ's glory.

To us, the crucifixion might not appear to have anything to do with "seeing his glory." But when we see what happened to Jesus by way of the cross, as compared to his lowly life of humiliation and servitude which he lived as the Son of man, we see glory unspeakable.

To Jesus, the cross was not a defeat, but a victory. Not a tragedy, but a glory. However, Jesus, being human, was sometimes inclined to think as we think: "Now my heart is troubled, and what shall I say? 'Father, save me from this hour'?" (John 12:27). That's what we might have prayed. But then on reflection, Jesus added, "No, it was for this very reason I came to this hour." Then immediately Jesus turned to the true meaning of the cross—GLORY! "Father, glorify your name!" Then a voice came from heaven, "I have glorified it, and will glorify it again."

Then in verses 31 and 32, Jesus said, "Now is the time for judgment on this world; now the prince of this world will be driven out. But I, when I am lifted up from the earth, will draw all men to myself." That's GLORY! "He said this to show the kind of death he was going to die" (v. 33). We may see only the cross; but Isaiah and Jesus saw glory.

Then immediately following, in this same 12th chapter, John applies the words quoted from Isaiah, adding that, "Isaiah said this because he saw Jesus' glory and spoke about him" (v. 41); not referring to his seeing Jehovah on the throne in heaven, but rather when he looked forward as a prophet or seer, and saw the cause, manner and result of Jesus' death on the cross, saw his resurrection in glory and power (1 Cor 15:43), and saw his ascension into heaven, crowned King of kings and Lord of lords, and enthroned at God's right hand. That's

GLORY! That's the glory Isaiah saw when he spoke prophetically about how Jesus would be rejected, crucified, and then glorified.

Isaiah was not the only prophet who saw his glory. Daniel, about 550 years before Christ, said, "In my vision at night I looked, and there before me was one like a son of man, coming with the clouds of heaven. He approached the Ancient of Days and was led into his presence. He was given authority, glory and sovereign power; all peoples, nations and men of every language worshiped him" (Dan 7:13-14). Like Isaiah, Daniel "saw his glory" when Christ would ascend into heaven.

To further behold Christ's glory, and to more fully understand what John meant when he said that Isaiah saw Christ's glory, we need only to review a few more of the many "glory passages" found in the NT:

> Matt 19:28, "I tell you the truth, at the renewal of all things, when the Son of Man sits on his glorious throne, you who have followed me will also sit on twelve thrones . . . ."
>
> Matt 24:30, "They will see the Son of Man coming on the clouds of the sky, with power and great glory." (see also Luke 21:27).
>
> Matt 25:31, "When the Son of Man comes in his glory, and all the angels with him, he will sit on his throne in heavenly glory."
>
> Luke 9:26, "If anyone is ashamed of me and my words, the Son of Man will be ashamed of him when he comes in his glory and in the glory of the Father and of the holy angels."
>
> Luke 24:26, Jesus said to the two men on the way to Emmaus, "Did not the Christ have to suffer these things and then enter his glory?"
>
> John 7:39, "Up to that time the Spirit had not been given, since Jesus had not yet been glorified." This obviously is a reference to the coming of the Holy Spirit on the apostles on Pentecost (Acts 2), just ten days after Jesus ascended to be glorified on his throne in heaven,
>
> John 11:4, When Jesus heard that Lazarus was sick, he said, "This sickness will not end in death. No, it is for God's glory so that God's Son may be glorified through it." The resurrection of Lazarus was what sparked a series of events which soon led Jesus to the cross, and then to his glory.
>
> John 12:16, "Only after Jesus was glorified did they realize that these things had been written."
>
> John 12:23, "The hour has come for the Son of Man to be glorified."
>
> John 13:31-32, After Judas had left Jesus and the other apostles at the Last Supper, Jesus said, "Now is the Son of Man glorified and God is glorified in him. If God is glorified in him, God will glorify the Son in himself, and will glorify him at once."

> John 17:1, The night Jesus was being betrayed by Judas, Jesus prayed, "Father, the time has come. Glorify your Son, that your Son may glorify you."
>
> John 17:5, And now, Father, glorify me in your presence with the glory I had with you before the world began."
>
> Acts 3:13, After Jesus had ascended into heaven, Peter could then declare that "the God of our fathers, has glorified his servant Jesus."
>
> John 12:41, "Isaiah said this because he saw Jesus' glory and spoke about him." As we might say today, "Isaiah *foresaw* his glory."

The obvious conclusion is that Isaiah's "seeing his glory" had nothing to do with his having seen the glory of Jehovah in Isaiah 6:1-5. But with prophetic vision, Isaiah saw the future glorification of Christ and prophesied of the conditions that would bring it about: blind eyes, closed ears and hardened hearts. Therefore a comparison of Isaiah 6 with John 12:41 in no way proves nor even suggests that Jesus Christ is the Jehovah of hosts, the Almighty, and should never be used as an argument in support of the doctrine of the Trinity by claiming that Jesus is Jehovah. He isn't.

But wait! Did God not say, "I am the LORD (Jehovah); that is my name! I will not give my glory to another"? (Isa 42:8; see also Isa 48:11). Therefore some have concluded that if Jehovah God shared his glory with Christ, then Christ could not have been "another," but would have been very Jehovah God himself. Such would mean that God merely shared his glory with himself who already had the glory. And such reasoning is why the doctrine of the Trinity is called a mystery. Truly, such would be a mystery indeed.

There are at least two other reasons why the foregoing conclusion is unwarranted: First, the context makes it quite clear that those others with whom God will not share his glory are the heathen gods which had won the hearts of Israel from time to time during their history. Contrasting the greatness of Jehovah God with them, Isaiah presents God as creator of the heavens, the earth and all things therein, as well as giver of breath and spirit to all people (Isa 42:5). Then he quotes Jehovah as saying, "I will not give my glory to another or my praise to idols" (v. 8). That compound statement is recognized by Bible students as one of the hundreds of biblical examples of what may be called "poetic parallelisms"; dual statements, the second of which broadens the concept or helps explain the first. In this parallelism "glory" corresponds with "praise," and "another" corresponds with "idols."

Whether or not God would, in the distant future, share that glory with his own Son at his right hand in heaven, was not even a remote consideration. Jehovah was thought of by the heathen world in general as just another one of the many gods created by the imaginations of idolatrous mankind. But God said he wouldn't share his glory or praise with any of them. Man could not serve both God and idols. *Matthew Henry's Commentary* at this place explains, "he *will not give his glory to another*, whoever it is that stands in competition with him, especially not to *graven images*."[19]

—Vol. IV, p. 229b.

But Christ was not one of those graven images which stood in competition with God, and therefore would not be classified as "another" with whom God would not share his glory.

Second, to share his glory with his own divine Son would in no way be giving up any glory at all that would not come back to God himself in the form of even greater praise and glory. Consider again some of those "glory passages" already quoted:

> "Now is the Son of Man glorified and God is glorified in him" (John 13:31).
> "Glorify your Son, that your Son may glorify you" (John 17:1).
> "Glorify me in your presence with the glory I had with you before the world began" (John 17:5).

The obvious conclusion is that any glory God gave to his Son continues to come back to God in the form of more glory and more praise. So by glorifying Christ, God becomes even more glorified, not less. By glorifying Christ, God does not give up his own glory. Speaking of Christ, John said, "We have seen his glory, the glory of the One and Only [Or *the Only Begotten*], who came from the Father, full of grace and truth" (John 1:14). Christ's glory is that of an only begotten divine Son, while God's glory is that of the one and only divine Father, Jehovah God the Almighty.

CHAPTER 38

SALUTATIONS, INVOCATIONS AND BENEDICTIONS

Within the first and last few verses of each of the epistles, Romans through Revelation, are contained what are commonly known as salutations, invocations and benedictions, a total of 72 such references (see Appendix D), in which the authors almost invariably invoke the name of deity as their source of authority, their fountain of benefits and blessings, and their objects of praise. And without attempting to make any technical distinction as to which references fit into those various categories, it should be most beneficial for us to see the frequency (or in the case of the Holy Spirit, the lack of frequency) with which each of those divine distinctions is mentioned.

Two of those 72 references are used most extensively by Trinitarians to support their idea of three coequal persons in the one God, only because both references make mention of God, Christ and the Holy Spirit, as follows:

> 2 Cor 13:14, "May the grace of the Lord Jesus Christ, and the love of God, and the fellowship of the Holy Spirit be with you all."
> 1 Pet 1:2, "Chosen according to the foreknowledge of God the Father, through the sanctifying work of the Spirit (in sanctification of the Spirit, ASV), for obedience to Jesus Christ."

These two Scriptures are examined at length in Part I, Chapter 35, entitled *First Person, Second Person, Third Person*, and need only a few further comments here, especially to remind the reader that neither passage states, nor even suggests that the one God is a triune being composed of three coequal persons—God the Father, God the Son, and God the Holy Spirit—even though the three distinctions mentioned do all have a vital and unified significance as pertains to the Christian system and community.

One other Scripture in this group of 72 references is sometimes used as a parallel, depending on one's interpretation of "the seven spirits": Rev 1:4-5, "Grace and peace to you from him who is, and who was, and who is to come, and from the seven spirits before his throne, and from Jesus Christ."

But this salutation, instead of supporting the idea of a triune God, is rather a refutation of the same. Who would deny that "him who is, and who was, and who is to come" (v. 4) is one and the same as the Lord God, "who is, and who was, and who is to come, the Almighty" in verse 8? There cannot be two or three Almighties, each more mighty than the other. But Jesus Christ (v. 5) is clearly distinguished from the

Lord God, the Almighty who is, and who was, and who is to come, Jesus being specifically identified as him "who is the faithful witness, the firstborn from the dead," a description which in no way can be applied to the Lord God Almighty, who has never been dead, and consequently has never been born from the dead. Therefore Jesus Christ is not that Almighty God, but is clearly distinguished from God.

And the seven spirits in verse 4 (whether they represent the Holy Spirit or not) are "before his throne," that is, before God's throne, and not part of a triune God who is on the throne. Those "seven spirits of God" are described as "seven lamps" that were blazing before the throne (Rev 4:5). If the only God, the Almighty, were a plural being composed of three coequal persons, then Christ and the Holy Spirit would be as much on the throne as was the Father. But instead—

> God was ON the throne (Rev 4:2; 5:1),
>
> the seven spirits were BEFORE the throne (Rev 1:4; 4:5),
>
> while Christ was on (or at) the RIGHT HAND of the throne (Heb 8:1; 12:2).

Other than those three passages listed among the 72 salutations, invocations and benedictions, none of the other 69 references make any mention of the Holy Spirit, a glaring inequity which should tell us something about the notion of three coequal persons in a plural being called God. Such a coequal personal Holy Spirit could not possibly have been thus excluded from 96% of all the 72 salutations, invocations and benedictions which invoke the names of only two divine persons.

In this list of 72 references, Jesus is mentioned 69 times. In 14 of them, Jesus alone is mentioned. Of the 58 times God is mentioned, 3 times he alone is mentioned. Fifty-two times Jesus and God are mentioned together without any reference to the Holy Spirit; while the Spirit is mentioned only three times total, even when including the apocalyptic "seven spirits" of Revelation 1:4-5.

Surely anyone who would read carefully all those 72 references (see Appendix D) must conclude that the conspicuous absence of the Holy Spirit in at least 96% of those references does raise an extremely high suspicion that the writers of those epistles did not consider the Holy Spirit to be a separate and distinct personal entity from the Father, as Jesus is a separate person from the Father. Consider just a few examples from Appendix D:

> Rom 1:7 (and at least 10 other references), "Grace and peace to you from God our Father and from the Lord Jesus Christ." Why not from the Holy Spirit also, if the Holy Spirit is a coequal person with God and Christ?
>
> 1 Cor 1:9, "God, who has called you into fellowship with his Son Jesus Christ our Lord." Why not also into the fellowship of the

Holy Spirit as well?

2 Cor 1:3, "Praise be to the God and Father of our Lord Jesus Christ, the Father of compassion and the God of all comfort" [*paraklesis*]. God is here identified as both the God and Father of Christ, and also the God of all comfort. If the Holy Spirit, (called "the Comforter" in John 15:26) were a distinct person from the Father, instead of God's Spirit "which proceedeth from the Father" (ASV), then why is it said that the Father, instead of the Holy Spirit, is the God of all comfort?

Titus 1:1, "Paul, a servant of God and an apostle of Jesus Christ." If Paul, as an inspired apostle, is guided by a personal Holy Spirit, a separate person from the Father, why did Paul not include the Holy Spirit along with God and Jesus Christ?

1 John 1:3, "Our fellowship is with the Father and with his Son, Jesus Christ." Why not also with the Holy Spirit? If the Holy Spirit is equally a personal entity as are the Father and his Son, then why is the Holy Spirit not here included as one of three persons with whom we have fellowship?

The absence of the Holy Spirit here should be sufficient to convince anyone that the fellowship (communion) of the Holy Spirit in 2 Corinthians 13:14 is not fellowship with a third personal entity, but is instead the Spirit of God, the power and influence through which our fellowship with God and Christ is effected. On and on we could go, pointing out these glaring inequities.

Of those 72 Scriptures listed in Appendix D, Christ is specifically distinguished from God at least 49 times; not just distinguished from the Father, whom Trinitarians believe to be one of three coequal persons in the one God, but distinguished from God himself. Furthermore, in those 72 Scriptures, God is specifically identified as the Father no less than 27 times; while neither Christ nor the Holy Spirit is even once identified as being God, much less, the God (*ho Theos*).

So instead of using only two, or possibly three of those 72 passages to support the doctrine of the Trinity, they as a whole should be used rather to refute such a doctrine.

For further exegesis of 2 Corinthians 13:14 and 1 Peter 1:2, see Part I, Ch. 39, *Communion and Sanctification of the Spirit*, as well as Part I, Ch. 35, *First Person, Second Person, Third Person*.

CHAPTER 39

COMMUNION AND SANCTIFICATION OF THE SPIRIT

"May the grace of the Lord Jesus Christ, and the love of God, and the fellowship [communion, ASV] of the Holy Spirit be with you all" (2 Cor 13:14).

"According to the foreknowledge of God the Father, through the sanctifying work of the Spirit [in sanctification of the Spirit, ASV], for obedience to Jesus Christ" (1 Pet 1:2).

Do these statements prove that the Holy Spirit is a person separate from the Father as Jesus is a person separate from the Father? They certainly do not say so; therefore they must be examined more closely with reason and logic.

Christians, whether individually or collectively, may enjoy "the communion of the Holy Spirit" and the "sanctification of the Spirit," whether that Spirit is the Spirit of Jehovah God, the Father, the means by which God himself is omnipotently omnipresent, or whether that Spirit is a person separate from the God of whom it is the Spirit. The communion of the Holy Spirit with the Christian, and the sanctification of the Spirit would be the same in either case. How could the Holy Spirit, as a person separate from the Father, have any greater significance, exercise any greater power, or be any more divine than it does (or is) as being the Spirit of God, "which proceedeth from the Father" (John 15:26)?

The word "communion" (2 Cor 13:14) is the Greek word *koinonia*, being translated elsewhere in the KJV as "communication," "contribution," "distribution," and most times, "fellowship"; and it has to do with "the share which one has in anything, participation."[7] (Thayer's *Greek-English Lexicon*).

Whether Paul here speaks of the participation of the Holy Spirit in a supernatural presence among the churches, or of the indwelling of that Spirit in the hearts and lives of individual Christians, or even in some other perceived manner, that participation has nothing to do with whether or not the Holy Spirit is a distinct personal being or entity separate from the Father, or if that Spirit is the means whereby God, the Father in heaven, is ever present with Christians individually, or with the church collectively.

Consider 1 Corinthians 10:16, "Is not the cup of thanksgiving for which we give thanks a participation in [communion of, ASV] the blood of Christ?" When Christians partake of the Lord's Supper, Paul says that they participate in, or have communion with the blood of Christ. That in no way means that Christ's blood is a distinct personal entity in order for us to participate in the benefits of that blood. So it is with the Spirit.

Phil 2:1, "If you have any encouragement from being united with Christ, if any comfort from his love, if any fellowship with the Spirit . ." Paul here does not expect us to conclude that the Spirit, in which we participate, or with which we have fellowship, is any more a personal entity, distinct from the Father, than the love that comforts us in that same passage is a distinct personal entity. Numerous other examples could be cited which show Christians having fellowship or communion with things that are not persons. Therefore the "communion of the Holy Spirit" in 2 Corinthians 13:14 in no way proves that the Holy Spirit is a personal entity apart from the Father. Paul simply desired that all the Christians at Corinth would participate in whatever came to them by means of the Holy Spirit, whether it came in the form of prophetic utterances, or the gift of tongues, or an attitude of heart or disposition of mind being influenced by the Spirit, or even by the word of God being delivered to them by inspiration of the Spirit.

Likewise, "in sanctification of the Spirit" (1 Pet 1:2) tells us only that in some way we become sanctified by the Spirit, whether that Spirit is a personal entity distinct from the Father, or if it is that Spirit which ever proceeds from the Father, being God's demonstrated power and influence to convict and convert mankind here on earth by miraculously confirming the apostles' words as being from God. (See Mark 16:20 and Heb 2:3-4).

Peter's statement may not even be saying that the Holy Spirit is that which sanctifies, even though other Scriptures might do so. It may not even be referring to the Holy Spirit at all, but rather to the spirit of man, as it is sanctified (set apart) from the things of this world to become the spirit of obedience, after which it receives figuratively the "sprinkling of the blood of Jesus Christ" (ASV), and is thereby cleansed and purified.

Do not conclude that it must refer to the Holy Spirit because of the capital "S." Remember that in the original there was no such distinction; and the capital "S" is the result of someone's interpretation, not an actual translation. If this be the case, the argument for the Trinity based on 1 Pet 1:2 is nullified.

Without eliminating the Holy Spirit from the process, 1 Corinthians 1:30 attributes sanctification, along with wisdom, righteousness and redemption, to Christ Jesus, not to the Holy Spirit.

2 Thess 2:13 (ASV), "God chose you from the beginning unto salvation in sanctification of the Spirit and belief of the truth." Again, the Spirit need not be the Holy Spirit doing the sanctifying, but rather our spirit which is being sanctified in believing the truth.

From Hebrews 10:29 we find that it is by "the blood of the covenant" that we are sanctified. And of course, that blood which sanctifies does not constitute a person distinct from Christ.

From Heb 13:12 we learn that it is Jesus who sanctifies the people "through his own blood" (ASV).

From John 17:17, we learn that God sanctifies us by his truth, for "your word is truth." (See also v. 19). So even the word of God sanctifies, without that word being a separate personal entity.

In 1 Thess 5:23, it is "God himself, the God of peace" who sanctifies. So in summation, it is Jehovah God himself who sanctifies us by having sent his Son Jesus Christ, who came to sanctify us by shedding his own blood, by which blood we are sanctified when we receive God's word of truth which was given by inspiration of the Holy Spirit, and when we believe and accept that truth, and allow that word to sanctify (set apart) our spirits from the corruptions of this world to serve the living God with a pure heart. That's sanctification OF the spirit, BY the Spirit; which no more requires that the Spirit be a personal being distinct from the Father than it requires the blood of Christ, the truth of God, or the word of God to be persons separate from the Father. Nor does it require my spirit which is sanctified to be a person separate from myself.

Therefore the Holy Spirit is not, as some have supposed, some personal being or entity who, apart from the Father, holds exclusively the ministry of sanctification. The NIV and some other versions seem to try to set forth such an idea in translating 2 Thessalonians 2:13 and 1 Peter 1:2. In both passages, the Greek phrase, *en hagiasmo pneumatos* (in sanctification of spirit) is translated in the NIV, "through the sanctifying work of the Spirit." To say the least, this rendition is obviously more of a paraphrased interpretation than a literal translation.

So when studying these passages in their context, and using those renditions which nearest reflect the literal translation, none of them offer any proof for the doctrine of the Trinity, inasmuch as they do not prove the distinct personal entity of the Holy Spirit, nor that the one God is a plural God composed of three coequal and coeternal persons.

CHAPTER 40

THE ANGEL OF JEHOVAH

God, whose memorial name is Jehovah (Exod 3:15; 6:2-3, ASV), therefore one and the same being or person, has from the beginning communicated with man in a variety of ways. It seems that in the beginning God may have communicated directly with Adam (Gen 3:9), with Eve (v. 13), with Cain (4:6), etc., without using some messenger to go between. But even that idea cannot be firmly established beyond question. Had it been stated later that God had communicated with them on those occasions by angels, nothing in those first few chapters would have been contradicted. Even when God sends an angel, a prophet, an apostle, or any other kind of messenger to deliver his message, it can still be proclaimed, "Jehovah God said it," without suggesting that the messenger doing the speaking is in any way Jehovah God. The message, not the messenger, is divine.

Because such messages were from God, the messenger oftentimes assumed the first-person singular mode as if he himself were the source of the message. In the case of angels, this was almost universally done. This practice added credence to the message and reverence to the occasion, implying that it was God himself doing the speaking, using the mouth and voice of the angel. Therefore, when an angel of Jehovah would say something like, "I will multiply your seed," it could be said that the angel said it, the angel being the spokesman or messenger. But it could also rightly be said that Jehovah said it, Jehovah being the source of the message. Then when such a seed promise was fulfilled, everyone knew that it was Jehovah, not the angel of Jehovah, who multiplied the seed.

This first-person mode of vicarious speech sometimes caused the recipient of the message to conclude that he or she had actually seen God, or at least was in direct communication with God himself; which, of course, would add still further to the solemnity of the occasion, and might on some occasions even produce attitudes or actions of worship toward the messenger, as a vicar of Jehovah.

Such a worshipful attitude might not necessarily be classified as angel worship; because in spite of such a case of possible mistaken identity, God would know that in the recipient's mind and heart, it was God himself, the source of the message, and not the angel, who was being worshiped. Only God could correctly assess the intent of the heart.

Unfortunately, some theologians have overlooked these very basic principles for interpreting angelic messages, and have therefore arrived at some untenable conclusions concerning certain angels' identities. It is believed and taught by some that "the angel of Jehovah," which appears numerous times in Scripture, is none other than the one they refer to as "the Second Person of the Trinity," the personal Word of God, later to be known as Jesus Christ, the Son of God. However, this concept presents numerous problems.

FIRST: It is purely an assumption that every time (or even occasionally), when "the angel of Jehovah" appears, it has reference to one and the same specific angel, supposedly Jesus Christ. That assumption apparently ignores the fact that Jehovah God has thousands of angels (Matt 26:53; Heb 12:22), any one of which might rightly be called "the angel of Jehovah," and any one of which, empowered by God, might possibly be able to handle any given assignment. And any one of those angels which God might assign to deliver a particular message would indeed be "the angel of Jehovah" for that particular occasion.

SECOND: Too much emphasis is placed on "the" angel of Jehovah, as though there were only one such angel of Jehovah for all occasions, that angel supposedly being the Second Person of the Godhead. Surely Genesis 32:1 dispels that idea of singularity: "Jacob also went on his way, and the angels of God met him." Since Jehovah is the name of God, then the angels of God would be the angels of Jehovah. Note the plural definite article, "the" angels of God in the Greek Septuagint (LXX), as well as in the translations. We are not told how many angels of Jehovah there were; but when Jacob saw them, he exclaimed, "This is the camp of God!" The Greek word here for "camp" is the same word applied to the encampment of the two or three million Israelites in the wilderness (Exod 29:14), referring to a camp or an army. A translation of the LXX has, "This is the camp of God."

Also, a look at the angel of Jehovah (Gen 16:7), which appeared to Hagar by a fountain of water, reveals no singular significance to the definite article as claimed by some. In the LXX, the Greek Septuagint Version of the OT, and also concurring with the Hebrew text, the "angel" at this point does not have the definite article "the," and is translated "an angel" (v. 7), not "the angel." Then in verses 9, 10 and 11, the angel is modified by the definite article in order to direct us back to that specific angel which was introduced in verse 7 as simply "an angel of Jehovah." God, no doubt, could have used any one of his thousands upon thousands of angels to be the angel of Jehovah for that particular assignment. It was not necessary that a divine person, such as Christ, carry the message.

At Hagar's second encounter with an angel (Gen 21:17-19), again we find the absence of the definite article in the LXX and Hebrew text, where it is translated "an angel of God." It is presumptuous on the part of anyone to assume that this angel is the same angel of Jehovah whom Hagar had encountered back in 16:7. There is no indication that Hagar recognized him as being the one she had seen previously.

So it was with Abraham when he offered Isaac: "an angel of the Lord" (LXX) called to him (Gen 22:11), not "the angel." There is no evidence that this is the same angel which had appeared to Hagar.

And again, "an angel of the Lord" (LXX) called unto Abraham a second time (v. 15), not "the angel," and possibly not even the angel which had spoken to him in verse 11.

When God encountered Moses in the wilderness (Exod 3:2), "an angel of the Lord" (LXX) appeared to him in a flame of fire out of the midst of the bush, not "the angel," and possibly one never before mentioned. (See also Acts 7:30).

The angel of God in Exod 14:19 is "the" one specific angel identified as the one "who had been traveling in front of Israel's army," and possibly the one who had encountered Moses from the bush, but not identified as otherwise having previously appeared on the scene.

Numbers 20:16 relates some of Israel's history, saying, "When we cried out to the LORD, he heard our cry and sent an angel and brought us out of Egypt." While this angel is not specifically called "the angel of Jehovah," it was definitely an angel sent by Jehovah, therefore "the angel of Jehovah" for that specific occasion; possibly, but not necessarily, the one so often referred to (but not in Scripture) as "the death angel" which God may have used to slay the firstborn of Egypt, resulting in the Exodus. But nothing specifically connects this angel of Jehovah with any previously mentioned angel.

The angel which appeared to Balaam's donkey, and then to Balaam himself (Num 22:21 ff), is here called "the angel of Jehovah" ten times, but without identifying him with any other angelic appearance.

The man with a sword whom Joshua saw (Josh 5:13-6:5), and who is presumed by many to be identical with the angel of Jehovah, identified himself simply as "commander of the army of the LORD," or "prince of the host of Jehovah" (ASV). This seems to have been a new character on the angelic scene, not identifiable with any previous angel. In fact, he might not have even been an angel at all, but simply a man with a prophetic message, revealing to Joshua God's military strategy for conquering Jericho. Fortunately for Israel, Joshua recognized the messenger as having been sent by God, and therefore reverenced his as one of higher rank than himself in the army of Jehovah, calling him "lord," as any underling would address his superior, especially in the militia.

It was "an angel of the Lord" (Judg 2:1), not "the angel" (according to the LXX), which brought a message to Israel at Bokim. When he said, "I brought you up out of Egypt," etc., who can be sure whether he was identifying himself as being that very angel which brought Israel forth out of Egypt (Num 20:16), or that he was rather speaking in the first-person singular mode for God, who had brought them forth?

Which angel was used for the task was of little or no significance. What was important was that God did it, by whatever means or agency he chose.

In Judges 6:11, "an angel of the Lord" (LXX), not "the angel," paid Gideon a visit.

In Judges 13:3, "an angel of the Lord" (LXX), not "the angel," appeared to Manoah's wife, the mother of Samson. She considered him to be "a man of God" (v. 6), whose countenance was like that of "an angel of God" (LXX). Manoah acknowledged that the angel was a man of God, sent by God (v. 8). And when the angel returned to Manoah's wife, unlike Hagar, she recognized him to be the same "man" she had seen before (v. 10).

The angel of Jehovah which came to Elijah (1 Kgs 19:7) was first identified simply as "an angel" (v. 5). In 2 Kings 1:3, Elijah was again approached by "an angel of the Lord" (LXX), not "the angel."

On and on we could go, pointing out the lack of evidence that might even suggest that "the angel of Jehovah" always referred to one and the same unique angel, supposedly the Second Person of the Godhead, Jesus Christ. And even in all those passages where the LXX and the Hebrew text have simply "an angel of the Lord," instead of "the angel of Jehovah" (ASV), "the angel" does nothing more than specify one particular angel chosen for each individual message being delivered.

THIRD: Even if it could be proved beyond question that on one of those occasions the angel of Jehovah was indeed the Christ (which cannot be proved), it still would not indicate, much less prove, that the angel of Jehovah was Christ in any or all of the many remaining cases. It was not necessary that Christ be the angel for any of those occasions. God's angels could handle them.

FOURTH: Positive proof that Jesus was not the angel of Jehovah, nor any other angel, is found in the rhetorical question presented in Hebrews 1:5, "For to which of the angels did God ever say, 'You are my Son; today I have become your Father [Or *have begotten you*]'?" (a quote from Ps 2:7). The true answer is obvious: NONE! NOT ONE, or else the question would never have been asked. God said this to Christ (we are not told when); but he never said it to any angel. Conclusion: Christ was not the angel of Jehovah. The Hebrew writer made no exception for the angel of Jehovah. He did not ask, "Unto which of the angels, except the angel of Jehovah, said he at any time . . . . ?"

Again, same verse, (To which of the angels did God ever say) "I will be his Father, and he will be my Son?" (a quote from 2 Sam 7:14). Similar question; same answer: NOT ONE!

And still again, a third question is asked for the same reason, "To which of the angels did God ever say, 'Sit at my right hand until I make your enemies a footstool for your feet'?" (v. 13, quoting from Ps

110:1). The answer is still the same: NONE! NOT ONE! According to the Hebrew writer, all these things Jehovah spoke to Christ. Never did he say these things to any of the angels. But he did say them to his own Son, Jesus Christ. Conclusion: Jesus was never an angel, therefore he could not have been the angel of Jehovah.

Someone might respond by pointing out that the word "angel" simply means "a messenger," and therefore supposedly renders invalid the foregoing conclusion. So let's change the question to read, "Unto which of the *messengers* said he at any time, 'You are my Son'?" Same answer: NOT ONE!

Not even to the angel or messenger of Jehovah did God ever make those statements.

In the Hebrew epistle, *aggelos* (angel or messenger) never refers to a human messenger, nor to Christ. Nowhere does the NT indicate that Christ had ever been an angel of Jehovah. In the NT the Greek word *aggelos* is never applied to Christ. Indeed, Christ is declared to be "much superior to the angels" (Heb 1:4), and was also made "a little lower than the angels . . . because of the suffering of death" (Heb 2:7, 9, ASV); but never was he said to be an angel, nor an angel's equal.

FIFTH: In pointing out the divine preexistence of Christ before he was born of Mary, Christ and the NT writers used several arguments to prove their point. If Jesus had been the angel of Jehovah, appearing so many times throughout the OT, and supposedly having such an important and obvious role in the history of Israel, it would be most inconceivable that neither Christ nor any of the NT writers ever identified any of those angels as being identical with Christ, nor ever offered that supposed role of Christ as proof of his preexistence. They proclaimed his preexistent role as creator, by or through whom all things were made, but never as the angel of Jehovah or any other angel. That silence is most revealing. Those today who herald Jesus as having been the angel of Jehovah have absolutely no NT evidence to support their claim.

In Stephen's final sermon (Acts 7), resulting in his immediate martyrdom, he recounted briefly the history of Israel and their forefathers, making reference to "an angel" that appeared to Moses in a flame of fire in a bush (v. 30), then to possibly the same angel which was with Moses in the wilderness after the Exodus (v. 38), and finally to the angels which ordained the law (v. 53). What an excellent opportunity for Stephen to have preached Christ as having been the angel of Jehovah on all those occasions, if indeed such had been the case. How could he possibly have missed such a splendid opportunity? Why didn't Stephen, full of the Holy Spirit (Acts 6:5, 8), use those same arguments which some are using today, to prove to the Jews that Christ is identical with the angel of Jehovah, and is also one of three persons in their plural God named Jehovah? The answer: Stephen knew that those were angels, and not Jesus Christ.

SIXTH: Instead of Jesus being an angel (a created being), he is identified as "the firstborn" (Heb 1:6); therefore, "let all God's angels worship him." Angels were created by Christ, but never born. Reproduction was never attributed to angels as having been born, nor as giving birth. And if Jesus were an angel, even the angel of Jehovah, Scripture would have one angel being worshiped by all the other angels. And carrying this scenario further, Christ, as an angel of Jehovah, would have worshiped himself, since all the angels worshiped him.

SEVENTH: The angel of Jehovah was seen numerous times by various people. But according to Exodus 33:20, God, who is Jehovah, said, "you cannot see my face, for no one may see me and live." And John 1:18 has, "No one has ever seen God." Therefore if "the angel of Jehovah," "Jehovah," and "God" all refer to the same being or person, as some have supposed, then the two Scriptures just quoted cannot be true, because "the angel of Jehovah" had been seen numerous times.

Did Hagar actually see God? Whether or not she thought she did is of no material significance. She asked the question, "Have I even here looked after him that seeth me?" (Gen 16:13, ASV). A possible paraphrase might be, "Have I actually seen God?" Instead of a question, the NIV has it a declarative statement, "I have now seen [Or *seen the back of*] the One who sees me." If she actually saw the person of God at all, then she, like Moses in the mount, must have seen only his back. Beyond that, it would be most unlikely that God would allow Hagar, the bondmaid, to see his face, but let Moses see only his back.

The "man" of Exodus 33:20 in the Greek LXX is *anthropos*, meaning any human being without regard to gender, including Hagar. So Hagar didn't see God. She evidently saw the angel, in whatever form, and rightly concluded that it was God speaking to her, even if the message was being transmitted through the angel; but she didn't see God.

The fact that this messenger to Hagar is called the "angel of Jehovah" four times in this one text (Gen 16:7-13), should be sufficient proof that even though Jehovah God was the source of the message, the messenger was an angel, and not Jehovah God, nor one of three persons in a supposed triune God.

As we have noted before, it was not at all uncommon—in fact it was almost universal—for such angels to speak in the first-person singular mode when delivering a message from God. So when the angel of Jehovah, bringing a message from Jehovah, said, "I will greatly multiply thy seed" (v. 10), it did not mean that the angel would be the person who would do the multiplying; nor did it mean that the angel was Jehovah God. So it is with all the appearance of the angel of Jehovah. This point can be made clear by examining a few angelic appearances:

Gen 16:7, "The angel of the LORD found Hagar near a spring in the desert . . . . And he said, 'the LORD has heard of your misery'" (v. 11). That is not to say that the angel did or did not hear. That wasn't important. What was important was that Jehovah (not the angel) heard her affliction. Jehovah and the angel of Jehovah are not identical. They are different beings. It was Jehovah who heard. It was the angel who said so.

Verse 13 tells us further that it was "the LORD who spoke to her," even though he spoke by the mouth of the angel. If Jehovah had spoken to her directly, there would have been no purpose for having an angel involved. Hagar concluded that it was "a God who sees," with whom she had communicated. Nothing here suggests that the angel she actually saw was Jehovah God.

Gen 18:1, Jehovah appeared unto Abraham in Mamre. Such is not to say that Abraham actually and literally saw God's person. As we have already seen, that would contradict Exodus 33:20 and John 1:18. However, God did appear to Abraham representatively, and the context explains how: Abraham lifted up his eyes and saw three men, who turned out to be angels. That's how God appeared to him. Abraham treated those strangers with his usual eastern hospitality before he realized that they were angels. Then they asked, "Where is your wife Sarah?" (v. 9). This does not mean that more than one of them did the asking. Any one of them could have represented the group by asking the question that was in the minds of all.

"Then the LORD [Hebrew *Then he*] said, 'I will surely return to you,'" possibly meaning that he (the angel) would return, but more probably meaning that Jehovah, who was speaking through him, would return to Abraham at the proper time, without signifying what particular angel, if any, might be used for the occasion. "Then the LORD said to Abraham" (v. 13), which he could have done directly from heaven; but then there would have been no need for these three men to be there as messengers from Jehovah. The fact that at least one of these messengers could predict the birth of Isaac, and know that Sarah secretly laughed, indicates no sign of deity on the part of any one of the three. Even some of the prophets performed greater signs than these. But these signs did establish that they were messengers from God, without even proving that they were heavenly beings. Evidently they didn't look very heavenly; and they actually ate a meal prepared for them by Abraham.

Then the men (who were angels, Gen 19:1) looked toward Sodom. And the LORD said (whether speaking himself from heaven, or speaking through the mouth of one or more of those men), "Shall I hide from Abraham what I am about to do?" (Gen 18:17). Again, what one or more of these men would or would not do was not the issue; the substance of the matter was what Jehovah God would or would not do, whether with or without the medium of men or angels. God used those angels as messengers, and spoke through them with the first-person singular "I," lest someone might get the idea that this delegation of men or angels was going to bring destruction to Sodom. And then when Sodom was destroyed, it was Jehovah God, not the angels, who did it. Obviously none of these three angels was Jehovah God. They were angels, appearing in the form of men; but they spoke messages from God. Thus it was God who spoke through them.

One must wonder why angels used the singular first-person pronoun "I," instead of the plural pronoun "we," when speaking for God, if indeed God were a plural being composed of three persons. Why did no angel, speaking for God, ever say, "We will do such and such," except when speaking for two or more angels.

EIGHTH: Some have become fancifully intrigued with the statement in Genesis 18:22, "The men turned away and went toward Sodom, but Abraham remained standing before the LORD." According to 19:1, only two of the three angels came to Sodom, apparently leaving one there to converse with Abraham. This one is supposedly referred to as "Jehovah," not "angel of Jehovah," causing some to conclude that this angel was very Jehovah God himself in presence, supposedly the Second Person of the Trinity, appearing in the likeness of a man. Based on this type of logic (or the lack thereof), one might as well surmise that it was rather Jehovah, the First Person of the Trinity, who stayed, while the Second and Third Persons of the Trinity, the Son and the Holy Spirit, went on to Sodom.

And if it be argued that for some reason the Jehovah who remained with Abraham could not have been the First Person of the Trinity, on what basis would one conclude that it had to be the Second Person of the Trinity, instead of the Third Person, the Holy Spirit? The two angels who went on to Sodom said, "We are going to destroy this place . . . . (Jehovah) has sent us to destroy it" (Gen 19:13). But Lot told his sons-in-law that Jehovah would destroy the city (v. 14). "Then the LORD rained down burning sulfur on Sodom and Gomorrah—from the LORD out of the heavens" (v. 24). The angels had said that they would do it; but it was Jehovah who did it. Therefore, both of these angels would be as much Jehovah as the angel who remained with Abraham. And if the one who remained with Abraham were the Second Person of the Godhead, as some have believed, then the two who went on to Sodom must have been the First and Third Persons of the supposed Trinity of the Godhead. Is it any wonder that the "Trinity" is called a mystery?

The simplest and most logical explanation is that all three "men" were angels in the likeness of men, all of whom were messengers or angels from Jehovah, and all acted as representatives of Jehovah, speaking in the first-person singular mode for Jehovah. Had it been either of the other two angels who stayed with Abraham, it still could have been said, "Abraham stayed yet before Jehovah." There is no indication that any one of the three represented Jehovah any more than the other two. They merely had different assignments. When all the various angelic appearances are interpreted with these basic understandings in mind, it will be apparent that there is no evidence that the angel of Jehovah is what some call the Second Person of the Trinity.

NINTH: "Do not forget to entertain strangers, for by so doing some people have entertained angels without knowing it" (Heb 13:2). This fits Abraham precisely. He entertained angels, thinking they were merely men. Soon he found them to be inspired messengers from God. (But so were the prophets). Then later it became evident that they were angels, heavenly beings. But we can be sure that none of them were divine beings, or else the Hebrew writer would surely have said, "for thereby some have entertained Jehovah unawares." This would have been a far greater reason for entertaining strangers than the fact that one might unknowingly entertain an angel. If Abraham entertained the Second Person of the Godhead, the Hebrew writer evidently didn't know it. But he did know that they were angels.

TENTH: Since the name "Jehovah" in the Hebrew OT is replaced with the title "Lord" in the LXX, both appellations referring to the same one Jehovah God, then when "the Lord" is used in the NT to identify deity, it must always refer to that same one supreme Almighty Jehovah God, unless there is reason to conclude that it refers rather to Christ, whom Jehovah God anointed to be our King of kings and Lord of lords. With this guiding principle in mind, and after Mary had already become pregnant with the body which was being prepared for Christ ("a body you prepared for me," Heb 10:5), consider that an angel of the Lord appeared to Joseph in a dream. If the angel of the Lord (Jehovah) were Christ in the OT, and the conception and birth of Jesus took place under that system and law, before that law was fulfilled in Christ's death, it would seem that it would still be that same angel of Jehovah who announced to Joseph in a dream, "What is conceived in her is from the Holy Spirit" (Matt 1:20). Such would indicate that one personal Jesus (the angel of Jehovah) was speaking to Joseph at the same time a body was being prepared for Jesus in Mary's womb. If this were the case, some would have to rethink their concept as to when the human embryo of Christ became the actual person of Christ, inasmuch as one supposed person of Christ (the angel of Jehovah) was delivering a message to Joseph about another personal Christ, who at that time was in the womb of Mary. Could there have been four persons in the Godhead during that time? And when Christ was born, what happened to the angel of Jehovah who supposedly had been the Second Person of the Godhead?

Mary, like most mothers, may have spoken of the infant Jesus as her "darling little angel." And she is known to have been called (but not in Scripture) "the mother of God," but never "the mother of the angel of God."

ELEVENTH: Further proof that "angel of Jehovah" is not identical with Christ, is found in Malachi 2:7, "For the lips of a priest ought to preserve knowledge, and from his mouth men should seek instruction—because he is the messenger (*aggelos*) of the LORD Almighty." The Greek text here is without the definite article, as in the numerous other places already mentioned. But this argument is being made here because of those who ignore that fact, and continue to insist that "the angel of Jehovah," with or without the definite article, is Christ.

Not only were the various angels individually called "the angel of Jehovah," but here in Malachi 2:7, even the priest is called "the *aggelos* of Jehovah." And the priest referred to cannot be Christ, but rather the OT priests from the tribe of Levi (vv. 8 and 9). Christ was from the tribe of Judah, and could not be a priest under that covenant. The priest was a messenger of God's word, and was therefore called "the *aggelos* of Jehovah."

In Malachi 3:1, the one being called God's *aggelos* (angel or messenger) is the prophet, John the baptizer. Therefore in these two references both priest and prophet are, in prophetic imagery, called *aggelos*, translated "messenger." Apparently in this same sense, Christ, being both priest and prophet (Heb 3:1; Acts 3:22), is called "the messenger of the covenant" (Mal 3:1), not the angel of Jehovah. Only here is Jesus ever referred to as *aggelos*, translated "messenger," being so-called as were both priests and prophets.

The Greek word for angel is *aggelos*, and the Hebrew word is *malak*, each of which is translated both "angel" and "messenger," depending on whether the messenger is believed to be an angelic heavenly being, or a human earthly being.

In addition to John, the forerunner of Christ, some of the OT prophets were thus called messengers. Some of Saul's messengers prophesied (1 Sam 19:20-21), making them prophets, at least temporarily. The prophet Haggai is also called a messenger (Hag 1:13). And other possible references to prophets as messengers are 2 Chronicles 36:15-16 and Nahum 2:13. But Christ was never identified as *aggelos* in the NT. Nor was he ever identified in the NT as having been the angel of Jehovah in the OT. That's why the Hebrew writer could ask, "To which of the angels did God ever say, 'You are my Son.'?" Knowing that Jesus had never been an angel, not even the angel of Jehovah, he could safely ask that question with full assurance that no one could produce an opposing reply. He proved his point conclusively; and his argument remains unchallenged. Christ is not the angel of Jehovah; he is the Son of God.

TWELFTH: There is a vast difference between the visit of the three angels to Abraham in Mamre, and the angels which Jacob saw going up and down a ladder (or stairway) that reached from earth to heaven. What Abraham saw was real. Abraham and Sarah were not dreaming; they were both wide awake. There is nothing to suggest that both Abraham and Sarah were seeing a vision or dreaming a dream. But what Jacob saw, he saw it in a dream (Gen 28:12). And in that dream he saw a ladder reaching from earth to heaven. There was no ladder; it was a dream. And going up and down the ladder he saw angels. But there were no angels; it was a dream. "There above it stood the LORD" (v. 13). But no one has ever seen Jehovah God (Exod 33:20; John 1:18). Jacob didn't actually see Jehovah; it was a dream. In fact, everything Jacob saw and heard that night was a dream. "When Jacob awoke from his sleep, he thought, 'Surely the LORD is in this place, and I was not aware of it" (v. 16). The mental picture he saw in his dream was what the Bible calls a "vision." But the message of promise was as real to Jacob as it had been to Abraham who was wide awake for his angelic encounter. Compare Jacob's dream with Daniel 7:1, "Daniel had a dream, and visions passed through his mind as he was lying on his bed." Reading the details of that dream, one sees the symbolic nature of the message delivered in a dream.

Furthermore, the person who spoke to Jacob in that dream is called "Jehovah" (Gen 28:13, ASV; see also "the angel of God," 31:11); which of course tells us nothing more than that it was Jehovah himself sending his message of promise to Jacob via one of his angels. This messenger was not the only angel of God present. All the angels who were going up and down the ladder are called "the angels of God" (Gen 28:12). It is pure speculation that one of these angels was any more the Second Person of the Trinity than any of the other angels. They did have different assignments: one delivered a verbal message, while the others went up and down the stairway, probably assuring Jacob by their presence that the host of heaven is ever present connecting heaven and earth, and able to assure that nothing would prevent the fulfilling of that divine promise.

But whether it was actually Jehovah God who stood at the top of the stairway, or the angel of Jehovah, is not the point. It was a dream. Whether God spoke the message directly from the top of the ladder, or if God spoke through his angel at the top of the ladder, the message of promise would be the same. And the fact remains, Jacob may have thought he saw God, but he didn't. "No one has ever seen God." Only in visions and dreams has God revealed his presence in any kind of visible form.

THIRTEENTH: If Jesus had been the angel of Jehovah, then it would have been proper for people to knowingly worship him as an angel; which, of course, would constitute angel worship. He was not an angel, for even angels were instructed to worship him. "When God brings his firstborn into the world, he says, 'Let all God's angels worship him'" (Heb 1:7, taken from Deut 32:43, according to the Dead Sea Scrolls and the LXX). But he is to be worshiped because he is God's firstborn, not because he is the angel of Jehovah.

In Revelation 22:8-9, John "fell down to worship at the feet of the angel," whereupon the angel rebuked him and said, "Worship God!" If the angel of Jehovah had been known to have been a second person in the Godhead, he no doubt would have been worshiped many, many times by those in OT history. But such was not the case. And why would God want to keep as secret the identity of such a significant person among them? One would think that God would want his identity known so that all could worship him.

But angel worship was specifically condemned by Paul (Col 2:18), as he apparently attempted to shield the church from the intrusion of gnosticism. *The NIV Study Bible* commenting here says, "Paul may refer to a professed humility in view of the absolute God, who was believed to be so far above man that he could only be worshiped in the form of angels he had created." An attempt to prove that the supposed second person of the Godhead was worshiped as the angel of Jehovah could possibly border on gnosticism.

Some have thought that Moses worshiped the angel which appeared to him in the bush, by removing his shoes while standing on "holy ground." He indeed obeyed the voice, whether it was the angel's voice or God's voice. He obeyed the message that came from God, regardless of the nature of the messenger. If Moses worshiped anyone there, it was God, not the angel. Furthermore, obedience to a command does not necessarily constitute worship. To obey a prophet is not to worship that prophet. To obey an apostle is not to worship that apostle. To obey Scripture is not to worship Scripture. And a son obeys his father without worshiping his father. So the angel in the bush cannot be said to be the Second Person in the Godhead, based on the idea that Moses worshiped him. He didn't.

When Balaam saw the angel of Jehovah standing in the way with his sword drawn in his hand, he bowed his head and fell on his face (Num 22:31), indicating submission, not worship. One may submit to any number of various authorities without worshiping them.

When the angel of Jehovah came from Gilgal to Bokim (Jud 2:1-5), the people sacrificed to Jehovah, not to the angel.

Gideon brought an offering and set it before "an angel" (LXX) of Jehovah (Jud 6:11-24). The angel, rather than receiving the offering as worship to himself, actually assisted Gideon in worshiping God by miraculously bringing fire out of the rock to consume the offering. When Gideon thus realized it was truly an angel, he declared, "Ah, Sovereign LORD! I have seen the angel of the LORD face to face." Then

Jehovah said to him, "Peace! Do not be afraid. You are not going to die. So Gideon built an altar to the LORD" (Jud 6:22-24). Thus Gideon worshiped God, not the angel.

Gideon knew he had not seen Jehovah; his own correct conclusion was that he had seen an angel, not God. To see even an angel face to face apparently was believed by some to bring death. But God corrected that by assuring, "You are not going to die." It was God's face, no the face of an angel, that one could not see and live.

From this we can conclude that when Jacob said, (after wrestling all night with a man, probably an angel, Hos 12:4), "I saw God face to face, and yet my life was spared" (Gen 32:30), the truth of the matter was that he, like Gideon, had seen an angel face to face, in the form of a man who apparently was not a champion professional wrestler, and who couldn't (or wouldn't) prevail over Jacob without delivering a low blow. To suppose that this was the Second Person of the Godhead might do an injustice to the omnipotence of God.

Jacob knew that the one with whom he wrestled was someone special, or else he wouldn't have insisted that he bless him. However, one did not have to be God in order to pronounce blessings from God. Patriarchs did it. Prophets, priests and kings did it. Anyone with authority from God could do it.

FOURTEENTH: At the giving of the law, God said, "I am sending an angel ahead of you to guard you along the way and to bring you to the place I have prepared. Pay attention to him and listen to what he says. Do not rebel against him; he will not forgive your rebellion, since my Name is in him" (Exod 23:20-21). It is argued by some that since only God can forgive sins, this angel must be Jehovah. But the idea that only God can forgive sins was Jewish theology, not biblical. God, who alone has the ultimate right or authority to forgive sins, can delegate that authority to anyone he chooses. Christ said, "The Son of Man has authority on earth to forgive sins" (Matt 9:5-6). And Christ continually taught us to forgive one another. To the apostles he said, "If you forgive anyone his sins, they are forgiven; if you do not forgive them, they are not forgiven" (John 20:23). And if Christ could give that authority to the apostles, surely God could give it to an angel. If an angel has been given authority by God to forgive or not to forgive, it doesn't mean that the angel is divine.

"My name is in him" (Exod 23:21), does not prove that the angel which went before Israel was actually Jehovah. The name of Jehovah "in" an angel does not mean that the angel's name is Jehovah (the existing one); it simply represents God's presence with the angel (see *The* NIV *Study Bible*). In the LXX the Greek preposition for "in" is not *en*, which usually means "in" or "within," but is rather *epi*, which usually means "on" or "upon." And the translation of the LXX here is, "my name is on him." This use of the preposition *epi* carries the idea of delegated authority; that is, "My authority is upon him," as in Luke 24:47, "Repentance and forgiveness of sins will be preached in (*epi*, upon, or by the authority of) his name to all nations." So the angel which went before Israel performed under the authority of God, but he wasn't God; just as the apostles performed under the authority of Christ; but they were not Christ.

Furthermore, to be called the angel of Jehovah is to have the name of Jehovah upon that angel. "Angel of Jehovah" automatically tells us by what authority that angel performs; it is the authority of Jehovah God.

The terms "angel of Jehovah," "Jehovah" and "God," simply distinguish between the messenger and the source of the message. So the ultimate conclusion from Scripture is that the angel of Jehovah was not Christ. Christ was not an angel; he was and is the divine Son of God.

Be not alarmed by the fact that some translations refer to angels as "sons of God." In Job 38:7 (see also 1:6 and 2:1) the NIV, following the Septuagint, has, "And all the angels shouted for joy." According to Adam Clarke's Commentary, the *Chaldee* has, "All the troops of angels."[3] But the KJV, ASV, NIV footnote and others have "sons of God" in place of *angels*.

Matthew Henry says, "The angels are called *the sons of God* because they bear much of his image, are with him in his house above, and serve him as a son does his father."[19] Realizing the poetic nature of this text in Job, we can understand how angels are here called *sons of God* figuratively, as easily as we can understand how "the morning stars sang together" (same verse).

Furthermore, Christ is not God's one and only Son in *every* sense, for even Adam (therefore all mankind by extension) is called "the son of God" (Luke 3:38). We are God's offspring (Acts 17:28), inasmuch as God is "the Father of our spirits" (Heb 12:9); but we do not possess God's divine nature, as does Christ. Christ is God's one and only begotten divine Son, because he alone was born of God in that unique sense, "the firstborn of every creature" (Col 1:15); born, not created.

So inasmuch as angels (though not divine) are intelligent spirit beings, and God is both the God and Father of spirits (Num 16:22; 27:16), in that sense even angels, like all mankind, may be called *sons of God*. But to none of them did God ever say, "Thou art my Son, this day have I begotten thee" (Heb 1:5, ASV).

CHAPTER 41

ONLY BEGOTTEN SON

"For God so loved the world that he gave his one and only Son [Or *his only begotten Son*]" (John 3:16). The words "only begotten" are the ASV translation of the Greek compound word *monogenes*. See also where *monogenes* is translated "only" son (Luke 7:12) and "only" daughter (8:42); and where it refers to Jesus as God's "only begotten" Son (John 1:14, 18; 3:18; 1 John 4:9); and to Isaac as Abraham's "only begotten (son)" (Heb 11:17).

From these nine references, the only occurrences of the word *monogenes* in the NT Greek text, we can see from the first eight, including those referring to Jesus, that *monogenes* may indeed, but not necessarily, refer to those who were literally "only begotten" as a result of being the one and only offspring of an immediate progenitor, whether human or divine. However, in the case of Isaac (Heb 11:17), *monogenes* cannot literally mean "only begotten," inasmuch as Ishmael, not Isaac, was Abraham's first offspring, making Isaac second, and certainly never the only begotten of Abraham. And while Isaac was not Abraham's only begotten son, he was indeed his one and only son who was born free, to be the recipient of the divine promise, unlike Ishmael, who was born of a bondwoman concubine, not to be heir of those said promises.

This irregularity, thus explained, lends credence to the conclusion of many Greek scholars that *monogenes* does not inherently necessitate the idea of progeny as is suggested by "only begotten," but instead means, "single of its kind, only . . . . used of only sons or daughters (viewed in relationship to their parents) . . . . used of Christ, denotes the only son of God or one who in the sense in which he himself is the son of God has no brethren."[7] (Thayer's *Greek-English Lexicon*, under *monogenes*).

This definition is accepted almost universally by Greek-to-English translators of the NT, at least as far back as the RSV, translating it simply as "only" Son, with the NIV translating it as the "one and only" Son. But even the NIV footnote allows the older rendition of "only begotten," as an acceptable alternative. So there does seem to be a cloud of uncertainty among translators as to whether *monogenes* necessarily includes, or merely allows the idea of Jesus' being begotten in addition to his being uniquely a one-of-a-kind Son.

Scripture speaks of sons of God in three different senses: First, all mankind are sons of God. Paul, speaking to the Athenians concerning mankind in general, gave sanction to the words of their own poets who had said, "We are his offspring" (Acts 17:28). And Luke, tracing the genealogy of Christ back to Adam, then calls Adam "the son of God"

(Luke 3:38), thereby making all of Adam's descendants "sons of God" by extension.

Second, those who have been "born again" (John 3:3), "born of water and the Spirit" (v. 5), are spiritual sons of God as distinguished from those who have not been thus reborn. "Those who are led by the Spirit of God are sons of God" (Rom 8:14; see also Gal 3:26-27). Such spiritual sons of God are also figuratively spoken of as having been adopted into the family of God. (See Rom 8:15; Gal 4:5-7; Eph 1:5).

Those who deny the divinity of Christ might concede that Christ is the Son of God, but then add, "Aren't we all?" If Christ were the Son of God in only those two senses, then he would be no more divine than we are. He would not be the *monogenes* (one of a kind, or one and only) Son of God. But Christ is uniquely the Son of God in that he is not only the "firstborn of all creation" (Col 1:15, ASV)—being born of God alone, as God was the only living being at that time—but is also the only being ever to be thus born of God without the instrumentality of any other being, therefore divine. And if he were not the Son of God in this way, then his Sonship, though unique, would not be proof of his divinity. His birth by Mary made him human, not divine. He was already divine.

Another compound Greek word which does mean "only begotten" is *monogennao* (a verb), but a word not found in Scripture. However, the word without the prefix *monos* (one or only) is *gennao* (begotten), which is found in Scripture, where Jehovah, speaking to Christ, says, "You are my Son; today I have become your Father [Or *have begotten you*]" (Ps 2:7; quoted again in Heb 1:5 and 5:5). Therefore Christ is not just God's *monogenes* (one and only, or one of a kind) Son, but he is also *gennao* (begotten) by God. The conclusion is that Christ is God's one and only begotten divine Son, whether or not John 3:16 and other such passages say so.

Another passage proving the deity of Christ is Matthew 1:20, the Lord speaking to Joseph in a dream, said, "Do not be afraid to take Mary home as your wife, because what is conceived (*gennao*, begotten) in her is from the Holy Spirit," corresponding with verse 18, "She was found to be with child through the Holy Spirit." Jesus is the Son of whatever person of whom he was begotten in Mary. Therefore if the Holy Spirit is that person, then Christ is the Son of the so-called Third Person of the Godhead instead of the so-called First Person of the Godhead. But if on the other hand, the Holy Spirit is not a person distinct from the Father, but is rather that Spirit which "proceedeth from the Father" (John 15:26), then truly God is his Father, having begotten (*gennao*) him by means of his omnipotent and omnipresent Spirit.

"Man shall not live by bread alone, but by every word that proceedeth out of the mouth of God" (Matt 4:4, ASV). If we can understand how the words of God proceed out of the mouth of God, without those words being a person distinct from God, then surely we should be able to understand how the Holy Spirit can continually proceed from the Father without that Spirit being a person distinct from the Father it proceeds from. Only in this way can Christ be the Son of God without the Holy Spirit being his personal Father when he was begotten in the virgin.

CHAPTER 42

THE FATHER IS GREATER THAN I

The Jews tried desperately to get Jesus to make the claim that he is God, but they failed. They even tried to twist some of Jesus' words to make it appear that he was claiming to be God. But they also failed in that effort. Jesus said, "I and the Father are one" (John 10:30). So the Jews—like many today, misunderstanding what it means for Jesus and his heavenly Father to be one—accused him of blasphemy, telling Jesus that "You, a mere man, claim to be God" (v. 33). That was their own erroneous conclusion; but Jesus denied the charge by responding, "I said, 'I am God's Son'" (v. 36), and that's not blasphemy against Israel's one and only Jehovah God Almighty. God could have a thousand such Sons, and there still be only one God.

Jesus used numerous occasions to rectify that false charge of blasphemy against him. One way he chose to defend himself against the charge was to proclaim that the Father is greater than he; meaning that he and his Father are two separate and distinct beings, persons or entities, and that the Father, who was recognized by all as being that one almighty Jehovah God, was greater than Jesus. So if Jesus taught that God is greater than himself, the conclusion should naturally follow that Jesus was denying that he is that God.

The equality that existed between God and his Son, as mentioned in Philippians 2:6-7, refers to the equality of their divine nature, as distinguished from human nature, animal nature, or even angelic nature (see Part I, Ch. 6, entitled *Equality With God*), and in no way insinuates that Christ is, ever was, or ever would be equal with God in such areas as Fatherhood, Sonship, sequence, begetting, being begotten, sending, being sent, sanctifying, being sanctified, supremacy, sovereignty, self-existence, authority and power. In fact, Jesus made it quite clear, "The Father is greater than I" (John 14:28). That is a denial that he himself is the God Almighty.

> John 10:29, "My Father, who has given them to me, is greater than all."
> John 5:19, "The Son can do nothing by himself: he can do only what he sees his Father doing." This Jesus said in response to the charge the Jews made that Jesus "was even calling God his own Father, making himself equal with God" (v. 18). Jesus' response did not deny equality with God in divine nature, but did deny equality with God in power and authority.
> John 8:29, "The one who sent me is with me; he has not left me alone, for I always do what pleases him."
> John 14:24, "These words you hear are not my own; they belong

to the Father who sent me."

John 12:49, "I do not speak of my own accord, but the Father who sent me commanded me what to say and how to say it."

John 6:38, "I have come down from heaven not to do my will but to do the will of him who sent me."

John 7:16, "My teaching is not my own. It comes from him who sent me."

John 8:26, "I have much to say in judgment of you. But he who sent me is reliable, and what I have heard from him I tell the world."

John 8:42, "I came from God and now am here. I have not come on my own; but he sent me."

Jesus had authority to judge man. But where did he get that authority? John 5:22, "The Father judges no one, but has entrusted all judgment to the Son." The one giving the authority to judge is greater than the one to whom that authority is given.

Luke 4:18, "The Spirit of the Lord (Jehovah, Isa 61:1) is on me, because he has anointed me to preach good news to the poor." God, who anoints a prophet, priest or king, is greater than the one being anointed.

Luke 10:22, "All things have been committed to me by my Father."

Jesus recognized that even the kingdom over which he would rule until the end of time was actually not his kingdom, but was rather the Father's kingdom, and referred to "that day when I drink it anew with you in my Father's kingdom" (Matt 26:29). Jesus ascended into heaven to be seated at God's right hand (Acts 2:34-35). To be seated at God's right hand shows subordination to him who sits on the throne.

Mark 12:36, "The Lord (Jehovah) said to my Lord (Christ), 'Sit at my right hand until I put your enemies under your feet.'" Even though Christ is crowned King of kings, and is enthroned at God's right hand, still it is God who will make Christ's enemies the footstool of Christ's feet. Why? Because "the Father is greater than I."

The disciples of Jesus got into a power struggle over who would be on his right hand and on his left hand in his kingdom. And the usual procedure in a kingdom was that the king would make that determination. But not so with the kingdom of Christ. His response was, "To sit at my right or left is not for me to grant. These places belong to those for whom they have been prepared by my Father" (Matt 20:23; see also Mark 10:40). How could this be? Because "the Father is greater than I."

One would think that in the kingdom of Christ the timetable for significant events would be determined by the king. Yet Jesus said, "No one knows about that day or hour, not even the angels in heaven, nor the Son, but only the Father" (Matt 24:36; Mark 13:32). The ASV footnote has: "Many authorities, some ancient, omit 'neither the Son.'" However, the admittance of the phrase in Mark 13:32 is not questioned. Furthermore, with or without the questionable addition, the fact remains that only the Father knows. Why? Because "the Father is greater than I."

John 13:20, "Whoever accepts anyone I send accepts me; and whoever accepts me accepts the one who sent me." The sender of those with authority is always greater than those who are sent.

When God said, "Let us make man in our image, in our likeness" (Gen 1:26), there had to be at least two persons, beings or entities in heaven who possessed the same image or likeness. Those two entities were none other than God and his Son; and man was made in their image. While there may be much speculation as to precisely what all that likeness included, it is evident from the Bible as a whole that the likeness must undoubtedly include individuality, personality, intellect, will, the power of choice, including the choice between right and wrong, to obey or to disobey. Even the angels supposedly possessed that likeness, some of whom apparently exercised those liberties of choice to their own destruction (Jude 6; 2 Pet 2:4). And we know also that man from the beginning has made the wrong choices at some point in life, "for all have sinned and fall short of the glory of God" (Rom 3:23).

It would be unthinkable that Christ would not also have that same power of choice at any point in his existence, whether before, during or after his life here on earth. Without the possibility to sin, Christ could never have been tempted to sin; and yet we know that Christ "has been tempted in every way, just as we are—yet was without sin" (Heb 4:15). Because God himself is the standard for right and wrong, it is therefore impossible for God to lie (Heb 6:18), and by implication impossible to commit any sin, and therefore impossible that he could be tempted to sin; "For God cannot be tempted by evil" (Jas 1:13).

But Jesus could be tempted, and was thus tempted. Had Jesus yielded to temptation, he could have at any time before, during or after his life on earth, rebelled against God as did some of the angels. Satan offered to Christ an alternative plan for receiving power and honor here on earth, apart from God's way, the way of the cross. And if Jesus had thus rebelled in a power struggle against God, is there any doubt as to which of the two would come out victorious? Would the conflict have ended in a standoff because of an equality that existed between the two? Of course it would be God, not Christ, (the Father, not the Son) who would be the victor. Why? Because "the Father is greater than I." When Christ said, "I and the Father are one," he was not describing a forced and compelled relationship, but rather a relationship which was the result of the exercise of his own power to choose that it be that way.

Had Jesus been, as Trinitarians claim, one of three coequal persons in a triune God, none of whom would be subordinate to another, then when man sinned against God, man would have sinned equally against all three supposed persons—the Father, the Son, and the Holy Spirit. Under this scenario, when the Father asked the Son to go down and reconcile man to the Father, the Son could have appropriately responded, "No, you go and reconcile man to me." Or he could have responded, "Let the Holy Spirit go and reconcile man to both of us."

But Adam and Eve had not sinned against Christ nor against a personal Holy Spirit. They had sinned against God, who is the Father. And it was to the Father that man needed to be reconciled (Rom 5:10; 2 Cor 5:18-20; Eph 2:15-16). Therefore God's Son was willing to come and reconcile man to God, his Father. Why? Because "the Father is greater than I."

The subordination of Christ to God is proven beyond question in Paul's epistle to the Corinthians at a time after which Christ had begun ruling as King of kings at God's right hand in heaven. Predicting the end of Christ's reign, Paul said, "Then the end will come, when he hands over the kingdom to God the Father after he has destroyed all dominion, authority and power. For he must reign until he has put all his enemies under his feet. The last enemy to be destroyed is death. For he 'has put everything under his feet.' Now when it says that 'everything' has been put under him, it is clear that this does not include God himself, who put everything under Christ. When he has done this, then the Son himself will be made subject to him who put everything under him, so that God may be all in all" (1 Cor 15:24-28).

If there were ever a time in which it might be said in any sense that Christ's power equals that of his Father, it would be only now in this Christian dispensation, the reign of Christ, after Jesus declared that "All authority in heaven and on earth has been given to me" (Matt 28:18). And even there, it is evident that he who gave him that authority must be greater than he who received it. For according to the quotation from 1 Corinthians 15, the authority given Christ was not given infinitely, without end, but rather indefinitely, for a period of time that shall come to an end, without specifying when that end shall be.

The fact that Christ is now enthroned at God's right hand (Mark 16:19; Luke 22:69; Eph 1:20; 1 Pet 3:22), and not actually taking God's place on God's throne, is proof positive of the subordination of Christ to God. And that's why he could say, "The Father is greater than I."

If Christ were inferior to God only in relation to his own incarnation, and if the Holy Spirit were a coequal person in the one God, a divine person who never became incarnate, one must wonder why Christ never said, "The Holy Spirit is greater than I." Nor did he ever say, "The Father and the Holy Spirit are greater than I." The fact that he never made any such statement about the Holy Spirit must surely tell us something about the non-personal nature of the Holy

Spirit. Only the Father, Jehovah God the Almighty, was, is, and shall ever be greater than the Son, Jesus Christ.

At the very time Christ was and is ruling in heaven, Paul could still declare that the chain of divine authority is as follows: "The head of every man is Christ, and the head of the woman is man, and the head of Christ is God" (1 Cor 11:3). So as man is subordinate to Christ, Christ is subordinate to God. How could Paul say such a thing? It's because Jesus said, "The Father is greater than I." Furthermore, if the Holy Spirit were a personal entity, coequal with God and Christ, surely, as such, the Holy Spirit would at least appear somewhere in that chain of divine authority. But it doesn't. The obvious reason is that the Holy Spirit is the Spirit of God, the Father, to whom Christ was and is subordinate.

Because the Holy Spirit is that part of God by which God is omnipresent, and the means by which God empowered his Son on earth, as well as the apostles and others—regardless what might be meant by "the blasphemy against the (Holy) Spirit," a sin which "will not be forgiven, either in this age or in the age to come" (Matt 12:31-32; Mark 3:28-29; Luke 12:10)—it is understandable that blasphemy against both Christ and man may be forgiven, while blasphemy against the Holy Spirit is blasphemy against God himself, and therefore causes one to be "guilty of an eternal sin." Otherwise, blasphemy against God, who is the Father, would not even be addressed in this discussion concerning blasphemy.

Thus blasphemy against God can be a more serious sin than blasphemy against Christ, because, as Jesus said, "The Father is greater than I."

CHAPTER 43

THE WORD BECAME FLESH

Closely related to those chapters entitled *Origin and Preexistence of Christ* and *Firstborn of All Creation*, this chapter also deals with the nature of that preexistence.

Within the Trinitarian camp there are at least two opposing theories concerning the nature of Christ's preexistence. While their common belief is that the Father, Son, and Holy Spirit are all coequal and coeternal persons in a triune God, they do not all agree on when that "Second Person" became the Son of the "First Person," nor do they agree on the nature of that preexisting "Second Person" prior to his birth via the virgin.

One theory is that the First Person and Second Person have always existed without beginning as Father and Son, a belief often referred to as the "Eternal Sonship" doctrine. But even common logic dictates that for one to be literally a Son, he must of necessity be preceded by the being or person who begot him, as well as by the act of his being begotten. Otherwise their Father-Son relationship would be a figurative relationship that would not literally have them existing as Father and Son.

The opposing theory is that the Second Person preexisted as the eternal personal Word (Gr. *Logos*) of God, and never became God's Son until that *Logos* was born of the Holy Spirit and Mary. "The Word became flesh and made his dwelling among us. We have seen his glory, the glory of the One and Only [Or *the Only Begotten*], who came from the Father" (John 1:14). The idea that the Son of God literally preexisted as the actual *Logos* of God is most incredible indeed; and the idea that the eternal *Logos* literally was conceived in and born of Mary, and literally died on a cross and was entombed for three days, defies all reasonableness. Surely there must be a more logical explanation for the statement under consideration: "The Word became flesh."

In the first place, no one seems to interpret that statement in an absolute literal sense, even though they might believe that the actual *Logos* of God became the actual Son of God. The Son of God on earth, just as any other man, was a distinct personal entity, composed of body (flesh) and spirit. The Scripture did not say that the *Logos* became such a human personal entity, but that it became "flesh." Yet all understand that to be a figure of speech (a synecdoche), speaking of a part (flesh) as though it were the whole (a human being), meaning that the spirit being who already existed became a human being by taking on a fleshly body via the virgin birth, for "a body you prepared for me" (Heb 10:5).

So if we can recognize the statement as being figurative in that way, we should also be able to recognize that the Word of God did not literally become flesh, but that the Son of God, "whose name is called The Word of God" (Rev 19:13, ASV), became a human being and dwelt among us. That, of course, is the more logical conclusion, as we shall see.

The Greek word *Logos* is a mystery to many, and therefore makes the doctrine of the Trinity even more a mystery by teaching that the *Logos* is one of three persons in the Trinity. Therefore, a better understanding of the *Logos* is necessary.

When we think of "word," we usually think of something either written or spoken. But *Logos* goes beyond that to include the reason or logic which underlies the word, whether or not that word is ever actually written or spoken. *The* NIV *Study Bible*, commenting on John 1:1 says, "Greeks used this term not only of the spoken word but also of the unspoken word, the word still in the mind—the reason." Therefore, in its broadest sense, *Logos*, as it pertains to God, could mean God's complete comprehension of all things at once; and that's omniscience, having infinite awareness, understanding and insight. Everything in the infinite mind of God is both reasonable and logical.

But the fact that God's reason or logic is infinite, is no reason to conclude that *ho Logos* (the Word) is a person distinct from the Father, any more than God's infinite and unchanging love is a person distinct from the Father. "Love Divine" is not a personal entity. Nor is the divine Word a personal entity. It is the Word of God.

In a vision John saw the rider on the white horse (Jesus Christ), whose "name is called The Word of God" (Rev 19:13, ASV). When, where, and by whom was Jesus ever called "The Word of God"? It was by John, and by none other, as recorded here and in John 1:1, 14; and 1 John 1:1. Only in these four references in Scripture does the "Word" have reference to the person of Christ, a total of only six times, all by the apostle John, and all toward the close of the First Century. During the first some 60 years of the history of Christ's personal ministry and the church, there is no record of Christ ever being called "the Word," not even by Christ himself. It was not until the latter part of that century, after the Gentiles, especially the Greeks, had become participants in Christianity, and when Greco-Christian theology was being born, that John, by divine inspiration, first made the connection between Christ and the *Logos*, other than the fact that Christ came to declare that word so completely and so authoritatively, as had never before been done.

For centuries Greek philosophers had cherished a certain fascination for *ho logos* (the word). "When they applied it to the universe, they meant the rational principle that governs all things" (*The* NIV *Study Bible*, commenting on John 1:1). It is also defined as "reason that in ancient Greek philosophy is the controlling principle in the universe."[20]

—Webster's Collegiate Dictionary.

Again, "LOGOS, a common term in ancient philosophy and theology. It expresses the idea of an immanent reason in the world . . . . To the Greek mind, which saw in the world a *kosmos* (ordered whole), it was natural to regard the world as the product of reason, and reason as the ruling principle in the world."[13]

—*Encyclopaedia Britannica*, Vol. XIV, p. 250a, under LOGOS.

It was in this philosophical and theological atmosphere that John by inspiration saw a striking likeness between the Greek *Logos* and the *Logos* of God, and could respond somewhat like this: "You're right! The universe is not the result of some spontaneous combustion nor a theoretical big bang, but is rather, as you Greeks say, a product of reason (*Logos*); and it is still that reason which is the ruling principle in the world." What *Logos* could possibly fit that concept better than the *Logos* of Jehovah God? And because Jesus came to declare that word so completely and so authoritatively, John could say in symbolic language, "His name is called The Word of God." It was by God and through Christ (called the Word) that all things were created (1 Cor 8:6).

The apostle Paul had used a similar approach with the Greeks at Athens, when he said, after seeing their inscription, To An Unknown God, "What you worship as something unknown I am going to proclaim to you" (Acts 17:23). Likewise John could say that the *Logos*, to which they attributed the creation and orderly control of the universe, is none other than the *Logos* of God as seen in the teachings of Christ. But to conclude that Christ is literally that eternal *logos*, instead of the Son of God who came to declare that *logos*, is an unreasonable conclusion indeed. Out of all the some 320 occurrences of the *logos* in the NT, 214 of them are translated "word" in the KJV, and only six of these are capitalized and recognized by scholars as references to the personal Christ. Within the remaining 314 occurrences of the *logos* are found statements too numerous to mention that prove that Jesus is not literally the *logos* of God, but is rather the Son of God who came to declare the *logos* of God, agreeing with John that he is "called The Word of God," without his literally being that word. The word was what Jesus spoke, not who he was.

When explaining to his disciples the meaning of the parable of the sower, Jesus referred to the seed as *"ho logos* of the kingdom" (Matt 13:19-23), whether that word would be spoken by himself or by his disciples. In either case it would be the word of God being planted in the hearts of men. According to Luke, Jesus said, "The seed is the *logos* of God" (Luke 8:11). "With many similar parables Jesus spoke the word to them" (Mark 4:33).

Mark 2:2, "And he (Jesus) preached the word to them." Jesus even cast out unclean spirits by the *logos* he spoke (Luke 4:36), not by the *logos* he was.

Luke 5:1, "The people crowded around him (Jesus) and listened to the *logos* of God." They heard what Jesus was speaking, the *logos*.

Luke 10:39 (ASV), Mary "sat at the Lord's feet, and heard his *logos*."

John 2:22, "Then they believed the Scripture and the words that Jesus had spoken." The *logos* is what Jesus spoke, not who he was.

John 12:48, Jesus said, "That very *logos* which I spoke (not the *logos* that I am) will condemn him at the last day." Jesus, who is called "the Word," will be the judge; but God's *logos*, proclaimed by Jesus, will be the basis upon which that judgment will be determined.

John 14:24 (ASV), "The *logos* which ye hear" (not the *logos* you see), "is not mine, but the Father's who sent me."

Acts 12:24 (ASV), "The *logos* of God grew and multiplied," which does not mean that the personal Jesus got bigger and bigger and produced more and more offsprings.

We could go on endlessly pointing out Scripture where *ho logos* is what Jesus spoke, and not who Jesus was. There is no more reason to conclude that Jesus is literally the *logos* of God than there is to conclude that he is a literal door or gate (John 10:7), literal bread (6:35), literal light (9:5), a literal vine (15:1), a literal rock (1 Cor 10:4), a literal lion or root (Rev 5:5), a literal morning star (22:16), or a literal lamb (26 times in the Revelation), etc. Jesus is not literally *ho logos*, but he is the Son of God who spoke the *logos*, and is therefore "called The Word of God."

To conclude that the eternal word of God, God's infinite wisdom, reason and comprehension, his word, is a personal entity distinguished from God himself, is as illogical as it would be to conclude that a man's *logos* is a personal entity distinct from the man it is the word of. It would be hard to imagine that the almighty Jehovah God, the Father, did not have as a part of his being a *logos*, a word, or divine infinite reason. And if Jesus were actually the personal *logos* of God, then by what *logos* did the voice speak from heaven at Jesus' baptism (Matt 3:17) and at his transfiguration (Matt 17:5), "This is my Son, whom I love"? If the *logos* of God had become flesh, then by what *logos* were those words spoken? It had to be by the word of God, the Father, because he called Jesus his beloved Son. Does God have another word by which he speaks, in addition to his word that supposedly became flesh and was baptized in the River Jordan? Does God have one *logos* that became flesh and another *logos* which did not? Inasmuch as the Word that became flesh is a distinct entity, does that Word, like all other personal entities, also have a word that is distinguished from the personal Word which Christ is claimed to be? And have you ever wondered why God did not say, "This is my beloved *Logos*, in whom I am well pleased"?

Jesus prayed, "Father, glorify your name!" Then a voice came from heaven, "I have glorified it, and will glorify it again" (John 12:28). If the word of God had literally become the Son of God on earth, then whose word was declared by the voice out of heaven on this occasion? The only reasonable conclusion is that God, who is the Father, has an infinite *logos* which is not a personal entity distinct from the God it is the word of, just as he has a Spirit which is also not a personal entity distinct from the God it is the Spirit of. But God does have a Son who is a person distinct from the God he is the Son of. It was that Son (called The Word of God) who "became flesh and dwelt among us." He was not literally God's word, but came to declare that word by the message he proclaimed.

We know that the Son of God was "called The Word of God" figuratively, because "you are to give him the name Jesus" (Matt 1:21). And when he was born, Joseph "gave him the name Jesus" (v. 25), fulfilling Isaiah's prophecy that "they will call him Immanuel" (vv. 22-23). So calling Jesus "The Word" was symbolically similar to calling him Immanuel; for his name was Jesus, as we see him called in Matthew 2:1.

CHAPTER 44

LORD

By far the most often used word translated "God" in the OT is *Elohim*, thus translated some 2,362 times. The memorial name by which Israel was to distinguish their God from the many false gods of the Gentiles is the Hebrew name *Yahweh*, which, when appearing with "Lord" in the KJV, is translated "God" (with all capitals) about 300 times, and otherwise translated "Lord" (with all capitals), probably over 6,000 times. Because Jews considered the name "Jehovah," known as the incommunicable name of God, a name too sacred to be spoken aloud by human lips, their Greek translation, the Septuagint (LXX), nearly always substituted the Greek word *Kurios* (Lord) for God's name, *Yahweh*, and its occasional contraction or shortened form, *Yah*, both meaning "the existing one." In the English translations, following the practice of the LXX, *Yahweh* is substituted by Lord (or sometimes God) with all capitals. However, the ASV does not make that substitution, but rather translates *Yahweh* as "Jehovah."

The word "lord" (owner, master or ruler) is not a name, but a title of respect, applied to anyone perceived to be, in some way, of higher rank, dignity or authority, and is translated from several Hebrew and Greek words, primarily *Adon* and *Adonai* (Hebrew) and *Kurios* (Greek). "It thus expresses all grades of dignity, honor, and majesty. It is not always possible to be sure of the sense in which the term is to be taken . . . . *Kurios* is freely used of both the Deity and men."[5]—*International Standard Bible Encyclopedia*, Vol. III, p. 1919a, under "LORD."

The following examples from the ASV illustrate the wide variety of uses of *Adon*, translated *Kurios* in the Greek LXX, and translated "lord" in the English versions: Sarah referred to Abraham as "my lord" (Gen 18:12). Lot called the two angels at Sodom "my lords" (Gen 19:2), but likely did not know at the time that they were angels, but were perceived as strangers to be treated with respect and hospitality. The children of Heth called Abraham "my lord" (Gen 23:6, 11). That is also what Rebekah called Abraham's servant (Gen 24:18), what Rachel called her father Laban (Gen 31:35), what Jacob called his brother Esau (Gen 32:4, 5, 18), and what Joseph's brothers called Joseph (Gen 42:10, 30, 33). The king of Egypt was called "lord" (Gen 40:1); Joseph was made "lord" of all Pharaoh's house (Gen 45:8), and then "lord" over all Egypt (v. 9).

Moses was called "my lord" by Aaron (Exod 32:22), by Joshua (Num 11:28), and by all the Israelites (Num 32:25, 27 and 36:2). Eglon was "lord" of Moab (Judg 3:25). "My lord" is what Jael called Sisera (Judg 4:18), Ruth called Boaz (Ruth 2:13), Hannah called Eli (1 Sam

1:15, 26), and what Gideon, Daniel and Zechariah called angels (Judg 6:13; Dan 10:16-18; and Zech 4:4, 5, 13), etc.

Jehovah God is also called *Adon* some 24 times, translated "Lord" with a capital "L" to show special respect, such as: "Thy males shall appear before the Lord Jehovah" (Exod 23:17; 34:23); "Jehovah your God, he is God of gods, and Lord of lords, the great God" (Deut 10:17); "Jehovah, the Lord of all the earth" (Josh 3:13); "do all the commandments of Jehovah our Lord" (Neh 10:29); etc.

Apparently Christ is likewise called *Adon* prophetically, also translated "Lord" with a capital "L": "Jehovah saith unto my Lord, Sit thou at my right hand" (Ps 110:1); and "the Lord, whom ye seek, will suddenly come to his temple; and the messenger of the covenant, whom ye desire, behold, he cometh" (Mal 3:1).

Jehovah God is also referred to in the OT with the Hebrew word *Adonai*, always translated "Lord" with a capital "L," more than 400 times, a title used in Scripture to refer exclusively to Jehovah God, with the possible exception of a few times when it is directed to angels as representatives of Jehovah God, such as when Abraham bargained with God over the proposed destruction of Sodom (Gen 18:27-32), and when Moses was called from the burning bush (Exod 4:10, 13), etc. But while Christ is called *Adon* possibly twice in the Hebrew OT, he is never called *Adonai*, which is reserved for Jehovah God alone.

Then in both the LXX and the Greek NT, both God and Christ are called *Kurios* (Lord), the Greek translation of both *Adon* and *Adonai*, as well as the Greek substitution of *Yahweh*. Therefore, the fact that *Kurios* represents *Adon*, as well as *Adonai* and *Yahweh*, proves that the title "lord" is not limited to Jehovah God. In fact, the Greek word *kurios* in the NT is translated "lord" 42 times, and "master" 11 times (KJV), when not referring to deity, such as found in the numerous parables taught by Jesus in which the owner or master is called "lord"; a servant (or slave) is said not to be above his lord (Matt 10:24); "Sarah obeyed Abraham, calling him lord" (1 Pet 3:6); etc. Therefore, for Jesus to be called *Kurios* (Lord) no more makes him Jehovah God than Sarah's calling Abraham "lord" makes Abraham Jehovah God.

Returning to the NIV, in the NT both God and Christ are called "Lord" too many times to mention; and yet we are told that there is only one Lord, just as there is only one God: "For even if there are so-called gods, whether in heaven or on earth (as indeed there are many 'gods' and many 'lords'), yet for us there is but one God, the Father, from whom all things came and for whom we live; and there is but one Lord, Jesus Christ, through whom all things came and through whom we live" (1 Cor 8:5-6); and "There is one body and one Spirit—just as you were called to one hope when you were called—one Lord, one faith, one baptism; one God and Father of all, who is over all and through all and in all" (Eph 4:4-6). In both of these passages Christ is clearly and emphatically distinguished from the one God, who is specifically identified as the Father. Yet on numerous other occasions both God and Christ are each called "Lord." How can this be, and yet there be only "one Lord"?

First, we have already seen that *kurios* (when translated from *adon*) can refer to anyone perceived to be, in some manner, of higher rank, dignity or authority. Both God and Christ, as well as Abraham and even Caesar (Acts 25:26), thus qualify to be called *Kurios*. We have also seen that *Kurios* (when translated from *Adonai*) refers uniquely to Jehovah God in a sense in which none other qualifies to be called *Kurios*. But then Jehovah God, identified exclusively as the Father, has the right and authority to empower anyone he chooses, specifically his own divine Son, with all authority in heaven and on earth (which he did, Matt 28:18), to make him King of kings and Lord of lords. Therefore, Peter could say to the multitude of Jews a few days later, "Therefore let all Israel be assured of this: God has made this Jesus, whom you crucified, both Lord and Christ" (Acts 2:36). "Lord and Christ" means that he is God's anointed ruler.

This royal transaction in no way reduces the power, authority and Lordship of God, but merely places God's anointed Son, and no one else, in charge of God's kingdom until all is accomplished. "Then the end will come, when he hands over the kingdom to God the Father" (1 Cor 15:24).

The reason God could make his Son uniquely Lord over his kingdom is that Christ had already proved himself to be faithful to his Father in all things; and God knew that his Son would rule the kingdom just as God himself would have it done. The Father knew that he could give his Son a blank check, and that his Son would never overdraw the account. In this way God can still be Lord, ruling through his Son, who is called the "one Lord" because of his unique position.

God is still the one God; and because of that, he continues to be called "Lord." Therefore Paul could say that to us there is one God, the Father, and one Lord, Jesus Christ, inasmuch as God anointed only his Son to be over his kingdom.

The apparent conclusion is that even though both God and Christ are called "Lord," that in no way proves, as Trinitarians would have us believe, that Christ is Jehovah God. It was God who anointed and empowered Jesus to be the one Lord over his kingdom. Jesus did not anoint himself. He is not the anointer; he is the anointed.

CHAPTER 45

MISCELLANEOUS ARGUMENTS CONSIDERED

I. *THE LORD SAID TO MY LORD:*

The inspired apostle Peter confirmed the obvious distinction between Jehovah and Christ on Pentecost (Acts 2:34-35) by quoting King David as saying, "The LORD (Jehovah) says to my Lord (Christ): 'Sit at my right hand until I make your enemies a footstool for your feet'" (Ps 110:1). It was Jehovah God (one being) speaking to Christ (another being). Then David further added, "The LORD (Jehovah) will extend your (Christ's) mighty scepter from Zion" (v. 2). And "The LORD (Jehovah) has sworn and will not change his mind: 'You (Christ) are a priest forever, in the order of Melchizedek'" (v. 4). Therefore Christ cannot be Jehovah who swore and spoke, but is rather our priest who goes between mankind and Jehovah. Surely none of the Jews on Pentecost got the idea from Peter's sermon that Christ is the Jehovah they had always worshiped, but is rather Jehovah's Son and anointed ruler over God's spiritual kingdom.

This declaration by Jehovah concerning Christ, our priest and king, must be kept in mind when considering other OT Scriptures which are often misused in trying to prove that Christ is literally Jehovah God.

II. *THE LORD IS GOOD:*

Psalm 34:8, "Taste and see that the LORD is good." Peter made reference to Christians who "have tasted that the Lord is good (1 Pet 2:3), causing some today to equate the Lord (possibly Christ) with the LORD (Jehovah), as if it would be impossible for both Christ and Jehovah to be good. The term "Lord" here, as elsewhere, may very well refer to either Christ or Jehovah, inasmuch as both are called "Lord" (see Part I, Chapter 44). Thus both may be said to be good (*chrestos*) without Christ and Jehovah being identical.

When Jesus rebuked the rich young man for calling him "good teacher," (Mark 10:17-18; see Part I, Chapter 36), the "good" under consideration was *agathos*, instead of *chrestos*, as used in 1 Peter 2:3. So Peter does not here contradict Jesus by saying that the Lord is good (*chrestos*), even if Jesus is the Lord being referred to. Both Jehovah and Christ can be *chrestos* (gracious, ASV; kind) without both being *agathos* (good) as was used by the rich young man. Christians have tasted that both Jehovah God and his Son Jesus Christ are good, gracious and kind. But Christ is not Jehovah.

III. *WHO CREATED EVERYTHING?*

Hebrews 1:10-12, borrowing David's acknowledgment to Jehovah

God in Psalm 102:25-27, has God saying to his Son, "In the beginning, O Lord, you laid the foundations of the earth, and the heavens are the work of your hands. They will perish, but you remain; they will all wear out like a garment. You will roll them up like a robe; like a garment they will be changed. But you remain the same, and your years will never end."

Comparing these two passages, it is claimed by some that the Son, to whom the Hebrew writer said God addressed this statement, is therefore identical with the LORD God to whom David addressed similar words, and that therefore Christ must be the Jehovah God of the OT. Such an argument might possibly have credibility, were it not for the fact that Christ was with God in the beginning (John 1:2), and "through him (Christ) all things were made" (v. 3; Col 1:16), Christ being the one to whom God spoke when he said, "Let us make man in our image" (Gen 1:26). And because all things were FROM God, but THROUGH Christ (1 Cor 8:6), it is evident that what David said concerning Jehovah, God could also say concerning Christ, without Christ actually being Jehovah. (See Part I, Chapter 12).

IV. *GOD HAS COME.*

In Zecharias' song at the circumcision of John the baptizer, he prophesied, "Praise be to the Lord, the God of Israel, because he has come and has redeemed his people" (Luke 1:68). This is not calling Christ the God of Israel, as some have supposed. God was coming to save Israel by sending his forerunner (John) to prepare his way, and by sending his Son (Christ) to provide the sacrifice. The very next verse actually tells us how God has come: "He (God) has raised up a horn of salvation for us in the house of his servant David" (v. 69). This "horn" is Christ, from the house of David, not John from the house of Levi. Furthermore, that horn is not God, for it was God who raised up the horn.

One's coming does not always mean literally and bodily in person. Jesus said at the Last Supper, "I will not leave you orphans; I will come to you" (John 14:18). And, "If anyone loves me, he will obey my teaching. My Father will love him, and we will come to him and make our home with him" (v. 23). This cannot have reference to Christ's Second Coming in the final judgment when "He is coming with clouds, and every eye will see him, even those who pierced him" (Rev 1:7); for Jesus continued, saying, "Before long, the world will not see me anymore, but you will see me" (v. 19), because that eminent coming of Christ and his Father would be a spiritual coming through the sending of the Holy Spirit, in which their presence would be spiritually felt and recognized by the disciples.

Therefore, when it is said that the God of Israel came to redeem his people, it does not mean that Christ is that God, but that Christ was sent as God's representative to redeem mankind. Otherwise, Scripture would have Jehovah God the Almighty dying on a cross and entombed for three days. One would hate to think what would happen to the entire creation if Jehovah were to die. It was Christ, not Jehovah, who said, "I was dead, and behold I am alive for ever and ever!" (Rev 1:18).

V. *THE STONE OF STUMBLING:*

In Isaiah 8:14, Jehovah God (v. 13) is called the one who "will be a stone that causes men to stumble and a rock that makes them fall." To both houses of Israel, God was either their sanctuary, their rock of refuge, or else he became to them a stone over which they stumbled. And what God was to Israel, Christ became to us. For the Sovereign LORD (Jehovah) later said: "See, I lay a stone in Zion, a tested stone, a precious cornerstone for a sure foundation" (Isa 28:16), which statement Peter applied to Christ (1 Pet 2:6).

Then in verse 7, Peter borrowed the words of David: "The stone the builders rejected has become the capstone" (Ps 118:22. See also Luke 20:17; Acts 4:11). And in verse 8 he borrowed Isaiah's words: "A stone that causes men to stumble and a rock that makes them fall" (Isa 8:14). Just as Israel had rejected Jehovah God in olden times, they later also rejected Christ.

We know that Peter is not saying that Christ is the Jehovah God of the OT, nor that Jehovah is the rock of which Peter speaks; for it was the Sovereign Jehovah who said, "I lay a stone in Zion." Christ, not Jehovah, was that stone; it was Jehovah who both chose the stone and then laid it. If Christ were Jehovah, we would offer our spiritual sacrifices to Christ. But instead, Peter says that we offer those sacrifices to God through Jesus Christ (v. 5). Christ is not our *ho Theos*, he is our High Priest through whom we reach God.

VI. *THAT ROCK WAS CHRIST:*

Because Paul said concerning the rock from which the Israelites drank in the Wilderness, " . . . that rock was Christ" (1 Cor 10:4), some see Christ as having been a literal and active participant in Israel's OT history, being literally transformed into that rock from which they literally drank. But a close look at this text reveals that Paul is here making a comparison between what happened to those whom God saved out of Egypt, and what might happen to us, since God "has rescued us from the dominion of darkness and brought us into the kingdom of the Son he loves" (Col 1:13). As they passed through the sea (v. 1), we pass through the waters of baptism. They were "baptized into (ASV: unto) Moses in the cloud and in the sea," dedicating themselves to the leadership of Moses, just as in water baptism we dedicate ourselves to the leadership of Christ.

"The manna and the water from the rock are used as figures

representing the spiritual sustenance that God continually provides for his people" (*The* NIV *Study Bible*, on vv. 3-4). The manna from heaven and the supernatural supply of water from the rock supplied their physical needs, just as Christ said, "I am the bread of life. He who comes to me will never go hungry, and he who believes in me will never be thirsty" (John 6:35), thereby supplying all our spiritual needs.

So when Paul said, "That rock was Christ," surely he must have meant that what that rock in the wilderness was to the Israelites, Christ, in a figure, is to us today; except that their rock provided physical sustenance, while our rock (Christ) provides spiritual sustenance. Therefore we should not conclude that Christ was back there in the Wilderness in the form of a literal rock being struck by Moses' rod and spewing out water.

VII. *THE LORD OUR RIGHTEOUSNESS:*

"The days are coming, declares the LORD, when I will raise up to David [Or *up from David's line*] a righteous Branch, a King who will reign wisely and do what is just and right in the land . . . . This is the name he will be called: The LORD Our Righteousness" (Jer 23:5-6).

Assuming that this prediction has reference to the promised Messiah, Jesus Christ, some have argued that Christ is here therefore called Jehovah, making Christ the Jehovah of the OT. First, it is Jehovah (one person) who would raise up this King (another person); and therefore Christ cannot be Jehovah raising up himself.

Second, we have seen that in the case of Immanuel (Isa 7:14), such expressions as "will call his name" or "his name shall be called," in prophetic language, often signifies some declaration found in the meaning of the name, rather than its being the actual proper name of some given person—such as Immanuel, fulfilled in the birth of Isaiah's son, Maher-Shalal-Hash-Baz (Isa 8:3), and centuries later in the birth of Jesus (Matt 1:21). The message in the name Immanuel (God with us), by which neither of them were ever actually called, was that their births as prophesied would mean that God was coming to man's rescue in both cases. (See Part I, Chapter 7).

The message in the name of the King raised up by Jehovah (Jer 23:6) would be that this King (Jesus) would rule in the righteousness of Jehovah, and not that he would actually be named Jehovah nor "Jehovah Our Righteousness." In the NT Jesus is never once called Jehovah. However, God did say about his Son, "Your throne, O God, will last for ever and ever [ASV fn. Or, *Thy throne is God for & c.*], and righteousness will be the scepter of your kingdom. You have loved righteousness and hated wickedness; therefore God, your God, has set you above your companions by anointing you with the oil of joy" (Heb 1:8-9).

Third, the translation of this passage has been the object of much controversy. A translation of the LXX has: "This is his name, which the Lord shall call him, Josedec among the prophets." The KJV has: "this is the name whereby he shall be called, THE LORD OUR RIGHTEOUSNESS."

Adam Clarke's Commentary lists a number of renderings: Dahler has: "And this is the name by which he shall be called; The Lord, *the Author of our happiness.*" Dr. Blayney translates thus: "And this is the name by which Jehovah shall call him, OUR RIGHTEOUSNESS." And again, "Literally, according to the Hebrew idiom—'And this is his name by which Jehovah shall call, Our Righteousness.'"[3]

To these, Adam Clarke, an obvious Trinitarian, adds, "I believe *Jesus* to be *Jehovah*; but I doubt much whether this text calls him so. No doctrine so vitally important should be rested on an interpretation so dubious and unsupported by the text."[3]

VIII. *CALLING ON THE NAME OF THE LORD:*

"And everyone who calls on the name of the LORD (Jehovah) will be saved" (Joel 2:32). When Peter quoted this prophecy on Pentecost, he used the word "Lord," not Jehovah (Acts 2:21), a title that can, and many times does apply to both God and Christ, without suggesting that Christ is the God (Jehovah) who made the prediction. But Paul specifically identifies "the name of our Lord Jesus Christ" as being the name on which we call (1 Cor 1:2), without suggesting that Christ is Jehovah.

We have learned from the Great Commission (Matt 28:19) that the "name" of the Father, Son and Holy Spirit is singular (See Part I, Chapter 29). The Son inherited his name from his Father. (See Heb 1:4). And inasmuch as both are one in agreement and purpose, Christ having come to do, not his own will, but the will of his Father (John 6:38), and because Jesus said, "I have come in my Father's name" (John 5:43), and "No one comes to the Father except through me" (John 14:6), therefore to call upon the name of either of the two is to call upon the name of both, without suggesting in any way that Christ is Jehovah. Reason dictates that Christ cannot be both Jehovah and the Son of Jehovah.

IX. *THE ONLY BEGOTTEN GOD:*

According to the NIV (John 1:18), "No one has ever seen God, but God the One and Only, who is at the Father's side, has made him known." The NIV translators, realizing the uncertainty of that rendition for "the One and Only," gave two alternate readings in the footnotes: [Or *the Only Begotten*] and [Some manuscripts *but the only* (or *only begotten*) Son]. Out of the seven Greek texts represented in Berry's *Interlinear Literal Translation* (ILT), only Tregelles has "the only begotten God" instead of "the only begotten Son." The English translations are greatly divided because of the difference in the ancient manuscripts as to whether it should be the *only begotten Son* or *the only begotten God* who has revealed the invisible God to man. Can there be two Gods, one begotten and one unbegotten?

According to the NWT footnote, as explained in its *Explanation of the Symbols* (pp. 28-30), ancient manuscripts having "God" include the Sinaitic (4th Century), the Vatican (4th Century), Codex Ephraemi (5th Century), and Peshitta Syriac (5th Century). And those having "Son" include the Alexandrine (5th Century), Latin Vulgate, and Curetonian Syriac (older than the Peshitta Syriac).

Several translations having such renditions as *the only Son, the only begotten Son, God's only Son, his only Son*, are found in the KJV, NKJV, ASV, RSV, JB, NEB, NCE, and Weymouth. Among these, the RSV, NEB, ASV, and Weymouth recognize in footnotes that the word *God* instead of *Son* could be intended. Some having *God*, instead of *Son*, in the actual text include the NASB, NWT (god), and Barclay, each of which recognizes in footnotes that the MSS differ.

Then several translations include in some form both *Son* and *God* in the text: Beck has, "the only Son who is God." The AB has, "the only unique Son, the only-begotten God." The TCNT has, "God the only Son." The TEV has, "The only One, who is the same as God." Goodspeed combines the two possible renditions in a logical and understandable way by translating *Theos* as *divine* rather than *God*: "It is the divine Only Son." This accords with his translation of John 1:1, "and the Word was divine." Only in this sense can Weymouth's footnote, "the only-born God," and the AB text, "the only-begotten God," be reasonably understood.

Barclay has, "It is the unique one, He who is God." But then commenting on his statement, "Jesus is *God*," in his *Daily Bible Study Series*, Barclay says—

Here we have the very same form of expression as we had in the first verse of the chapter. This does not mean that Jesus is identical with God; it does mean that in mind and character and being Jesus is one with God. In this case it might be better if we thought of it as meaning that Jesus is divine. To see him is to see what God is.

(See Part I, Ch. 15, *And the Word Was God*).

Such a questionable Greek text as here considered should never be used to support the doctrine of the Trinity, supposing that Christ, God's only begotten Son, is the one God (*ho Theos*) he is the Son of. For there is no other God, in the absolute sense, than the Father. And even though "No one has ever seen God," God's one and only begotten divine Son, "who is at the Father's side, has made him known" (v. 18). There are not two Gods in the absolute sense (*ho Theos*), one the Father and the other his Son. Neither is there a visible God whom man has seen, and an invisible God whom no man has ever seen. Rather, the one invisible God is the Father of his divine Son, Jesus Christ.

X. *ICE-WATER-STEAM*:

The relationship between the Father, Son, and Holy Spirit is often pictured by both Trinitarians and Unitarians as being like ice, water, and steam, in that those three distinctions are simply three different manifestations of the same substance—two parts hydrogen and one part oxygen (H_2O). They see the one God as a divine substance or being who manifests himself in three different forms as Father, Son, and Holy Spirit.

This could be an excellent illustration of their concept of the Trinity, but is no proof whatsoever that such a Trinity of persons actually exists. It does nothing to prove that the one God is composed of three persons. And surely they would not insist that those three supposed persons can change forms back and forth, as do ice, water and steam.

XI. *THIS DAY HAVE I BEGOTTEN THEE*:

King David declared, "Jehovah said unto me, Thou art my Son; This day have I begotten thee" (Ps 2:7, ASV). Even though Jehovah's statement is made to David, it is universally accepted as a messianic prophecy, based on its divine application to Christ on at least three occasions in the NT.

Reading Acts 13:33 (ASV), one might get the idea that "this day" has reference to the day Christ was raised from the dead, and that "begotten thee" has reference to his being begotten from the dead. As we learned earlier in Part I, Chapter 8, *Using Prophetic Expressions*, it would not be strange for this statement from the Psalms to be applied to Christ's resurrection, inasmuch as at least part of the statement seems to somewhat fit the occasion of the resurrection, paralleling Paul's declaration that Christ is "the firstborn from among the dead" (Col 1:18). However, that approach would have Jesus becoming God's Son by being begotten (raised) from the dead, rather than being begotten before all things, or being born of Mary.

A much better explanation may be found in Romans 1:4, concerning God's Son, who "was declared with power to be the Son of God by his resurrection from the dead." The resurrection did not cause Jesus to become God's Son; but rather, it proved that Jesus was who he said he was, that he was already God's Son, without signifying when, where, or how that birth took place.

Proving the superiority of Christ over the angels, that declaration from Psalm 2:7 is again quoted in Hebrews 1:5. If "this day" (ASV), or "today" (NIV) had reference to any point in existence AFTER angels were created by Christ, then the implication would be that Christ was not the Son of God when he created the angels. And if he became God's Son AFTER the angels were created, the implication is that Christ was not superior to the angels until he was begotten by God. So "this day have I begotten thee" must refer to a point in existence prior to the angels, so that Christ would always be their superior. His Sonship, not just his existence, made him superior to the angels.

In Hebrews 5:5, the Psalm 2:7 statement is again applied to Christ as our high priest. Not that Christ appointed himself—which he could have done if he had been God—but that it was God, the one who had said to him, "You are my Son; today I have become your Father [Or *have begotten you*]." Again, we are not told when "this day I have begotten thee" occurred.

Whether or not there was any such thing as a "day" (as we know a day) back there in eternity when the Son was begotten by God, we cannot tell; nor does it matter. By "accommodative language" God has let us know that there was a point in God's existence that he did not have a Son to love and to be loved by, but that God produced a Son, who, in the course of time, would eventually become our high priest, and be the firstborn among us as his brethren in the family of God forever and ever. Surely "this day" did not refer to Christmas as we know Christmas.

PART II

GOD AND HIS SPIRIT

CHAPTER 1

THE HOLY SPIRIT PERSONIFIED

Thus far we have dealt primarily with God and his Son, with only an occasional reference to God's Spirit, as when the Trinity was being discussed. We now turn more specifically to the study of God and his Spirit.

A great host of exegetic literary compositions have flooded the theological market in which most treatises concerning the Holy Spirit begin with something which conveys the following idea: "In order to properly understand the significance and work of the Holy Spirit, it is absolutely necessary that one first understand the personal nature of the Holy Spirit, that is, that the Holy Spirit is a person, a distinct personal entity." Such is then usually followed by a series of stereotyped arguments intended to support that man-invented premise, even though the Scriptures never specifically say so. In this composition concerning *God and His Spirit*, all such arguments will be thoroughly considered and shown to be invalid. And we contend that there is absolutely nothing which the Holy Spirit can do, does, or should do, as a personal entity distinct from the Father, which the Father cannot or does not do by means of his omnipotent and omnipresent Spirit which ever proceeds from the Father. There is absolutely no spiritual, psychological, theological, nor just plain logical advantage in perceiving the Holy Spirit to be an individual personal entity separate from the Father and his Son.

We have already established that the one God is the Father; and therefore when we speak of the Spirit of God, we are speaking of the Spirit of the Father. We have also established that Jehovah is the name of that one God; and therefore when we speak of the Spirit of God, we are speaking of the Spirit of Jehovah. And since Jehovah God's title is "Lord," when we speak of the Spirit of God, we are speaking of the Spirit of the Lord.

Furthermore, that Spirit is characterized as being holy, thus "the Holy Spirit of God" (Eph 4:30). So when we speak of the Holy Spirit, we are speaking of the Spirit of the Father, Jehovah God, the Lord Almighty. It is the Spirit of God, never the Spirit of the Godhead, nor the Spirit of the Trinity.

God's Spirit is that Spirit which "goes out from the Father" (John 15:26), or "which proceedeth from the Father" (ASV), "the Spirit of truth" (same verse); that Spirit of God which in the beginning "was hovering over the waters" (Gen 1:2), and the means by which God is omnipresent (Ps 139:7-10); the power by which God inspired the prophets of old (2 Pet 1:21), and by which Mary became pregnant (Matt 1:18; Luke 1:35); that Spirit which descended upon Jesus when he was baptized (Luke 3:22), the Spirit with which God anointed Jesus (Acts 10:38), and with which the apostles were baptized on Pentecost (Acts 1:5; 2:4); that power which was promised to the apostles (Acts 1:8), and which Jesus called "the Counselor" (John 14:26; or "the Comforter," ASV); that Spirit which indwells God's children (Rom 8:11), and by which we cry, "*Abba, Father*" (v. 15).

The relationship between God and his Spirit should be no mystery: Just as I have a son, a separate and distinct person from myself, Jehovah God likewise has a Son, a separate and distinct person from God himself, namely Jesus Christ, the Son of God. And just as I have a spirit which is NOT a separate person from myself as my son is a separate person, but is rather an essential and composite part of the person I am, Jehovah God likewise has a Spirit which is NOT a separate person from the Father as Christ is a separate person from the Father, but is rather an essential and composite part of the person which the Father is.

In the sense that my spirit may be called a person (a synecdoche: speaking of a part as the whole), just as my body likewise may be called a person (also a synecdoche), so may the Spirit of God be thought of as a person, God being that person it is the Spirit of. This comparison should not seem strange to anyone who realizes that man is made in God's image, even though man does not possess God's divine nature. But when theologians, particularly Trinitarians, speak of the Spirit of God as being a person, they are not using a figure of speech. They mean that the Holy Spirit is a separate personal entity from the Father, just as Christ is a separate person from the Father, a separation existing between God and his Spirit which does not exist between me and my spirit.

When a man's spirit separates from his body, that man dies. We learn that at death, "the dust returns to the ground it came from, and the spirit returns to God who gave it" (Eccl 12:7), the word "death" itself meaning primarily a separation. And it is common knowledge that "the body without the spirit is dead" (Jas 2:26). Therefore, it would seem from this fact that if God's Spirit were separated from God himself in such a way as to actually be a separate person from God, then God, being left without his Spirit, would, as some have supposed, be dead. Or does God have another Spirit by which he lives, in addition to his Holy Spirit, which is supposedly a personal entity separate from the Father? And if so, is that Spirit also holy? Does God have two Holy Spirits, one of which is a personal entity distinct from God himself, and another Holy Spirit which is not such a distinct person? And if the Holy

Spirit is such a distinct personal entity, just as the Father and Son are distinct persons, does the Holy Spirit likewise have a Spirit, just as the Father, Son, and every other person who has ever lived, each has a spirit? And if so, then is the Spirit of the Holy Spirit also a distinct person from the Holy Spirit it is the Spirit of, just as the Spirit of the Father is supposedly a distinct person? Or is the Holy Spirit the only person who has ever existed who does not have a spirit?

Let it not be concluded that the Holy Spirit does not have a spirit because the Holy Spirit IS a spirit; for remember that God also is spirit, or a spirit (John 4:24), and yet God has a Spirit, the Holy Spirit. Therefore, if two Spirit persons of the supposed Trinity have Spirits, then why would not the supposed Third Person also have a Spirit? And we could go on and on endlessly asking such unanswerable questions. But one can see that the doctrine of the Trinity is indeed a mystery, creating more questions than it is ever able to answer. That doctrine insists that the Holy Spirit is a coequal person with the Father and the Son, which cannot be true if the Holy Spirit is the Spirit of the Father.

In Scripture, even when God's Spirit is personified as "the Counselor" (John 15:26), it is described as that "which proceedeth from the Father" (ASV). The Greek word for "proceedeth" is a verb in the durative present tense, which means that God's Spirit is something which continually keeps on proceeding from the Father, which would not be said if the Holy Spirit were an eternally separate person from the Father.

Not all scholars and theologians have accepted the theory that the Holy Spirit is a distinct personal entity. Joseph Henry Thayer, world renowned Greek lexicographer, tells us that—

> In some pass, the Holy Spirit is rhetorically represented as a person: Mt 28:19; Jn 14:16 sq. 26; 15:26; 16:13-15 (in which pass. fr. Jn. the personification was suggested by the fact that the Holy Spirit was about to assume with the apostles the place of a person, namely of Christ . . .)[7]
> —*Greek-English Lexicon of the NT*, p. 522b, under "*pneuma*."

We will show beyond any reasonable doubt that Thayer is entirely correct in concluding that the Holy Spirit is "rhetorically represented as a person" in the Great Commission and at the Last Supper, calling it a "personification."

Personification is a figure of speech in which personal qualities are attributed to a thing or an idea which are not persons. For example: The United States is a country, a nation, not a person. But when that "posterized" Uncle Sam, dressed in red, white and blue, from his billboard habitat points a finger straight at you and says, "Uncle Sam wants you!" meaning that the U.S. government needs you for its military, that's personification. That's letting the U.S. government speak as though it were a person. We speak of the U.S.A. as "it" (or possibly sometimes "she"), but never as "he." But when the U.S. government becomes personified in Uncle Sam, "it" becomes "he." That's personification.

Or when the spirit of Christmas, the spirit of love, sharing and giving, comes all wrapped up in red trimmed in white as a corpulent jolly old gentleman with white hair and beard, descending once each year from his workshop site at the North Pole, spreading cheer and happiness throughout the world, that's personification. We speak of the spirit of Christmas as "it," never as "he." But when the spirit of Christmas is personified in Santa Claus, "it" becomes "he." That's personification.

Or when Paul speaks of love as though love were a person who is patient, kind, does not envy nor boast, is not proud, rude nor self-seeking, not easily angered, keeps no record of wrongs, does not delight in evil but rejoices with the truth, and always protects, trusts, hopes and preserves (1 Cor 13), that's personification. Weymouth's *NT in Modern Speech* in this passage consistently refers to love with the feminine pronoun "she"; and the KJV has "seeketh not her own" in verse 5. That's love personified in the person of anyone who loves.

So it is when Jesus tells his apostles that he is going away; but that after he leaves them, God will send his Holy Spirit as a Comforter, a Counsel for their defense, the power of God to do for them what Jesus as a person had been doing for them. That's personification of the Spirit of God. In the Greek language, the Spirit is always spoken of as "it" or "itself"; but when the Spirit is personified as a "Comforter" (a Counsel for the defense of the apostles in the presence of "the powers that be") then "it" or "itself" becomes "he" or "himself." That's personification.

Therefore we can unhesitatingly say with Thayer that here, "the Holy Spirit is rhetorically represented as a person . . . . the personification (being) suggested by the fact that the Holy Spirit was about to assume with the apostles the place of a person, namely of Christ," in the role of a Comforter. The Holy Spirit was the power they needed, and that power they received.

The Spirit of God appears some 105 times in the OT, and some 269 times in the NT, a total of 374 times, if we include a number of references where the identity of the Spirit as being identical with the Holy Spirit might be questionable. The word "spirit" (Gr. *pneuma*) in Scripture is always neuter gender. There is no masculine form for *pneuma*. And when "spirit" is preceded by the definite article, "the" Spirit, which is in a majority of those references, "the" is always in the neuter gender, as is required by the Greek language when modifying a neuter noun. Furthermore, when the Spirit is characterized by the adjective "Holy," that adjective is also always in the neuter gender.

These truths are without exception in the Greek text.

So when personal qualities or characteristics are attributed to the neuter Holy Spirit, the obvious implication points to one of two possible conclusions: (1) those personal qualities belong to the person from whom the Spirit proceeds, namely God, the Father; or else (2) the Spirit is being personified as though the Spirit is the person causing something to happen; when in reality, God is the person causing such to happen by means of his omnipotent and omnipresent Spirit. Such personal qualities attributed to the Holy Spirit in no way prove that the Holy Spirit is a personal entity, distinct from the person of the Father.

Without the two references mentioned by Thayer (the Great Commission and the Last Supper), it is most likely that no one would have ever gotten the idea that the Holy Spirit is a person, distinct from the Father, any more than they would conclude that love is a distinct personal entity, based on love's appearing in the feminine gender, having personal qualities, and being referred to with a feminine possessive pronoun (1 Cor 13:5, see Greek). For this reason Thayer singles out those two references from all the 374 references to the Spirit, and says that in these two cases the Spirit is personified; for these two references, especially the Last Supper, are the ones most often used in attempts to prove the person of the Holy Spirit. There are several other occasions where the Holy Spirit apparently is personified; but because no personal pronouns are there used in the Greek text, those occasions, without the two named by Thayer, likely would never have been used to prove personal entity.

But when the Last Supper conversations are examined in the Greek text, it is clear that the masculine pronouns never modify the neuter Holy Spirit, but rather always modify the masculine Counselor, which is here endowed with personal qualities as an advocate, teacher, witness, convicter, guide, speaker, hearer, announcer, glorifier, etc., and therefore receives the masculine articles, masculine adjectives and masculine pronouns.

But the neuter Holy Spirit which appears in these texts as parenthetical explanations of that which is being personified in the masculine Counselor, and which we are here setting off in brackets [ ], is not being pictured as having any personal qualities in its unpersonified state, and therefore receives the neuter articles, neuter adjectives and neuter pronouns. These quotations are from the ASV, except that the genders are sometimes changed to correspond with the Greek text. For clarity's sake, we are here placing the Greek MASCULINE genders in ALL CAPITALS, and are placing the Greek *neuter* genders in *italic* type, all from the Gospel of John, as follows:

14:16-17 MASC: "And I will pray the Father, and he shall give you ANOTHER COMFORTER, that HE (the Comforter) may be with you forever,

Neut: [even *the Spirit* of truth: *which* the world cannot receive; for it (the world) beholdeth *it* (the Spirit) not, neither knoweth *it*; for *it* (the Spirit) abideth with you, and shall be in you]."

14:26 MASC: "But THE COMFORTER,

Neut: [even *the Holy Spirit, which* the Father will send in my name],

MASC: HE (the Comforter) shall teach you all things . . . ."

15:26 MASC: "But when THE COMFORTER is come, WHOM I will send unto you from the Father,

Neut: [even *the Spirit* of truth, *which* proceedeth from the Father],

MASC: HE (the Comforter) shall bear witness of me."

16:7-8 MASC: " . . . for if I go not away, THE COMFORTER will not come unto you; but if I go, I will send HIM unto you. And HE, when HE is come, will convict the world . ."

16:13-15 MASC: "Howbeit when HE (the Comforter),

Neut: [*the Spirit* of truth],

MASC: is come, HE (the Comforter) shall guide you into all the truth; for HE shall not speak from HIMSELF: but what things soever HE shall hear, these shall HE speak: and HE shall declare unto you the things that are to come. HE shall glorify me: for HE shall take of mine, and shall declare it unto you. All things whatsoever the Father hath are mine: therefore said I, that HE (the Comforter) taketh of mine, and shall declare it unto you."

This conversation by Jesus, on this singular occasion, the Last Supper, and recorded only by John, is the only time God's Spirit is ever personified with masculine pronouns in the Greek text. And technically speaking, it is the Comforter, the personification of the Spirit, not the Spirit in its unpersonified state, which receives the masculine pronouns. Therefore it is unreasonable to suggest that the Holy Spirit must be a distinct personal entity to be referred to as "he," "him," "himself" or "whom"; for it is the Comforter, not the unpersonified Spirit, which is identified by those masculine pronouns. Otherwise, the Holy Spirit is always addressed with neuter adjectives and pronouns.

The other mentioned occasion, the Great Commission, also listed by Thayer as containing a personification of the Spirit when referring to the "name of the Holy Spirit," as though the Spirit were a personal entity with a name, is discussed at length in Part I, Chapter 29, *The Name of the Father, Son, and Holy Spirit*, and needs no further comments here, except to emphasize Thayer's added possible explanation for "the name of the Holy Spirit" as being a personification of the Holy Spirit.

Some may wonder how the Holy Spirit can be God's means of omnipresence, while the Spirit is spoken of as *coming upon* or *being poured out upon* someone, being sent to the apostles from the Father, or descending like a dove and lighting upon Jesus. All such expressions seem to necessitate the Spirit's moving from one given place to another, which would not be literal omnipresence. For if God's Spirit were to move from one place to another, it would no longer be present in the place where the Spirit moved from. But it is possible for God's Spirit to be literally omnipresent in one sense, and yet be pictured as moving from one place to another in a different sense.

In reality, it is not actually God's Spirit moving from place to place, but rather God's Spirit causing something to happen in one place as distinguished from another place, or to some people as distinguished from others. More specifically, if an apostle or prophet received from God's Spirit a power which he did not previously possess, that power was what came upon him, or was poured out upon him. But because God, by his omnipotent and omnipresent Spirit, gave such powers to men, those transactions were spoken of as the Spirit *coming upon* or *being poured out upon* the recipients. God's Spirit is neither a dove descending on Jesus at his baptism (Matt 3:16), nor cloven tongues like fire resting on each of the apostles on Pentecost (Acts 2:3). God's Spirit is invisible. So God gave in each case, a visible sign to demonstrate the coming of God's power on each, powers which would subsequently be demonstrated by their performing many miracles, from speaking in languages they had never learned, to even raising the dead. It was that power, not the omnipresent Spirit, that took up residence where it had not previously been in that particular context.

So God, by his Spirit, can be omnipresent, giving powers to whom God wills, without the Spirit being a distinct personal entity.

CHAPTER 2

"HE" OR "IT"

Many people have argued that because the Spirit in the English translations is often referred to as "he" or "himself," the Holy Spirit therefore must be a person. As was pointed out in Part II, Ch. 1, each of the 374 occurrences of the Spirit in the Greek text is always neuter gender, as well as its definite article "the," and its modifying adjective "Holy." And there are no exceptions. However, this fact in itself is not presented as proof that the Holy Spirit cannot therefore be a person. Persons may appear in the neuter gender (which grammarians call an exception) such as *paidion* (a young child, a little boy, a little girl), especially where the greater significance is age rather than gender (see Matt 14:21; Mark 7:28; *et al*). But because so many have placed such great significance to the masculine pronouns referring to the Spirit in the English translations, it is therefore compelling that we point out the reasons for such exceptional translations of Greek neuter pronouns with English personal masculine pronouns.

In such passages as Romans 8:16, 26, we see, as in the KJV, Goodspeed, the NWT, and Berry's *Interlinear Literal Translation*, reference to "the Spirit itself" (Gr. *auto*, neuter gender), while others, including the ASV, RSV, NIV, NASB, the NCE, etc., translate the passage in the masculine gender, "the Spirit himself," as though it were *autos*, the Greek masculine form of the reflective pronoun. But the pronoun is not *autos*, it is *auto* (neuter), and should be translated "itself," unless it is a proven fact that the Holy Spirit is a masculine personal entity. Only with such compelling proof would such a breach in literal translating be justified. This uncertainty has therefore produced the conflicting renditions of the pronouns referring to the Spirit.

An interesting reversal takes place in Acts 8:16, where the KJV, which refers to the Holy Spirit in Romans 8:16, 26 as "itself," here refers to the Holy Spirit thus: "For as yet HE was fallen upon none of them." While on the other hand, the ASV and RSV, which refer to the Holy Spirit in Romans 8:16, 26 as "himself," here refer to the Holy Spirit thus: "For as yet IT was fallen upon none of them." What an interesting and perplexing reversal on the part of these translators. The obvious conclusion is that these various translations of the pronouns are not the result of variations in the Greek text, but are due rather to the various theological perceptions in the minds of the translators. The fact is that there is nothing compelling in the Greek text that requires these pronouns in either case to be translated in the masculine gender. Every pronoun modifying the Spirit in Scripture may be translated in the neuter gender without violating any rule of Greek grammar, if indeed the Holy Spirit is not a personal entity.

Such a rendering might violate someone's Trinitarian theology, but would not affect one's scholastic stature in the NT Greek language, in the absence of proof that the Holy Spirit is a person. Had no one concluded from the Last Supper or the Great Commission that the Holy Spirit is a person, then all pronouns referring to the Spirit would no doubt have been translated in the neuter gender, as with man's spirit in Eccl 12:7 (*auto*, it; see LXX and NIV), never in the masculine gender; always "it" or "itself," and never "he" nor "himself." Therefore it should never be argued that the Holy Spirit is a distinct person because of the masculine pronouns in the translations; for the only reason they are sometimes rendered as masculine is because some translators believe that the Holy Spirit is a person, or because they believe that "he" would be more acceptable to those who believe the doctrine of the Trinity, and on whom the translators depend to purchase their publications.

Conflicting renditions are also even found in some places where no pronoun actually exists in the Greek text; as in Num 11:17, where Jehovah said to Moses, "I will take of the Spirit which is upon thee, and will put IT upon them," the 70 men of the elders of Israel (ASV, KJV, the NCE and the AB). See also verse 25.

Surely this Spirit that was upon Moses was the Holy Spirit, empowering Moses as a prophet. And when part of that Spirit was then put upon the 70, they also prophesied. So here, several English translations call the Holy Spirit "it," even though the pronoun does not appear at this point in the LXX.

In Judges 6:34, "the Spirit of Jehovah came upon Gideon" (ASV), where a marginal note adds, "Heb. *Clothed itself with*," meaning that the Holy Spirit clothed ITSELF with Gideon. (See also 2 Chr 24:20).

Again, "his Spirit, IT hath gathered them" (Isa 34:16, ASV). And John 1:32, "John bare witness, saying, I have beheld the Spirit descending as a dove out of heaven; and IT abode upon him" (ASV). "It" cannot refer to the dove because "dove" is feminine gender. But the Spirit is neuter gender; therefore "it" must refer to the Spirit.

These passages cannot be used to prove that the Holy Spirit either is or is not a person. But they do show the nonpersonal nature of the Holy Spirit in the minds of those who would thus refer to the Holy Spirit as "it" rather than "he." Surely no one would think that God would take part of a person, (the Holy Spirit) from Moses and put that part of a person on the Seventy. Consequently, inasmuch as only a few, if any of the translators hold strictly to a literal translation of those neuter pronouns referring to the Spirit, they cannot be used as a conclusive guide as to the gender of the Holy Spirit, whether "he" or "it."

Even if it could be established from the Greek text that those Holy Spirit neuter pronouns should be translated "he" or "him," such masculine pronouns could refer to the Father, who manifests himself and his power through his omnipresent Spirit, instead of referring to the Holy Spirit as a distinct personal entity apart from the Father.

It is a misapplication of context to interpret the Spirit in 1 Cor 12:11 as being the "he" who "determines" and "gives" the spiritual gifts mentioned in that chapter. It is God, as distinguished from the Spirit and the Lord, who "works all of them (the different gifts, services and workings) in all men" (vv. 4-6). "To each one the manifestation of the Spirit is given for the common good" (v. 7). The Spirit is not the giver, but is rather the means through which God gives those said gifts. God gives all those gifts "through the Spirit," or "by means of the same Spirit" (v.8). "All these (gifts) are the work of one and the same Spirit" (v. 11), the Spirit of God, who "works all of them in all men" (v. 6). "And he (God, who works all of them in all men) gives them (the spiritual gifts) to each one, just as he (God) determines" (v. 11).

Furthermore, no masculine Greek pronoun occurs in verse 11; but if there were such, surely it would refer back to the masculine *Theos* (God, v. 6) and not to the neuter *pneuma* (Spirit, v. 11).

In this same context, it is God (not the Holy Spirit) who gives the special gifts (v. 24), and makes the special appointments (v. 28); therefore "he" (v. 11) must refer to God, and not to the Holy Spirit.

CHAPTER 3

THE HOLY SPIRIT AS A WITNESS

One of the several ways in which the Holy Spirit is personified is as a witness. And because the Holy Spirit is portrayed as a witness, many have erroneously concluded that the Holy Spirit must therefore be a personal entity, believing that only a person can be a witness or testify. Several Scriptures portray the Holy Spirit as a witness, which necessitates one of two possible conclusions: (1) Either the Holy Spirit is a personal entity, or (2) the Holy Spirit, proceeding from the Father, is personified as a witness, usually because of something which the Holy Spirit has empowered some person to testify.

One who testifies is called a witness. So when the Holy Spirit empowered the prophets, apostles and others to give testimony from God or about God, that made them witnesses of God or for God. But it also made the Holy Spirit a witness figuratively, inasmuch as the Holy Spirit was the means or power by which God in heaven transmitted his message or testimony to a select few persons on earth. And when such persons on earth received that testimony from God by the power of the Holy Spirit, those persons also became known as witnesses.

As we have already seen in the previous chapters, in Jesus' conversation at the Last Supper, Jesus promised that the Father would send his Holy Spirit which "goes out from the Father," as a Counselor, and said, "he will testify about me" (John 15:26), and "will teach you all things . . . ." (John 14:26). Thus it was by the power of God's omnipotent and omnipresent Spirit that God's message or testimony was transmitted into the minds of the apostles of Christ, just as it had been done for centuries with the prophets in OT times; "For prophecy never had its origin in the will of man, but men spoke from God as they were carried along by the Holy Spirit" (2 Pet 1:21). In this way the Holy Spirit delivered testimony from God to mankind.

But those prophets and apostles were never to keep that testimony unto themselves; they, too, were to become witnesses by declaring that God-given and Holy-Spirit-confirmed testimony to the whole world. Just before Christ ascended back to heaven from whence he had come, and just after giving to his chosen apostles that Great Commission to be transmitted to the whole world, he told his apostles, "You are witnesses of these things" (Luke 24:48; see also John 15:27). And furthermore, "you will receive power when the Holy Spirit comes on you; and you will be my witnesses in Jerusalem, and in all Judea and Samaria, and to the ends of the earth" (Acts 1:8). That power they received just ten days later on the day of Pentecost (Acts 2:4) and began testifying that same day (vv. 14-40).

Shortly thereafter the apostles informed the Jewish Council, "We are witnesses of these things, and so is the Holy Spirit, whom [or, which] God has given to those who obey him" (Acts 5:32), without specifying whether it was given to the obedient individually, collectively or representatively. By this the apostles no doubt meant that not only were they witnesses of that which they proclaimed, but that the power by which "many miraculous signs and wonders (were performed) among the people" (Acts 5:12) was the Holy Spirit thus confirming the testimony they proclaimed. For they "went out and preached everywhere, and the Lord worked with them and confirmed his word by the signs that accompanied it" (Mark 16:20). The Hebrew writer spoke of "This salvation, which was first announced by the Lord, was confirmed to us by those who heard him. God also testified to it by signs, wonders and various miracles, and gifts of the Holy Spirit distributed according to his (God's) will" (Heb 2:3-4). It is God who is here declared to have borne witness with the apostles, but he did so by the power of his Spirit working in the apostles. Such does not require the Holy Spirit to be a distinct personal entity. God himself could handle it through the power of his omnipresent Spirit.

Does "bearing witness" necessarily mean that everything which bears witness is a personal entity? Consider 1 John 5:6-9, "This is the one who came by water and blood—Jesus Christ. He did not come by water only, but by water and blood. And it is the Spirit who [that, ASV] testifies, because the Spirit is the truth. For there are three that testify: the Spirit, the water and the blood; and the three are in agreement. We accept man's testimony, but God's testimony is greater." Thus the witness of God is here identified as the witness of "the Spirit, the water and the blood." If the witness of the Spirit proves that the Holy Spirit is a person, then why does the witness of the water and the blood not also prove that both the water and the blood are likewise personal entities whose witness agrees with the supposed personal Holy Spirit? It is obvious that the Spirit, the water and the blood are here personified as witnesses who all bear testimony to corroborate the fact that Jesus is the Son of God, and that life is in the Son. That popular old adage is certainly true here: "That which proves too much, proves nothing"; for if the Spirit is a person, so are the water and the blood also persons, based on the same mode of reasoning.

Again, in Romans 8:16 we find that "The Spirit himself [Gr. *auto*, itself] testifies with our spirit that we are God's children." Here we have not just one witness, which under the Law would not have been sufficient to establish a thing as being true (Deut 17:6; Matt 18:16), but instead we have two witnesses, (1) the Holy Spirit, and (2) our spirit. If the witness of the Holy Spirit makes the Holy Spirit a distinct personal entity, then likewise the witness of my spirit also makes my spirit a distinct personal entity.

Some would have this passage say that the Spirit bears witness TO our spirit, instead of WITH our spirit; but the Greek word here means "to testify or bear witness together with another; to add testimony," as in Romans 9:1 (ASV), "I lie not, my conscience bearing witness with me in the Holy Spirit." (See also 2:15). Does this statement mean that Paul's witness-bearing conscience is a distinct personal entity from Paul himself? Not all such witnesses are persons. Therefore it is no more necessary that the Holy Spirit be a person than it would be necessary that Paul's conscience be a person.

Divine Scripture reveals at least twenty-one things, other than persons, which are said to be witnesses, including those already mentioned: (1) the Holy Spirit, (2) man's spirit, (3) the water, (4) the blood, and (5) man's conscience. Others include (See ASV): (6) Abraham's seven ewe lambs given to Abimelech (Gen 21:30); (7) Laban's and Jacob's heap of stones (Gen 31:48); (8) their stone pillar (v. 52); (9) a neighbor's goods, specifically a torn animal (Exod 22:13); (10) the song of Moses (Deut 31:19,21); (11) the book of the Law (v. 26); (12) the altar of Reuben, Gad and Manasseh (Josh 22:27, 28, 34); (13) Joshua's stone of witness (Josh 24:27); (14) Job's wrinkles (Job 16:8 KJV); (15) Job's leanness (same verse); (16) the eye that saw Job (Job 29:11); (17) the show of the countenance of ruined Jerusalem and fallen Judah (Isa 3:9); (18) a prophetic altar to Jehovah in the midst of Egypt (Isa 19:19-20); (19) a prophetic pillar to Jehovah at Egypt's border (same reference); (20) the works of Jesus (John 5:36; 10:25); and (21) the law (Rom 3:21).

All these are said to have witnessed or to be witnesses. They are not persons, but each had a message, a testimony, a witness, a story to tell. Not all witnesses are persons. So it is with the Holy Spirit. All these are personified as though they are seated on the witness stand, having sworn to tell the truth, the whole truth, and nothing but the truth. As sworn witnesses, they tell their story.

Every time the apostles performed a sign, wonder or miracle by the power of God's Spirit, that supernatural event was testimony by the Spirit to the world that the message they spoke was from God. In that way the Holy Spirit corroborated (was witness to) the testimony of the apostles.

The Holy Spirit is God's power which educated, informed, empowered and enabled the apostles to fulfill that commission given them by Christ. God could do that by the power of his omnipotent and omnipresent Spirit. And God's Spirit didn't have to be a distinct personal entity for God to do so.

CHAPTER 4

THE HOLY SPIRIT SPEAKS

Closely related to the previous chapter, *The Holy Spirit as a Witness*, we now further consider the Holy Spirit personified as one who speaks, in addition to those passages already considered, wherein the Holy Spirit is personified as a witness. In the 105 OT Spirit references (see Appendix E) the Spirit of God is never called a witness, nor one who testifies. Nor is it ever said in the OT that the Spirit speaks, except where David said, "The Spirit of the LORD spoke through me; his (Jehovah's) word was on my tongue" (2 Sam 23:2), showing that it was actually David doing the speaking, but doing so by the power of the Spirit. It is not said that the Spirit spoke *to* David, but *through* David. Or when Zedekiah asked, "Which way did the spirit from the LORD go when he went from me to speak to you?" (1 Kgs 22:24; 2 Chr 18:23), in which case Zedekiah sarcastically spoke in a fit of anger, not actually believing that Jehovah had spoken to the prophet Micaiah, and therefore not a statement by divine inspiration. And lest someone may think that the masculine pronoun "he" in these two passages in the NIV refers to the Spirit instead of Jehovah, it should be pointed out that the pronoun is not even found in the original text (See LXX, ASV, *et al*). To say that the Spirit speaks was not OT terminology, even though it is known that God did speak through prophets who were moved by the Holy Spirit (2 Pet 1:21). It was by the power of God's Spirit that God's message reached those prophets, whether (1) by the Spirit literally speaking the words of God into the hearing ears of the prophets, as one person would speak to another, or (2) by God supernaturally implanting his message into the minds of the prophets by the power of his Spirit, or (3) by God, through the power of his Spirit, putting his words directly into the mouths of the prophets as implied in the case of Balaam, when he said to Balak, "Must I not speak what the LORD puts in my mouth?" (Num 23:12). In none of these three possible scenarios must it be concluded that the Holy Spirit is a distinct personal entity because the Spirit speaks.

While the OT nowhere says that the Spirit speaks, except in the two aforementioned references to David and Zedekiah, the following two references in the NT, referring to the OT, do so: "The Holy Spirit spoke long ago through the mouth of David concerning Judas" (Ac 1:16); and "Well spake the Holy Spirit through Isaiah the prophet unto your fathers, saying, . . ." (Acts 28:25, ASV). And if the Holy Spirit spoke through David and Isaiah, it is only reasonable that the same may be said concerning other prophets as well. But the obvious implication is that God, by the power of his Spirit, used those prophets, and speifically the mouths of the prophets, to do the actual speaking.

Therefore it may be said that the prophets' mouths spoke, or that the prophets themselves spoke, or that the Holy Spirit spoke, or that God spoke, none of which would require that the Holy Spirit, any more than the prophet's mouth, be a personal entity. God could empower his prophets without requiring the aid or medium of another personal entity to do so.

Several passages in the NT do present the Holy Spirit as a speaker: "It will not be you speaking, but the Spirit of your Father speaking through you" (Matt 10:20; Mark 13:11); "he (the Counselor) will not speak on his own; he will speak only what he hears" (John 16:13); "The Spirit told Philip, 'Go to the chariot and stay near it'" (Acts 8:29); "While Peter was still thinking about the vision, the Spirit said to him" (Ac 10:19); the Holy Spirit said, "Set apart for me Barnabas and Saul for the work to which I have called them" (Ac 13:2); the prophet Agabus said, "The Holy Spirit says," (Ac 21:11); "the Spirit clearly says that in later times some will abandon the faith" (1 Tim 4:1); "Yes," says the Spirit, "they will rest from their labor" (Rev 14:13); and finally, "The Spirit and the bride say, 'Come!'" (Rev 22:17). And if the Spirit is a person because the Spirit says, "Come," then by the same reasoning the bride, which is the church (Eph 5:22-32), would likewise be a person. If the church, which is not a person, may be personified, so also the Spirit, which is not a distinct person, may likewise be personified.

Only these few passages, none of which are found in the OT, out of all the 374 Spirit passages, have the Spirit speaking as though the Holy Spirit were a person. But is it the Spirit as a distinct entity doing the speaking? Or is it God speaking through or by the power of his Spirit? The latter is obvious from the host of other passages, such as, "When the Spirit rested on them, they prophesied" (Num 11:25, 26); "I wish that all the LORD's people were prophets, and that the LORD would put his Spirit on them" (v. 29); *et al.*

By far the most used phrase in the OT to show the power and inspiration of God in the prophets is "the Spirit of God came upon" them. The Spirit of God "came upon" Balaam (Num 24:2), Othniel (Jud 3:10), Gideon (6:34), Jephthah (11:29), Samson (14:6), Saul (1 Sam 10:6, 10; 11:6; 19:23), David (16:13), the messengers of Saul (19:20), Amasai (1 Chr 12:18), Azariah (2 Chr 15:1), Jahaziel (20:14), Zechariah (24:20), *et al.* In such cases it doesn't say that the Spirit spoke to those prophets, but that the Spirit came upon them, indicating that the Spirit empowered them, as it did the apostles on Pentecost (Ac 2:4), to say the proper thing as they were "carried along by the Holy Spirit" (2 Pet 1:21). A parallel to "came upon" is the idea of God pouring out his Spirit upon certain ones (ASV). "Behold, I will pour out my Spirit upon you," which is then explained as, "I will make known my words unto you" (Pr 1:23. See also Isa 32:15; 44:3; Ezek 39:29; and Joel 2:28, 29, a prophecy fulfilled in Ac 2:17-18 and 10:45).

Even if every Spirit passage had said that the Spirit speaks, it would not necessarily mean that the Spirit does so as one person speaks to another. The idea is that God, by the power of his Spirit, conveyed his message into the minds and/or mouths of certain persons, especially apostles and prophets.

Furthermore, there are numerous things which are not persons, that are said to speak, without making them persons. In such figures of speech, nonperson things become personified. The following (according to the ASV) is a list of nonperson things, in addition to the Holy Spirit, that speak: Feet speak (Prov 6:13), the sea speaks (Isa 23:4), a horn speaks (Dan 7:11), righteousness speaks (Rom 10:6), exhortation speaks (Heb 12:5), the blood of sprinkling speaks (Heb 12:24), the tongue speaks (Ps 35:28; 119:172), lips speak (1 Pet 3:10), and the mouth speaks (Ps 37:30; Prov 8:7; Dan 7:8, 20; Isa 9:17; Matt 12:34; Luke 6:45; Rev 13:5), none of which are persons.

Usually it is a person who speaks, but may be said to do so by means of things that are not distinct persons: by his lips, his tongue, his mouth. But when it is actually said that lips, tongues or mouths speak, that's personifying those parts of a person's anatomy which are used when that person speaks, specifically one's lips, tongue or mouth. God has spoken by the mouths of all his holy prophets. By the power of God's Spirit, whether that Spirit is a distinct person from the Father, or if it is the Spirit of God which ever proceeds from the Father and by which God is omnipotently omnipresent, the result is the same. Holy men of God spoke as they were being moved by the Holy Spirit.

Figuratively, anything that conveys a message, even though not a person, may be said to speak. So it is with the Spirit of God. Because God conveys his message by the power of his Spirit, it may be said that the Spirit speaks, without suggesting that the Spirit is a person.

If the Holy Spirit literally speaks, as one person speaks to another, it would seem that there would be a host of Scriptures that say so. Yet the vast majority of the 374 Spirit passages present the Spirit as "coming upon" or "being poured out upon" a person, or a person being "filled with the Holy Spirit," each of which points toward influence and empowerment, not personality. The idea of one person being poured out upon another person, or one person being baptized in or with another person (Mark 1:8; Ac 1:5), is unthinkable. But the idea of God overwhelming some person with the power and influence of his Spirit perfectly accords with the idea that the Spirit "came upon," or "came mightily upon," or "was poured out upon" that person. This concept makes understandable God's statement that, "I will take of the Spirit that is on you (Moses) and put the Spirit on them" (Num 11:17). "Then the LORD came down in the cloud . . . and he took of the Spirit that was on him and put the Spirit on the seventy elders. When the Spirit rested on them, they prophesied" (11:25). Nothing is said about the Spirit speaking to the seventy, but instead, it was put upon them, empowering them with the gift of prophecy. To take part of a person that was on Moses and put that part of a person on the seventy would be unthinkable. But to do so with the power of prophecy which was upon Moses is completely understandable. That's theology simplified.

Then finally, if the Holy Spirit as a person speaks, one would think that someone would at least occasionally speak in return to the Holy Spirit, as man speaks to both God and Christ. But nowhere in the 4,000 years of Bible history, nor in the 374 Spirit passages, did anyone ever speak to the Holy Spirit; nor was anyone ever told or encouraged to do so. Both God and Christ, on occasions far too numerous to mention, spoke to one another as one person speaks to another person. But never did either of them ever speak to the Holy Spirit. Doesn't that seem strange, if the Holy Spirit is a coequal person with God and Christ in the Godhead as claimed by Trinitarians? This should definitely tell us something about the nonpersonal nature of the Holy Spirit as compared with God and Christ. So it should never be said that the Holy Spirit must be a personal entity because the Spirit speaks.

Surely angels must be considered as distinct personal entities. And God used such angels to deliver certain messages in both the OT and NT. However, the apostles were baptized with the Holy Spirit on Pentecost (Acts 1:5, 8 and 2:1-4), which would teach them all things, would remind them of everything Jesus had said to them (John 14:26), would testify about Jesus (15:26), and would guide them into all truth (16:13). If the Holy Spirit were a distinct personal entity abiding with or in the apostles, teaching them ALL things, and guiding them into ALL truth, it would seem that there would be no need for the presence of angels delivering messages to, and performing miracles for the apostles. A personal Holy Spirit could handle any situation.

However, it was an angel, not the Holy Spirit, which opened the prison doors for the apostles, and said, "Go, stand in the temple courts, and tell the people the full message of this new life" (Acts 5:19-20). See also where Peter was again delivered from prison by an angel of the Lord (Acts 12:7-10). If the apostle Paul were guided and counseled by an abiding personal Holy Spirit, why was it an angel, and not the Holy Spirit, who spoke to Paul a message in the night when shipwrecked? (Acts 27:23-24).

Furthermore, the Revelation of Jesus Christ to the apostle John was delivered by an angel, not by a personal Holy Spirit (Rev 1:1). However, that message did contain "what the Spirit says to the churches" (Rev 2:7, et al). Therefore, even though the apostles were guided by revelations from God's Spirit, and empowered by that Spirit to perform miracles, sometimes those revelations were made to appear more personal by the medium of angels from the Lord. Such probably would not have been done if the Holy Spirit in the apostles had been perceived to be a personal messenger from God, as were angels. But instead, the Father sent those messages by the power of his Holy Spirit in the apostles, sometimes using angels to make the message or event more personal.

If the Holy Spirit were a personal entity appearing at Jesus' baptism in the likeness of a dove, and on Pentecost in the likeness of flames of fire, why not appear as a person as did the angels?

CHAPTER 5

THE MIND OF THE SPIRIT

It is claimed by some that the Holy Spirit is a personal entity, based on their belief that the Spirit has a mind, which is indeed a characteristic of personality. In support of this idea, the main (if not the only) Scripture appealed to is the statement made by Paul in Romans 8:27, "He who searches our hearts knows the mind of the Spirit." This statement is only a portion of the larger declaration of verses 26 and 27, a text over which even the most learned scholars, including translators, are divided. The entire statement will be discussed in our next chapter, *The Intercession of the Spirit.* We shall here show how "the mind of the Spirit" has been grossly misinterpreted and misapplied by separating it from the greater text of the entire 8th chapter of Romans, apparently by those seeking desperately to prove that the Holy Spirit is a personal entity.

First, who is it that "searches the hearts"? We know that God has the power to search hearts, otherwise God would not be omniscient. The thoughts of our minds and the intents of our hearts cannot be held secret from God. The biblical heart (Gr. *kardia*) is regarded as the seat of feeling, impulse, affection and desire, the inner and mental frame, the center and seat of spiritual life, the conscience. God knows man from the inside out. "God knows your hearts" (Luke 16:15). "God is greater than our hearts, and he knows everything" (1 John 3:20).

But inasmuch as God anointed Christ "with the Holy Spirit and power" (Ac 10:38), and exalted him "far above all rule and authority, power and dominion" (Eph 1:21), Christ likewise knows the heart of every person. "Knowing their thoughts, Jesus said . . ." (Matt 9:4; 12:25; see also Luke 11:17). And "Jesus knew in his spirit that this is what they were thinking in their hearts" (Mark 2:8). "Jesus knew what they were thinking" (Luke 6:8); "He did not need man's testimony about man, for he knew what was in a man" (John 2:25). Jesus' disciples prayed, "Lord, you know everyone's heart. Show us which of these two you have chosen" (Acts 1:24), a statement which could have been directed to either God or Christ. But knowing that it was Christ who chose the original apostles, they no doubt looked toward him to choose the replacement for Judas, inasmuch as Christ had been given all authority.

The NT pictures Christ as the one who searches the hearts, more than it thus pictures God. And rightly so, for it is Christ who is our only mediator between God and man (1 Tim 2:5), and the one who makes intercession to God on our behalf. "Christ Jesus, who died—more than that, who was raised to life—is at the right hand of God and is also interceding for us" (Rom 8:34). For Christ to be able to successfully intercede for us as our mediator at the right hand of God, he must be able to search our hearts, and to relay even those innermost feelings, desires and concerns to his Father on the throne. Not that the Father doesn't have the power to know our concerns; but God chose that all mankind must come to him, for whatever purpose, through his Son.

So it is Christ who searches our hearts and knows what is the mind of the Spirit. To conclude that Christ searches the mind of the Holy Spirit, and that the Holy Spirit therefore has a mind, and is therefore a personal entity, misses the whole point altogether. But if "the mind of the Spirit" does not mean that the Holy Spirit has a mind, then what does it mean?

The "mind" here is from the Greek word *phronema*, which is defined as frame of thought, mind, will, purpose or inclination; while the heart generally has to do more with feeling, impulse, affection or desire. So one's mind would include his thoughts and his will; his will to do evil or to do good; his will to follow the flesh or to follow the Spirit.

The first part of this text in Romans, chapter 8, deals with two contrasting classes of people: those who walk after the flesh, and those who walk after the Spirit (v. 4). "Those who live according to the sinful nature have their minds set on what that nature desires; but those who live in accordance with the Spirit have their minds set on what the Spirit desires" (v. 5). "The mind of sinful man is death, but the mind controlled by the Spirit is life and peace" (v. 6); "the sinful mind [Or *the mind set on the flesh*] is hostile to God" (v. 7).

So it is clear that the text is not talking about the Holy Spirit's mind; it is talking about the mind of man, whether it be a mind that follows after, and is concerned with the flesh, fulfilling the desires of the flesh, or if it is a mind that follows after and is concerned with the Spirit, fulfilling the desires of the Spirit. In either case, it is the mind of man, described as the mind of the flesh or the mind of the Spirit, depending on each individual person as to which kind of mind would control his life. It is not saying that the flesh is a distinct personal entity because it has a mind, nor that the Spirit (whether God's Spirit or man's spirit) is a distinct personal entity because it has a mind. That's not the subject at all. It's talking about the mind of man, whether the mind of the flesh or the mind of the Spirit. We here use the capital "S" for Spirit, not because of the Greek text; for the original text was written in all capitals. But we try to capitalize the one unique Spirit of God, just as we capitalize the one unique Son of God. And here we are not concerned with making the distinction between the Spirit of God, and the spirit of man when it is led by or filled with the Spirit of God. In either case, with or without the capital "S," neither the spirit of man nor the Spirit of God is a distinct personal entity.

"The mind of the Spirit" (v. 6, ASV) is the literal translation of the

Greek text, "*to phronema tou pneumatos,*" the exact same Greek phrase as found in verse 27, where he who searches the hearts knows what is "the mind of the Spirit." In order for Christ to make intercession for us, it is imperative that he know whether our mind is the mind of the flesh or the mind of the Spirit. Christ can properly make that judgment because he searches our hearts, he knows the mind of the Spirit when he sees one, and then makes intercession to God accordingly.

"He that searcheth the hearts knoweth what is the mind of the Spirit, because he maketh intercession for the saints" (v. 27, ASV) "He" who makes intercession in this statement is not the Spirit, but rather Christ, the one who searches the hearts, the one who knows if our mind is the mind of the Spirit, and the one who makes intercession to God for us (v. 34). The NIV, in place of "he maketh intercession," has, "the Spirit intercedes," which is not a translation, but is rather an interpolation, inserting "the Spirit" where it does not occur in the Greek text, and changing the meaning entirely without justification. Verse 26 does speak of the intercession of the Spirit, which will be discussed at length under that heading. But the simple and most logical explanation herein given for "the mind of the Spirit" should help immensely in understanding the intercession of the Spirit. So the theology-simplified conclusion is that Romans 8:27 does not prove that the Holy Spirit is a person with a mind.

CHAPTER 6

INTERCESSION OF THE SPIRIT

The fact that Romans 8:26-27 has been so variously interpreted, and the fact that it is used in support of so many conflicting ideas and doctrines, suggest to us that surely it must be somewhat toward the top of the list of difficult passages in the Bible. A "difficult passage" may be described as one which, on the surface, and in the light of certain prevalent concepts, seems to be saying something which apparently contradicts the general idea often expressed elsewhere in Scripture. Looking at this passage we can agree with the apostle Peter who said of Paul, "His letters contain some things that are hard to understand" (2 Pet 3:16). However, since the words used by Paul were inspired by the Holy Spirit, we would not question the wisdom of the use thereof, but rather try our best to understand them.

But one should be very careful not to base any doctrine, such as the intercession of the Holy Spirit, on a passage so singular and so controversial as Romans 8:26-27. Only here is the claim made by some that the Holy Spirit, in addition to Christ, personally intercedes for man, and is therefore necessarily a personal intercessor, just as Christ is, even though verse 26 refers to the Spirit "itself" (Gr. *auto*, the impersonal neuter gender), and does so without specifying whether it is the spirit of man, the Spirit of God, or both, which helps our infirmity and makes intercession for us.

The text under consideration (vv. 26 and 27) is found in the ASV as follows (except that the reflective pronoun referring to the Spirit is changed to conform to the Greek text, as in the KJV): "And in like manner the Spirit also helpeth our infirmity: for we know not how to pray as we ought; but the Spirit *itself* maketh intercession for us with groanings which cannot be uttered; and he that searcheth the hearts knoweth what is the mind of the Spirit, because he maketh intercession for the saints according to the will of God." We have already established in the previous chapter that he who searches the hearts and makes intercession for the saints in verse 27 is Christ Jesus, as confirmed by verse 34. So that brings us to the identity of the intercessor in verse 26.

The word "also" is significant in this text, and should be considered. "The Spirit also helpeth" (v. 26). "Also" means, in addition to some other help already mentioned, namely "hope" (vv. 24-25). We are saved in hope; and hope produces patience while we await the redemption of our body (v. 23). So "in like manner the Spirit also (in addition to our hope, and the patience produced by hope) helpeth our infirmity."

Another "also" is found in verse 34, which some have removed from its immediate context in such a way as to place Christ in somewhat of a second-rate position in the matter of intercession. They claim that verse 34 is saying that in addition to the Holy Spirit making intercession (v. 26), Christ also makes intercession (v. 34). But such an association of the two ignores the immediate context of verse 34, where it says that Christ, who is at the right hand of God, also makes intercession for us. Not in addition to the Holy Spirit making intercession, but in addition to his being at the right hand of God. The message of verse 34 is that Christ not only died but was also raised; and not only was raised, but he is also at the right hand of God. And he is not just at the right hand of God (there to forget about the saints he left behind), but he is also making intercession for us.

There is a tendency, especially in the present-day charismata, to exalt the Holy Spirit to a position equal to, or possibly even above that of Christ, even to the point of worshiping the Holy Spirit in song and otherwise, even though there is absolutely no biblical record of the Holy Spirit ever being worshiped in any manner by anyone, and no instructions for anyone to ever do so. And to do so is completely without any Scriptural precedence or authority whatsoever.

Unfortunately, many seem to have come to think in terms of the dispensation of Christ as being that short period of time while Jesus was on earth, or even more specifically that three-year period of his personal ministry. Then after his ascension and the coming of the Holy Spirit on Pentecost, we are now supposedly in the dispensation of the Holy Spirit, an age in which the Holy Spirit is viewed as a personal entity, distinct from both the Father and the Son, just as the Son is a distinct person from the Father, a Spirit who supposedly takes up his personal residence in the Christian, supernaturally motivating, moving and controlling the Christian's life, making his decisions for him, interpreting Scripture for him, and praying for him, even to the point of serving as a personal intercessor between the Christian and God. That's why they sing and pray to the Spirit, praise and worship the Spirit, even though such was never done in all the 4,000 years of Bible history, and is never mentioned anywhere in the 374 Spirit passages. Such a concept tends to dethrone Christ by giving to the Holy Spirit the role of divine personal intercessor.

Making the Holy Spirit a personal intercessor with Christ suggests that Christ does not have all power, and is not able to handle the job by himself. It is not denied that the Holy Spirit, as the Spirit of God, is the power by which Christ is able to do all that he does, including making intercession for us, and can therefore, by personification, be said to intercede. But remember that it is Christ, not the Holy Spirit, who is at God's right hand making intercession for us, while it is by the power of God's Spirit that Christ is able to search our hearts.

We have only one mediator between God and man, the man Jesus

Christ (1 Tim 2:5). A mediator is "one who intervenes between two, either in order to make or restore peace and friendship, or to form a compact, or for ratifying a covenant; a *medium of communication, arbitrator*," and one who "does not belong to one party but to two or more, Gal 3:20."[7]—Thayer's *Greek-English Lexicon*, p. 401a. Only Christ, who is both the Son of God and the Son of man, thus qualifies.

There are two main functions of a mediator between God and man: The first is atonement, offering the necessary sacrifice. That has already been accomplished for the Christian Dispensation. It was offered once, never to be offered again. "We have been made holy through the sacrifice of the body of Jesus Christ once for all" (Heb 10:10), never to be repeated. "When this priest (Christ) had offered for all time one sacrifice for sin, he sat down at the right hand of God" (v. 12). "Because by one sacrifice he has made perfect forever those who are being made holy" (v. 14).

But what is Christ now doing there at God's right hand as our mediator? He is performing the only other function required of our mediator; that is, pleading to God on our behalf. That's the only function of our one mediator that continues. As Lord and King, Christ has other functions. But as priest, only intercession continues. To intercede is "*to go to* or *meet a person*, esp. *for the purpose of conversation, consultation*, or *supplication . . . to pray, intreat*."[7]

—Thayer's *Greek-English Lexicon*, p. 219a.

Or to "plead the cause of."[21]

—*The Analytical Greek Lexicon*, Harper & Brothers.

"Therefore he is able to save completely those who come to God through him, because he always lives to intercede for them" (Heb 7:25). The noun form for "intercession" is used of prayer to God, where food "is consecrated by the word of God and *prayer*" (1 Tim 4:5). And "I urge, then, first of all, that requests, prayers, *intercession* and thanksgiving be made for everyone" (1 Tim 2:1). So when we pray to God through Christ, we, in a sense, intercede to God on behalf of those for whom we pray. But because we cannot search man's heart, we cannot intercede directly to God, but must direct our intercessions through Christ who can, and who is the only one who knows our hearts, and is therefore our only personal and divine intercessor, just as he is our only mediator.

If the Holy Spirit personally makes intercessions for us, to whom does he intercede? Does the Holy Spirit intercede to God through Christ? Or do we have two coequal personal divine intercessors? The answer is found in the priesthood of Christ. The function of intercessor is reserved exclusively for priesthood. The reason Christians can pray (intercede) in behalf of others is that all Christians are priests (Rev 1:6; 5:10; 1 Pet 2:5); they have the ministry of intercession, but in a very limited sense, not to be compared with Christ, our only high priest. Only Christ, not even the Holy Spirit, qualifies for that position. There is not the slightest indication that the Holy Spirit is now, ever has been, or ever will be a priest, much less our high priest, to make intercession for us. "Fix your thoughts on Jesus, the apostle and high priest whom we confess" (Heb 3:1).

Furthermore, in addition to the fact that Jesus is our only high priest, he is the only person qualified to be so. "For this reason he had to be made like his brethren in every way, in order that he might become a merciful and faithful high priest in service to God, and that he might make atonement for the sins of the people. Because he himself suffered when he was tempted, he is able to help those who are being tempted" (Heb 2:17-18). The Holy Spirit never became a man, never suffered, was never tempted and therefore does not qualify to be our personal intercessor.

"Therefore, since we have a great high priest who has gone through the heavens [Or *gone into heaven*], Jesus the Son of God, let us hold firmly to the faith we profess. For we do not have a high priest who is unable to sympathize with our weaknesses (same as in Rom 8:26, 'the Spirit helps us in our weakness'), but we have one who has been tempted in every way, just as we are—yet was without sin" (Heb 4:14-15). Again, the Holy Spirit just doesn't qualify as a personal high priest to make intercession for us. Only Jesus could say, "Been there; done that!"

"The point of what we are saying is this: We do have such a high priest, who sat down at the right hand of the throne of the Majesty in heaven" (Heb 8:1). But what is Jesus doing there? For sure, he is not offering sacrifice in the form of his own blood, for that was done once for all. Instead, he is doing the only other thing that a mediator, who is a high priest, has to do; he is making intercession for men. "He always lives to intercede for them" (Heb 7:25). Such was never said of the Holy Spirit.

Then how can "the Spirit itself" be said to "make intercession for us," if the Spirit is not our personal intercessor? There are at least two possible answers, neither of which requires that the Holy Spirit be a distinct personal entity: First, this activity by the Holy Spirit may be understood in the same sense as the Holy Spirit's part in begetting Jesus in the virgin. Mary "was found to be with child through the Holy Spirit" (Or "child of the Holy Spirit," Matt 1:18, ASV), making Jesus the child of the supposed Third Person of the supposed Trinity, if indeed the Holy Spirit were a personal entity. But if Jesus, as a man, is the Son of God, then he had to become such by the power (not the person) of the Holy Spirit, or else the Holy Spirit would be Jesus' personal Father. Otherwise Jesus would be begotten by proxy, by a Third Person, the Holy Spirit, which would be a denial that Christ is the actual and literal Son of God the Father.

Anyone who can understand Matthew 1:18 should be able to understand Romans 8:26. For just as God in heaven could become the personal Father of Jesus here on earth by the power (not the person) of the Holy Spirit, likewise Jesus in heaven can be mediator for us here on earth by the power (not the person) of that same Holy Spirit. And remember that if "beareth witness" in verses 16 and 26 means that the Holy Spirit is a person, then that same action, "beareth witness," in verse 16 should be used likewise to prove that my spirit (which bears witness with God's Spirit) is a separate person from me.

In this first explanation of the intercession of the Spirit, the power of God is personified as a person who intercedes for man, while in reality the Spirit is not WHO intercedes, but rather HOW Christ intercedes; that is, by the power of God's Spirit. The passage may be interpreted thus: In addition to the other considerations mentioned before, including the hope which keeps us waiting patiently, the Spirit of God—not the person, but the power given Jesus to enable him to effectively search our hearts and intercede for us, in addition to such things as bearing witness with our spirit (v. 16)—keeps on helping our weaknesses, one of which Paul then proceeds to explain; that is, we neither know what is best for us, nor what God wants us to have; but Christ, by the power of God's Spirit, keeps on making intercession for us, not with the groans of the Holy Spirit, nor the groans of Christ, but our own groans, our deep feelings and intense anxieties within our oppressed and burdened hearts—not some ecstatic utterance that cannot be understood, but which cannot even be uttered, cannot be expressed in articulate language. But by the power of God's Spirit, Christ knows our desires, our needs and our deep longings, and therefore can plead our cause before God's throne. Christ, by the power of God's Spirit, knows whether we are led by the flesh or by the Spirit, knows for whom to intercede, and does so according to God's foreordained plan. That explanation makes the intercession of the Spirit understandable without the Holy Spirit being the person doing the interceding.

However, there is still another most plausible explanation, stated by Joseph Henry Thayer in his *Greek-English Lexicon*, under *pneuma*, as follows:

> (*The Spirit intercedes with groanings inexpressible*) in Rom 8:26 means, as the whole context shows, nothing other than this: 'although we have no very definite conception of what we desire, and cannot state it in fit language in our prayer but only disclose it by inarticulate groanings, yet God receives these groanings as acceptable prayers inasmuch as they come from a soul full of the Holy Spirit.'[7]

—p. 522b.

The mind of the Spirit is determined by what is in one's heart. And just as the Spirit bears witness with our spirit (v. 16), without making the Holy Spirit a person, any more than it makes my spirit a person, so our spirit, being influenced by, and filled with God's Spirit, not with the desires of the flesh, is able to communicate to God through Christ our deep longings and intense desires, our spirits filled with God's Spirit interceding on behalf of our souls, without requiring either our spirit or God's Spirit to be a distinct personal entity.

Because the mind of the Spirit is man's spirit when filled with God's Spirit, no distinction is made in this text between man's spirit and God's Spirit. Our spirit, bearing witness with, and being led by God's Spirit, conveys without articulate utterances the deep yearnings of our heart. And Christ, by the power of God's Spirit to search our hearts, reads the message loud and clear. That's "intercession of the Spirit," whether it is man's spirit influenced by God's Spirit, or God's Spirit influencing man's spirit, or both. In either case, whether the spirit of man or the Spirit of God, neither spirit needs to be a distinct personal entity.

CHAPTER 7

PERSON? OR MERE INFLUENCE?

Someone—it has not been determined who nor when—evidently determined that if the Holy Spirit is not a distinct personal entity, it necessarily has to be no more than a "mere influence," as though there were no other possible category by which the Holy Spirit may be identified. That two-category either/or concept has since been promoted by almost all Trinitarians, and by any others who may possibly attempt to promote the personal-entity concept of the Spirit. They state that the works and characteristics of the Holy Spirit cannot be attributed to a "mere influence," a statement to which we heartily agree; but some explanation is in order.

A study of the Holy Spirit reveals that it can be, and is, far more than a mere influence. First of all, it is the Spirit of God, a composite part of God himself, just as my spirit is a composite part of me, and without which I would not be a complete person. The designation itself, "the Spirit of God," should be enough within itself to tell us that the Spirit is a part of the person it is the Spirit of. But for the benefit of those who are not able to discern the significance of that implication, we proceed further: Jehovah God the Father, the person (not the Trinity, and not the Godhead), would not be a complete person without his Spirit. The omnipresent Spirit of God is God's means by which God is omnipresent. That's why God's presence and his Spirit are used interchangeably, such as in Psalm 139:7-10, where David, speaking to Jehovah, said, "Where can I go from your Spirit? Where can I flee from your presence? If I go up to the heavens, you are there; if I make my bed in the depths, you are there. If I rise on the wings of the dawn, if I settle on the far side of the sea, even there your hand will guide me, your right hand will hold me fast."

Here, God, God's presence, and God's Spirit are used interchangeably because, even though God is in heaven in a sense in which he is nowhere else (see Part I, Ch. 24, *The Omnipresence of God*), yet by his Spirit God is everywhere and cannot be escaped, avoided nor hidden from. If God's Spirit were a separate person from God himself, then it appears that God would be confined, in a sense, to his throne in heaven where Jesus said his Father was when teaching his disciples how to pray, "Our Father in heaven" (Matt 6:9). But because God has a Spirit that is part of God himself, therefore wherever God's Spirit is, God is; meaning therefore that God is everywhere. "The Spirit of God was hovering over the waters" (Gen 1:2). That speaks of God's presence by his Spirit. Thus the Holy Spirit is not a "mere influence," it is part of God himself, just as my spirit is part of me. Nor is the Holy Spirit a person distinct from God, just as my spirit is not a person distinct from me, but is rather a part of God, the person. For this reason, the works of the Holy Spirit are the works of God which God performs by his omnipotent and omnipresent Spirit.

Second, the Holy Spirit is an influence; that is, God influences mankind in various ways by his omnipresent Spirit, just as my spirit is an influence, whether bad or good, depending on whether my mind is the mind of the flesh, or the mind of the Spirit. But my spirit is more than an influence; it is an essential and composite part of myself, part of that which makes me the person I am. So is the Holy Spirit more than a mere influence; it is an essential and composite part of God, part of that which makes God the person God is. And every influence exhibited by the Holy Spirit is the influence of God, influenced by his omnipresent Spirit.

The same can likewise be said of the power of God. The Holy Spirit is often associated with, used interchangeably with, and presented as the power of God, whether the power of prophecy, the power of tongues, the power of healing, or any other power associated with the gifts of the Holy Spirit. Consider these few passages from the NT: John the Baptist "will go on before the Lord, in the spirit and power of Elijah" (Luke 1:17). It was told Mary, "The Holy Spirit will come upon you, and the power of the Most High will overshadow you" (Luke 1:35). "Jesus returned to Galilee in the power of the Spirit" (Luke 4:14). "You will receive power when the Holy Spirit comes on you" (Acts 1:8). "God anointed Jesus of Nazareth with the Holy Spirit and power" (Acts 10:38). "That you may overflow with hope by the power of the Holy Spirit" (Rom 15:13). "By the power of signs and miracles, through the power of the Spirit" (Rom 15:19). "My message and my preaching were . . . a demonstration of the Spirit's power" (1 Cor 2:4). "Our gospel came to you not simply with words, but also with power, with the Holy Spirit" (1 Thess 1:5). Some "who have shared in the Holy Spirit, who have tasted the goodness of the word of God and the powers of the coming age" (Heb 6:4-5).

Besides these, the Holy Spirit is also associated with power by implication on occasions far too numerous to mention, both in the OT and NT. Every time the Spirit came upon, or was poured out upon, or filled someone, power came to that person. That's why it could be said that the kingdom would come with power (Mark 9:1), because the kingdom came when the Holy Spirit came upon the apostles, giving them power (Acts 1:8; 2:4).

However, while this evidence shows that the Holy Spirit is the power of God, inasmuch as when and where the Holy Spirit came, the power came, it is not claimed that the Holy Spirit is identical with the power, but is the medium through which God administered his power. The Holy Spirit is far more than the power and influence of God; it is the Spirit of God. There is no influence or power attributed to the Holy

Spirit as a supposed personal entity that has not, is not, or cannot be accomplished by God the Farther by or through his ever-proceeding and omnipresent Holy Spirit.

And while God's Spirit is far more than a mere influence, in today's absence of miraculous demonstrations of the power of that Spirit in the realm of religion, the Spirit's influence by God's word continues to operate in the hearts and lives of God's children, who have "received the spirit of adoption [or sonship], whereby we cry, Abba. Father" (Rom 8:15, ASV). Therefore, "be made new in the attitude [spirit, ASV and Gr.] of your minds" (Eph 4:23). And continue to be influenced by the Spirit-confirmed message (God's word) to produce "the fruit of the Spirit" as listed in Gal 5:22, "love, joy, peace," etc. Such is to be led by the influence (not the overpowering compulsion) of God by his ever-proceeding Holy Spirit.

So, is the Holy Spirit an influence? YES! Is the Holy Spirit merely an influence? NO! It is the Spirit of God.

CHAPTER 8

THE HOLY SPIRIT AND DEITY

Is the Holy Spirit divine? As a background for this subject one should read, or reread Chapter 27 of Part I, titled *Godhead*. It appears that many have concluded that "deity" necessarily means "person"; that is, if something is divine, that means it is God, and is therefore a person. So it is believed that if one can prove that the Holy Spirit is divine, that means that the Holy Spirit is a person, a distinct personal entity.

In the NT there are three Greek words, found in only five passages, which are indiscriminately translated "Godhead," "divinity" or "deity," depending on the translation used. These Scriptures apply deity, divinity, or divine nature to Christ (Col 2:9), to God (Rom 1:20; Acts 17:29), to God's power (2 Pet 1:3), and to God's nature (v. 4). The Holy Spirit is nowhere mentioned in connection with these five passages that specifically refer to divine nature; but that does not mean that the Holy Spirit is not divine. The Spirit's deity can be proved in other ways without these passages, the only ones that use the words "deity," "divinity" and "Godhead."

If God is divine, which of course he is, and inasmuch as "divine" means "having the nature of God," then everything of which God consists must be divine. And since it has been established that the Holy Spirit is the Spirit of God, an essential part of the person God is, therefore the fact that the Holy Spirit is divine goes unchallenged.

But not everything that is said to be divine is a personal entity. In those passages under consideration, four distinctions are specifically mentioned as being divine: Christ, God, God's power and God's nature. And then if we were to add to these the Holy Spirit as a divine distinction, which it is, we would then have five distinctions of deity instead of only three. But that would not mean that the Godhead is composed of five persons, including God's power, God's nature and God's Spirit. We know that power and nature are not persons, but they are divine if they have to do with God. So to prove that something is divine, even including the Holy Spirit, is not to prove that it is a distinct person in a plural being called God. Therefore deity, divinity and Godhead are not words to be equated with "person," for they only identify the particular nature of a person or thing, as distinguished from the nature of man, animals, angels, etc.

The scope of deity takes a very wide range, because all things pertaining to God, whether his being or essence, his characteristics, his Spirit, his one and only Son, etc., are divine; but not all are necessarily personal entities. Being divine is not what makes something a person. Even though not specifically stated in Scripture, there are things which may be said to be divine, besides God, his Son, his nature and his power as already mentioned.

The word of God is divine because it is God's word, and not man's word. "The word of God is living and active . . . it judges the thoughts and attitudes of the heart" (Heb 4:12). God's word is divine; and here it is even given characteristics of personality, the power "to judge the thoughts and attitudes of the heart." But other than the fact that God's word is personified in the person of Christ ("His name is called The Word of God," Rev 19:13, ASV), God's word, although divine, is not a person. (See Part I, Chapter 43, *The Word Became Flesh*).

So it is with both the wisdom and the knowledge of God (Rom 11:33). Both are divine because they both pertain to God; they are part of God. A God without knowledge and wisdom would not be the Almighty God we know and worship. And yet, even though divine, neither knowledge nor wisdom are persons. And even though wisdom may be personified in Christ (Prov 8:22-31; see verse 12 to find that it is wisdom speaking), and is given several characteristics of personality, divine wisdom is not a personal entity.

Similar things may be said of the grace of God (1 Cor 15:10), the kindness of God (Titus 3:4), his mercy (v. 5), his patience (1 Pet 3:20), his righteousness (Ps 103:17), his glory (Exod 40:34), *et al.* And surely there can also be added God's truth, his compassion, goodness, justice, holiness, majesty, sovereignty, *et al.* All these are divine, but none of them are to be worshiped except God and his Son, because only God and his Son are divine persons; and we have been told to worship them. But because the Holy Spirit is not a distinct personal entity, God has never told us to worship his Spirit; consequently no one in Scripture ever did.

The church of God is a divine institution, composed of persons who are not divine; but the church, even though personified as the bride of Christ (Eph 5:25-27; Rev 21:2), is not a person and is not to be worshiped.

We sing of the love of God as "Love divine, all love excelling." But love is not a personal entity to be worshiped, even though divine love has many personal characteristics, some of which, when applied to the Holy Spirit, are used by some in an effort to prove that the Holy Spirit is a person. Why not love, a person? For love divine is eternal, long-suffering, kind, rejoices, believes, hopes, endures, appears in the feminine gender, and is modified by feminine articles and pronouns (1 Cor 13). Love "seeketh not HER own" (v. 5, KJV and Greek text). But even though God's love is divine, and has all those personal characteristics, divine love is not a personal entity to be worshiped. Nor is the Holy Spirit. Not everything that is divine is a person; but those who are to be worshiped are personal entities, specifically God and Christ, Father and Son, but do not include the Holy Spirit, nor all those other things that may be said to be divine.

Furthermore, like man, Jehovah God has a soul, according to at least 14 passages in the OT and 2 in the NT, as follows (ASV): Lev 26:11, 30; Isa 1:14; 42:1; Jer 5:9, 29; 6:8; 9:9; 14:19; 15:1 (translated "mind"); 32:41; 51:14 (translated "self"; also Amos 6:8); Ezek 23:18; Matt 12:18 and Heb 10:38. Naturally God's soul is divine because it is God's soul, and not a human soul.

Likewise, the Son of God, just as his divine Father, also has a soul, according to at least 4 passages in the OT and 10 in the NT, as follows: Ps 16:10; Isa 53:10, 11, 12; Matt 26:38; Mark 14:34; John 12:27; Acts 2:27; and Matt 20:28 (translated "life"; see also Mark 10:45; John 10:11, 15, 17 and 1 John 3:16). And naturally Christ's soul, like his Father's soul, is also divine because it is the soul of the divine Son of God. But for God's soul and Christ's soul to be divine does not mean that the soul of God and the soul of Christ are personal entities distinct from God and Christ, just as my soul is not a distinct personal entity from me.

Every person, whether human or divine, has (or is) a soul. According to Trichotomists, every person is composed of spirit, soul and body (whether a physical body or a spiritual body); and according to Dichotomists, every person IS a soul, composed of a spirit and a body. But regardless of one's concept of the soul (Heb. *Nephesh*; Gr. *psuche*), the word "soul" is never once applied to the Holy Spirit of God, even though those 30 passages from both the OT and NT show that both God and Christ have souls. The reason must be obvious: the Holy Spirit, though divine, is not a personal entity as are God, Christ and man, each of whom has a soul. If the Holy Spirit were such a person, it would surely have a soul, just as every other person has a soul; yet the Scriptures never say so.

Of all the 374 Spirit passages, not one of them calls the Holy Spirit "God." And even if the Holy Spirit were said to be *Theos* (God), it would not necessarily be saying that the Holy Spirit is *ho Theos* (THE God). The difference is that *ho Theos*, with the definite article, refers to "the God," the being, the person, the God we worship; while *Theos*, without the definite article, may refer to the nature of anything that pertains to God. (See Part I, Chapter 15, *And the Word Was God*, for a more complete explanation of the significance of the definite article in the Greek text). "Man" can mean "human" or "mankind," distinguished from God, angels or animals; but "the man" has reference to a single personal human being. So it is with God. The Holy Spirit can be "God" in the sense of being divine, not human, not animal, and not angelic. But the Holy Spirit is neither called "God" nor "the God."

Some have misapplied Acts 5:3-9 to make it appear that the Holy Spirit is called "God." Peter asked Ananias, "How is it that Satan has filled your heart that you have lied to the Holy Spirit?" (v. 3). "You have not lied to men but to God" (v. 4). Obviously Peter is not here denying that Ananias had lied to him and to the other apostles, for that was the obvious intent of Ananias. But Peter is saying that the apostles were not the only ones being lied to, and by far not the most significant. If only the apostles were being lied to, that is, if the apostles had not been miraculously endowed by the Holy Spirit to know that Ananias was lying, he might have gotten by undetected. But he lied to Holy-Spirit-endowed apostles; therefore he lied to the Holy Spirit which endowed them. And because the Holy Spirit is the Spirit of God, therefore Ananias lied to God himself. Peter is not here saying that the Holy Spirit is a distinct personal entity called God. He did not say, "You have lied to God the Spirit"; for he had lied to the Spirit of God, therefore to God himself. There is a difference.

While the Holy Spirit is nowhere called either "God" or "the God," an effort is sometimes made to prove that the Holy Spirit is God, thinking that the Spirit is here called "Lord," as follows: "The Lord is the Spirit" (2 Cor 3:17); and, "which comes from the Lord, who is the Spirit" (v. 18). But since both God and Christ wear the title "Lord," it may be significant that the "Lord" here may refer to Christ, and not to God; in which case it would be saying, "Christ (not God) is the Spirit."

Furthermore, it says, "the Lord is the Spirit," not "the Spirit is the Lord." There can be a difference. William Barclay's *Daily Study Bible* at this place says, "In this passage Paul has set for many a theological problem . . . . He seems to identify the Risen Lord and the Holy Spirit. We must remember that Paul was not writing theology; he was setting down experience. And it is the experience of the Christian life that the works of the Spirit and the works of the Risen Lord are one and the same. The strength, the light, the guidance we receive come alike from the Spirit and from the Risen Lord." More specifically, these blessings come from Christ by the power of God's Spirit.

Concerning "the Lord is the Spirit," Albert Barnes' *Notes on the NT* here says that "expositors have been greatly divided in regard to its meaning."[6] That alone should cause one to be extremely cautious about using such an uncertain and controversial passage as a proof text for the personal entity of the Spirit.

Paul said that he and others were "ministers of a new covenant—not of the letter, but of the Spirit; for the letter kills, but the Spirit gives life" (v. 6). Then he calls the old covenant "the ministry that brought death," and distinguishes it from the new covenant, "the ministry of the Spirit" (vv. 7-8). Paul also said that "the law of the Spirit of life (in Christ Jesus) set me free from the law of sin and death" (Rom 8:2). So the Spirit under consideration here is the Spirit of life; and that life is in the Son. Consequently, to be in the Son is to possess that life, called the Spirit of life. Thus the Lord is that Spirit. The Lord, with his new covenant, called the Spirit of life, is here contrasted against Moses, with the administration of death, with the idea that Christ, not Moses, is that Spirit.

The Spirit here, as in numerous other places in Scripture, may be presented as one's perception, one's own attitude or disposition of mind, whether the attitude of bondage and death, which is the spirit of the old covenant, or the attitude of sonship and life, which is the spirit of Christ's new covenant. Concerning the latter, Christ is that spirit; the law of Christ brings that attitude and disposition of mind. "For you did not receive a spirit that makes you a slave again to fear (the attitude of a slave), but you received the Spirit of sonship (the attitude of a son). And by him [whereby, ASV] we cry, 'Abba, Father'" (Rom 8:15). (Note: The masculine pronoun "him" does not appear here in the Greek text). Christ, the Son, is that spirit, that attitude and disposition of mind in sons of God. To those who seemingly had not yet attained that attitude (spirit), or who had attained it and then lost it, Paul said, "be made new in the attitude of your minds" (Eph 4:23; Or, "in the spirit of your mind," ASV). Christ and all he stands for is that spirit.

Whatever is the proper interpretation of "the Lord is the Spirit," it is evident that nothing in 2 Cor 3:17 teaches that the Holy Spirit is called "God," "the God," or anything that means "God"; nor does it teach that the Holy Spirit is a distinct personal entity in a plural being called "God." But the Holy Spirit is the divine Spirit of God. He has no other kind.

CHAPTER 9

THE SPIRIT KNOWS AND TEACHES

One of the characteristics of personality is the power to know, to perceive, to understand, to be cognizant, to be aware of something. Therefore any Scripture which indicates that the Spirit of God is able to know something, that Scripture is used extensively by Trinitarians to teach that the Holy Spirit is a distinct personal entity. Just such a Scripture is found in 1 Corinthians 2:11, "No one knows the thoughts of God except the Spirit of God."

Several violations of reasonable interpretation are committed when using this text to prove that the Holy Spirit is a person. First, the contextual subject under consideration is what God had prepared for those who love him (v. 9). Inasmuch as Paul is the writer here, we turn to him for an explanation as to whom he means by "God." Reading onward in this letter to Corinth, Paul explains that, "for us there is but one God, the Father, from whom all things came . . . and there is but one Lord, Jesus Christ, through whom all things came" (1 Cor 8:6), letting us know that when he says "God," he means "the Father," and then distinguishes God from Christ in such a way as not to be misunderstood by even those who are unskilled in theology. In this one epistle alone, Paul makes a clear distinction between God and Christ no less than 13 times (see Appendices A, B and C), in addition to the statement already quoted, where he asserts that the one God is the Father; not Christ, not the Holy Spirit, not the Godhead, and not the Trinity, but the Father. Therefore, the things of the Father are known only by the Father's Spirit, the Holy Spirit of God.

But even though God had prepared something special for those who love him, those things had been hidden from man's knowledge from the beginning (1 Cor 2:7). There was no way for man to uncover that mystery without divine help, because that was one of those "things of God." However, when God was ready for man to know and understand the details of that mystery which was hidden through the ages, "God has revealed it to us by his Spirit" (v. 10). It was God, the Father, who revealed this knowledge, but he did so by the power of his Holy Spirit, which ever proceeds from the Father (John 15:26), by revealing the message to mankind through Holy-Spirit-inspired apostles and others, as he had so inspired his prophets of old. God's Spirit need not be a separate person from God in order to empower the apostles to verbalize such a revelation.

It is evident that Paul here does somewhat personify the Spirit as one who "searches all things, even the deep things of God" (v. 10), meaning simply that there is no mystery so hidden that God cannot make it known by the Spirit of prophecy working in the apostles. There is nothing that the Holy Spirit as a separate person could reveal, which the Father himself could not reveal through the apostles by the power of his Spirit which ever proceeds from the Father himself. Man cannot know what is in the mind of God; those things of God have to be revealed to us by the supernatural power of God's Spirit. Thus only the Spirit of God knows the things of God (v. 11). If taken literally, this passage would have one coequal person in the Godhead (the Spirit) searching into the things of one or more other coequal persons in the Godhead, as though the Spirit didn't already have infinite knowledge about that eternal plan without making a diligent search to find out from others, who theoretically knew no more about it than he himself knew, inasmuch as all persons in the Godhead were supposedly coequal, including the matter of omniscience.

But the first part of verse 11 is carefully avoided by Trinitarians, because it asks, "Who among men knows the thoughts of a man except the man's spirit within him?" In this statement the spirit of man is likewise said to have the power of knowledge, just as God's Spirit has the power of knowledge in the statement immediately following. In fact, that first statement is used by Paul to illustrate the sense in which God's Spirit knows, as he then presents in the statement that follows. So if the power of knowledge in God's Spirit makes God's Spirit a separate person from the God it is the Spirit of, then according to common logic, the power of knowledge in man's spirit would also make man's spirit a separate person from the man it is the spirit of. That conclusion seems inevitable. And if both God's Spirit and man's spirit were distinct personal entities, just what kind of persons would they be?

Paul's illustration here is saying that only a man (besides God, of course) knows what he himself is thinking or what is in his own mind. One man cannot know what is in the mind of another man. Such a man must reveal it for it to be known by others. Likewise, only God knows what God himself is thinking or what is in God's own mind. Surely God could have revealed his own mind to man by speaking directly from heaven as he possibly did at Jesus' baptism (Matt 3:17), and at his transfiguration (Matt 17:5); but instead, God chose to reveal his mind through the apostles and prophets by the power of his Holy Spirit. To say that only the Spirit of God knows the things of God means no more than the fact that the hidden things of God are revealed to man only by the power of his Spirit working supernaturally through the apostles and prophets. And God's Spirit need not be a distinct person from God himself in order to accomplish that transmission of information from God to man.

In this passage (1 Cor 2:11) we are told that "no one knows the thoughts of God except the Spirit of God," which means that only the Spirit of God knows the things of God. Do we have a contradiction in Matthew 11:27 and Luke 10:22? Christ said, "No one knows the Father except the Son and those to whom the Son chooses to reveal him." There does seem to be a very real contradiction here, if indeed the Holy Spirit were a distinct personal entity. While one passage is saying that only the Spirit knows the things of God, who Paul said is the Father, the other passage is saying that only the Son knows the Father, plus such other persons to whom the Son wills to reveal him. Which one is correct? Well, they both are correct. Inasmuch as the Holy Spirit is not a personal entity as is Christ, Christ could correctly say that the Son is the only person who knows the Father in that unique sense. But were it not for the revealing power of the Holy Spirit, not even Christ would have thus known the Father. So it was by the ultimate power of God's Spirit that Christ knew his heavenly Father; and by the power of that same Spirit he was able to reveal the Father to mankind. The Holy Spirit need not be a distinct personal entity in order to reveal God, or the things of God, to and through his divine Son.

David once said, "My heart mused and my spirit inquired" (Ps 77:6). The ASV has, "I commune with mine own heart; and my spirit maketh diligent search." Presumably David's spirit was searching for some form of knowledge, more specifically a remembrance of things gone by. But who would say that David's heart and his spirit were both distinct personal entities apart from the person of David himself? The fact that David's heart mused, and his spirit diligently searched and inquired, does not mean that David consisted of three persons, one of which was his heart and another his spirit. David, his heart and his spirit were three distinctions, but not three persons. As with any man, there are three distinctions: body, soul and spirit; but only one person. So it is with God, his Son and his Spirit; three distinctions, but only two persons: God the Father, and Christ his Son. Not all distinctions are persons.

Then our text in 1 Corinthians 2 goes on, speaking of the things that are freely given to us from God: "This is what we speak, not in words taught us by human wisdom, but in words taught by the Spirit" (vv. 12-13). This latter statement is also used by Trinitarians to prove that because the Spirit teaches, the Spirit is therefore a distinct personal entity, because only a person can teach. But the same passage says that man's wisdom teaches, therefore making man's wisdom a separate person from the man it is the wisdom of. Surely one can realize the figures of speech being used here. In either case, the message is being spoken by Paul and his companions. They are the persons involved. But the message they spoke had to be learned either from man's wisdom or from God. Paul was saying that they got it from God. They, as apostles and prophets, were divinely inspired of God by the power of God's Spirit.

There are numerous other things in Scripture which are said to teach; such as, "Age should speak; advanced years should teach wisdom" (Job 32:7). That does not mean that "advanced years" is a person. Again, "Ask the animals, and they will teach you, or the birds of the air, and they will tell you; or speak to the earth, and it will teach you, or let the fish of the sea inform you" (Job 12:7-8). All these, the beasts and birds, the fish, all teach their message; but they are not persons, even though they are personified as teachers.

Again, "Thy right hand shall teach thee terrible things" (Ps 45:4, ASV). And "The heart of the wise instructeth his mouth" (Prov 16:23, ASV). Also, "Does not the very nature of things teach you that if a man has long hair, it is a disgrace to him?" (1 Cor 11:14). And even the grace of God teaches us (Tit 2:11-12). Surely no one would conclude that one's right hand, one's heart, nature and grace are all persons because they teach. Many such things, including the Spirit of God, are personified as teachers. They might all have a message to impart, but that doesn't mean that they are therefore personal entities.

God's Spirit and man's spirit are personified far more than other things because God's Spirit and man's spirit are composite parts of the persons they are the spirits of. Thus they lend themselves more to that type figure of speech than do other inanimate objects such as those considered above.

CHAPTER 10

WORSHIPING THE HOLY SPIRIT

Many fundamental churches for the past two centuries have held to the idea that everything we do, concerning how to worship, must have biblical authority from God. That authority must come from the Scriptures in the form of (1) a direct command, which requires obedience, (2) a divinely approved example, which grants permission, or (3) a necessary inference that such a command or approval exists. Silence of the Scriptures therefore is not considered an acceptable reason for doing anything as worship without meeting at least one of those three criteria. Otherwise there would be nothing that we could not do as worship toward God, as long as what is done does not violate some moral or spiritual law, even including burning incense and offering burnt sacrifices. For this reason we worship God by prayer and thanksgiving, by singing praise and making melody in our hearts unto God, by observing the Lord's Supper, thereby remembering and proclaiming the Lord's death, etc.

Those same criteria are also used in distinguishing between required specifics and mere expediencies in performing such worship, such as whether to stand, sit or kneel for prayer; whether or not to pray through or in the name of Christ, Mary, the saints, etc.; whether to have a choir, or congregational singing, or both; whether to have a cappella singing, or mechanical instruments of music, or both; whether or not to use anything in the Lord's Supper except unleavened bread and the fruit of the vine; or even the time, place and sequence for observing the Lord's Supper, etc.

Those same criteria are furthermore used in determining whether or not to reject from our worship the presence of priestly robes, christening, holy water, infant baptism, candle lighting, bead counting, incense burning, hand holding, interpretive dancing, banner waving, theatrics, sign of the cross, foot washing, tongue speaking, hand clapping, snake handling, ash daubing, etc. And while there may be differences in opinions as to how those criteria are to be adapted in certain specific cases, it seems that the legitimacy of those standards, when properly understood, go virtually unchallenged. Without such guidelines there would be almost nothing we could not do in the name of "worshipping God."

But if we are to use those principles in determining *how* we are to acceptably worship God, then surely we should use those same guidelines in determining *what* or *whom* we should worship. If one can be more important than the other, surely *what* or *whom* we worship is of greater significance than *how* we worship. So by using those same criteria, we reject the worship of idols, icons, statues, crosses, saints, popes, and even angels. Idolatry may include the worship of any person or thing which God has not specifically directed us to so worship.

The whole Bible is filled with commands and examples of people talking to God, praying to God, singing to God, praising God, and worshiping God. Then when Christ appeared overtly onto the scene through the virgin birth, God said, "Let all God's angels worship him" (Heb 1:6). Even as an infant, Jesus was worshipped by the Magi from the East (Matt 2:11). And throughout his earthly ministry, as well as after his reglorification to the right hand of God in heaven, Jesus continually accepted worship.

Throughout the NT people talked to Jesus, made requests of Jesus, praised Jesus, and worshiped Jesus. Besides God and Christ (Father and Son), no person or thing in heaven or on earth is authorized to be an object of our worship today. God has told us whom to worship; and we don't need a "thou shalt not" to determine who else may or may not be worshiped; just as we don't need God to say, "Thou shalt not have beef steak and coffee in the Lord's Supper." When we were told what to eat and drink in the Lord's Supper, that excluded all other items of food, in the absence of any scriptural authority or precedence otherwise.

Through the centuries, hymns and spiritual songs have been composed and used in worship, some of which composers have not necessarily been guided by the principles and criteria as earlier stated; and therefore the songs do occasionally contain statements and sentiments contrary to those aforesaid criteria. Sometimes words have to be changed or eliminated to keep a hymn from being anti-scriptural. This should be done only after making considerable allowance for "poetic license," considering all the various possible implications of the wording used.

One noted hymn which comes to mind is Reginald Heber's "Holy, Holy, Holy!" The last phrase in the first and last verses, "God in Three Persons, blessed Trinity," has been changed in many nondenominational hymnals to read, "God over all, and blessed eternally." Many of the more recent songs of praise are products of Charismatic influence, and therefore often present the Holy Spirit as an object of worship. One such song, titled "Glorify Thy Name," the third verse of which is an expression of praise to the Spirit (obviously the Holy Spirit), states, "Spirit, we love you, we worship and adore you. Glorify thy name in all the earth." And another song from much earlier times, Thomas Ken's "Doxology," ends with, "Praise Father, Son, and Holy Ghost."

But before we praise, love, worship, adore and glorify the Holy Spirit, certainly we should be able to produce specific authority from the Scriptures to do so. However, in all the some 374 Spirit references in the Bible, not one time did anyone ever talk to the Holy Spirit, pray to the Holy Spirit, sing to the Holy Spirit, praise the Holy Spirit, or worship the Holy Spirit. Furthermore, no one was ever even told to do so; and to do so is therefore without any scriptural precedence or authority whatsoever.

So in the absence of such scriptural authority, the practice should be opposed as much, or even more than we would oppose beef steak and coffee in the Lord's Supper. At least the Lord's Supper grew out of, or was instituted at the time of the last Passover feast where the meat of roast lamb was eaten, whereas there is no scriptural evidence that worshiping the Holy Spirit has ever been either commanded or allowed. Inasmuch as it cannot be proved that the Holy Spirit is as much a personal entity as the Father and Son are, and because idolatry may be defined as worshiping anything or anybody without God's command or permission to do so, worshiping the Holy Spirit could possibly be a form of idolatry.

Even if it could be established that the Holy Spirit is a distinct personal entity, there still would be no scriptural authority for worshiping the Holy Spirit. We would not even worship Christ, the Son of God, without authority from God to do so; while at God's command we would even worship a serpent on a pole.

Some may suppose that to be baptized in (or into) the name of the Holy Spirit is an act of worshipful obedience to the Holy Spirit. We are indeed authorized and expected to obey the Holy Spirit, but not to worship, praise, sing to nor pray to the Holy Spirit. Baptism may be an act of worshipful obedience to God and Christ, but not to the Holy Spirit. Scripture tells us that baptism is a lot of things, but never that it is an act of worship toward the Holy Spirit. And the First-Century Christians never considered it to be so.

When the OT prophets, or Christ's apostles responded to the inspiration and guidance of the Holy Spirit, that was never considered as worshiping the Holy Spirit. Obedience to a Scripture is not worshiping Scripture. Neither is obedience to the apostles worshiping the apostles. Nor was obedience to one of God's angels ever classified as angel worship. Obeying Moses was not considered as worshiping Moses.

Lest it be argued that worshiping the Holy Spirit is worshiping God, be reminded that if such were the case, surely somewhere during that 4,000 years of Bible history, and in at least one of those 374 references to the Spirit in Scripture, someone would have worshiped the Holy Spirit, or would have at least been told or permitted to do so. But such is not the case. The psalmist never mentioned anything about praising or worshiping the Holy Spirit in that God-inspired Hebrew hymnal containing 150 psalms. And if it has always been God's will that the Holy Spirit be worshiped on an equal basis with God and Christ, then all of God's people in the OT, as well as all NT Christians of the First Century must have missed the point entirely; for none of them ever worshiped the Holy Spirit. Christ worshiped God, his Father; but he never worshiped the Holy Spirit. So why should anyone today think that such should be done? And if it be argued that God wants us to worship the Holy Spirit because the Holy Spirit is God, we have been doing a very poor job of it, inasmuch as only a very few Christian songs are written to do so, in comparison with those numerous songs that worship God and Christ. For some reason nearly all our worship and praise songs are directed toward God and Christ. And surely for that same reason or reasons, most Christians never speak to nor worship the Holy Spirit. Seldom does anyone, except in the Catholic faith and a few others, ever direct a public prayer to the Holy Spirit. Many who have been Christians for decades have never once heard a prayer directed to the Holy Spirit, and would be shocked to hear one. Have you ever wondered why? It's because it's unscriptural.

To try to please everyone in a congregation by sometimes including in song the worship of the Holy Spirit, and at other times eliminating it, would be similar to preparing the Lord's Supper as a smorgasbord so everyone can eat whatever he or she pleases. If someone in his own privacy chooses to sing praise to the Holy Spirit, and to even set aside a day of special worship to the Holy Spirit, and maybe even offer burnt sacrifices and offerings to the Holy Spirit, that's between him and God. But to do so in the church's public worship assemblies violates our very basic interpretation of acceptable worship, and wrongfully involves those who might oppose for the reasons stated herein. We would deplore the idea of offering burnt sacrifices, animal or otherwise, in the church's public assemblies, not because God has specifically said not to do so, but because there is no New Testament authority or precedence for doing so, even though such sacrifices were both authorized and commanded in the Old Testament.

The absolute lack of Holy Spirit worship in Scripture, as in all biblical history, should forever settle the question as to whether or not the Holy Spirit is a third and coequal person in a Godhead called the Trinity. If the Holy Spirit were such a separate personal entity as are the Father and Son, he surely would have been worshiped, and we would have been told about it in Scripture.

CHAPTER 11

THE COMFORTER

Because of the present familiarity with the term "Comforter" as found in the KJV and ASV, we are sometimes using that term in lieu of the better rendition, "Counselor," as found in the RSV and NIV. The Greek word is *paraclete*, and means "Advocate" or "Helper," according to the ASV footnote.

On the night of the last Passover with his disciples, Jesus promised to send, in his absence, the Holy Spirit as a Comforter (John 14:16-17, 26; 15:26; 16:7-8, 13-15). These passages have already been referred to rather extensively in Part II, Chapter 1, *The Holy Spirit Personified*, and Chapter 2, *He or It*, as well as brief references in most of the other Spirit chapters. Here we shall discuss to whom and for what the Holy Spirit was given as a Comforter. The main thrust of *Theology Simplified* deals with the relationship of the Father, Son and Holy Spirit with each other, while a study of the Comforter deals primarily with the Holy Spirit's relation to man, a subject that would fill another book. But because so many Christians are led to believe that the Holy Spirit as a person comes into and personally indwells each Christian as his Comforter, supernaturally motivating, moving and controlling the Christian's life, making his decisions for him, interpreting Scripture for him, and even praying for him, basing their belief on Jesus' promise to send the Comforter, it seems necessary at this point to deal more specifically with that subject.

The first thing that needs to be understood about the Comforter is that it was promised only to those who were with Jesus at the Last Supper; namely, the twelve apostles (Matt 26:20; Mark 14:17; Luke 22:14), less Judas Iscariot who had left the group (John 13:27-31) before the promise of the Comforter was given. Then after the death and resurrection of Jesus, and just before ascending into heaven, Jesus instructed the apostles (Acts 1:2), "Do not leave Jerusalem, but wait for the gift my Father promised, which you have heard me speak about" (v. 4). That promise was to be the Holy Spirit in the form of a Comforter. Then he added, "For John baptized with water, but in a few days you will be baptized with the Holy Spirit" (v. 5). Furthermore, he told the apostles, "You will receive power when the Holy Spirit comes on you" (v. 8).

Then after Jesus was received up into heaven, the apostles went back to Jerusalem as they were told to do; and there they abode in an upper chamber, only the eleven remaining apostles as are specifically named in verse 13. For ten days they waited to be baptized with the Holy Spirit, the power that would serve as a Comforter for them. During that waiting period they continued steadfastly in prayer with other disciples of Jesus, including the women, on various occasions. At one time there were about 120 present, at which time Matthias was chosen to take Judas' place. So Matthias "was added to the eleven apostles" (Acts 1:26).

"When the day of Pentecost came, they (the twelve apostles) were all together in one place" (Acts 2:1). It is unreasonable to conclude that the 120 disciples were with the apostles all that time, and that they were all in the house where the apostles were sitting when the Holy Spirit came. We are told by name the ones who were abiding in the upper chamber, namely the apostles. And even though others were with them on one or more occasions, whether at their abode, or elsewhere, to think that the 120 disciples were present in the house when the Holy Spirit came is purely speculation. And even if they were present, it is obvious that the baptism of the Holy Spirit as the Comforter came only upon the apostles to whom it had been promised. The Spirit caused them to speak in other tongues (v. 4). The crowd recognized that all those who were thus speaking were Galileans (v. 7). Most likely many of the 120 were not Galileans.

"Then Peter stood up with the Eleven, raised his voice and addressed the crowd: 'Fellow Jews . . . These men are not drunk, as you suppose" (vv. 14-15). "These" had reference to the eleven apostles standing with Peter and speaking in other tongues. And even though Joel's prophecy, here quoted by Peter, made mention that both sons and daughters, servants and handmaidens would prophesy (vv. 17-18), neither Joel nor Peter were claiming that everything Joel predicted would take place on that very day, nor that everyone who would eventually prophesy as a result of the coming of the Spirit would have received the Holy Spirit as a Comforter.

At the conclusion of Peter's message to the multitude, 3,000 were baptized (v. 41). "Everyone was filled with awe, and many wonders and miraculous signs were done by the apostles" (v. 43). The conclusion is that the power was promised to the apostles; that the apostles received that power when they were baptized in the Holy Spirit, causing them to speak with other tongues; that the apostles, by the power of the Spirit, were able to perform many wonders and signs. All this could be said of the apostles only. The Holy Spirit as the Comforter was promised only to the apostles, and only the apostles received it as such. To say that every Christian is given the Holy Spirit as "the Comforter," just because it was given to the apostles as their Comforter, is without biblical authority. The Bible nowhere refers to the Holy Spirit as a "Comforter" for anyone except the apostles.

This is not to infer that the church then or now, whether collectively or individually, was not or is not "comforted" as a result of the apostles having been baptized with the Holy Spirit; but the indwelling of the Holy Spirit in each Christian (1 Cor 6:19; Rom 8:9,

11; Eph 3:16) is never referred to in the Bible as "the Comforter." The same can also be said even concerning those who received supernatural powers through the laying on of the apostles' hands (Ac 8:14-19; 19:6; 2 Tim 1:6). The supernatural endowments in such cases are never referred to as either "the baptism of the Holy Spirit" or "the Comforter."

The Greek word which is translated "Comforter" appears in its various forms in the NT 141 times. *Parakletos*, comforter, a noun referring to one who (or which) comforts, is defined by Thayer's *Greek-English Lexicon* as follows: "In the widest sense, *a helper, succorer, aider, assistant*; so of the Holy Spirit destined to take the place of Christ with the apostles (after his ascension to the Father), to lead them to a deeper knowledge of the gospel truth, and to give them the divine strength needed to enable them to undergo trials and persecutions on behalf of the divine kingdom."[7] *Parakletos* appears only five times, four of which were used by Jesus at the last supper when speaking only to the apostles.

But then toward the end of the Apostolic Age, nearing the completion of the NT writings, and probably after all the other apostles were dead, the remaining apostle, John, said to Christians in general, "My little children, these things write I unto you, that ye sin not. And if any man sin, we have an advocate [*parakletos*, comforter] with the Father, Jesus Christ the righteous" (1 John 2:1, ASV). So it is Jesus Christ, not the Holy Spirit, who is said to be our "comforter."

Paraklesis, comfort, also a noun, refers to the comfort provided by some person or thing. This word appears 29 times, many of which refer to the "comfort" which God gave the apostles, but never refers to the Holy Spirit as given to anyone else. As a result of the personal presence of the apostles among the congregations, performing signs, wonders and miracles by the power of the Holy Spirit (the Comforter) given only to them, the congregations are said to have been "walking in the fear of the Lord, and in the comfort of the Holy Spirit" (Acts 9:31, ASV). Thus the churches were comforted by the power in the apostles (not in others), as is described in the remainder of that chapter, where Peter healed a man with palsy (vv. 32-34), and raised Tabitha from the dead (vv. 36-41). The result of such confirmation of the message being demonstrated by the apostles is seen in the fact that so many were converted to Christ (vv. 31, 35, 42).

Another way in which Christians both then and now receive comfort is by God's word, the Scriptures. "Whatsoever things were written aforetime were written for our learning, that we through patience and comfort [*paraklesis*] of the Scriptures might have hope" (Rom 15:4, ASV). Not by the comfort of the Holy Spirit, but by the comfort of the Scriptures, which of course were delivered and confirmed by the power of the Holy Spirit in the apostles, even as in the prophets of old. "For prophecy never had its origin in the will of man, but men spoke from God as they were carried along by the Holy Spirit" (2 Pet 1:21).

Resulting from the Jerusalem conference (Acts 15), it was not the Holy Spirit, but rather a letter from the apostles, elders and brethren at Jerusalem (v. 23), a letter having the sanction of the Holy Spirit (v. 28), which brought comfort to the troubled brethren at Antioch; for verse 31 (ASV) says, "When they had read it, they rejoiced for the consolation [*paraklesis*, comfort]." Our comfort is to be found in God's word. Hebrews 13:22 speaks of "my word of exhortation [*paraklesis*], for I have written you only a short letter."

Parakaleo, a verb meaning "to comfort," occurs 107 times in the NT. Sometimes God's ministers (but never the Holy Spirit) are said to have comforted Christians: "God . . . comforted [*parakaleo*] us by the coming of Titus" (2 Cor 7:6). Also, "That he (Tychicus) may comfort [*parakaleo*] your hearts" (Eph 6:22, ASV). But whatever brings such comfort, does so by bringing God's word; for it is that word (not the Holy Spirit) that comforts. "Therefore encourage [*parakaleo*] each other with these words" (1 Thess 4:18).

The Holy Spirit was to comfort the apostles in a unique way that was never promised to other Christians. In Matthew 10, the twelve apostles named in verses 2-4 were sent forth on a limited commission (vv. 5-7), giving to them a temporary taste of the power of the Holy Spirit (v. 8) which they would later receive permanently, as Jesus promised them in John 14:16, "I will ask the Father, and he will give you another Counselor (the Spirit of truth) to be with you (apostles) forever"; and verse 17, "for he (Gr. it, the Spirit) lives with you and will be in you." The Comfort to be provided by the Holy Spirit is described in Matthew 10:19-20, "When they arrest you, do not worry about what to say or how to say it. At that time you will be given what to say, for it will not be you speaking, but the Spirit of your Father speaking through you." Not the Spirit of the Godhead, not the Spirit of the Trinity, not the Spirit of Christ, but the Spirit of the Father.

"When you are brought before synagogues, rulers and authorities, do not worry about how you will defend yourselves, or what you will say, for the Holy Spirit will teach you at that time what you should say" (Luke 12:11-12).

When Jesus said, "He will give you another Counselor" (John 14:16), the word "another" is from the Greek word *allos*, as distinguished from *heteros*. Both words mean "another"; but *allos* indicates that which is simply numerically distinct, as the distinction of one person or thing from another person or thing, as adding one besides or in place of; while *heteros* indicates that which is generically distinct, different, denoting one of two, involving the secondary idea of difference of kind. Because *allos* suggests another person or thing of the same kind, Trinitarians have concluded that inasmuch as Christ is a person, therefore the Holy Spirit as "another" Comforter must therefore mean that the Holy Spirit is likewise a person, as if that were the only way the two distinctions could possibly be of the same kind. They fail to realize that two persons or things may have at least one thing in common while having any number of things quite different, and yet one be characterized as *allos*, another of the same kind.

Any number of examples, biblical and otherwise, could be cited to illustrate this fact. When *allos* is used as an adjective, the noun it modifies reveals what it is that the two distinctions have in common so that either may be referred to as "another." The Magi "returned to their country by another [*allos*] route" (Matt 2:12). They had two choices: go back by way of Jerusalem, or go another way. The way they chose was *allos*, another of the same kind; that is, both were "ways." However, other than that, those ways could have been altogether different: one through the city, the other through the countryside; one a crowded thoroughfare, the other a lonely country lane; one paved with stone, the other a dusty path. Yet they both had something in common: both were "ways" to get from where they were back to their own country. So instead of going back by way of Herod and Jerusalem, they went another (*allos*) way.

"Jesus told them another [*allos*] parable" (Matt 13:24, 31, 33). Those stories told by Jesus were different stories teaching different lessons. There were the sower, the tares, the mustard seed, and the leaven; all different stories, and all teaching different but not conflicting lessons. Yet all those stories were of the same kind in that they were all parables. Thus each could be introduced as another (*allos*), another story of the same kind, another parable, yet different in every other way.

One more example should suffice: "All flesh is not the same: Men have one kind of flesh, animals have another [*allos*], birds another [*allos*] and fish another [*allos*]" (1 Cor 15:39). Paul says that all these are different, yet they are each introduced as "another" (*allos*), another of the same kind. How can this be? It's because although the flesh of men, of beasts, of birds and of fishes are different kinds of flesh, yet they all have one thing in common, they are all flesh. Thus each could be introduced as "another flesh."

So it is with "another Comforter." There are many things that distinguish between Christ and the Holy Spirit, things that make them different. One is God's Son, the other is not. One became the Son of man, the other did not. One died on a cross, the other did not. One appeared in the likeness of a dove, and as cloven tongues of fire, the other did not. One prayed to the Father, the other did not. One was worshiped, the other was not, etc. Then how can either of these two distinctions be called "another" (*allos*), another of the same kind? What do they both have in common? The answer is simple. Both served as Counselors for the apostles. Christ, while on earth, was their Comforter, their advocate, their counsel for defense. But after Jesus went away, the Holy Spirit was sent to take his place as "another" (*allos*) Comforter. They were different in that Christ was a distinct personal entity, while the Holy Spirit was not. One is the Son of God, while the other is the Spirit of God. But they were still both of the same kind in that both were Comforters for the apostles. The Holy Spirit did for the apostles what Christ had been doing for them.

Surely this evidence should be enough to demonstrate how Trinitarians have abused and misused "another Comforter" and the Greek language, in an effort to prove that the Holy Spirit is another personal entity, just like Christ.

The obvious conclusion is that the Holy Spirit as a Comforter was for the apostles only; but the Christian's comfort is God's word, which was supernaturally revealed and confirmed to us by those Holy-Spirit-guided apostles. Nowhere does the Bible teach that the Holy Spirit is the Christian's comforter for today, except for the fact that Christians find their comfort in the Scriptures, which are a product of the Holy Spirit which worked through the apostles.

CHAPTER 12

THE SPIRIT LEADS AND GUIDES

"Then Jesus was led by the Spirit into the desert to be tempted by the devil" (Matt 4:1; Luke 4:1-2). Thus the Spirit leads, assuming that this is the Holy Spirit, the Spirit of God, and not Jesus' own spirit, being drawn and tempted by Satan. Mark says, "the Spirit driveth him forth into the wilderness" (Mark 1:12, ASV). If this Spirit were the Holy Spirit as a person, it would either lead Christ into the wilderness, or drive Christ into the wilderness, but not both. However, as God was the person who influenced Christ by the power of his Spirit to go into the wilderness for that purpose, then that Spirit could be described as either a leading influence or a driving influence. Whichever is correct, it can be said that the Spirit leads.

"Those who are led by the Spirit of God are sons of God" (Rom 8:14). Therefore the Spirit leads. But whether the Spirit as a distinct personal entity does the leading, or whether God is the person doing the leading by the power of his Spirit, this text does not tell us.

"But if you are led by the Spirit, you are not under law" (Gal 5:18). Thus the Spirit leads; but none of these texts tell us how the Spirit leads, nor if it is simply God leading by his Spirit. And to conclude that the Spirit necessarily leads as a personal entity is a virtual denial that God has the power to lead by his own omnipresent Spirit. Nevertheless, many Trinitarians have come to that conclusion, erroneously thinking that only a person can lead.

But in the Scriptures, several things which are not persons are said to lead. David said to Jehovah, "Even there your hand will guide me, your right hand will hold me fast" (Ps 139:10). Thus the hand of Jehovah leads, without the hand of Jehovah being a personal entity, separate from Jehovah himself. And if the hand of Jehovah can lead without being a personal entity, then so can the Spirit of Jehovah lead without being a personal entity. But the hand of God is a part of God himself, someone might say. Yes, but so is the Spirit of God a part of God himself, just as my spirit is a part of myself.

"Keep your father's commands and do not forsake your mother's teaching . . . . When you walk, they will guide you" (Prov 6:20-22). Thus a father's and mother's commandment and law are said to lead or guide. But commandments and laws, regardless of origin, are not persons. The same can be said of God's commandments and laws. Again, "God's kindness (goodness, ASV), leads you toward repentance" (Rom 2:4). Kindness leads; but kindness is not a person. Surely one can see from all such references that God is the person who leads and guides by using his hand, his commandment, his law, his kindness, his goodness, as well as his Spirit.

"The integrity of the upright guides them" (Prov 11:3). Integrity guides; but integrity is not a person. It is a person who has integrity that guides.

"By day the pillar of cloud did not cease to guide them, nor the pillar of fire by night to shine on the way they were to take" (Neh 9:19). The pillar of cloud and pillar of fire led Israel through the wilderness; but those pillars were not persons. Then what person did lead them? Exodus 13:21-22 explains: "By day the LORD went ahead of them in a pillar of cloud to guide them on their way and by night in a pillar of fire to give them light." Jehovah was the person who led them, but he did so by the two pillars. So it is with God's Spirit. God is the person who leads and guides us, but he does so by his Spirit. If God could be the person in the pillar of fire in the wilderness, whether literally or figuratively, without that pillar being a personal entity, then God could also be the person in the cloven tongues as of fire on Pentecost, whether literally or figuratively, without those tongues being a personal entity.

Was it the Holy Spirit as a personal entity which kept Paul from going into Asia? (Acts 16:6). Or was it God, by his Holy Spirit in Paul, directing him in where to speak, as well as what to speak? So let it never be said that the Holy Spirit is a person because it leads and guides. It is God who leads and guides; but he does so by his Spirit. And if God still leads us by his Spirit today, in some way other than by the influence of God's word having its effect in our hearts and lives, then God failed to tell us *how* his Spirit still leads us.

CHAPTER 13

THE LOVE OF THE SPIRIT

"I urge you, brothers, by our Lord Jesus Christ and by the love of the Spirit, to join me in my struggle by praying to God for me" (Rom 15:30). Here we see reference to "the love of the Spirit," which has caused some to conclude that the Holy Spirit has a personality that includes affections, specifically love, and is therefore a personal entity who loves and who is to be loved, adored, and even worshiped. This conclusion is without foundation for more than one reason.

First of all, the genitive case, "of the Spirit," may grammatically allow possession, as though the Spirit possesses love as an attribute. It would, in that way, have reference to the Spirit's love; that is, love that belongs to and therefore characterizes the Spirit, as though the Spirit is an affectionate being or person. This has traditionally been the Trinitarian's interpretation, as though there could be no other. Then too, the English translation, "love of the Spirit," could even have reference to the love and affection which a Christian might have toward the Spirit.

But to adopt either of these two interpretations completely ignores the context, which is the only logical guide for determining the significance of the statement. For the genitive case may also, as it obviously does here, have reference to the Christians' love for one another, specifically their love for Paul, which is generated by God operating through his Spirit; a love that had been produced in the Christian by God's Spirit. Hence, "the love of the Spirit." Paul was appealing to their love toward him, a love produced by the influence of the Spirit, to get them to pray to God for him, that he might be delivered from his enemies in Jerusalem.

Secondly, we do not stand alone in this appraisal of the passage under consideration. Consider the following translations: William F. Back's translation has, "By our Lord Jesus Christ and the love we have from the Spirit I urge you to join me in my struggle." Edgar J. Goodspeed's translation has, "I beg you, brothers, for the sake of our Lord Jesus Christ, and of the love that the Spirit inspires, join me in most earnest prayer to God for me." The TEV has, "by the love that the Spirit gives." The NEB, Williams, and Weymouth all have, "by the love that the Spirit inspires." The TCNT has, "by the love inspired by the Spirit." These all are in accord with the context under consideration.

Furthermore, consider also some noted Commentaries: According to Adam Clarke, "the love of the Spirit" means, "By that love of God which the Holy Spirit sheds abroad in your hearts."[3] According to Albert Barnes, it means, "By the mutual love and sympathy which the Spirit of God produces in the minds of all who are the friends of God."[6]

Matthew Henry has, "as a proof and instance of that love which the Spirit works in the hearts of believers one to another."[19] And Moses E. Lard has, "The love of the Spirit is that love for one another which the Spirit pours out in the hearts of those in whom it dwells."[22]

—*Commentary on Romans*, p. 448.

Therefore it is not the Holy Spirit that loves; it is God who loves, and who therefore by his Spirit inspires and produces that same kind of love in us toward one another. God's Spirit need not be a distinct person in order for that to happen.

THE INEVITABLE CONCLUSION

So the inevitable conclusion concerning the identity of the one only Almighty God is that he is not a triune being composed of three coequal and coeternal persons, God the Father, God the Son, and God the Holy Spirit, as taught by Trinitarians. Neither is he one being or person manifesting himself in three personalities, as taught by some Unitarians. But the one God (*ho Theos*), is the Father to the exclusion of all other beings or persons, Jehovah God the Lord Almighty, who has a one-and-only divine Son, Jesus Christ (born, not created), as well as an ever-proceeding Spirit by which the infinite, omniscient and omnipotent God is omnipresent.

As far as we have been able to determine, all the various known arguments, both old and new, that have been put forth by Trinitarians and Unitarians, as set forth herein, have each been successfully shown to be invalid, therefore leaving those doctrines without any substantial support whatsoever. And while unskilled minds may not understand all the terminology invented by theologians as set forth herein, most of them are able to understand the simple concept that the one God is the Father, who, like man, has a Son and a Spirit. That's *Theology Simplified*, conforming to both Scripture and reason.

APPENDIX A

GOD IS DECLARED TO BE THE FATHER (56 times)

Note: Those 44 references marked with an asterisk (*) are references where God, who is declared to be the Father, is also specifically distinguished from Christ. The word "Lord" is herein being replaced with "Jehovah" in the comments and explanations, as in the ASV text.

OT REFERENCES:

Seven of the OT references declaring God to be the Father, also identify that God as Jehovah, thereby showing that Christ, the Son, cannot be Jehovah God the Father.

* 2 Sam 7:14, "I (Jehovah, v. 11) will be his Father, and he will be my Son." When applying the "son" in this passage to Christ, as is done by the writer of Heb 1:5, Jehovah is clearly the God who is thus distinguished from Christ. Therefore, Christ is not the Jehovah of the OT.
  Ps 89:26, "He (David, v. 20) will call out to me Jehovah God Almighty, v. 8), 'You are my Father, my God, the Rock my Savior.'"
  Isa 9:6, "And he (Christ) will be called . . . Mighty God, Everlasting Father . . . ." Of all the 56 references where God is declared to be the Father, only here is Christ identified as "Father," which, if taken literally and absolutely, instead of representatively, Christ would be his own personal Father. Only representatively can Christ be called "Mighty God" and "Everlasting Father." See where this Scripture is explained extensively in Part I, Chapter 9.
    63:16, "But you (Jehovah) are our Father . . . you, O Lord, are our Father . . . ."
  Jer 31:9, "I (Jehovah, v. 7) am Israel's father . . . ."
  Mal 1:6, "'If I (Jehovah) am a Father, where is the respect due me?' says the Lord Almighty."

NT REFERENCES:

The following three references not only show that God is the Father, but that the Father, as distinguished from Christ, is the ONE and ONLY true God:

* John 17:3, Jesus praying to his Father (v. 1), prayed, "that they may know you, the only true God, and Jesus Christ, whom you have sent."

* 1 Cor 8:6, " . . . for us there is but one God, the Father, from whom all things came . . . and there is but one Lord, Jesus Christ, through whom all things came . . . ."
* Eph 4:5-6, " . . . one Lord, one faith, one baptism; one God and Father of all . . . ."

OTHER NT REFERENCES showing that God is the Father:

* John 5:18, " . . . but he (Jesus) was even calling God his own Father."
* 6:27, "On him (Jesus) God the Father has placed his seal of approval."
  8:41,The only Father we have is God himself."
* 8:54, "My (Jesus') Father, whom you claim as your God . . . ."
* Rom 1:7, "Grace and peace to you from God our Father and from the Lord Jesus Christ."
  8:14-15, " . . . those who are led by the Spirit of God are Sons of God . . . . And by him (or *whereby*, ASV) we cry, '*Abba*, Father.'"
* 15:6, " . . . you may glorify the God and Father of our Lord Jesus Christ."
* 1 Cor 1:3, "Grace and peace to you from God our Father and the Lord Jesus Christ."
* 15:24, " . . . when he (Christ) hands over the kingdom to God the Father . . . ."
* 2 Cor 1:2, "Grace and peace to you from God our Father and the Lord Jesus Christ."
* 1:3, "Praise be to the God and Father of our Lord Jesus Christ . . ."
* 1:3, " . . . the Father of compassion and the God of all comfort . ."
* 11:31, "The God and Father of the Lord Jesus . . . ."
* Gal 1:1, " . . . by Jesus Christ and God the Father . . ."
* 1:3, Grace and peace to you from God our Father and the Lord Jesus Christ . . . ."
  1:4, " . . . according to the will of our God and Father . . . ."
* Eph 1:2, "Grace and peace to you from God our Father and the Lord Jesus Christ."
* 1:3, "Praise be to the God and Father or our Lord Jesus Christ . . ."
* 1:17, " . . . the God of our Lord Jesus Christ, the glorious Father . ."
* 5:20, " . . . giving thanks to God the Father . . . in the name of our Lord Jesus Christ."
* 6:23, " . . . love with faith from God the Father and the Lord Jesus Christ."
* Phil 1:2, "Grace and peace to you from God our Father and the Lord Jesus Christ."
* 2:11, ". . . confess that Jesus Christ is Lord, to the glory of God the Father."

4:20, "To our God and Father be glory for ever and ever."

Col 1:2, "Grace and peace to you from God our Father."

*   1:3, "We always thank God, the Father or our Lord Jesus Christ."

*   3:17, " . . . do it all in the name of the Lord Jesus, giving thanks to God the Father . . . ."

*   1 Thess 1:1, " . . . in God the Father and the Lord Jesus Christ . . . ."

*   1:3, " . . . before our God and Father . . . in our Lord Jesus Christ."

*   3:11, "Now may our God and Father himself and our Lord Jesus clear the way . . . ."

*   3:13, " . . . in the presence of our God and Father when our Lord Jesus comes . . . ."

*   2 Thess 1:1, " . . . in God our Father and the Lord Jesus Christ . . . ."

*   1:2, "Grace and peace to you from God the Father and the Lord Jesus Christ."

*   2:16, "May our Lord Jesus Christ himself and God our Father, who loved us . . . ."

*   1 Tim 1:2, "Grace, mercy and peace from God the Father and Christ Jesus our Lord."

*   2 Tim 1:2, "Grace, mercy and peace from God the Father and Christ Jesus our Lord."

*   Titus 1:4, "Grace and peace from God the Father and Christ Jesus our Savior."

*   Phlm 1:3, "Grace to you and peace from God our Father and the Lord Jesus Christ."

*   Heb 1:5, "I (God) will be his Father, and he will be my Son" (quotation from 2 Sam 7:14, which see in this Appendix).

Jas 1:27, "Religion that God our Father accepts as pure . . . ."

*   1 Pet 1:2, " . . . according to the foreknowledge of God the Father . . for obedience to Jesus Christ and sprinkling by his blood."

*   1:3, "Praise be to the God and Father or our Lord Jesus Christ!"

*   2 Pet 1:17, "For he (Christ) received honor and glory from God the Father . . . ."

*   2 John 1:3, " . . . peace from God the Father and from Jesus Christ, the Father's Son . . . ."

*   Jude 1:1, " . . . loved by God the Father and kept by Jesus Christ."

*   Rev 1:6, "(Christ, v. 5) made us to be a kingdom and priests to serve his God and Father . . . ."

Of these 56 references declaring God to be Christ's Father, 7 of them (according to both the NIV and ASV) furthermore declare him to be also the GOD of Christ; not just his Father, but also his God. (See Rom 15:6; 2 Cor 1:3; 11:31; Eph 1:3, 17; 1 Pet 1:3; Rev 1:6).

APPENDIX B

JESUS CHRIST IS DECLARED TO BE THE SON OF GOD (77 times)

As Jesus is declared to be the Son of God, he is thereby distinguished from the God he is the Son of. "Son of God" no more makes Jesus GOD than "Son of David" makes him David. But "Son of God" does give Jesus the *nature* of God (divinity), just as "Son of David" gives him the *nature* of David (humanity).

NOTE: Those four references marked with an asterisk (*) show that the God whom Jesus is the Son of, is Jehovah, proving that Jesus is not Jehovah God, but is rather the Son thereof.

NT REFERENCES:

* Matt 2:15, "And so was fulfilled what the Lord had said through the prophet. 'Out of Egypt I called my son.'" (A quotation from Hos 11:1. "Lord," in this passage, refers to Jehovah, Hos 1:1).

4:3, "The tempter came to him and said, 'If you are the Son of God . . . .'"

4:6, "If you (Jesus) are the Son of God . . . throw yourself down."

8:29, "What do you (Jesus) want with us, Son of God?"

14:33, "Then those who were in the boat worshiped him, saying, 'Truly you are the Son of God.'"

16:16, "Simon Peter answered, 'You are the Christ, the Son of the living God.'"

26:63, "Tell us if you are the Christ, the Son of God."

27:40, "Come down from the cross, if you are the Son of God!"

27:43, " . . . for he said, 'I am the Son of God.'"

27:54, "Surely he was the Son of God."

Mark 1:1, "The beginning of the gospel about Jesus Christ, the Son of God."

5:7, "What do you want with me, Jesus, Son of the Most High God?"

15:39, "Surely this man was the Son of God!"

Luke 1:32, "He will be great and will be called the Son of the Most High."

1:35, "So the holy one to be born will be called the Son of God."

4:3, "If you are the Son of God, tell this stone to become bread."

4:9, "If you are the Son of God . . . throw yourself down from here."

4:41, " . . . demons came out of many people, shouting, 'You are the Son of God!'"

8:28, "What do you want with me, Jesus, Son of the Most High God?"

22:70, "They all asked, 'Are you then the Son of God?'"

John 1:34, "I have seen and I testify that this (Jesus) is the Son of God."

    1:49, "Rabbi, you are the Son of God; you are the King of Israel."

    3:16, "For God so loved the world that he gave his one and only Son" [fn and ASV: or *God's only begotten Son*].

    3:17, "For God did not send his Son into the world to condemn the world . . . ."

    3:18, " . . . he has not believed in the name of God's one and only Son" [fn and ASV: or *God's only begotten Son*].

    5:25, " . . . the dead shall hear the voice of the Son of God . . . ."

    9:35, "Do you believe in the Son of Man?" [ASV: *Son of God*].

    10:36, " . . . I said, 'I am God's Son.'"

    11:4, " . . . that God's Son may be glorified through it."

    11:27, "I believe that you are the Christ, the Son of God . . . ."

    19:7, " . . . he claimed to be the Son of God."

    20:31, "But these are written that you may believe that Jesus is the Christ, the Son of God."

Acts 3:13, "The God . . . has glorified his servant Jesus." [ASV fn: Or *Child*].

    3:26, "When God raised up his servant . . . ." [ASV fn: Or *Child*].

    9:20, "At once he began to preach in the synagogues that Jesus is the Son of God."

*   13:33, "You are my (God's, v. 32) Son . . . ." (A quote from Ps 2:7, where it is Jehovah who said, "You are my Son").

Rom 1:1-3, " . . . the gospel of God . . . regarding his Son . . . ."

    1:4, Christ (v. 1) " . . . was declared with power to be the Son of God . . . ."

    1:9, "God, whom I serve with my whole heart in preaching the gospel of his Son . . . ."

    5:10, " . . . we were reconciled to him (God) through the death of his Son . . . ."

    8:3, " . . . God did by sending his own Son in the likeness of sinful man . . . ."

    8:29, " . . . he (God) also predestined to be conformed to the likeness of his Son . . . ."

    8:32, "He (God) who did not spare his own Son . . . ."

1 Cor 1:9, "God, who has called you into fellowship with his Son Jesus Christ . . . ."

    15:28, " . . . then the Son himself will be made subject to him who put everything under him, so that God may be all in all."

2 Cor 1:19, "For the Son of God, Jesus Christ, who was preached among you by me . . . ."

Gal 1:15-16, " . . . God . . . revealed his Son in me . . . ."

256

2:20, " . . . Christ lives in me. The life I live in the body, I live by faith in the Son of God . . . ."

4:4, " . . . God sent his Son, born of a woman . . . ."

4:6, " . . . God sent the Spirit of his Son into our hearts . . . ."

Eph 4:13, " . . . until we all reach unity in the faith and in the knowledge of the Son of God . . . ."

1 Thess 1:9-10, "They tell how you turned to God from idols to serve the living and true God, and to wait for his Son from heaven . . . ."

Heb 1:1-2, " . . . God . . . has spoken to us by his Son . . . ."

* 1:5, "You are my Son; today I have become your Father." [fn and ASV: Or *have begotten you*]. (A quote from Ps 2:7, where it is Jehovah who said, "You are my Son").

4:14, " . . . since we have a great high priest . . . Jesus the Son of God . . . ."

* 5:5, "But God said to him, 'you are my Son'" (see 1:5 above).

6:6, " . . . they are crucifying the Son of God all over again . . . ."

7:3, " . . . like the Son of God he (Melchizedek) remains a priest forever."

10:29, " . . . who has trampled the Son of God under foot . . . ."

2 Pet 1:17, "For he (Christ) received honor and glory from God the Father when the voice came to him from the Majestic Glory, saying, 'This is my Son . . . .'"

1 John 1:5-7, "God is light . . . . and the blood of Jesus, his Son, purifies us from all sin."

3:8, "The reason the Son of God appeared was to destroy the devil's work."

3:21-23, " . . . we have confidence before God . . . to believe in the name of his Son, Jesus Christ . . . ."

4:9, "He (God) sent his one and only Son into the world . . . ."

4:10, " . . . he (God) loved us and sent his Son as an atoning sacrifice for our sins."

4:15, "If anyone acknowledges that Jesus is the Son of God, God lives in him . . . ."

5:5, "Only he who believes that Jesus is the Son of God."

5:9, " . . . God's testimony is greater . . . which he has given about his Son."

5:10, "Anyone who believes in the Son of God has this testimony . . . ."

5:10, " . . . the testimony God has given about his Son."

5:11, "God has given us eternal life, and this life is in his Son."

5:12, " . . . he who does not have the Son of God does not have life."

5:13, "I write these things to you who believe in the name of the Son of God . . . ."

5:20, "We know also that the Son of God has come . . . ."

5:20, "We are in him who is true—even in his Son Jesus Christ."

2 John 1:3, "Grace, mercy and peace from God the Father and from Jesus Christ, the Father's Son."

Rev 2:18, "These are the words of the Son of God . . . ."

APPENDIX C

JESUS IS DISTINGUISHED FROM GOD (326 times)

Jesus is not herein merely distinguished from the Father, a distinction of persons even recognized by Trinitarians who claim that both Jesus and the Father are separate persons in a plural being they call God; but Jesus is even more specifically distinguished from God, the being himself, in a way in which the Father is never once thus distinguished from God. If Jesus and the Father were coequally God in the same absolute sense, then it would be as appropriate to call the Father "the Father of God" as it is to call Jesus "the Son of God." But Jesus is distinguished from God these 326 times, in addition to those 77 times in Appendix B, while the Father is consistently spoken of in Scripture as being identical with God. The Father is never once called "the Father of God," as some (though not in Scripture) call Mary "the mother of God," but is identified as "God, the Father."

+ Those 46 references marked with a plus sign (+) are NT quotations from the OT where the God whom Jesus is distinguished from is Jehovah, proving that Jesus is not Jehovah God, but is rather the Son thereof.

\# Those 21 references marked with a pound sign (#) show that God is not only distinguished from Jesus, but is also even the God of Jesus. Six of these, all in the Revelation, show that God is still Jesus' God, even after his ascension and reglorification in heaven.

* Those 118 references marked with an asterisk (*) show further that Jesus is still distinguished from God, even after his ascension and reglorification in heaven.

+ Matt 4:6, "If you are the Son of God . . . throw yourself down." Then Satan quotes from Ps 91:11-12, "For he (Jehovah, see vv. 2, 9) will command his angels concerning you (Jesus)."

+# 4:7, "Do not put the Lord your God to the test." Jesus here quotes from Deut 6:16, "Do not test the LORD your God as you did at Massa." Jesus is not here saying that Satan should not be tempting Jesus, but that Jesus should not tempt Jehovah as Satan was trying to get him to do. Jesus thus recognized Jehovah as being his God.

+# 4:10, "For it is written: 'Worship the Lord your God, and serve him only.'" This quotation is from Deut 6:13, where "the Lord your God" is "the LORD (Jehovah) your God." Jesus therefore told Satan that Jehovah is the only being Jesus is authorized to worship. Thus Jesus hereby denied being either Jehovah or God.

5:8, " . . . for they will see God." But they were already seeing Jesus continually.

5:9, " . . . for they will be called the sons of God." If Jesus were as much God (*ho Theos*) as anyone else, then we would be as much sons of Jesus as we would be sons of anyone else.

\+ 8:17, "He took up our infirmities and carried our diseases." This quotation is from Isa 53:4, where it also says, " . . . we considered him stricken by God," thus distinguishing Jesus from God (who is called Jehovah in Isa 53:1).

9:8, " . . . they praised God, who had given such authority to men." (Specifically to Christ).

\+ 12:18, "Here is my servant whom I have chosen, the one I love, and he will proclaim justice to the nations." This quotation is from Isa 42:1, where it is Jehovah speaking (Isa 1:2), calling Jesus "my servant," etc. "I (Jehovah) will put my Spirit on him . . . ." So Jesus is here again distinguished from Jehovah.

\+ 22:44, "The Lord said to my Lord: 'Sit at my right hand until I put your enemies under your feet.'" This quotation is from Ps 110:1, where, "The Lord (Jehovah) says to my Lord (Christ) . . . ."

\+ 26:31, "I will strike the shepherd, and the sheep of the flock will be scattered." This is taken from Zech 13:7, where Jesus is prophetically referred to as Jehovah's shepherd.

\# 27:46, On the cross Jesus cried out, "My God, my God, why have you forsaken me?"

Mark 1:24, An evil spirit cried out to Jesus, "I know who you are—the Holy One of God!"

2:7, Some teachers of the law were thinking to themselves, "He's blasmpheming! Who can forgive sins but god (*ho Theos*) alone?" In verse 10 Jesus responded, " . . . the Son of Man has authority on earth to forgive sins . . . ." Here Jesus did not claim to be God who forgives sins, but rather that he had authority from that God to forgive sins.

10:18, Jesus asked, "Why do you call me god? . . . No one is good—except God alone."

\+ 12:36, "David himself, speaking by the Holy Spirit, declared: 'The Lord said to my Lord: "Sit at my right hand . . . ."'" (See explanation of Matt 22:44).

\+ 14:27, "I will strike the shepherd, and the sheep will be scattered." (See explanation of Matt 26:31).

\# 15:34, "My God, my God, why have you forsaken me?"
* 16:19, " . . . he was taken up into heaven and he sat at the right hand of God."

Luke 1:32, "The Lord God will give him (Jesus) the throne of his father David . . . ."

1:68-69, "Praise be to the Lord, the God of Israel, because he has

. . . raised up a horn of salvation (Jesus) in the house of his (God's) servant David . . . ."

+ 2:22-23, " . . . Joseph and Mary took him to Jerusalem to present him to the Lord . . . ."

In Exod 13:2, 12, it is Jehovah to whom all the firstborn were to be presented. Therefore Jesus was presented to Jehovah, proving that Jesus is not Jehovah.

2:40, " . . . and the grace of God was upon him (Jesus)."

2:52, "And Jesus grew in wisdom and stature, and in favor with God and men."

3:23-38, "He (Jesus) was the son, so it was thought, of Joseph . . the son of God."

+# 4:8, "Jesus answered . . . 'Worship the Lord your God . . . .'" (See explanation of Matt 4:10).

+ 4:10, "He will command his angels concerning you . . . ." (See explanation of Matt 4:6).

+# 4:12, "Do not put the Lord your God to the test." (See explanation of Matt 4:7).

+ 4:18, "The Spirit of the Lord (Jehovah, according to Isa 61:1) is on me (Jesus) . . . . He (Jehovah) has sent me . . . ."

4:34, A demon said to Jesus, "I know who you are—the Holy One of God!"

5:17, "And the power of the Lord was present for him (Jesus) to heal the sick."

5:21-24, "Who can forgive sins but God alone? . . . the Son of Man has authority on earth to forgive sins . . . ." (See explanation of Mark 2:7-10).

6:12, Jesus " . . . spent the night praying to God."

9:20, "Peter answered, 'The Christ of God.'"

11:20, "But if I (Jesus) drive out demons by the finger of God."

18:19, "Why do you call me good? . . . No one is good—except God alone." (See explanation of Mark 10:18).

+ 20:42, "David himself declares . . . 'The Lord said to my Lord . . .'" (See explanation of Matt 22:44).

23:35, " . . . let him save himself if he is the Christ of God, the Chosen One."

24:19, "He (Jesus) was a prophet, powerful in word and deed before God . . . ."

John 1:1, " . . . the Word was with God (Gr: *ho Theos*), and the Word was God (*Theos*, divine)."

1:2, "He (Jesus) was with God in the beginning."

1:18, "No one has ever seen God, . . ." yet thousands had seen Jesus.

1:29, "Look, the Lamb of God, who takes away the sin of the world!"

1:36, "Look, the Lamb of God!"

1:51, " . . . and the angels of God ascending and descending on the Son of Man."

3:2, "Rabbi, we know you are a teacher who has come from god. For no one could perform the miraculous signs you are doing if God were not with him."

3:34, "For the one whom God has sent speaks the words of God . . . ."

5:18, " . . . he (Jesus) was even calling God his own Father, making himself equal with God." This was a conclusion drawn by the Jews, but does show that Jesus is distinguished from God as any son is distinguished from his father.

6:27, "On him (Jesus) God the Father has placed his seal of approval."

6:29, "The work of God is this: to believe in the one (Jesus) he (God) has sent."

6:33, 35, "For the bread of God is he who comes down from heaven . . . ."

6:46, "No one has seen the Father except the one who is from God . . . ."

6:69, "Peter said, "We believe and know that you (Jesus) are the Holy One of God."

7:17-18, " . . . he will find out whether my (Jesus') teaching comes from God or whether I speak on my own. He who speaks on his own does so to gain honor for himself . . . ."

8:40, " . . . the truth that I (Jesus) heard from God."

8:42, " . . . I (Jesus) came from God and now am here."

9:16, "Some of the Pharisees said, 'This man (Jesus) is not from God . . . ."

9:33, "If this man (Jesus) were not from God, he could do nothing."

11:22, "But I know that even now God will give you (Jesus) whatever you ask."

13:3, " . . . he (Jesus) had come from God and was returning to God . . . ."

13:31, "Now is the Son of Man glorified, and God is glorified in him."

13:32, " . . . God will glorify the Son in himself, and will glory him at once."

14:1, "Trust in God; trust also in me (Jesus)."

16:30, "This makes us believe that you (Jesus) came from God."

17:3, " . . . that they may know you (the Father, v. 1), the only true God, and Jesus Christ, whom you have sent."

+ 19:24, "They divided my garments among them and cast lots for my clothing." This quotation is from Ps 22:18, where, in verse

19, Jesus asks for help from Jehovah.

\#   20:17, "I am returning to my Father and your Father, to my God and your God."

Acts 2:22, "Jesus . . . accredited by God to you . . . ."

     2:22, " . . . signs, which God did among you through him (Jesus)."

     2:24, "But God raised him (Jesus) from the dead . . . ."

     2:25, "I saw the Lord always before me." Jesus here quotes from Ps 16:8-11. The first person I, ME and MY refer to Jesus as proved in Acts 2:29-33. And the Lord is Jehovah, according to Ps 16:8.

+   2:25, "Because he (Jehovah) is at my right hand, I (Jesus) will not be shaken."

+   2:27, " . . . because you (Jehovah) will not abandon me to the grave . . . ."

+   2:27, " . . . nor will you (Jehovah) let your Holy One (Jesus) see decay."

+   2:28, "You (Jehovah) have made known to me (Jesus) the paths of life . . . ."

+   2:28, " . . . you (Jehovah) will fill me with joy in your presence."

     2:32, "God has raised this Jesus to life . . . ."

*   2:33, Jesus being "Exalted to the right hand of God . . . ."

+   2:34, "The Lord (Jehovah, Ps 110:1) said to my (David's) Lord (Christ): 'Sit at my right hand.'"

+   2:35, " . . . until I (Jehovah) make your (Christ's) enemies a footstool for your feet."

*   2:36, "God has made this Jesus, whom you crucified, both Lord and Christ."

     3:15, "You killed the author of life, but God raised him (Jesus) from the dead."

     3:18, " . . . God fulfilled what he foretold . . . that his Christ would suffer."

*   3:20, " . . . that he (God) may send the Christ . . . ."

+   3:22, "The Lord (Jehovah, Deut 18:15) your God will raise up for you a prophet (Christ) . . . ."

     4:10, " . . . Jesus Christ . . . whom God raised from the dead . . . ."

+   4:26, " . . . the rulers gather together against the Lord (Jehovah, Ps 2:2) and against his Anointed One."

     4:27, " . . . to conspire against your (God's, v. 24) holy servant [ASV fn: Or *Child*] Jesus . . . ."

*   4:3, " . . . through the name of your (God's, v. 24) holy servant (or Child) Jesus."

     5:30, "The God of our fathers raised Jesus from the dead . . . ."

*   5:31, "God exalted him (Jesus) to his own right hand as Prince and Savior . . . ."

     7:37, "God (Jehovah, Deut 18:15) will send you a prophet (Jesus) . . . ."

* 7:55, Stephen saw "Jesus standing at the right hand of God."

* 7:56, " . . . the Son of Man standing at the right hand of God."

10:36, "You know the message God sent . . . the good news of peace through Jesus Christ . . ."

10:38, " . . . how God anointed Jesus of Nazareth with the Holy Spirit and power . . . ."

10:38, " . . . because God was with him (Jesus)."

10:40, " . . . but God raised him (Jesus) from the dead . . . ."

10:41, "He (Jesus) was not seen by all the people, but by witnesses whom God had already chosen—by us who ate and drank with him . . . ."

10:42, " . . . he (Jesus) is the one whom God appointed as judge."

13:23, " . . . God has brought to Israel the Savior . . . ."

13:30, "But God raised him (Jesus) from the dead . . . ."

13:33, "What God promised our fathers he has fulfilled for us . . . by raising up Jesus."

+ 13:33, "You are my Son; today I (Jehovah, Ps 2:7) have become your Father." [fn and ASV: Or *have begotten you*].

+ 13:34, A quotation from Isa 55:3, where Jehovah is speaking (Isa 1:20. Thus, "I (Jehovah) will give you (Jesus) the holy and sure blessings promised to David."

+ 13:35, A quotation from Ps 16:10. "You (Jehovah, Ps 16:8) will not let your Holy One see decay."

* 17:31. "For he (God) . . . will judge the world . . . by the man (Jesus) he has appointed."

17:31, "He (God) has given proof to this . . . by raising him (Jesus) from the dead."

20:21, " . . . they must turn to God in repentance and have faith in our Lord Jesus."

* 22:14, "The God of our fathers has chosen you (Paul) . . . to see the Righteous One (Jesus) . . . ."

* Rom 1:7, "Grace and peace to you from God our Father and from the Lord Jesus Christ."

* 1:8, "First, I thank my God through Jesus Christ for all of you . ."

* 2:16, " . . . God will judge men's secrets through Jesus Christ . . . ."

3:25, "God presented him (Jesus) as a sacrifice of atonement . . ."

4:24, " . . . for us who believe in him (God) who raised Jesus our Lord from the dead."

* 5:1, " . . . we have peace with God through our Lord Jesus Christ."

5:8, "But God demonstrates his own love . . . While we were still sinners. Christ died for us."

* 5:11, " . . . we also rejoice in God through our Lord Jesus Christ."

5:15, " . . . how much more did God's grace and the gift that came by the grace of the one man, Jesus Christ . . . ."

  *   6:10, " . . . but the life he (Christ) lives, he lives to God."

  *   6:11, " . . . but alive to God in Christ Jesus."

  *   6:23, " . . . but the gift of God is eternal life in Christ Jesus our Lord."

  *   7:25, "Thanks be to God—through Jesus Christ our Lord."

        8:11, "And if the Spirit of him who raised Jesus from the dead is living in you . . . ."

  *   8:17, " . . . heirs of God and co-heirs with Christ . . . ."

  *   8:27, "And he who searches our hearts (Jesus) . . . intercedes for the saints in accordance with God's will." The questionable translations and interpretations of this passage are discussed in Part II, Chapter 6, *Intercession of the Spirit.*

  *   8:34, "Christ Jesus, who died . . . is at the right hand of God . . . ."

  *   8:39, " . . . from the love of God that is in Christ Jesus our Lord."

  +   9:33, A quotation from Isa 28:16. "See, I (Jehovah) lay in Zion a stone that causes men to stumble . . . the one who trusts in him (Jesus) will never be put to shame."

        10:9, " . . . confess with your mouth, 'Jesus is Lord,' and believe in your heart that God raised him from the dead, you will be saved."

  *   14:18, " . . . anyone who serves Christ in this way is pleasing to God . . . ."

  #   15:6, " . . . you may glorify the God and Father of our Lord Jesus Christ."

        15:7, " . . . Christ accepted you, in order to bring praise to God."

  *   16:27, " . . . to the only wise God be glory forever through Jesus Christ!'

    1 Cor 1:1, " . . . an apostle of Christ Jesus by the will of God . . . ."

  *   1:3, "Grace and peace to you from God our Father and the Lord Jesus Christ."

        1:4, "I always thank God for you because of his grace given you in Christ Jesus."

        1:24, " . . . Christ the power of God and the wisdom of God."

        1:30, " . . . you are in Christ Jesus, who has become for us wisdom from God . . . ."

  *   3:23, " . . . you are of Christ, and Christ is of God."

        6:14, " . . . God raised the Lord from the dead, and he will raise us also."

  *   8:6, " . . . there is but one God, the Father, from whom all things came and for whom we live; and there is but one Lord, Jesus Christ, through whom all things came and through whom we live."

  *   11:3, " . . . the head of every man is Christ . . . and the head of Christ is God."

        15:15, " . . . we have testified about God that he raised Christ from the dead."

*   15:24, "Then the end will come, when he hands over the kingdom to God the Father . . . ."

     15:27, A reference to Ps 8:6, referring to Jehovah (v. 1). "For he (Jehovah) 'has put everything under his (Christ's) feet.'"

*   15:27, ". . . this does not include God himself, who put everything under Christ."

     15:57, "But thanks be to God! He gives us victory through our Lord Jesus Christ."

  2 Cor 1:1, "Paul, an apostle of Christ Jesus by the will of God . . . ."

*   1:2, "Grace and peace to you from God our Father and the Lord Jesus Christ."

\#   1:3, "Praise be to the God and Father of our Lord Jesus Christ . ."

     1:21, "Now it is God who makes both us and you stand firm in Christ."

*   2:14, "But thanks be to God, who always leads us in triumphal procession in Christ . . . ."

     2:15, "For we are to God the aroma of Christ among those who are being saved . . . ."

*   2:17, ". . . in Christ we speak before God with sincerity . . . ."

     3:4, "Such confidence as this is ours through Christ before God."

*   4:4, ". . . the glory of Christ, who is the image of God."

     4:14, ". . the one (God) who raised the Lord Jesus from the dead."

     5:18, "All this is from God, who reconciled us to himself through Christ . . . ."

     5:19, ". . . God was reconciling the world to himself in Christ . . ." This shows that Christ was God representatively.

     5:20, "We implore you on Christ's behalf: Be reconciled to God."

\#   11:31, "The God and Father of the Lord Jesus . . . ."

*   12:19, "We have been speaking in the sight of God as those in Christ . . . ."

*   13:4, ". . . he (Christ) was crucified in weakness, yet he lives by God's power."

*   13:14, "May the grace of the Lord Jesus Christ, and the love of God . . . ."

*   Gal 1:1, ". . . sent not from men nor by man, but by Jesus Christ and God the Father . . . ."

*   1:3, "Grace and peace to you from God our Father and the Lord Jesus Christ . . . ."

     1:4, ". . . who gave himself for our sins . . . . according to the will of our God and Father . . . ."

*   3:26, "You are all sons of God through faith in Christ Jesus . . . ."

  Eph 1:1, "Paul, an apostle of Christ Jesus by the will of God . . . ."

*   1:2, "Grace and peace to you from God our Father and the Lord Jesus Christ."

\#   1:3, "Praise be to the God and Father of our Lord Jesus Christ . ."

         1:3, " . . . who (God) has blessed us . . . in Christ."

         1:5, "In love he (God) predestined us to be adopted as his sons through Jesus Christ . . . ."

         1:6, " . . . which he (God) has freely given us in the One (Christ) he loves."

\#   1:17, " . . . the God of our Lord Jesus Christ, the glorious Father."

         1:20, " . . . which he (God) exerted in Christ when he raised him from the dead . . . ."

*   1:20, " . . . and seated him (Christ) at his (God's) right hand in the heavenly realms . . . ."

*   1:22, "And God placed all things under his (Christ's) feet . . . ."

*   2:5, "God, who is rich in mercy, made us alive with Christ . . . ."

         2:7, " . . . he (God) might show the incomplete riches of his grace . . . in Christ Jesus."

         2:10, "For we are God's workmanship, created in Christ Jesus to do good works . . . ."

         2:16, Christ's purpose was "to reconcile both of them to God through the cross . . . ."

         2:19-20, " . . . you are . . . fellow citizens with God's people . . . with Christ Jesus himself . . . ."

         3:11, " . . . according to his eternal purpose which he (God) accomplished in Christ Jesus . . . ."

*   3:21, ". . to him (God) be glory in the church and in Christ Jesus."

*   4:5-6, "There is . . . one Lord, one faith, one baptism; one God and Father of all . . . ."

         4:32, " . . . just as in Christ God forgave you."

         5:2, " . . . just as Christ loved us and gave himself up for us as a fragrant offering . . . to God."

         5:20, " . . . giving thanks to God the Father for everything, in the name of our Lord Jesus Christ."

*   6:23, " . . . and love with faith from God the Father and the Lord Jesus Christ . . . ."

*   Phil 1:2, "Grace and peace to you from God our Father and the Lord Jesus Christ."

         1:8, "God can testify how I long for all of you with the affection of Christ Jesus."

         1:11, " . . . through Jesus Christ—to the glory and praise of God."

         2:26, "Who (Christ), being in very nature [fn and ASV: Or *in the form of*] God, did not consider equality with God something to be grasped . . . ."

         2:9, "Therefore God exalted him (Christ) to the highest place . ."

*   2:11, " . . . and every tongue confess that Jesus Christ is Lord, to the glory of God the Father."

         3:9, " . . . that which is through faith in Christ—the righteousness that comes from God . . . ."

    3:14, " . . . God has called me heavenward in Christ Jesus."

*   4:7, "And the peace of God . . . will guard your hearts and your minds in Christ Jesus."

*   4:19, "And my God will meet all your needs . . . in Christ Jesus."

Col 1:1, "Paul, an apostle of Christ Jesus by the will of God . . . ."

    1:3, "We always thank God, the Father of our Lord Jesus Christ."

*   1:15, "He (Christ) is the image of the invisible God, the firstborn over all creation."

    2:12, " . . . raised with him (Christ) through your faith in the power of God . . . ."

*   3:1, " . . . where Christ is seated at the right hand of God."

*   3:3, " . . . your life is now hidden with Christ in God."

*   3:17, " . . . do it all in the name of the Lord Jesus, giving thanks to God the Father through him."

* 1 Thes 1:1, " . . . in God the Father and the Lord Jesus Christ."

    1:3, " . . . before our God and Father . . . and . . . in our Lord Jesus Christ."

    2:15, " . . . who killed the Lord Jesus . . . . They displeased God . ."

*   3:11, "Now may our God and Father himself and our Lord Jesus clear the way for us . . . ."

*   3:13, " . . . in the presence of our God and Father when our Lord Jesus comes . . . ."

*   4:1, " . . . to please God . . . we ask you and urge you in the Lord Jesus . . . ."

    4:2-3, " . . . by the authority of the Lord Jesus. It is God's will that you should be sanctified . . . ."

*   4:14, " . . . God will bring with Jesus those who have fallen asleep in him."

    5:9, "For God did not appoint us to suffer wrath but to receive salvation through our Lord . . . ."

    5:18, " . . . give thanks in all circumstances, for this is God's will for you in Christ Jesus."

*   5:23, "May God himself, the God of peace, sanctify you through and through. May your whole spirit, soul and body be kept blameless at the coming of our Lord Jesus Christ."

* 2 Thes 1:1, " . . . in God our Father and the Lord Jesus Christ."

*   1:2, "Grace and peace to you from God the Father and the Lord Jesus Christ."

    1:12, " . . . according to the grace of our God and the Lord Jesus Christ."

*   2:16, "May the Lord Jesus Christ himself and God our Father . ."

1 Tim 1:1, " . . . by the command of God our Savior and of Christ Jesus our hope . . . ."

*   1:2, "Grace, mercy and peace from God the Father and Christ

268

Jesus our Lord."

* 2:5, "For there is one God and one mediator between God and men, the man Christ Jesus . . . ."

* 5:21, "I charge you, in the sight of God and Christ Jesus and the elect angels . . . ."

* 6:13, "In the sight of God, who gives life to everything, and of Christ Jesus . . . ."

2 Tim 1:1, "Paul, an apostle of Christ Jesus by the will of God . . . ."

* 1:2, "Grace, mercy and peace from God the Father and Christ Jesus our Lord."

1:9, " . . . God, who has saved us . . . . in Christ Jesus before the beginning of time . . . ."

* 4:1, "In the presence of God and of Christ Jesus . . . ."

Titus 1:1, "Paul, a servant of God and an apostle of Jesus Christ . ."

* 1:4, "Grace and peace from God the Father and Christ Jesus our Savior."

* 2:13, " . . . the glorious appearing of our great God and Savior, Jesus Christ . . . ." [ASV: "of the great God and our Savior Jesus Christ"]. The questionable translations and interpretations of this passage are discussed in Part I, Chapter 19, *The Great God and Savior*.

3:6, " . . . he (God, v. 4) poured out on us generously through Jesus Christ . . . ."

* Phlm 1:3, "Grace to you and peace from God our Father and the Lord Jesus Christ."

Heb 1:2, " . . . Son, whom he (God) appointed her of all things . . . ."

1:2, " . . . through whom (Christ) he (God) made the universe . . . ."

1:3, "The Son is the radiance of God's glory . . . ."

* 1:3, "After he (Christ) had provided purification for sins, he sat down at the right hand of the Majesty in heaven."

+ 1:5, "For to which of the angels did God ever say, 'You (Christ) are my (God's, v. 1; Jehovah's Ps 2:7) Son . . . ."

+ 1:5, " . . . today I (God, Jehovah) have become your Father." [fn and ASV: Or *have begotten you*].

+ 1:5, A quotation from 2 Sam 7:14, (where in verse 11 it is Jehovah speaking): "I will be his Father, and he will be my Son."

1:6, " . . . when God brings his firstborn (Christ) into the world . ."

1:6, "Let all God's angels worship him (Christ)."

* 1:8, "But about the Son he (God) says, 'Your throne, O God, will last for ever and ever . . . .'" [ASV fn: Or, *Thy throne is God for & c.*]. This quotation is from Ps 45:6 where the ASV footnote says [Or, *Thy throne is* the throne of *God & c.*]. See Part I, Chapter 20 for a full explanation as to why these alternate translations better fit the context.

\#   1:9, " . . . therefore God, your God, has set you above your companions by anointing you . . . ."

\+   1:13, A quotation from Ps 110:1, where it is Jehovah who said, "Sit at my right hand until I make your enemies a footstool for your feet."

     2:3-4, "This salvation, which was first announced by the Lord (Christ), was confirmed to us by those who heard him. God also testified to it by signs . . . ." (2:6-9, A quotation from Ps 8:4-6, where in verses 1 and 9 "you" and "your" refer to Jehovah. "Son of man" in Heb 2:6 may refer to man in general, but is applied to Jesus in verse 9).

\+   2:6, "What is . . . the son of man that you (Jehovah) care for him (Christ)."

\+   2:7, "You (Jehovah) made him a little lower than the angels . . . ."

\+   2:7, " . . . you (Jehovah) crowned him with glory and honor . . . ."

\+   2:7, ASV: "And (you, Jehovah) didst set him over the works of thy hands." [fn: Many authorities omit *And didst . . . hands*].

\+   2:8, And you (Jehovah) "put everything under his (Christ's) feet."

\+   2:8, "God left nothing that is not subject to him."

\+   2:9, Jesus "was made a little lower than the angels . . . so that by the grace of God he (Christ) might taste death for everyone."

\+   2:13, "Here am I (evidently Christ), and the children God has given me." (A quotation from Isa 8:18, where God is Jehovah).

*   2:17, " . . . the he (Christ) might become a . . . high priest in service to God . . . ." We know that Christ's priesthood came after his ascension, for "If he were on earth, he would not be a priest (Heb 8:4)." He was from the wrong tribe (Heb 7:14).

*   3:1-2, " . . . fix your thoughts on Jesus, the apostle and high priest . . . . He was faithful to the one who appointed him, just as Moses was faithful in all God's house."

     3:6, "But Christ is faithful as a son over God's house."

*+   5:4-5, "No one takes this honor (of highest priest) upon himself; he must be called by God . . . . So Christ also did not take upon himself the glory of becoming a high priest. But God (Jehovah, Ps 2:7) said to him, 'You are my Son; today I have become your Father.'"

*   5:10, " . . . and (Christ) was designated by God to be high priest in the order of Melchizedek."

*+   7:17, "You (Christ) are a priest forever . . . ." This quotation is from Ps 110:4, where it was Jehovah who swore and would not change his mind: "You are a priest forever . . . ."

*+   7:21, " . . . he (Christ) became a priest with an oath when God (Jehovah, Ps 110:4) said to him: . . . 'You are a priest forever.'"

*   7:25, "Therefore he (Christ) is able to save completely those who come to God through him, because he always lives to intercede for them."

*   8:1, "We do have such a high priest (Christ), who sat down at the right hand of the throne of the Majesty in heaven . . . ."

   9:14, " . . . Christ . . . offered himself unblemished to God . . . ."

*   9:24, " . . . he (Christ) entered heaven itself, now to appear for us in God's presence."

+   10:5, "Sacrifice and offering you did not desire, but a body you prepared for me . . . ." This quotation is from Ps 40:6, where it is Christ speaking to Jehovah God, verse 5.

10:7, "I (Christ) have come to do your will, O God." A quotation from Ps 40:7-8.

   10:9, "Here I (Christ) am, I have come to do your (God's) will."

*   10:12, " . . . he (Christ) sat down at the right hand of God."

*   12:2, " . . . fix our eyes on Jesus . . . who . . . sat down at the right hand of the throne of God."

*   12:23-24, "You have come to God, the judge of all men . . . to Jesus the mediator . . . ."

*   13:15, "Through Jesus, therefore, let us continually offer to God a sacrifice of praise . . . ."

   13:20, "May the God of peace, who . . . brought back from the dead our Lord Jesus . . . ."

*   13:21, " . . . may he (God, v. 20) work in us what is pleasing to him through Jesus Christ . . . ."

   Jas 1:1, "James, a servant of God and of the Lord Jesus Christ . . . ."

   1 Pet 1:2, " . . . according to the foreknowledge of God the Father, through the sanctifying work of the Spirit, for obedience to Jesus Christ and sprinkling by his blood."

1:3, "Praise be to the God and Father of our Lord Jesus Christ!"

*   2:5, " . . . offering spiritual sacrifices acceptable to God through Jesus Christ."

+   2:6, "A quotation from Isa 28:16, where we are told that the statement is made by the Sovereign Jehovah. Thus Jehovah said, "See, I lay a stone in Zion, a chosen and precious cornerstone, and the one who trusts in him (Christ) will never be put to shame."

   3:18, "For Christ died for sins once for all . . . to bring you to God."

   3:21, " . . . a good conscience toward God. It saves you by the resurrection of Jesus Christ . . . ."

*   3:22, " . . . Jesus Christ, who has gone into heaven and is at God's right hand . . . ."

*   4:11, " . . . in all things God may be praised through Jesus Christ."

   5:10, "And the God of all grace, who called you to his eternal glory in Christ . . . ."

2 Pet 1:1, "To those who through the righteousness of our God and Savior Jesus Christ . . . ." [ASV: "of our God and *the* Savior Jesus Christ."]

1:2, " . . . through the knowledge of God and of Jesus our Lord."

1:17, "For he (our Lord Jesus Christ, v. 16) received honor and glory from God the Father when the voice came to him from the Majestic Glory, saying, 'This is my Son . . . .'"

2 John 1:9, "Anyone who . . . does not continue in the teaching of Christ does not have God."

* Jude 1:1, " . . . loved by God the Father and kept by Jesus Christ."

* 1:25, " . . . to the only God our Savior be glory . . . through Jesus Christ our Lord . . . ."

* Rev 1:1, "The revelation of Jesus Christ, which God gave him to show his servants . . . ."

* 1:2, " . . . the word of God and the testimony of Jesus Christ."

* 1:4-5, "Grace and peace to you from him who is, and who was, and who is to come . . . and from Jesus Christ, who is the faithful witness, the firstborn from the dead . . . ."

*# 1:5-6, "To him who loves us and has freed us from our sins by his (Christ's) blood, and has made us to be a kingdom and priests to serve his God and Father . . . ."

1:8, "'I am the Alpha and the Omega,' says the Lord God, 'who is, and who was, and who is to come, the Almighty.'" (See verse 4 where this one is distinguished from Jesus Christ).

1:9, "I, John . . . was on the island of Patmos because of the word of God and the testimony of Jesus."

*# 3:2, " . . . I (Jesus) have not found your deeds complete in the sight of my God."

*# 3:12, "Him . . . I (Jesus) will make a pillar in the temple of my God."

*# 3:12, "I (Jesus) will write on him the name of my God . . . ."

*# 3:12, " . . . and the name of the city of my (Jesus') God . . . ."

*# 3:12, " . . . the new Jerusalem, which is coming down out of heaven from my (Jesus') God . . . ." Chapter 4 through 5:4 is a description of God on the throne, as distinguished from Christ:

4:8, "Holy, holy, holy is the Lord God Almighty, who was, and is, and is to come."

4:11, "You are worthy, our Lord and God, to receive glory and honor and power . . . ." Chapter 5:5 and following is a description of Jesus as distinguished from God:

* 5:6, "Then I saw a Lamb . . . standing in the center of the throne . . . ." (Not ON the throne).

* 5:7, "He (the Lamb, Christ) came and took the scroll from the right hand of him (God) who sat on the throne."

* 5:9-10, "You (Christ) are worthy . . . because you were slain, and with your blood you purchased men for God . . . . You have made them . . . to serve our God . . . ."

* 6:16. " . . . hide us from the face of him who sits on the throne and from the wrath of the Lamb."

* 7:9, " . . . standing before the throne (God) and in front of the Lamb (Christ)."

* 7:10, "Salvation belongs to our God, who sits on the throne, and to the Lamb."

* 7:14-15, " . . . they have washed their robes and made them white in the blood of the Lamb . . . . Therefore, 'they are before the throne of God and serve him day and night . . . .'"

* 7:17, "For the Lamb at the center of [ASV fn: Or, *before*] the throne will be their shepherd . . . . And God will wipe away every tear from their eyes."

* 11:15, "The kingdom of the world has become the kingdom of our Lord and of his Christ . . . ."

* 12:5, "She gave birth to a son, a male child, who will rule all the nations with an iron scepter. And her child was snatched up to God and to his throne."

* 12:10, "Now have come the salvation and the power and the kingdom of our God, and the authority of his Christ."

12:17, " . . . those who obey God's commandments and hold to the testimony of Jesus."

* 14:4, " . . . offered as firstfruits to God and the Lamb."

* 14:10, " . . . he, too, will drink of the wine of God's fury . . . . He will be tormented with burning sulfur in the presence of the holy angels and of the Lamb."

14:12, "This calls for patient endurance on the part of the saints who obey God's commandments and remain faithful to Jesus."

15:3, " . . . and sang the song of Moses the servant of God and the song of the Lamb."

20:4, "And I saw the souls of those who had been beheaded because of their testimony for Jesus and because of the word of God."

* 20:6, " . . . but they will be priests of God and of Christ . . . ."

* 21:22, "I did not see a temple in the city, because the Lord God Almighty and the Lamb are its temple."

* 21:23, "The city does not need the sun or the moon to shine on it, for the glory of God gives it light, and the Lamb is its lamp."

* 22:1, "Then the angel showed me the river . . . as clear as crystal, flowing from the throne of God and of the Lamb . . . ."

* 22:3, "The throne of God and of the Lamb will be in the city . . ."

APPENDIX D

SALUTATIONS, INVOCATIONS, AND BENEDICTIONS

Note: Asterisks (*) indicate those 49 passages which clearly distinguish between God and Christ.

Rom 1:1, "Paul, a servant of Christ Jesus, called to be an apostle and set apart for the gospel of God . . ."

*   1:7, "Grace and peace to you from God our Father and from the Lord Jesus Christ."

*   1:8, "I thank my God through Jesus Christ for all of you . . ."

*   1:9, "God, whom I serve with my whole heart in preaching the gospel of his Son, is my witness . . ."

*   16:27, " . . . to the only wise God be glory forever through Jesus Christ!"

*   1 Cor 1:1, "Paul, called to be an apostle of Christ Jesus by the will of God, and our brother Sosthenes . . ."

*   1:3, "Grace and peace to you from God our Father and the Lord Jesus Christ."

*   1:4, "I always thank God for you because of his grace given you in Christ Jesus."

*   1:9, "God, who has called you into fellowship with his Son Jesus Christ our Lord, is faithful."

     1:10, "I appeal to you, brothers, in the name of our Lord Jesus Christ . . ."

     16:23, "The grace of the Lord Jesus be with you."

     16:24, "My love to all of you in Christ Jesus."

*   2 Cor 1:1, "Paul, an apostle of Christ Jesus by the will of God . . ."

*   1:2, "Grace and peace to you from God our Father and the Lord Jesus Christ."

*   1:3, "Praise be to the God and Father of our Lord Jesus Christ, the Father of compassion and the God of all comfort (*paraklesis*) . . ."

     13:11, "And the God of love and peace will be with you."

*   13:14, "May the grace of the Lord Jesus Christ, and the love of God, and the fellowship of the Hollywood with you all."

*   Gal 1:1, "Paul, an apostle—sent . . . by Jesus Christ and God the Father . . ."

*   1:3-4, "Grace and peace to you from God our Father and the Lord Jesus Christ . . . according to the will of our God and Father . . ."

     6:18, "The grace of our Lord Jesus Christ be with your spirit . . ."

*   Eph 1:1, "Paul, an apostle of Christ Jesus by the will of God . . ."

*   1:2, "Grace and peace to you from God our Father and the Lord Jesus Christ."

*   1:3, "Praise be to the God and Father of our Lord Jesus Christ . ."

*   6:23, "Peace to the brothers, and love with faith from God the Father and the Lord Jesus Christ."

    6:24, "Grace to all who love our Lord Jesus Christ with an undying love."

* Phil 1:2, "Grace and peace to you from God our Father and the Lord Jesus Christ."

*   4:19, "And my God will meet all your needs according to his glorious riches in Christ Jesus."

    4:20, "To our God and Father be glory for ever and ever."

    4:23, "The grace of the Lord Jesus Christ be with your spirit."

* Col 1:1, "Paul, an apostle of Christ Jesus by the will of God, and Timothy our brother."

    1:2, "Grace and peace to you from God our Father."

*   1:3, "We always thank God, the Father of our Lord Jesus Christ, when we pray for you . . ."

* 1 Thess 1:1, "To the church of the Thessalonians in God the Father and the Lord Jesus Christ: Grace and peace to you."

*   5:23, "May God himself, the God of peace, sanctify you through and through . . . at the coming of our Lord Jesus Christ."

    5:28, "The grace of our Lord Jesus Christ be with you."

* 2 Thess 1:1, "To the church of the Thessalonians in God our Father and the Lord Jesus Christ."

*   1:2, "Grace and peace to you from God the Father and the Lord Jesus Christ."

*   2:16-17, "May our Lord Jesus Christ himself and God our Father . . . encourage your hearts . . ."

    3:16, "Now may the Lord (Jesus Christ) himself give you peace . . . . The Lord (Jesus Christ) be with all of you." ("The Lord" in this passage could possibly refer to God, 1 Thess 5:23).

    3:18, "The grace of our Lord Jesus Christ be with you all."

* 1 Tim 1:1, "Paul, an apostle of Christ Jesus by the command of God our Savior and of Christ Jesus our hope . . ."

*   1:2, "Grace, mercy and peace from God the Father and Christ Jesus our Lord."

* 2 Tim 1:1, "Paul, an apostle of Christ Jesus by the will of God, according to the promise of life that is in Christ Jesus . . ."

*   1:2, "Grace, mercy and peace from God the Father and Christ Jesus our Lord."

    4:22, "The Lord (Christ) be with your Spirit." ("The Lord" here could possibly refer to God).

* Titus 1:1, "Paul, a servant of God and an apostle of Jesus Christ . . ."

*   1:4, "Grace and peace from God the Father and Christ Jesus our Savior."

Phlm 1:1, "Paul, a prisoner of Christ Jesus, and Timothy our brother . . . ."

* 1:3, "Grace to you and peace from God our Father and the Lord Jesus Christ."

1:4, "I always thank my God . . . because I hear about your faith in the Lord Jesus . . ."

1:25, "The grace of the Lord Jesus Christ be with your spirit."

* Heb 1:1-2, "God . . . in these last days he has spoken to us by his Son . . ."

13:20, "May the God of peace, who through the eternal covenant brought back from the dead our Lord Jesus, that great Shepherd of the sheep . . ."

* Jas 1:1, "James, a servant of God and of the Lord Jesus Christ . . ."

* 1 Pet 1:2, " . . . chosen according to the foreknowledge of God the Father, through the sanctifying work of the Spirit (in sanctification of the Spirit, ASV) for obedience to Jesus Christ."

* 1:3, "Praise be to the God and Father of our Lord Jesus Christ!"

* 5:10, "And the God of all grace, who called you to his eternal glory in Christ . . ."

5:14, "Peace to all of you who are in Christ."

* 2 Pet 1:1, "Simon Peter, a servant and apostle of Jesus Christ, To those who through the righteousness of our God and Savior Jesus Christ [and the Savior Jesus Christ, ASV] . . ."

* 1:2, "Grace and peace be yours in abundance through the knowledge of God and of Jesus our Lord."

3:18, "But grow in the grace and knowledge of our Lord and Savior Jesus Christ. To him be glory both now and forever!"

1 John 1:1-2, "This we proclaim concerning the Word of life . . . which was with the Father and has appeared to us."

1:3, "And our fellowship is with the Father and with his Son, Jesus Christ."

* 5:20, "And we are in him who is true—even in his Son Jesus Christ. He is the true God and eternal life."

* 2 John 1:3, "Grace, mercy and peace from God the Father and from Jesus Christ, the Father's Son."

* Jude 1, "Jude, a servant of Jesus Christ and a brother of James, To those who have been called, who are loved by God the Father and kept by Jesus Christ."

* 25, "To the only God our Savior be glory, majesty, power and authority, through Jesus Christ our Lord, before all ages, now and forevermore!

* Rev 1:1, "The revelation of Jesus Christ, which God gave him to show his servants . . ."

1:2, " . . . who testifies to everything he saw—that is, the word of

God and the testimony of Jesus Christ."

*   1:4-5, "Grace and peace to you from him who is, and who is to come, and from the seven spirits before his throne, and from Jesus Christ, who is the faithful witness . . ."

*   1:5-6, "To him (Christ) who loves us and has freed us from our sins by his blood, and has made us to be a kingdom and priests to serve his God and Father—to him be glory and power for ever and ever!"

22:21, "The grace of the Lord Jesus be with God's people.

Amen."

APPENDIX E

SPIRIT PASSAGES
(105 OT References)

To avoid omitting any possible references to God's Spirit, some questionable references may be included. Some references may be man's spirit when filled with the influence of God's Spirit, in which cases the capital "S" is questionable. All quotes are from the NIV unless otherwise stated. NIV footnotes are placed in brackets [ ]. Other translations and explanations gathered from the context are placed in parentheses ( ).

Gen 1:2, and the Spirit of God was hovering over the waters

6:3, the LORD said, "My Spirit will not contend with man forever" [Or *My spirit will not remain in*]

41:38, Pharaoh asked them, "Can we find anyone like this man, one in whom is the spirit of God?" [Or *of the gods*]

Exod 28:3, (ASV) thou shalt speak unto all that are wise-hearted, whom I (Jehovah) have filled with the spirit of wisdom

31:3, I (Jehovah) have filled him (Bezalel) with the Spirit of God, with skill, ability and knowledge in all kinds of crafts

35:31, he (Jehovah) has filled him (Bezalel) with the Spirit of God

Num 11:17, I (Jehovah) will take of the Spirit that is on you (Moses) and put the Spirit (ASV: it) on them (the seventy).

11:25, he (Jehovah) took of the Spirit that was on him (Moses) and put the Spirit on the seventy elders

11:25, When the Spirit rested on them (the seventy), they prophesied, but they did not do so again.

11:26 Yet the Spirit also rested on them (Eldad and Medad), and they prophesied in the camp.

11:29, I (Moses) wish that all the LORD's people were prophets and that the LORD would put his Spirit on them!

24:2, the Spirit of God came upon him (Balaam) and he uttered his oracle

27:18, So the LORD said to Moses, "Take Joshua son of Nun, a man in whom is the spirit" [Or *Spirit*]

Deut 34:9, Now Joshua son of Nun was filled with the spirit [Or *Spirit*] of wisdom because Moses had laid his hands on him

Judg 3:10, The Spirit of the LORD came upon him (Othniel), so that he became Israel's judge

6:34, The Spirit of the LORD came upon Gideon

11:29, Then the Spirit of the LORD came upon Jephthah

13:25, the Spirit of the LORD began to stir him (Samson)

14:6, The Spirit of the LORD came upon him (Samson) in power so that he tore the lion apart with his bare hands

14:19, Then the Spirit of the LORD came upon him (Samson) in power

15:14, The Spirit of the LORD came upon him (Samson) in power

1 Sam 10:6, The Spirit of the LORD will come upon you (Saul) in power, and you will prophesy

10:10, a procession of prophets met him (Saul); the Spirit of the God came upon him (Saul) in power, and he joined in their prophesying

11:6, the Spirit of God came upon him (Saul) in power

16:13, from that day on the Spirit of the LORD came upon David in power.

16:14, Now the Spirit of the LORD had departed from Saul

19:20, The Spirit of God came upon Saul's men and they also prophesied.

19:23, But the Spirit of God came even upon him (Saul), and he walked along prophesying

2 Sam 23:2, The Spirit of the LORD spoke through me; his word was on my tongue.

1 Kgs 18:12, I (Obadiah) don't know where the Spirit of the LORD may carry you (Elijah) when I leave you.

22:24, Which way did the spirit from [Or *Spirit of*] the LORD go when he went from me (Zedekiah) to speak to you (Micaiah)?

2 Kgs 2:9, Let me (Elisha) inherit a double portion of your (Elijah's) spirit

2:15, The spirit of Elijah is resting on Elisha.

2:16, Perhaps the Spirit of the LORD has picked him (Elijah) up and set him down on some mountain

1 Chr 12:18, Then the Spirit came upon Amasai, chief of the Thirty

28:12, He (David) gave him (Solomon) the plans of all that the Spirit had put in his mind for the courts of the temple

2 Chr 15:1, The Spirit of God came upon Azariah

18:23, Which way did the spirit from [Or *Spirit of*] the LORD go when he went from me (Zedekiah) to speak to you (Micaiah)?

20:14, Then the Spirit of the LORD came upon Jahaziel . . . as he stood in the assembly.

24:20, Then the Spirit of God came upon Zechariah

Neh 9:20, You (God) gave your good Spirit to instruct them (Israel)

9:30, By our (God's) Spirit you admonished them through your prophets

Job 26:13, (ASV) By his Spirit (NIV: breath) the heavens are garnished

32:8, But it is the spirit [Or *Spirit*] in a man, the breath of the Almighty that gives him understanding.

32:18, For I am full of words, and the spirit [Or *Spirit*] within me compels me

33:4 The Spirit of God has made me, the breath of the Almighty gives me life.

34:14, If it were his intention and he withdrew his spirit [Or *Spirit*] and breath, all mankind would perish together and man would return to the dust.

Ps 51:11, Do not cast me from your presence or take your Holy Spirit from me.

51:12, Restore to me the joy of your salvation and grant me a willing spirit, to sustain me.

104:30, When you send your Spirit, they are created, and you renew the face of the earth.

106:33, they rebelled against the Spirit of God, and rash words came from Moses' lips [Or *against his spirit / and rash words came from his lips*]

139:7-8, Where can I go from your (Jehovah's) Spirit? Where can I flee from your presence? If I go up to the heavens, you are there; if I make my bed in the depths, you are there.

143:10, you are my God; may your good Spirit lead me on level ground.

Prov 1:23, (ASV) Behold, I (Wisdom) will pour out my spirit upon you; I will make known my words unto you.

Isa 4:4, he (the Lord) will cleanse the bloodstains from Jerusalem by a spirit [Or *the spirit*] of judgment and a spirit [Or *the Spirit*] of fire.

11:2, The Spirit of the LORD will rest on him (the Messiah)

11:2, the Spirit of wisdom and of understanding, the Spirit of counsel and of power, the Spirit of knowledge and of the fear of the LORD

28:6, He (the LORD Almighty) will be a spirit of justice to him who sits in judgment

29:10, (ASV) Jehovah hath poured out upon you the spirit of deep sleep, and hath closed your eyes, the prophets

30:1 Woe . . . to those who carry out plans that are not mine, forming an alliance, but not by my Spirit

32:15, till the Spirit is poured upon us from on high

34:16, For it is his (the LORD's) mouth that has given the order, and his Spirit will gather them together.

40:13, Who has understood the mind [Or *Spirit*; or *spirit*] of the LORD, or instructed him as his counselor?

42:1, I will put my Spirit on him (the Messiah) and he will bring justice to the nations.

44:3, I (the LORD) will pour out my Spirit on your offering, and my blessing on your descendants.

48:16, the Sovereign LORD has sent me, with his Spirit.

59:19, For he (the LORD) will come like a pent-up flood that the breath of the LORD drives along. [Or *When the enemy comes in like a flood / the Spirit of the LORD will put him to flight*]

59:21, My Spirit, who (ASV: that) is on you, and my words that I have put in your mouth will not depart from your mouth

61:1, The Spirit of the Sovereign LORD is on me

63:10, Yet they rebelled and grieved his (the LORD's) Holy Spirit.

63:11, Where is he who set his Holy Spirit among them

63:14, they were given rest by the Spirit of the LORD.

Ezek 1:12, Wherever the spirit would go, they (the four living creatures) would go, without turning as they went.

1:20, Wherever the spirit would go, they would go

2:2, As he spoke, the Spirit came into me and raised me to my feet

3:12, Then the Spirit lifted me up, and I heard behind me a loud rumbling sound

3:14 The Spirit then lifted me up and took me away

3:24, Then the Spirit came into me and raised me to my feet.

8:3, The Spirit lifted me up between earth and heaven and in visions of God he took me to Jerusalem

11:1, Then the Spirit lifted me up and brought me to the gate of the house of the LORD

11:5, Then the Spirit of the LORD came upon me, and he told me to say . . .

11:19, I will give them an undivided heart and put a new spirit in them

11:24, The Spirit lifted me up and brought me to the exiles in Babylonia in the vision given by the Spirit of God.

36:26, I will give you a new heart and put a new spirit in you

36:27, And I will put my Spirit in you and move you to follow my decrees

37:1, and he brought me out by the Spirit of the LORD and set me in the middle of a valley

37:14, I will put my Spirit in you and you will live

39:29, I will no longer hide my face from them, for I will pour out my Spirit on the house of Israel

43:5, Then the Spirit lifted me up and brought me into the inner court, and the glory of the LORD filled the temple.

Dan 4:8, (Nebuchadnezzar speaking) and the spirit of the holy gods is in him (Daniel)

4:9, (Nebuchadnezzar speaking) I know that the spirit of the holy gods is in you (Daniel)

4:18, (Nebuchadnezzar speaking) But you can, because the spirit of the holy gods is in you.

5:11, (King Belshazzar's queen speaking) There is a man in your kingdom who has the spirit of the holy gods in him (Daniel).

5:12, (The queen speaking) This man Daniel . . . was found to have a keen mind (ASV: an excellent spirit) and knowledge and understanding, and also the ability to interpret dreams

5:14, I (Belshazzar) have heard that the spirit of the gods is in you (Daniel)

6:3, (ASV) this Daniel was distinguished above the presidents and the satraps, because an excellent spirit was in him

Joel 2:28, I will pour out my Spirit on all people (ASV: all flesh)

2:29, Even on my servants, both men and women, I will pour out my Spirit in those days.

Micah 2:7, Is the Spirit of the LORD angry? Does he do such things?

3:8, I am filled with power, with the Spirit of the LORD

Hag 2:5, And my (the LORD's) Spirit remains among you.

Zech 4:6, "Not by might nor by power, but by my Spirit," says the LORD Almighty.

6:8, Look, those going toward the north country have given my Spirit [Or *spirit*] rest

7:12, and would not listen to the law or to the words that the LORD Almighty had sent by his Spirit through the earlier prophets.

12:10, I will pour out on the house of David and the inhabitants of Jerusalem a spirit [Or *the Spirit*] of grace and supplication.

(269 NT References)

Matt 1:18, before they came together, she (Mary) was found to be with child through (ASV: of) the Holy Spirit.

    1:20, what is conceived in her is from (ASV: of) the Holy Spirit.

    3:11, He (Jesus) will baptize you with the Holy Spirit and with fire.

    3:16, As soon as Jesus was baptized . . . he saw the Spirit of God descending like a dove and lighting on him.

    4:1, Then Jesus was led by the Spirit into the desert to be tempted by the devil.

    10:20, it will not be you speaking, but the Spirit of your Father speaking through you.

    12:18, (Quoting from Isa 42:1) I (Jehovah) will put my Spirit on him (Christ), and he will proclaim justice to the nations.

    12:28, But if I (Jesus) drive out demons by the Spirit of God, then the kingdom of God has come upon you.

    12:32, anyone who speaks against the Holy Spirit will not be forgiven, either in this age or in the age to come.

    22:43, David, speaking by the Spirit, calls him (Jesus) "Lord"

    28:19, baptizing them in [Or *into*] the name of the Father and of the Son and of the Holy Spirit

Mark 1:8, I baptize you with [Or *in*] water, but he (Christ) will baptize you with the Holy Spirit

    1:10, As Jesus was coming up out of the water, he saw heaven being torn open and the Spirit descending on him like a dove.

    1:12, At once the Spirit sent him (Christ) out into the desert

    2:8, Immediately Jesus knew in his spirit that this was what they were thinking

    3:29, But whoever blasphemes against the Holy Spirit will never be forgiven; he is guilty of an eternal sin.

    8:12, (ASV) And he (Christ) sighed deeply in his spirit, and saith, Why doth this generation seek a sign?

    12:36, David himself, speaking by the Holy Spirit, declared, "The Lord said to my Lord . . . ."

    3:11, Just say whatever is given you at that time, for it is not you speaking, but the Holy Spirit.

Luke 1:15, and he (John the Baptist) will be filled with the Holy Spirit even from birth.

    1:17, And he will go on before the Lord, in the spirit and power of Elijah

    1:35, The Holy Spirit will come upon you (Mary), and the power of the Most High will overshadow you. So the holy one to be born will be called the Son of God.

    1:41, the baby (John the Baptist) leaped in her (Elizabeth's) womb, and Elizabeth was filled with the Holy Spirit.

1:67, His father Zechariah was filled with the Holy Spirit and prophesied

2:25, He (Simeon) was waiting for the consolation of Israel, and the Holy Spirit was upon him.

2:26, It had been revealed to him by the Holy Spirit that he would not die before he had seen the Lord's Christ.

2:27, Moved by the Spirit, he went into the temple courts.

3:16, He (Christ) will baptize you with the Holy Spirit and with fire.

3:22, the Holy Spirit descended on him in bodily form like a dove.

4:1, Jesus, full of the Holy Spirit, returned from the Jordan

4:1, and was led by the Spirit in the desert

4:14, Jesus returned to Galilee in the power of the Spirit

4:18, The Spirit of the Lord is on me (Christ)

10:21, At that time Jesus, full of joy through the Holy Spirit, said . .

11:13, how much more will your Father in heaven give the Holy Spirit to those who ask him!

12:10, anyone who blasphemes against the Holy Spirit will not be forgiven.

12:12, the Holy Spirit will teach you at that time what you should say.

John 1:32, I (John) saw the Spirit come down from heaven as a dove and remained on him.

1:33, The man on whom you see the Spirit come down and remain is he who will baptize with the Holy Spirit.

3:5, no one can enter the kingdom of God unless he is born of water and the Spirit.

3:6, Flesh gives birth to flesh, but the Spirit [Or *but spirit*] gives birth to spirit

3:8, So it is with everyone born of the Spirit.

3:34, For the one (Christ) whom God has sent speaks the words of God, for God gives the Spirit without limit.

4:23, the true worshipers will worship the Father in spirit, and truth

4:24, God is spirit

4:24, his (God's) worshipers must worship in spirit and in truth.

6:63, The Spirit gives life; the flesh counts for nothing. Jesus had not yet been glorified.

6:63, The words I have spoken to you are spirit [Or *Spirit*] and they are life.

7:39, By this he meant the Spirit, whom (ASV: which) those who believed in him were later to receive

7:39, Up to that time the Spirit had not been given, since Jesus had not yet been glorified.

11:33, When Jesus saw her weeping . . . he was deeply moved in spirit and troubled.

13:21, After he had said this, Jesus was troubled in spirit and testified

14:16-17, I will ask the Father, and he will give you another Counselor to be with you forever—the Spirit of truth.

14:26, But the Counselor, the Holy Spirit, whom (KJV and Gr neut: which) the Father will send in my name

15:26, When the Counselor comes, whom I will send to you from the Father, the Spirit of truth, who (KJV and Gr neut: which) goes out from the Father, he will testify about me.

16:13, But when he, the Spirit of truth, comes, he will guide you into all truth. (See our Part II, Chapter 1, for explanation of John 14:16 through 16:13).

20:22, he (Jesus) breathed on them and said, "Receive the Holy Spirit."

Acts 1:2, until the day he was taken up to heaven, after giving instructions through the Holy Spirit to the apostles he had chosen.

1:5, For John baptized with [Or in] water, but in a few days you will be baptized with the Holy Spirit.

1:8, But you will receive power when the Holy Spirit comes on you

1:16, the Scripture had to be fulfilled which the Holy Spirit spoke long ago through the mouth of David concerning Judas

2:4, All of them were filled with the Holy Spirit . . . and began to speak in other tongues as the Spirit enabled them.

2:17, I will pour out my Spirit on all people.

2:18, I will pour out my Spirit in those days, and they will prophesy.

2:33, he (Christ) has received from the Father the promised Holy Spirit and has poured out what you now see and hear.

2:38, And you will receive the gift of the Holy Spirit.

4:8, Then Peter, filled with the Holy Spirit, said to them

4:25, You spoke by the Holy Spirit through the mouth of your servant, our father David (ASV fn: The Greek text in this clause is somewhat uncertain).

4:31, And they were all filled with the Holy Spirit and spoke the word of God boldly.

5:3-4, Ananias, how is it that Satan has filled your heart that you have lied to the Holy Spirit . . . . You have not lied to men but to God.

5:9, How could you agree to test the Spirit of the Lord?

5:32, We are witnesses of these things, and so is the Holy Spirit, whom (Gr neut: which) God has given to those who obey him.

6:3, choose seven men from among you who are known to be full of the Spirit and wisdom.

6:5, They chose Stephen, a man full of faith and of the Holy Spirit

6:10, they could not stand up against his wisdom or the Spirit by whom (ASV: which) he spoke.

7:51, You are just like your fathers: You always resist the Holy Spirit!

7:55, But Stephen, full of the Holy Spirit, looked up to heaven

8:15, When they arrived, they prayed for them that they might receive the Holy Spirit

8:16, because the Holy Spirit had not yet come upon any of them (ASV: for as yet it was fallen upon none of them).

8:17, Then Peter and John placed their hands on them, and they received the Holy Spirit.

8:18, When Simon saw that the Spirit was given at the laying on of the apostles' hands, he offered them money

8:19, Give me also this ability so that everyone on whom I lay my hands may receive the Holy Spirit

8:29, The Spirit told Philip, "Go to that chariot and stay near it."

8:39, When they came up out of the water, the Spirit of the Lord suddenly took Philip away

9:17, Jesus . . . has sent me (Ananias) so that you (Saul) may see again and be filled with the Holy Spirit.

9:31, It (the church) was strengthened; and encouraged by the Holy Spirit, it grew in numbers

10:19, While Peter was still thinking about the vision, the Spirit said to him . . .

10:38, God anointed Jesus of Nazareth with the Holy Spirit and power

10:44, While Peter was still speaking these words, the Holy Spirit came on all who heard the message.

10:45, The circumcised believers who had come with Peter were astonished that the gift of the Holy Spirit had been poured out even on the Gentiles.

10:47, They have received the Holy Spirit just as we have.

11:12, The Spirit told me (Peter) to have no hesitation about going with them.

11:15, As I (Peter) began to speak, the Holy Spirit came on them as he had come on us at the beginning. (ASV: fell on them, even as on us at the beginning). (No Greek pronoun for "he" is found in this passage).

11:16, John baptized with [Or *in*] water, but you will be baptized with the Holy Spirit.

11:24, He (Barnabas) was a good man, full of the Holy Spirit and faith

11:28, Agabus, stood up and through the Spirit predicted that a severe famine would spread over the entire Roman world.

13:2, While they were worshiping the Lord and fasting, the Holy Spirit said . . .

13:4, The two of them, sent on their way by the Holy Spirit, went down to Seleucia

13:9, Then Saul, who was also called Paul, filled with the Holy Spirit, looked straight at Elymas

13:52, And the disciples were filled with joy and with the Holy Spirit.

15:8, God . . . showed that he accepted them by giving the Holy Spirit to them, just as he did to us.

15:28, It seemed good to the Holy Spirit and to us not to burden you

16:6, Paul . . . having been kept by the Holy Spirit from preaching the word in the province of Asia.

16:7, they tried to enter Bithynia, but the Spirit of Jesus would not allow them to. (Some Greek texts omit "of Jesus").

18:25, He (Apollos) had been instructed in the way of the Lord, and he spoke with great fervor [Or *with fervor in the Spirit*]

19:2, Did you receive the Holy Spirit when [Or *after*] you believed?

19:2, No, we have not even heard that there is a Holy Spirit.

19:6, When Paul placed his hands on them, the Holy Spirit came on them, and they spoke in tongues and prophesied.

19:21, Paul decided (ASV: purposed in the spirit) to go to Jerusalem

20:22, And now, compelled by the Spirit, I am going to Jerusalem

20:23, I only know that in every city the Holy Spirit warns me that hardships are facing me.

20:28, Keep watch over yourselves and all the flock of which the Holy Spirit has made you overseers.

21:4, Through the Spirit they urged Paul not to go on to Jerusalem.

21:11, The Holy Spirit says, "In this way the Jews of Jerusalem will bind the owner of this belt and will hand him over to the Gentiles.

28:25, The Holy Spirit spoke the truth to your forefathers when he said through Isaiah the prophet (No Greek pronoun for "he" is found in this passage. See ASV).

Rom 1:4, who (Christ) through the Spirit [Or *who as to his spirit*] of holiness was declared with power to be the Son of God.

2:29, circumcision is circumcision of the heart, by the Spirit, not by the written code.

5:5, God has poured out his love into our hearts by the Holy Spirit, whom (ASV: which) he has given us.

7:6, we have been released from the law so that we serve in the new way of the Spirit, and not in the old way of the written code.

8:1, [Some later manuscripts *Jesus, who do not live according to the sinful nature but according to the Spirit*]

8:2, through Christ Jesus the law of the Spirit of life set me free from the law of sin and death.

8:4, who do not live according to the sinful nature [Or *the flesh*] but according to the Spirit

8:5, but those who live in accordance with the Spirit have their minds set on what the Spirit desires.

8:9, You, however, are controlled not by the sinful nature [Or *the flesh*] but by the Spirit, if the Spirit of God lives in you.

8:9, And if anyone does not have the Spirit of Christ, he does not belong to Christ.

8:11, And if the Spirit of him who raised Jesus from the dead is living in you

8:11, he who raised Christ from the dead will also give life to your mortal bodies through his Spirit, who (ASV: that) lives in you.

8:13, but if by the Spirit you put to death the misdeeds of the body, you will live

8:14, because those who are led by the Spirit of God are sons of God.

8:15, but you received the Spirit of sonship [Or *adoption*].

8:16, The Spirit himself (KJV: itself; Gr: *auto*, neut.) testifies with our spirit that we are God's children.

8:23, we ourselves, who have the firstfruits of the Spirit, groan inwardly as we wait eagerly for our adoption as sons, the redemption of our bodies

8:26, In the same way, the Spirit helps us in our weakness.

8:26, We do not know what we ought to pray for, but the Spirit himself(See 8:16 above) intercedes for us with groans that words cannot express.

8:27, And he who searches our hearts (Christ, our intercessor, v. 34) knows the mind of the Spirit, because the Spirit (ASV: he [Christ]) intercedes for the saints in accordance with God's will. (See our Part II, Chapters 5 and 6 for further explanation of 8:26-27).

9:1, I am not lying, my conscience confirms it in the Holy Spirit

14:17, For the kingdom of God is not a matter of eating and drinking, but of righteousness, peace and joy in the Holy Spirit

15:13, so that you may overflow with hope by the power of the Holy Spirit.

15:16, the Gentiles might become an offering acceptable to God, sanctified by the Holy Spirit.

15:19, by the power of signs and miracles, through the power of the Spirit.

15:30, I urge you . . . by the Lord Jesus Christ and by the love of the Spirit, to join me in my struggle by praying to God for me.

1 Cor 2:4, My message and my preaching were not with wise and persuasive words, but with a demonstration of the Spirit's power

2:10, God has revealed it to us by his Spirit.

2:10, The Spirit searches all things, even the deep things of God.

2:11, no one knows the thoughts of God except the Spirit of God.

2:12, We have not received the spirit of the world but the Spirit who (ASV: which) is from God

2:13, not in words taught us by human wisdom but in words taught by the Spirit

2:14, The man without the Spirit does not accept the things that come from the Spirit of God

3:16, Don't you know that you yourselves are God's temple and that God lives in you?

5:3, Even though I (Paul) am not physically present, I am with you in spirit.

5:4, When you are assembled in the name of our Lord Jesus and I am with you in spirit, and the power of our Lord Jesus is present

6:11, you were justified in the name of the Lord Jesus Christ and by the Spirit of our God.

6:17, But he who unites himself with the Lord is one with him in spirit.

6:19, Do you not know that your body is a temple of the Holy Spirit, who (ASV: which) is in you, whom (ASV: which) you have received from God?

7;40, I (Paul) think that I too have the Spirit of God.

12:3, Therefore I tell you that no one who is speaking by the Spirit of God says, "Jesus be cursed"

12:3, and no one can say, "Jesus is Lord," except by the Holy Spirit.

12:4, There are different kinds of gifts, but the same Spirit.

12:7, Now to each one the manifestation of the Spirit is given for the common good.

12:8, To one there is given through the Spirit the message of wisdom

12:8, to another the message of knowledge by means of the same Spirit

12:9, to another faith by the same Spirit

12:9, to another gifts of healing by that one Spirit

12:11, All these are the work of one and the same Spirit, and he (God, v. 6) gives them (through the Spirit, v. 8) to each one, just as he (God) determines.

12:13, For we were all baptized by [Or *with*; or *in*] one Spirit into one body

12:13, and we were all given the one Spirit to drink.

14:2, Indeed, no one understands him; he utters mysteries with his spirit [Or *by the Spirit*].

14:14, For if I pray in a tongue, my spirit prays, but my mind is unfruitful.

14:15, So what shall I do? I will pray with my spirit, but I will also pray with my mind

14:15, I will sing with my spirit, but I will also sing with my mind.

14:16, If you are praising God with your spirit, how can one who finds himself among those who do not understand say "Amen"

14:32, The spirits of the prophets are subject to the control of the prophets.

15:45, "The first man Adam became a living being"; the last Adam, a life-giving spirit.

2 Cor 1:22, (God) set his seal of ownership on us, and put his Spirit in our hearts as a deposit (ASV: earnest), guaranteeing what is to come.

3:3, you are a letter . . . written not with ink but with the Spirit of the living God

3:6, as ministers . . . not of the letter but of the Spirit

3:6, for the letter kills, but the Spirit gives life.

3:8, will not the ministry of the Spirit be even more glorious?

3:17, Now the Lord is the Spirit, and where the Spirit of the Lord is, there is freedom.

3:18, being transformed into his likeness with ever-increasing glory, which comes from the Lord, who is the Spirit. (See our Part II, Chapter 8, for further explanation of vv. 17-18)

5:5, Now it is God who has made us for this very purpose and has given us the Spirit as a deposit (ASV: earnest), guaranteeing what is to come.

6:6, in hard work, sleepless nights and hunger; in purity, understanding, patience and kindness; in the Holy Spirit and in sincere love

12:18, Did we not act in the same spirit (ASV fn: Or, *by the same Spirit*) and follow the same course?

13:14, May the grace of the Lord Jesus Christ, and the love of God, and the fellowship of the Holy Spirit be with you all.

Gal 3:2, Did you receive the Spirit by observing the law, or by believing what you heard?

3:3, After beginning with the Spirit, are you now trying to attain your goal by human effort?

3:5, Does God give you his Spirit and work miracles among you because you observe the law, or because you believe what you heard?

3:14, so that by faith we might receive the promise of the Spirit

4:6, Because you are sons, God sent the Spirit of his Son into our hearts, the Spirit who calls out, "*Abba*, Father." (ASV: into our hearts, crying Abba, Father) (In the NIV, "the Spirit who calls out" is without textual basis).

4:29, the son born in the ordinary way (Ishmael) persecuted the son (Isaac) born by the power of the Spirit.

5:5, But by faith we eagerly await through the Spirit the righteousness for which we hope.

5:16, live by the Spirit, and you will not gratify the desires of the sinful nature [Or *the flesh*].

5:17, For the sinful nature [Or *the flesh*] desires what is contrary to the Spirit, and the Spirit what is contrary to the sinful nature [Or *the flesh*].

5:18, But if you are led by the Spirit, you are not under law.

5:22, But the fruit of the Spirit is love, joy, peace . . . .

5:25, Since we live by the Spirit, let us keep in step with the Spirit.

6:8, the one who sows to please the Spirit, from the Spirit will reap eternal life.

Eph 1:13-14, Having believed, you were marked in him with a seal, the promised Holy Spirit, who is a deposit guaranteeing our inheritance (ASV: sealed with the Holy Spirit of promise, which is an earnest of our inheritance). (In the NIV, "who is a deposit" is without textual basis).

1:17, I keep asking that the God of our Lord Jesus Christ, the glorious Father, may give you the Spirit [Or *a spirit*] of wisdom and revelation

2:18, For through him we both have access to the Father by one Spirit.

2:22, And in him you too are being built together to become a dwelling in which God lives by his Spirit.

3:5, it has now been revealed by the Spirit of God's holy apostles and prophets.

3:16, he (the Father) may strengthen you with power through his Spirit in your inner being

4:3, Make every effort to keep the unity of the Spirit through the bond of peace.

4:4, There is one body and one Spirit

4:23, to be made new in the attitude (ASV: spirit) of your minds

4:30, And do not grieve the Holy Spirit of God, with (ASV: in) whom (Gr: masc. or neut.) you were sealed

5:18, Instead, be filled with the Spirit.

6:17, Take the helmet of salvation and the sword of the Spirit, which is the word of God.

6:18, And pray in the Spirit on all occasions

Phil 1:19, for I know that through your prayers and the help given by the Spirit of Jesus Christ

1:27, stand firm in one spirit, contending as one man for the faith of the gospel

2:1, if any fellowship with the Spirit, if any tenderness and compassion

3:3, For it is we who are the circumcision, we who worship by the Spirit of God, who glory in Christ Jesus

Col 1:8, and who (Epaphras) also told us of your love in the Spirit.

1 Thess 1:5, our gospel came to you not simply with words, but also with power, with the Holy Spirit and with deep conviction.

1:6, you welcomed the message with the joy given by the Holy Spirit.

4:8, he who rejects this instruction does not reject man but God, who gives you his Holy Spirit.

5:19, Do not put out the Spirit's fire

2 Thess 2:2, we ask you, brothers, not to become easily unsettled or alarmed by some prophecy (ASV: spirit), report (ASV: word) or letter supposed to have come from us

2:13, from the beginning God chose you to be saved through the sanctifying work of the Spirit (ASV: in sanctification of the Spirit) and through belief in the truth.

1 Tim 3:16, He appeared in a body [Or *in the flesh*], was vindicated by the Spirit, was seen of angels

4:1, The Spirit clearly says that in later times some will abandon the faith

2 Tim 1:7, God did not give us a spirit of timidity, but a spirit of power, of love

1:14, guard it with the help of the Holy Spirit who (ASV: which) lives in us.

Titus 3:5-6, He saved us through the washing of rebirth and renewal by the Holy Spirit, whom (ASV: which) he poured out on us generously through Jesus Christ our Savior

Heb. 2:4, God also testified to it by signs, wonders and various miracles, and gifts of the Holy Spirit distributed according to his (God's) will.

3:7, So, as the Holy Spirit says: "Today, if you hear his voice . . . ."

6:4, It is impossible for those who have once been enlightened, who have tasted the heavenly gift, who have shared in the Holy Spirit

9:8, The Holy Spirit was showing by this that the way into the Most Holy Place had not yet been disclosed

9:14, the blood of Christ, who through the eternal Spirit offered himself unblemished to God

10:15, The Holy Spirit also testifies to us about this.

10:29, and who has insulted the Spirit of grace

Jas 4:5, Or do you think Scripture says without reason that the spirit [Or *Spirit* . . .] he caused to live in us envies intensely?

1 Pet 1:2, through the sanctifying work (ASV: in sanctification) of the Spirit, for obedience to Jesus Christ

1:11, trying to find out the time and circumstances to which the Spirit of Christ in them was pointing

1:12, by those who have preached the gospel to you by the Holy Spirit sent from heaven.

3:18, He was put to death in the body but made alive by the Spirit

4:6, but live according to God in regard to the spirit.

4:14, you are blessed, for the Spirit of glory and of God rests on you.

2 Pet 1:21, but men spoke from God as they were carried along by the Holy Spirit.

1 John 3:24, We know it by the Spirit he gave us.

4:1, do not believe every spirit, but test the spirits to see whether they are from God

4:2, This is how you can recognize the Spirit of God

4:2, Every Spirit that acknowledges that Jesus Christ has come in the flesh is from God

4:6, This is how we recognize the Spirit [Or *spirit*] of truth

4:13, We know that we live in him and he in us, because he has given us of his Spirit.

5:6, And it is the Spirit who (ASV: that) testifies, because the Spirit is the truth.

5:7-8, For there are three that testify: the Spirit, the water and the blood; and the three are in agreement.

Jude 19, These are the men who divide you, who follow mere natural instincts and do not have the Spirit.

20, But you, dear friends, build yourselves up in your most holy faith and pray in the Holy Spirit.

Rev 1:4, Grace and peace to you from him who is, and who was, and who is to come, and from the seven spirits [Or *the sevenfold Spirit*] before his throne

1:10, On the Lord's Day I was in the Spirit

2:7, He who has an ear, let him hear what the Spirit says to the churches.

2:11, (Same as 2:7).

2:17, (Same as 2:7).

2:29, (Same as 2:7).

3:1, These are the words of him who holds the seven spirits [Or *the sevenfold Spirit*] of God and the seven stars.

3:6, (Same as 2:7).

3:13, (Same as 2:7).

3:22, (Same as 2:7).

4:2, At once I was in the Spirit, and there before me was a throne in heaven

4:5, These are the seven spirits [Or *the sevenfold Spirit*] of God.

5:6, He (the Lamb) had seven horns and seven eyes, which are the seven spirits [Or *the sevenfold Spirit*] of God sent out into all the earth.

14:13, "Yes," says the Spirit, "they will rest from their labor, for their deeds will follow them."

17:3, Then the angel carried me away in the Spirit into a desert.

19:10, Worship God! For the testimony of Jesus is the spirit of prophecy.

21:10, And he carried me away in the Spirit to a mountain great and high

22:17, The Spirit and the bride say, "Come!"

SCRIPTURE INDEX

Scripture	Page	Scripture	Page
GENESIS		19:24	167
1:1	34, 141	21:15	128
1:2	141, 199, 225	21:17-19	161
1:5	127	21:30	210
1:26	34, 35, 36,	22:2	128
	82,105, 179, 191	22:11	162
1:26-27	119	22:15	162
2:3	34	23:6	187
2:4	127	23:11	187
2:21	127	24:9	33
3:9	160	24:10	33
3:13	160	24:18	187
3:15	141	24:51	33
3:22	34	25:24-26	92
4:1	45	28:12	170
4:6	160	28:13	170
4:19	128	28:16	170
11:6	127	31:11	170
11:7	34	31:35	187
13:15	83	31:48	210
16:7	161, 166	31:52	210
16:7-13	58, 165	32:1	161
16:9	161	32:4	187
16:10	161	32:5	187
16:11	161, 166	32:18	187
16:13	166	32:24-30	58
17:1	133	32:30	172
18:1	166	39:2	33
18:9	166	39:3	33
18:12	187	39:7	33
18:13	166	39:8	33
18:17	166	39:16	33
18:22	167	39:19	33
18:27-32	188	39:20	33
19:1	166, 167	40:1	187
19:2	187	40:5	128
19:13	167	41:51	93
19:14	167	42:10	187

42:11 128
42:13 128
42:16 128
42:30 ....33, 187
42:33 ....33, 187
44:8 33
45:8 187
45:9 187
48: 93

EXODUS
3:2 162
3:14 ....84, 133
3:15 160
4:10 188
4:13 188
4:22 92
6:2-3 160
7:1 32
12:24 83
13:1-2 91
13:21-22 248
14:19 162
22:13 210
23:17 188
26:6 127
26:11 127
27:20-21 83
28:42-43 83
29:14 161
29:27-28 83
30:18-21 83
32:4 32
32:8 32
32:22 187
33:20 ....126, 148, 165, 166, 170
33:20-21 172
34:19-20 91
34:23 188
40:34 229

LEVITICUS
6:14-18 83
10:9 83
16:29-30 83
23:10-14 83
26:11 230
26:30 230

NUMBERS
3:13 92
11:17 206,213
11:25 ....206,212, 213
11:26 212
11:28 187
11:29 212
16:22 173
20:16 162
22:21 162
22:31 171
23:12 211
24:2 212
27:16 173
32:25 187
32:27 187
36:2 187

DEUTERONOMY
4:35 122
6:4 ....67, 122, 123, 127, 129
6:16 12
10:17 188
17:6 ....128, 129, 209
19:15 129
21:16-17 93
21:17 92
31:19 210
31:21 210
31:26 210
32:43 171

JOSHUA
3:13 188
5:13-6:5 162
17:1 93
22:27 210
22:28 210
22:34 210
24:27 210

JUDGES
2:1 162
2:1-5 171
3:10 212
3:25 187
4:18 187
6:11 163
6:11-24 171
6:13 188
6:22-24 172
6:31 32
6:34 ....206, 212
8:33 32
9:5 23
9:27 32
11:24 32
11:29 212
13:3 163
13:6 163
13:8 163
13:10 163
13:21-22 58
14:6 212
16:23-24 32

RUTH
2:13 187

1 SAMUEL
1:15 187
1:26 188
5:7 32
10:6 212

10:10 212
11:6 212
16:13 212
19:20 212
19:20-21 169
19:23 212

2 SAMUEL
7:11 10
7:14 ....10, 69,163
7:22 122
23:2 211

1 KINGS
11:5 32
11:33 32
18:27 32
19:5 163
19:7 163
22:19 34
22:24 211

2 KINGS
1:2 32
1:3 ....32, 163
1:6 32
1:16 32
12:21 24
19:37 33
22:1 23

1 CHRONICLES
5:1 93
12:18 212
12:20 23
17:20 122

2 CHRONICLES
15:1 212
18:23 211
20:14 212
24:20 ....206, 212

32:21 33
36:15-16 169

EZRA
3:2 24

NEHEMIAH
9:18 32
9:19 248
10:29 188

JOB
1:6 173
2:1 173
12:7-8 236
16:8 210
18:13 94
29:11 210
32:7 236
38:7 173

PSALMS
2:7 ....97, 163, 175, 196, 197
16:10 230
25:8 147
34:8 ....147, 190
35:28 213
37:30 213
40:7-8 67
45:4 236
45:6 ....68, 69
77:6 235
82:1 15
82:6 15
83:18 122
86:5 147
86:6 122
86:10 122
86:11 122
89:27 94
100:5 147
102:1 69

102:25 69
102:25-27 191
102:26 69
102:27 69
103:17 229
106:1 147
107:1 147
110:1 ....11, 103, 163, 188, 190
110:2 190
110:4 190
118:1 147
118:22 192
118:29 147
119:68 147
119:172 213
135:3 147
136:1 147
139:7-8 112
139:7-10 ....76, 199, 225
139:10 247

PROVERBS
1:23 212
6:13 213
6:20-22 247
8:7 213
8:12 229
8:22-31 ....86, 88, 229
11:3 248
16:23 236

ECCLESIASTES
12:7 ....75, 113, 199, 206

ISAIAH
1:14 230
3:9 210
5:13 21
6: 149
6:1 148
6:1-5 152
6:3 148

6:5 ....34, 148
6:6-7 148
6:8 ....34, 148
7:8 21
7:14 ....21, 22, 23, 25, 193
8:3 ....22, 193
8:4 22
8:5-8 23
8:13 192
8:14 192
9:6 ....10, 28
9:17 213
19:19-20 210
23:4 213
28:16 192
32:15 212
34:16 206
37:38 33
40:3 79
40:5 80
42:1 230
42:5 152
42:8 152
44:3 212
44:6 ....122, 138
45:18 122
48:11 152
48:12 138
53: 149
53:1 148
53:2 148
53:4 149
53:6 149
53:10 ....149, 230
53:11 ....149, 230
53:12 ....149, 230
57:15 75
61:1 178

JEREMIAH
5:9 230
5:29 230

6:8 230
9:9 230
14:9 230
15:1 230
23:5-6 193
23:24 76
31:9 93
31:15 ....25, 26
31:17 26
32:41 230
40:1 25
51:14 230

EZEKIEL
23:18 230
39:29 212

DANIEL
1:2 33
7:1 170
7:8 213
7:11 213
7:13-14 151
7:20 213
10:16-18 188

HOSEA
12:4 172

JOEL
2:28 212
2:29 212
2:32 194

AMOS
6:8 230

JONAH
1:5 33

MICAH
5:2 ....82, 84

5:4 84

NAHUM
2:13 169

HAGGAI
1:13 169

ZECHARIAH
4:4 188
4:5 188
4:13 188

MALACHI
2:7 169
2:8 169
2:9 169
3:1 ....169, 188

MATTHEW
1:1 103
1:18 ....53, 76, 175, 199,
                                 222, 223
1:20 ....76, 168, 175
1:21 ....23, 28, 186, 193
1:22-23 186
1:23 23,25
1:25 186
2:1 186
2:11 238
2:12 245
2:18 ....25, 26
3:2 79
3:3 79
3:6 108
3:15 79
3:16 ....19, 204
3:16-17 ....4, 139, 142
3:17 ....6, 112, 185, 234
4:1 ....12, 247
4:3 7
4:4 175

4:6 7
4:7 12
4:17 80
6:9 ....73, 225
9:4 216
9:5-6 172
10:2-4 244
10:5-7 244
10:8 244
10:19-20 244
10:20 212
10:24 188
11:27 234
12:18 230
12:25 216
12:31-32 181
12:34 213
13:19-23 184
13:24 245
13:31 245
13:33 245
14:21 205
16:15 6
16:16 6
16:17 6
16:18 60
16:27 66
17:5 ....4, 112, 185, 234
17:6 4
18:16 209
19:16-17 143
19:28 151
20:23 178
20:28 230
21:33-41 ....2, 29
22:30 35
22:42-46 103
22:44 11
23:9 28
24:30 ....66, 151
24:36 179
25:21 143

25:31 151
26:20 241
26:29 178
16:38 230
26:53 161
28:18 ....106, 109, 113, 180, 189
28:19 ....114, 139, 194, 200
28:19-20 107

MARK
1:3 79
1:8 213
1:10-11 4
1:12 ....79, 247
1:24 7
2:2 184
2:8 216
3:28-29 181
4:33 184
7:28 205
9:1 226
10:17 147
10:17-18 ....143, 190
10:20 144
10:33 144
10:40 178
10:45 ....144, 230
12:6 103
12:29 ....122, 123, 129
12:36 178
13:11 212
13:32 179
14:17 241
14:34 230
15:34 12
16:15-18 107
16:19 ....11, 73, 180
16:20 ....158, 209

LUKE
1:7 226
1:35 ....54, 76, 105, 199, 226

1:68 191
1:69 191
2:33 131
3:4 79
3:22 ....4, 199
3:23-38 18
3:38 ....16, 84, 173, 175
4:1-2 247
4:14 226
4:18 178
4:36 184
4:41 131
5:1 185
6:8 216
6:12 11
6:45 213
7:12 174
7:30 79
8:11 184
8:19 131
8:30 131
8:42 174
9:26 151
10:20 178
10:22 234
10:39 185
11:17 216
12:10 181
12:11-12 244
16:15 216
18:18-19 143
20:13 103
20:17 192
21:27 151
22:14 241
22:69 180
23:46 113
24:26 151
24:39 77
24:43 77
24:46-49 107
24:47 ....109, 173

24:48 208
24:51 74

JOHN
1:1 ....5, 41, 43, 58, 63, 71, 77,
           84, 88, 124, 183, 195
1:1-2 42
1:1-3 ....35, 104
1:2 ....84, 136, 191
1:3 ....19, 29, 34, 35, 84, 88, 191
1:14 ....5, 35, 42, 71, 153, 174,
           182, 183
1:18 ....5, 11, 41, 42, 148, 165,
           166, 170, 174, 194, 195
1:29 42
1:32 206
1:32-34 5
1:34 42
1:41 5
1:49 42
2:11 20
2:16 42
2:19 75
2:21 75
2:22 185
2:25 216
3:2 143
3:3 ....94, 111, 175
3:5 ....94, 111, 175
3:13 74
3:16 .... ix, 1, 43, 68, 103, 106,
           174, 175
3:17 ....ix, 43
3:34-35 ....19, 120
4:24 ....77, 200
5:18 177
5:19 177
5:22 178
5:36 210
5:43 194
6:35 ....185, 193
6:38 ....178, 194

6:62 73
7:16 178
7:39 151
8:26 178
8:29 177
8:32 i
8:42 178
8:58 ....81, 84, 85, 137
9:5 185
10:7 ....123, 185
10:11 ....123, 230
10:15 230
10:17 230
10:24-38 ....15, 43
10:25 ....109, 210
10:29 177
10:30 ....122, 177
10:30-36 85
10:31 123
10:33 ....4, 123, 177
10:33-36 58
10:34 43
10:34-36 15
10:35 15
10:35-36 43
10:36 ....4, 15, 18, 85, 123,
           144, 177
11:4 151
12:16 151
12:23 151
12:27 ....150, 230
12:28 186
12:31-32 150
12:33 150
12:39-43 149
12:40 149
12:41 ....149, 150, 152
12:44 109
12:48 ....5, 185
12:49 ....109, 124, 178
13:20 179
13:27-31 241

13:31 153
13:31-32 151
14:6 109,194
14:8 126
14:9 126
14:10 109
14:16 ....200, 244
14:16-17 ....203, 241
14:17 ....120, 244
14:18 191
14:23 191
14:24 ....109, 124, 177, 185
14:26 ....199, 200, 203, 208,
                214, 241
14:28 177
15:1 185
15:26 ....113, 156, 157, 175,
                198, 200, 203, 208,
                214, 233, 241
15:27 208
16:7-8 ....203, 241
16:13 ....212, 214
16:13-15 ....200, 203, 241
17:1 ....4, 19, 122, 152, 153
17:3 ....4, 104, 122
17:5 ....11, 19, 35, 65,
                81, 152, 153
17:8 124
17:11 125
17:17 159
17:19 159
17:21 126
17:21-22 125
17:23 ....125, 126
20:17 ....59, 73
20:18 59
20:23 172
20:28 ....43, 58
20:31 ....5, 42, 47, 59, 104

ACTS
1:2 241

1:4 241
1:5 ....199, 213, 214, 241
1:8 ....199, 208, 226, 241
1:9 73
1:13 241
1:16 211
1:24 216
1:26 242
2: 141, 151
2:1 242
2:1-4 214
2:3 204
2:4 ....120, 199, 208, 212,
                226, 242
2:7 242
2:14-15 242
2:14-40 208
2:17-18 ....212, 242
2:21 194
2:27 230
2:34-35 ....178, 190
2:36 189
2:38 114
2:41 242
2:43 242
3:13 152
3:22 169
4:11 192
5:3-9 230
5:4 231
5:12 209
5:19-20 214
5:32 209
6:5 164
6:8 164
7:30 ....162, 164
7:38 164
7:53 164
8:14-19 243
8:16 ....114, 205
8:29 212
8:36-39 108

9:31 243
9:32-34 243
9:35 243
9:36-41 243
9:42 243
10:19 212
10:37-38 19
10:38 ....20, 139, 142, 199,
                              216, 226
10:45 212
10:48 114
11:14 131
12:7-10 214
12:24 185
13:2 212
13:33 196
15:23 244
15:28 244
15:31 244
16:6 248
17:23 184
17:27-28 75
17:28 ....16, 173, 174
17:29 ....117, 118, 120, 228
19:5 114
19:6 243
20:28 ....29, 60, 61
21:9 22
21:11 212
25:26 189
27:23-24 214
28:25 211

ROMANS
1:3-4 103
1:4 196
1:7 ....63, 155
1:8 63
1:20 ....117, 118, 120, 228
2:4 247
2:15 210
2:16 63

3:21 210
3:23 179
3:25 63
5:10 ....81, 180
6:3 ....94, 114
8:2 231
8:3 103
8:4 217
8:5 217
8:6 217
8:7 217
8:9 242
8:11 ....199, 243
8:14 ....175, 247
8:15 ....175, 199, 227, 232
8:16 ....205, 209, 223, 224
8:17 63
8:23 219
8:24-25 219
8:26 ....205, 216, 218,
                              220, 222, 223
8:26-27 219
8:27 ....216, 218
8:29 90
8:34 ....63, 216, 218, 219, 220
9:1 210
9:5 ....43, 63, 64, 65
10:6 213
11:33 229
15:4 243
15:13 226
15:19 226
15:30 249
16:16 60

1 CORINTHIANS
1:2 194
1:9 155
1:13 114
1:23-24 87
1:30 ....88, 158
2:4 226

2:7 233
2:9 233
2:10 233
2:11 ....233, 234
2:12-13 235
3:5 126
3:6 126
3:8 126
5:3 74
6:19 ....75, 120, 242
6:20 75
8:4 ....122, 123
8:5-6 188
8:6 ....6, 34, 35, 53, 63, 104, 106,
            112, 121, 122, 123, 133,
                136, 184, 191, 233
10:2 114
10:3-4 193
10:4 ....185, 192
10:16 157
11:3 181
11:14 236
12:4-6 207
12:7 207
12:8 ....207, 88
12:11 207
12:24 207
12:28 207
13: 201
13:5 ....202, 229
13:13 50
15:10 229
15:20 97
15:24 ....136, 189
15:24-25 137
15:24-28 ....149, 180
15:39 245
15:42-44 ....30, 77
15:43 150
15:50 77
16:19 131

2 CORINTHIANS
!:3 156
3:6 231
3:7-8 231
3:17 ....231, 232
3:18 231
5:18-20 ....81, 180
6:18 133
7:6 244
13:14 ....50, 139, 154, 156,
....157, 158

GALATIANS
3:20 221
3:26-27 175
3:27 ....94, 114
4:4 103
4:5-7 175
5:18 247
5:22 227

EPHESIANS
1:4-5 82
1:5 175
1:20 180
1:21 216
1:23 30
2:15 83
2:15-16 81,180
3:16 243
3:19 30
4:4-6 ....6, 188
4:6 122,123
4:23 ....227, 232
4:30 198
5:22-32 212
5:25-27 229
6:22 244

PHILIPPIANS
2:1 158

2:2 126
2:6-7 17,177
2:7 19

COLOSSIANS
1:1 192
1:3 10
1:13 96,192
1:14 96
1:15 84,86,90,95,96,97,98,
102,124,134,173,175
1:15-16 17,89,105
1:16 19,34,35,82,84,88,91,
95,96,134,191
1:16-17 104
1:17 96
1:18 96,97,98,196
1:19-20 81
2:3 88
2:9 30,117,118,120,228
2:14 83
2:16 83
2:18 171
3:16 88
4:14 131

1 THESSALONIANS
1:5 226
3:11 130,132
4:18 224
5:23 50,159

2 THESSALONIANS

2:13 158,159
2:16-17 130,132

1 TIMOTHY
1:1 50
1:2 50
1:20 132
2:1 221

2:5 11,122,123,
134,216,221
3:16 1,40,41
4:1 212
4:5 221

2 TIMOTHY
1:6 243
1:15 132
2:7 132

TITUS
1:1 156
1:3 65
1:4 65
2:10 65
2:11-12 236
2:13 43,65,66
3:4 229
3:4-6 65
3:5 229
3:6 65

HEBREWS
1:2 103,104
1:3 123,124
1:4 97,112,164,194
1:4-5 70
1:5 10,67,97,163,
173,175,196
1:6 98,165,238
1:7 171
1:8 43,67,68
1:8-9 193
1:8-10 70
1:9 67
1:10 69
1:10-12 190
1:13 163
2:3-4 158,209
2:7 18,164
2:9 164

2:17-18 222
3:1 68,134,169,222
4:12 229
4:14 134
4:14-15 222
4:15 179
5:5 175,197
6:4-5 226
6:18 179
7:25 221,222
8:1 155,222
10:5 18,81,104,120,168,182
10:7 67
10:10 221
10:12 221
10:14 221
10:29 158
10:38 230
11:17 174
11:28 98
12:2 155
12:5 213
12:9 173
12:22 161
12:23 94
12:24 213
13:2 168
13:12 158
13:22 244

JAMES
1:13 7,179
1:17 146
2:26 199
3:9 125

1 PETER
1:2 139,154,156,
157,158,159
1:3 139
2:3 190
2:5 192,221

2:6 192
2:7 192
2:8 192
2:22 143
3:6 188
3:10 213
3:20 229
3:22 180

2 PETER
1:1 66
1:2 66
1:3 120,228
1:3-4 117
1:4 120,121,228
1:21 110,199,208,211,
212,244
2:4 34,179
3:10 136
3:10-11 83
3:16 219

1 JOHN
1:1 124,183
1:1-2 35
1:3 156
2:1 243
3:16 230
3:20 216
4:9 174
4:15 71
5:5 38,71
5:6-9 209
5:7-8 37,128
5:8 50
5:18 71
5:19 71
5:20 ....43, 71

JUDE
6..34, 179

REVELATION
1:1 ....138, 214
1:4 ....133, 134, 155
1:4-5 ....154, 155
1:5 ....10, 98, 138
1:6 ....10, 136, 138, 221
1:7 191
1:8 ....133, 134, 135, 136, 154
1:10-11 136
1:11 ....135, 136
1:17-18 136
1:18 192
1:19 191
2:7 214
2:8 136
2:18 138
3:2 138
3:12 ....12, 138
3:14 ....136, 138
4:2 155
4:5 155
4:8 ....133, 134
5:1 155
5:5 ....138, 185
5:10 221
6:10 138
11:8 138

11:16-17 133
11:17 134
12:9 34
13:15 213
14:13 212
15:3 ....133, 134
16:5-7 133
16:7 ....133, 134
16:14 ....133, 134
17:14 ....138, 141
19:6 133
19:11 138
19:11-15 134
19:13 ....71, 124, 138, 143,
                        183, 229
19:15 133
19:16 ....138, 141
21:2 229
21:6 ....135, 137
21:7 137
21:22 ....133, 134
22:8-9 171
22:10 137
22:12 137
22:13 ....135, 137
22:16 ....137, 138, 185
22:17 212

BIBLIOGRAPHY

Bible Versions, including those accompanied by their authors' comments, are listed under VERSIONS AND TRANSLATIONS, p. vii, and are identified in *Theology Simplified* by their names and/or initials, but without superscripts. References with superscripts are listed here.

[1] Mathes, Elder James M. *Works of Elder B. W. Stone*, ed. John Allen Hudson. Rosemead, CA: Reproduced and Distributed by The Old Paths Book Club, 1953.

[2] Young, Robert. *Analytical Concordance To the Bible* (KJV). Peabody, MA: Hendrickson Publishers.

[3] Clarke, Adam. *Clarke's Commentary*. 6 vols. New York: Abingdon Press.

[4] Peloubet, F. N. *Peloubet's Bible Dictionary*. Philadelphia, PA: The John C. Winston Co., 1925.

[5] *The International Standard Bible Encyclopaedia*. 6 vols. Grand Rapids: Wm. B. Eerdmans Publishing Co., 1949.

[6] Barnes, Albert. *Notes On the New Testament*. 11 vols. Grand Rapids: Baker Book House, 1956

[7] Thayer, Joseph Henry. *Greek-English Lexicon Of the New Testament*. New York: American Book Co.; Harper & Brothers, 1889.

[8] Robertson, A. T. and W. Hersey Davis. *A Short Grammar Of the Greek Testament*. 10th edition. Grand Rapids: Baker Book House, 1977.

[9] Zodhiates, Spiros. *Was Christ God?* Grand Rapids: Wm. B. Eerdmans Publishing Co., 1966.

[10] *The Ante-Nicene Fathers*. 10 vols. New York: Charles Scribner's Sons, 1925.

[11] Boles, H. Leo. *The Holy Spirit*. Nashville: Gospel Advocate Co., 1942.

[12] *The American People's Encyclopedia*

[13] *Encyclopaedia Britannica*. 23 vols. Chicago: William Benton, Publisher, 1970.

[14] *Schäff Encyclopaedia Of Religious Knowledge*.

[15] Cohen, A. *Everyman's Talmud*. New York: Schocken Books, 1975.

[16] Johnson, B. W. *The People's New Testament With Notes*. 2 vols. St. Louis: Christain Board Of Publication, 1889.

[17] Vincent, Marvin R. *Word Studies In the New Testament*. Vol. III. Reprint. Grand Rapids: Wm. B. Eerdmans Publishing Co, 1973.

[18] Machen, J. Gresham. *New Testament Greek For Beginners*. New York: The Macmillan Co., 1953.

[19] Henry, Matthew. *Matthew Henry's Commentary*. 6 vols. McLean, VA: MacDonald Publishing Co.

[20] *Webster's Seventh New Collegiate Dictionary*. Springfield, MA: G. & C. Merriam Co., 1972.

[21] *The Analytical Greek Lexicon*. Harper & Brothers.

[22] Lard, Moses E. *Commentary on Romans*. Cincinnati: The Standard Publishing Co.

Made in the USA
Monee, IL
06 March 2021

62103730R00184